THE TWILIGHT
OF FRANCE

THE TWILIGHT
OF FRANCE

1933-1940

by

Alexander Werth

Edited with an Introduction by
D. W. Brogan

'*Mais que sert de lui sauver la vie, si l'on perd son âme?
Et parfois m'envahit une tristesse sans nom à contempler
ce clair miroir de vérité qu'était la France, se ternir.*'

André Gide, JOURNAL

NEW YORK

Howard Fertig

1966

HOWARD FERTIG, INC. EDITION 1966

Published by arrangement with the author

All rights reserved.

First published in the United States in
1942 by Harper & Brothers

Library of Congress Catalog Card number: 66-24358

PRINTED IN THE UNITED STATES OF AMERICA
BY NOBLE OFFSET PRINTERS

To
Nancy Alexandra

Introduction

A MONG the disasters of the London *Blitz* was the destruction of so
many millions of books, and among the valuable records of our age
thus destroyed were the stocks of *The Destiny of France* and *France and
Munich*. These books are now permanently out of print, so that the most
valuable contemporary record of the last years of the parliamentary
republic in France is not available at a time when, for the present conduct
of the war and the preparation for the peace, it is most important that the
British and American publics should be well informed on French matters.
It seemed well worth while, then, to make of these two books (with the
epilogue of *The Last Days of Paris*) an omnibus volume, and in the
absence of Mr. Werth in Russia it fell to me to cut down, with a reluctant
but necessary ruthlessness, this detailed record of the most critical and
depressing years in modern French history. The extraordinary journalistic flair of the Paris Correspondent of the *Manchester Guardian* is best
seen from the importance he already attached, in 1934 and 1935, to men
like Déat, Brinon, Doriot, Abetz and others who, at that time, seemed of
little consequence, but were to become leading villains in 1940.

I have called this period the 'most critical and depressing' in modern
French history. Not the most tragic, that period began on May 10, 1940.
But it was in the years that preceded 1940 that the preparations for the
tragedy were completed. Marx said of Louis Napoleon's *coup d'état*
that history repeats itself, 'first as tragedy, then as farce.' It is one of
history's favourite jokes to invert Marxian prophecy and it has done so
here. For much of what Mr. Werth has to tell is, taken apart from its
consequences, farcical. The characters are farcical, the solutions of the
situation have the temporarily final character of a good farce. Then the
curtain goes up again and the actors resume their buffoonery. But this
farce was being played on a great stage and involved great issues. The
tragedy followed the farce when the stage was suddenly invaded by
characters out of Wagner, and the characters out of Sacha Guitry suddenly found themselves at a loss.

This is primarily a political chronicle, a first-class political chronicle.
The political life of a nation does not often illustrate its virtues and
achievements at their best. Even those philosophers who have thought
politics the highest art practised by man have not underestimated the
difficulties, moral and material, that stand in the way of its good practice.
And in the France of the last twenty years the difference between the

vii

achievements of the French nation and the French state was even more striking than usual. It was not merely that France was as fertile as ever in talent and in genius, that her primacy in the arts was undisputed, her leadership in the sciences contested by few. Her moral life, too, seemed to be renewing itself; there were everywhere signs of a second spring.

Not quite everywhere; the state, the political organization, seemed unchanged or changed only for the worse. The French state was still capable of great material achievements: the restoration of the devastated regions, the development of the Empire. These were among the greatest successful efforts in construction of our times. But the political direction of these plans grew feebler and the political machine functioned more and more slowly, was less and less capable of mechanical efficiency. Where it acted effectively, it was in an extremely wasteful fashion, and often, in the most important spheres, it did not act at all. It is this depressing aspect of French affairs that is the main subject of this book. The rest of French life is there in the background, not neglected as a foundation, sometimes brought forward in those interviews with 'the people' who were—and remain—the chief ground of hope in France. But, as I have said, this is a political chronicle. And it is inevitably, therefore, a chronicle of failure. It is a picture of a machine slowing down, seizing up, of a machine so well provided with brakes and safety-valves that it comes slowly to a state of immobility. What is being described here is the process that Daniel Halévy described and lamented, the 'decline of the French state.'

Such a decline had happened before and had gone to extreme lengths before it was noticed. Louis XVI was still issuing edicts *de par le roi*,' still dismissing the Parliament of Paris in the manner of Louis XIV, at a time when his authority was already a sham. And so Prime Ministers sat in the place of Ferry and Clemenceau and Poincaré, Ministers of the Interior in the place of Rouher and Constans, Foreign Ministers in the place of Vergennes and Delcassé, when the effective powers of these offices had evaporated. With a fine dramatic sense, Dumas opens *Twenty Years After* in the Palais Royal, with Mazarin as the shade of Richelieu. But the change from Richelieu to Mazarin was as nothing to the change whose consequences are illustrated here. The authority of the executive had been destroyed. Thinkers (that is sophists) like 'Alain' might try to make the flesh creep with visions of the transient and embarrassed phantoms who passed through the Quai d'Orsay or the Rue Saint Dominique being infected with the authoritarian microbes left by Delcassé or Clemenceau. They need not have worried.

Political authority had passed (for what it was worth) to Parliament, to the thousand deputies and senators. The Third Republic, in its last years, was a parliamentary republic as the old Polish Republic in its last generations was a nobleman's republic. And the French politicians were the equivalent of the Polish gentry whose power of impeding action, whose *liberum veto*, we have all learned to denounce and despise—but not necessarily to recognize in fundamentally identical if superficially different forms.

It is this governing (hardly ruling) class that provides almost the whole of the *dramatis personae* of this book. Most of the senators and deputies were neither fools nor knaves. But they were members of a morally dangerous trade. The French have a proverb that 'a door must be open or shut.' The French parliamentary system existed to confute this belief. Had France been a physical as well as psychological island, her happy state might have made her the envy of the world. She had her problems, her stresses and strains, but her natural wealth, the industry and tenacity of her inhabitants, the stabilizing effect of widely distributed property, the comparative absence of that wrecker of modern states, prolonged and general unemployment, made it possible to avoid answering some of the most difficult questions put to the rulers of the great industrial states. French politics could, therefore, be about 'principles,' not about the application of those principles. They could be, and were, passionate, stirring, entertaining, but they did not reflect the urgency of modern economic problems. Elections could still be fought on fine old irrelevant slogans, and whole communes of *Kulaks* vote the Communist ticket without provoking more than an indulgent smile.

For there was a sense in which politics in France had become very pure, had acquired some, though not all, of the character of art for art's sake that was shown by American politics in the boom days of Coolidge. It was often as difficult to explain, on rational grounds of choice, the political colour of similar French regions as it was to explain why the slum dwellers of Philadelphia voted the Republican and their brethren in New York the Democratic ticket. Elections, the right to vote, the legal equality of Frenchmen, these were an important part of French social life. There was not much reason to complain of indifference or of failure to vote. But what was being voted for or against was harder to define. Men still voted for and against the Revolution, the Church, the Commune, but what they voted for or against in the current situation was harder to discover. And although France had its share of politicians of the Ledru-Rollin school who would have said with him, 'I must follow them, I am their leader,' it was harder in 1939 than in 1849 to find followers to give a lead—even to the most importunate party chief. All that one could safely say of the results of a general election was that it changed to some degree the political personnel, and gave an indication of the names which the President of the Republic would have to consider *for the first few months* of the Parliament in looking for ministers. But there was nothing that Rousseau would have called a general will revealed by the consultation of the electors—as the language of politics unconsciously revealed.

There used to recur in French political jargon, above all on the Left, a technical term whose popularity was depressingly significant. How often has a measure been opposed in the name of 'universal suffrage'; how often has a politician (whose own weight was light) proudly spoken as the 'delegate of universal suffrage'; how often has what is, after all, a term describing a piece of electoral machinery, been hypostatized into an independent power whose presumed will was to be blindly obeyed! Such verbal idolatry was not insignificant. The older French republican tradition spoke of 'the sovereign people' as the Constitution of the United States speaks of 'We, the People of the United States "who" *do* ordain and establish' the form of government which is to give effect to their continuing sovereign will. To a philosopher, the fiction of the People having a continuing will may be distasteful, but it is as a working political idea more real and more dignified than 'universal suffrage.' You can make a song about it. The soldiers of the Revolution could sing *'le peuple souverain s'avance'* as they dethroned kings and liberated peoples. Try to sing *'le suffrage universel s'avance'* as a battle-cry!

The verdict of universal suffrage was a verdict in favour of a number of candidates professing certain doctrines and making certain promises over a number of candidates professing not very different doctrines and making very similar promises. It had no more positive content, as was speedily found by such victors as put on airs as mandatories of the popular will. French elections never produced landslides of the American or British types. A defective electoral system gave exaggerated parliamentary majorities which never represented overwhelming majorities in votes cast. And in a country where women played so decisive a role in family and economic life, women did not vote. The sole animating force of the French political system was a Parliament so chosen. Once the elections were over, it remained for the successful candidates to give the machine of government, it would be too much to say its impetus, but those little jerks forward and backward that gave the electors an impression of something happening. French politics took a fairly uniform development, at any rate, from 1924 on, when the 'Left' recovered its normal electoral predominance. Electors returned a coalition majority which began by promising and even trying to put into effect some of the promises made during the campaign. Within a period that was never more than two years long, the balance of power in the Chamber had shifted towards the Right and the electors learned with more or less resignation that, for various 'technical,' i.e. financial reasons, the goods promised could not be delivered. If the technical problems were really serious, Parliament abandoned any pretence of dealing with them, and gave 'full powers' to a Prime Minister to do by decree what the deputies could not bring themselves to do by law. The responsibility was thus put on the shoulders of Poincaré or Doumergue or Laval or Daladier. When the crisis was over, politics were resumed, credit taken and responsibility disowned.

In normal times, the damage done by such a system could be exaggerated by the captious critic. The elector was less deceived than it was customary to pretend. He wanted his deputy or senator to do his best, but he did not expect much, and in rural France did not want much, in the way of change. The elected did not really deceive the electors. No doubt there were hundreds of thousands of sincere *militants* on the Left who suffered from these repeated deceptions, as they saw their leaders make necessary, if ignominious, compromises. No doubt there were hundreds of thousands of sincere pessimists on the Right who believed that, to use the old Bonapartist phrase, it was necessary first to 'strangle the slut' before France could be restored to political health. But the average Frenchman had the resigned pessimism of the peasant. Good harvests mean bad prices; no autumn ever fully justifies the hopes of spring.

The temptation this attitude put in the way of the politician was very great. He knew that profound changes were not wanted and that even substantial changes were very difficult. He knew that all sections of the French political world would combine against a man, a section, or a group, that seemed to have a chance to use the machinery of the state vigorously. All parties, therefore, agreed that, since they could not have their own way, no one should. What was left was too often what Burke called 'a confused and scuffling bustle of local agency.' Each deputy and senator did his best for his constituents, in the hope that the aggregate of these competing bests would add up to the good of the French state. But that is the kind of political arithmetic of which states die. Again and again in these pages the reader will see schemes of reform or of change boldly proposed and not so much rejected as smothered. The fate of Tardieu was the fate of Blum; the fate of Briand was the fate of Paul-Boncour and would probably have been the fate of Barthou had he lived. The policies of these men differed; what they had in common was a desire to give effect to a policy—and the chambers were not ready to support the effort necessary to make any real, coherent, decisive policy work.

It was this situation that made possible the career of what in seventeenth-century England was called the 'undertaker,' the manipulator of parliament whose pretensions to policy or principle were hardly taken seriously even by his own electoral committee, but who was a master of what Italians call *combinazioni*. There are several of these masters of parliamentary manipulation in this book. There is, for example, Chautemps, highly cultivated, with hereditary claims to Radical loyalty, master of passing the responsibility for decision on to others. But the perfect specimen of the type is, of course, Laval. Here he is, with his teeth not much dirtier than his 'white' cravat or his hands. Like so many agents of the Right, he got his start by the profession of the most violent, intolerant Left-wing sentiments. But once elected to the Chamber, he made friends, friends on all sides—and it must be remembered that he *kept* friends on all sides. Even when he was the incarnation (for the purposes of public meetings) of all that the Left detested, he did not break off his useful connections with his old friends on the Left—either in Aubervilliers or Auvergne. He was a lawyer, and it was impossible for him to make fine distinctions between his clients in Parliament and in the Courts. But Laval, if the most finished specimen of the political adventurer, was only the most successful representative of a class. And that he had friends on all sides was not surprising, for the Chamber was a club; it was suspicious of members who were not on easy terms of familiarity with the other members. Barrès might object to being *tutoyé* by strangers who were merely colleagues, but Barrès was not a typical deputy. No, outside the Communist party (if that exception is valid) it was true in 1939 as it was when Robert de Jouvenel laid down the law before the war of 1914: 'There is more in common between two deputies, one of whom is a revolutionary, than between two revolutionaries, one of whom is a deputy.'

For all its faults and falseness, the French political system might have continued to permit good, the development of the humane, critical, rich French civilization, and not have done irremediable harm, if France had been, let us say, an island more isolated than New Zealand is from the stormy outside world. But France was a neighbour of Germany. By a combination of heroism, skill and luck, France had been the victor in 1918. But, intrinsically, for the purposes of modern war, France was hopelessly inferior to her formidable neighbour. Once Austria was added to the Reich, there were twice as many Germans as there were Frenchmen. Nor was this all; because her population of military age in 1914 was disproportionately *lower* than that of Germany (as a pioneer in birth control, the population of France was older), the fact that her military losses were disproportionately *higher* made the position of France *vis à vis* Germany still worse. And because in modern war, industrial potential is even more important than man-power, France was still weaker. Then, although this grim truth was hidden from all but the few real experts like General de Gaulle, who understood modern war, the weaker, less completely prepared nations would not, this time, be given a chance to pull themselves together. In 1914, the machine-gun, the quick-firing field-gun, were the weapons that made the defensive possible and made vain the German dream of 'a battle without a morrow.' In 1940, the dive-bomber and the tank had given reality to the dreams of Schlieffen.

That France was beaten in 1940 was not surprising; only a miracle could have prevented that. But not only had the world come to expect miracles of France, the world was dazzled by the victory of 1918. That victories do not keep, that they must be renewed incessantly—that truth was even less understood in London than in Paris. The French defeat was not surprising; what was surprising was the failure to preserve the fruits of victory, those minimum guarantees of French security which were wrung with such difficulties from the British and American optimists protected from Germany (as they unconsciously thought) by impassable seas and oceans.

As far as the fundamental question of these years is concerned, the attitude France took or failed to take in the face of Nazi Germany, Mr. Werth's story makes depressing but educational reading. There were, possibly, two policies to be adopted towards Germany. While there was yet time, the Weimar Republic might have been buttressed and threatened; helped on promises of effective good behaviour. Or, when that policy had been tried and failed, or simply not tried, the realities of the Hitlerian Revolution might have been faced. The enemies of Hitler in Germany told the German people that he was asking them to commit suicide, that Germany's neck was in a rope, and that, if the hands which held it in Paris, Warsaw, Prague, were frightened by Nazi threats, they would pull the rope. Hitler called that bluff; it was his greatest internal victory.

All the former victors were to blame, but the French failure was inherent in the French political system. To choose one or other line of action was to commit the French state to one resolute policy, carried out without flinching, without compromise. At home and abroad the Third Republic had lost all power to carry out any coherent, long-term policy. No doubt, as Mr. Werth maintains, Barthou saw what needed to be done. But had he not been physically assassinated at Marseilles he would have been politically assassinated in Parliament. The fact that the French talked of Hitler, even after 1934, as 'Chancellor Hitler' was a disquieting symptom. So he was just a politician like Brüning or Blum? Alas! he was not.

The failure of the French to understand, in time, what was the full import of the Nazi revolution was due to virtues as well as to vices. Accustomed in their own country to vehement words covering moderate and reasonable projects, the genuine German extravagance, an extravagance of content as well as of form, was discounted by the man in the shop and on the farm who, for too long, took the bellowings of the Führer as bluff and bluster. How could a primary schoolteacher, convinced that the only real obstacle to the spread of enlightenment, of rational pacifism, of the religion of humanity was the Church, understand the daemonic power of the Nazi religion? His education narrowed him by its very generality. Men could not because they should not believe such things, and if, by an incredible hypothesis, they *did* believe them, their belief need have no result in action. It was both natural and disastrous that the schoolteachers, all over rural France the moulders of the political mind of the country, should have been uncritical and optimistic pacifists. From this well-meaning, but as far as the outside world was concerned, ill-equipped body, came some of the most effective pacifist propaganda of 1938 as is here set out. Not until it was too late did the profession that regarded itself as, in a special sense, the guardians of the Republic realize that it had helped to destroy its own work.

But it was not only the primary schoolteachers who were at fault. The master whom the Left intelligentsia among the university and secondary schoolteachers most delighted to honour, 'Alain,' was a dangerous dissolvent of the sense of realism. For the France, tolerant, sceptical, anarchical which Alain wished to preserve or create, was a Utopia in the modern world of heavy industry and nationalist passion. And it was another university teacher, Déat, here shown in his political aspects, who has moved from the candid if impracticable selfishness of 'Why die for Dantzig?' to preaching to the Frenchmen of 1941 the duty of dying to make Moscow German.

There was even some justice in the criticism passed on a leading *universitaire* who, in his role as a statesman, never fell into the more absurd or base aberrations of Alain or Déat. It was of M. Herriot, confronted with Germanic hysteria, that Bainville wrote, 'A Cartesian Frenchman like M. Herriot will rub his eyes when he has read these documents. He will ask himself if he is dreaming. It is another world of ideas, another universe. Without a preliminary study, you might believe it was an affair of a bet, of a paradox or of an aberration.' The gullible English spectator of the madness of the Third Reich thought that all this extravagance covered a fundamental soundness of practice and aims, that the frenzies of a Nuremberg party-day were merely a Teutonic version of an Aldershot tattoo plus a Scout jamboree. The gullible Frenchman thought they were mere declamation. He thought the ideals proclaimed were detestable, but he thought they had no chance of being put into practice. It was a more respectable error, but its consequences were the same—and in France they were not mitigated by the existence of the Channel.

But this was not all. Those sections of French opinion which had boasted of their realism, which had prided themselves on their knowledge of the modern world, a world in which the optimistic generalities of 1789 had no place, were incapable of putting their realism to any good use. As German power grew, as the primary need of the French state was a most vigorous, uncontested, and rapid assertion of its dwindling military superiority, the Right in France found other fish to fry. It feared, or professed to fear, that Russia was as great a danger as Germany; in some cases it was found convenient to pretend that Russia was a greater danger. And, suffering from an illusion common to the Right in all countries (and not confined to the Right), the revolutionary character of Nazism was ignored. In Germany Hitler was a 'restorer of order'—as soon as it became evident that that task was not to be carried out by a soldier in whom the French Right, after a century of hopes deceived, continued to put their hopes. That Schleicher had no chance and that Hitler was not another Schleicher was a truth learned too late. The popular basis of Nazism, those elements in it which gave it its explosive power, were underestimated by the Right to whom they were in fact too much like the emotional forces behind the *Front Populaire* to be palatable. The idea of a European order in which Germany would preserve the existing class structure was an illusion which clouded some professedly clear minds. And more were blinded by the fantastic vision of an Italian counterpoise to Germany, by ideas of a Latin union based on classical virtues of order and clarity. It was a literary illusion. No amount of mythical nonsense about the German language and the German race would have mattered much, if there had not been so many Germans, if there had not been German heavy industry to arm them and the

Prussian military tradition to make the *Wehrmacht* something that rhetoric could not alone have made, and once made could not alone destroy.

It was a bewildered and anguished country that had to face both the disasters of 1940 and the problem of what was to be done to repair or to palliate them. It was the third successful invasion of France in seventy years. True, the invaders of 1914 had finally been expelled, but that victory had been far more costly in wealth, and still more in lives, than the defeat of 1870. And now after the victory had come the new invasion, more terrible than ever before. Was victory with such short-lived fruits, so dearly bought, worth the price—even if it were certain?

In the crisis of June 1940 what was lacking to set against a natural resentment and despair was *political* authority. The defeatism of the generals was natural enough. They had done all they knew how to do—and it had not been enough. They were chess-players who knew that they had lost. But the art of war is more than a military art, and statesmen of authority might have countered the professional despair of the soldiers. They might have estimated, more justly, the power and will of Britain to resist. They might have estimated, more justly, the possibilities of imperial resistance. Above all, they might have denounced as suicidal illusion that pathetic belief in an honourable peace 'between soldiers,' that professional self-deception of Marshal Pétain, that ignorant refusal to see the Nazi revolution as it really was. But it was just this independent political authority that was lacking. M. Paul Reynaud had shown foresight and energy, but his own political position was weak. A man of the Right, he had been disowned by his own supporters without being accepted by the Left. The President of the Republic was filling, worthily, an office which had long since lost all authority and had only formal prestige. Parliament was a body which had failed to carry out the policy of the *Front Populaire* without finding any substitute, which had not even openly ratified the declaration of war, and which was soon to perform its final abdication, to crown its series of resignations of responsibility by giving dictatorial powers to Marshal Pétain.

There was no centre of authority left. A generation of open fear of great personalities, a generation of temporary alliances to weaken any over-mighty minister, had reduced the personal authority of the parliamentarians to nothing. Against the palace revolution of the Bordeaux cabinet crisis, only a political counter-revolution could have been effective. And where were the leaders of such a counter-revolution to be found? Only Georges Mandel was of the stuff of which Gambettas are made—and Mandel, even less than Reynaud, had a political position worthy of his talents and courage. He had been the right-hand of Clemenceau—and the Left had spent twenty years explaining and explaining away its sin in producing the dictator who, in 1917 and 1918, had saved France. No precaution had been omitted which would help to make it certain that no new Clemenceau could appear. Nor did one.

Louis Veuillot once wrote of Montalembert, '*M. de Montalembert se croit libéral, il est simplement orateur.*' Both the Chamber and the Senate were too well provided with men who, because they were orators, thought themselves statesmen, and who thought that a successful speech was a solution in itself, a complete action. There are, of course, speeches that are complete acts, speeches that secure for a moment the emotional and moral adherence of the audience, that prevent a collapse or generate a new and necessary burst of energy. Such have been the most successful speeches of Mr. Churchill. In the age of Hitler and Roosevelt, Churchill and Mussolini, we are not likely, if we are wise, to neglect that power of speech which, a generation ago, seemed to so many forward-thinkers an accomplishment of diminishing importance in would-be rulers of men and re-makers of society. But the great and effective orators of to-day are popular orators, the movers of great masses, the dominators of great crowds or the men who, at the microphone, can hold the attention and control the judgment of many millions. Such were not the masters of the French tribune. No more than so many eminent lawyers did the *virtuosi* of the Chamber have an equivalent power of effective speech outside the arena whose rules and temper they knew so well. This had not always been so. Gambetta, Déroulède, Clemenceau, above all, Jaurès, could dominate both the senate and the people. But in the period between the two wars, the leaders of French politics were less and less concerned with the outside world, less and less able to repeat their parliamentary successes outside. Their rhetoric was often generous, even moving, as it was when M. Herriot appealed to the great and true commonplaces of the republican tradition, but it was not a call to action, at best it was an appeal for resistance.

This decline in the power of the political leaders to move the man in the street was crucial in a country where government by speech was so important. As long as power went to the masters of parliamentary tactics (of which a great part was the skilful use of parliamentary oratory) this did not much matter. But in a crisis where it was no longer enough to modify or to express the opinion of the Palais Bourbon, when the Chamber had no opinion or dared not express what opinion it had, the lack of tribunes of the people was felt. France was provided with masters of formal rhetoric, fit for the 14th of July; she was even better

xvii

provided with masters of debate fit for the daily rhetorical games of Parliament. She was not provided, as both Britain and America were provided in their great crises, with masters of public and general speech. The country of Danton and Lamartine had now nothing but Guizots and Ferrys—at best. For Guizot and Ferry were men of ability, of courage, of character. Not all of the spokesmen of the regime in its critical years could lay claim to be all these epithets. Political questions were, indeed, discussed at a higher level than they usually were at Westminster or at Washington. But it was not unimportant that the most brilliant debater and reasoner of the Left, M. Blum, was not merely lacking in popular appeal, but normally and wisely did not pretend to have it. And as far as the Right had a master of doctrine and an inspirer of action, it was Charles Maurras, almost stone deaf, a man of the study and of the docile, listening group.

One of the most revealing episodes of these pages is Mr. Werth's account of the short career of M. Doumergue as the saviour of Society (and possibly, if it could be managed, of the Republic as well). It was not merely that the restorer of political purity had been the ally, the assistant, the accomplice of M. Caillaux when that master of the political game was most clearly revealing his indifference to petty scruples. That was quite a long time ago, and evil communications do not always corrupt political good manners. It was from Tammany Hall, that Governor Al Smith and Senator Wagner came—and more austere organizations have produced far less upright and far less useful statesmen. The ex-President of the Republic, the great sinecurist of the Suez Canal, appearing as the new Cato the Censor, had its comic side, but a good deal could be allowed to meridional powers of acting and something, perhaps, to a lingering Huguenot fondness for outward respectability. What really angered and terrified the old comrades of the new saviour of public order and public solvency was his appearance as a demagogue. He was not a demagogue in the vulgar sense of the term; it was not that he stirred up evil passions against the rich or the Jews or any other minority. It was his methods, not his objects, that angered and even frightened the politicians. For he insisted on speaking directly to the people, over the air, breaking through the elaborate barriers erected, by law and custom, between the sovereign people and its executive mandatories. It was not that Papa Doumergue's fireside chats were very stirring or in themselves likely to inspire more than mild agreement or disagreement in those in whom they did not inspire boredom. But if Doumergue, why not others? The French political system, for two generations, had been increasingly organized to neutralize the powers of the orator or leader who could move men to action, not merely to voting on a motion of confidence according to parliamentary rules. Had the Chamber had such members on February 6, they might have been outside haranguing the mob as it threatened to invade the Palais Bourbon. But equally they might have been outside haranguing the mob to induce it to invade the Chamber. That kind of talent was dangerous; so it was distrusted and hamstrung. And it was as naive to expect the French politicians to encourage that talent, to give its possessors opportunities to exercise it, as to expect the courtiers of Versailles to give Mirabeau his chance to save the monarchy—and them—while there was yet time. So Doumergue was treated as if he were at least another Boulanger, if not a first or second Bonaparte on his way to absolute power based on a popular plebiscite. Alas! for France and the Republic, there were no parliamentary politicians who were a danger to the Republic or to Parliament in 1934—and none who could arouse the people to save France from the Germans and the generals in 1940.

It was not that there were not men of courage and ability, of understanding and energy, but how was the people to distinguish between the forcible and the forcible-feeble, between the men whose energies were aroused by dangers and the men who were numbed by it? The creation of such personal, non-parliamentary reputations was made as difficult as possible. So when the great crisis came, the bewildered, desperate, betrayed French people turned to the one emblem of independent authority that remained to a Marshal of France. There were so few Marshals[1]; there were so many ex-Prime Ministers, leaders of the Chamber and the House, masters of the arts that control debating bodies, parliaments and party congresses, *voces et praeterea nihil*. It was, in fact, the politicians, MM. Lebrun, Herriot, Reynaud, who were in favour of carrying on the war from Africa; as happened in Germany in 1918, it was the nerves and resolution of the great military chiefs which snapped first. Ludendorff preceded Pétain, both in despairing of the military situation, in throwing up the sponge and in placing the blame on civilian shoulders. But that the French people took the word of the Marshal, that the Third Republic collapsed with as little resistance as the Second Empire, is a lesson that Frenchmen and friends of popular government everywhere must ponder. In 1871, Daumier drew his Bonapartist peasant looking at the ruins of his house and reflecting on the overwhelming support he and his class had given to Napoleon III less than a year before: 'We didn't vote for that.' So said the Frenchman of 1940; so would have said the Englishman or the American had he had to face such disasters under such leadership.

[1] Franchet d'Esperey was the only other Marshal living in 1940. He was a complete invalid.

For to return to the theme suggested in nearly every chapter of this book, the French political system increasingly made rapid and effective decision impossible. It was, indeed, more and more designed to make *any* fundamental decision impossible. The whole Parliament, not merely the nominal executive, had been slowly transformed into a constitutional monarch who reigned but did not rule. But in a great nation, some body or bodies must rule, openly or covertly. In easy, settled times, the issue may be evaded as it was evaded for the old principalities and republics of the eighteenth century before the conquering and crusading Republic asked of them, 'By what authority?' When there is this vacuum of authority, it is sooner or later filled from without or within. In 1940 it was filled from without as it was in the Venice of 1797. The Third Republic, like the Venetian Republic, has many claims on our gratitude and respect:

> 'Men are we and must grieve when even the Shade
> Of that which once was great is pass'd away.'

But what remains? That can best be answered by an anecdote. In 1870, the main French Army was shut up in Metz under Marshal Bazaine who, after the news of Sedan, refused to have any belief in the effectiveness of the resistance of Paris, or in the new armies summoned from the soil of France by the genius of Gambetta. So, as soon as it was decently possible, he surrendered his great force which could thus be preserved intact 'to restore order.' But for the premature surrender of Metz, it is probable that Paris would have been relieved by the amateurs who took over when the professionals failed. For this crime against the nation, Marshal Bazaine was tried by court martial. His defence was simple. After Sedan, the Emperor prisoner, the legitimate government destroyed, a mere insurrectionary *camarilla* professing to resist those Prussian armies which had triumphed over the imperial troops, what was there left to trust in, to fight for? It was a soldier who was a Prince of the Blood, who answered him. *'Monsieur le maréchal, il y avait la France.'*

There was France; there is France, and a France that less than ever is likely to forget the need of a faith in the Rights of Man and the Citizen in the presence of the armed enemies of France—and of all other nations. The present rulers of Vichy may have hoped to tame the wild beast by making him at home; if they have not learned better, the French people have. They will recover their liberties and their pride, but they are hardly likely to embody them in the political system whose last years are the theme of this book.

February, 1942   D. W. BROGAN

Contents

BOOK I: 1933-36

BOOK II: 1937–39

EPILOGUE

THE TWILIGHT
OF FRANCE

BOOK I: 1933–36

I. NON-STOP 1919–32

THE church bells were ringing in the old rue St. Jacques; and the Paris crowds were frantic with joy. The Armistice had been signed at Rethondes that morning. Like all other officers and soldiers who happened to be on leave in Paris that day, Lieutenant Jean Piot[1] was loudly cheered by the people in the street. *'Vous faites une drôle de tête!'* somebody in the crowd remarked. 'What are you making that face for? Aren't you pleased it's over?' *'C'est aujourd'hui que ça commence!'* said Jean Piot.

Anyway, that's what he told us very late one night during a Radical Congress at the Bar Basque at Biarritz.

Whatever Jean Piot may have thought of it at the time, most of his countrymen thought of the Armistice as an end, not as a beginning. For several months afterwards France was in a state of blissful repose. The nightmare was over. Fifteen hundred thousand young Frenchmen were dead; France was bled white by the War; but anyway, it was over— and France had won. Germany had been brought to her knees, and Mr. Lloyd George said she had been knocked out for sixty years. Clemenceau was at the height of his glory. Strasbourg gave him and Poincaré a rousing welcome; and, seeing the French troops enter Strasbourg, even Marcel Cachin, the future Communist leader, wept with joy.

There was all the fearful devastation in the North; but it would now be repaired. After the Armistice came the lengthy peace negotiations; and the spring of 1919 was marked by great labour unrest, until Clemenceau agreed to introduce the eight-hour working day—which made him unpopular with the Conservatives. His popularity declined still further when it was found that the peace treaty, by leaving the Left Bank of the Rhine to Germany, was not giving France the one thing she really needed —a safe Eastern frontier.

On June 28, the day the Treaty of Versailles was signed, there were large crowds in the streets of Paris, and the town was illuminated at night; but the people were not nearly as joyful as they had been on the 11th of November. Many besides Lieutenant Jean Piot must have said to themselves: *'C'est aujourd'hui que ça commence.'*

[1] Until the War Editor of *L'Œuvre* and Vice-President of the Radical Party.

I

France was less happy on the day the Peace Treaty was signed than on Armistice Day. She had, as the phrase went, won the War, but lost the peace. Foch had asked, for the sake of France's future security, the annexation of the Left Bank of the Rhine or, failing that, the creation of a buffer state under French control; Clemenceau abandoned this claim in exchange for an Anglo-American convention guaranteeing militarily France's Rhine frontier. But soon afterwards, when the Versailles Treaty was signed, America denounced the convention and England followed suit.

The United States also refused to enter the League of Nations. France felt cheated. She had been left face to face with Germany with a frontier between them which, after the end of the Rhineland occupation, would be little better than the frontier of 1914. As for the League, it was still an unknown quantity, after America's departure; and Poincaré treated it as a joke. It is true that, at the time of the Cannes Conference, Mr. Lloyd George offered to make amends for the rejection of the Anglo-American convention; but the Briand Government was overthrown before the proposed British guarantee was given any careful consideration. After that, relations with England went from bad to worse—which in turn encouraged Germany not to pay reparations; and, in the end, Poincaré decided to invade the Ruhr in order to obtain reparations, or better still (if only it were possible), to disrupt German unity, before she had time to regain her political and military strength. But the separatist movement in the Rhineland, though supported by France, proved a complete failure; the immediate material benefits that France derived from the Ruhr occupation were negligible (they were later estimated at one milliard francs net), and the tension between England and France almost reached breaking-point.

When this became clear, the French people, though not perhaps unfavourable to the Ruhr occupation at first, turned against Poincaré. They were also annoyed with him because he had increased what little taxation there was in France, by 20 per cent. The movement was led by Edouard Herriot, who believed in the possibility of a reconciliation with Germany, and who considered a reconciliation with England essential, and believed in giving the League a fresh start.

.   .   .   .

The Cartel des Gauches, who won the election of 1924, were to suffer severely for the extravagance of their predecessors. Financial difficulties caused the downfall of the first Herriot Government which had lasted from June 1924 to April 1925, and of the six Radical or semi-Radical

Governments which fell in increasingly rapid succession between April 1925 and July 1926, when Poincaré returned.

Inflation was in full swing, and sent down the franc at a spectacular rate. Caillaux—'le traître Caillaux'—was brought back by M. Painlevé in May 1925; the 'financial wizard' made a spectacular *rentrée* but could do nothing. The *mur d'argent*—or, to use a more modern phrase, the Two Hundred Families—was sabotaging the Left-Wing Governments; though it is only fair to say that the Chamber itself could not make up its mind on any coherent programme of financial salvation. The Socialists demanded a capital levy, and the Radicals would not hear of it and hated all forms of tax-increases.

.   .   .   .

If this second post-War phase was full of internal difficulties, it opened up hopeful prospects in the international field. Luck had it, in 1924, that France and England both had Left-Wing Governments. The Ruhr was evacuated, and the Dawes plan was agreed upon—the only satisfactory reparations settlement (as M. Herriot afterwards claimed) that France had ever obtained; a settlement which was to bring France twenty-five milliard francs. During the same year the Herriot Government hoped to place the League on a solid basis by giving its full support to the Geneva Protocol (mainly the work of Dr. Beneš) designed to render the League Covenant—and particularly Article Sixteen—an instrument of practical politics. Unfortunately, a storm was set loose against the Protocol by the British Conservative Press, which declared it monstrous that the British Navy should be used as 'the world's policeman.' A few weeks later the Labour Government was defeated, and the new Tory Government under Mr. Baldwin, with Austen Chamberlain as Foreign Secretary, rejected the Protocol *en bloc*.

Together with Stresemann and Lord d'Abernon, the British Ambassador in Berlin, Mr. Chamberlain devised a new plan for 'keeping the French quiet.' Herriot frankly disliked the scheme—which, in its final form, became the Treaty of Locarno—and considered it a miserably poor substitute for his beloved Protocol; but Briand, who, in the middle of 1925, took possession of the Quai d'Orsay—a position he was going to retain for the next six years—thought better of it.

In subsequent years, without ever abandoning security as his first principle, Briand made numerous concessions to Germany, and British opinion encouraged and flattered him by proclaiming him the Apostle of Peace. So strong was the 'Briand myth' in Europe that Poincaré, though disliking Briand at heart, and all that he stood for, did not attempt to replace him at the Quai d'Orsay and return to the 'strong' policy of the Ruhr Occupation.

.   .   .   .

The third post-War period, 1926–9, may aptly be called the Poincaré-Briand period. In home politics everything went very smoothly. Poincaré formed a National Government, and being a man of great tact, he managed to reduce to a minimum the friction between its component parts. Briand and Herriot, though men of the Left, both members of his Cabinet, got on well with the Premier for, unlike the Premiers of certain other 'National' Governments (such as Doumergue and Laval), Poincaré was always loyal to his colleagues, and was in every sense a true Republican. Since 1922 France had been in a state of economic prosperity, in spite of, and partly because of, the falling currency. Her trouble had been monetary, not economic. Poincaré, aided by an obedient Chamber, put the Budget right in a few days, by getting Parliament to vote nine milliards of new taxation.

The years 1926–9 were the happiest and most prosperous of post-War France. The one unhealthy element—the falling currency—had been eliminated; and the hectic years of the currency crisis were succeeded by four years of economic and financial stability. Trade was brisk; French exports reached record figures in 1928–9, and tourism during those years represented an annual item of invisible exports of over ten milliard francs, and the years were marked by an unprecedented devèlopment in the new French industries, such as motor-cars. Between 1919 and 1929 the number of cars in France had increased tenfold. The *bourgeois* youth of Paris became motor-mad; motoring, jazz, cinema and cocktail bars became the chief interest of a large part of their lives, and older Parisians shook their heads at this Americanization of Paris. The Loucheur Building Act started an unprecedented building boom all over France, and transformed much of the country round Paris into a mass— an incoherent mass—of ugly red-roofed suburban houses and villas. The old ring of fortifications built in 1840 was razed to the ground, and blocks of flats were built in their place, and the old boundary between Paris and its surroundings became largely a fiction. Paris, the town of three million people, now surrounded by a ring of industrial suburbs full of active new industries, became a vast conglomeration of nearly six million people. A large number of the new inhabitants of this greater Paris were foreigners, whom the trade boom and shortage of labour had attracted to France.

The finances of the State had never been more prosperous than during

1926–9. The enormously fat 'Papa' Chéron was M. Poincaré's Minister of Finance; and the thrifty old Norman managed to pile up in three years a surplus of something like nineteen milliard francs. About one-third of this money was spent on the so-called 'Maginot Line,' which France began to build in 1928—the year in which the military service in the French Army was reduced from eighteen months to one year. Its purpose was to make up for the eventual shortage of recruits—for 1935–40, the lean recruiting years, resulting from the low birth-rate during the War were not far ahead; and, anyway, it was better to take precautions for the future, Stresemann or no Stresemann.

. . . .

The election of April 1928, held at the height of the economic boom, was little more than a plebiscite for Poincaré. The Right and Centre Parties got a small majority. The effort of getting Parliament in July 1929 to ratify the Mellon-Béranger and Churchill-Caillaux debt agreements, put a heavy strain on Poincaré's health, and early in August he resigned his Premiership. He underwent two serious operations, and was never to return to public life again. He retired to his country house at Sampigny in Lorraine, and, opening the window with trembling hands, he would look anxiously at the Eastern horizon. He felt 'they would come again.'

M. Briand became Premier, but only to be overthrown at the re-assembly of Parliament in October.

But although he lost the Premiership, he remained at the Quai d'Orsay.

Briand had been the master of France's foreign policy since 1925. He had no illusions about France's lasting hegemony. He knew only too well that France had neither Germany's population, nor her industrial resources. If peace was to be preserved, it could only be by coming to terms with Germany. His rhetoric was magnificent and had a profound effect on French public opinion. On one occasion, alluding to the Press subsidized by the armaments firms, he said that there were 'pens made of the same steel as guns.'

Briand's programme of Franco-German reconciliation would have made greater headway had he not been constantly restrained by his critics at home. That was why the famous Thoiry programme, agreed upon between Stresemann and Briand, came to nothing. That is also why all French concessions to Germany were made with hesitation and bad grace. The Germans thanked England for her pressure, and France got no thanks. As for Stresemann, he was attacked by his own Nationalists for being too slow in obtaining the required concessions. Especially since

5

the publication of the Stresemann Papers, it has been assumed in France that Stresemann was insincere and that Briand allowed himself to be duped. Perhaps Germany, as she grew in strength, would have abandoned the League of Nations and repudiated Locarno in any case, Hitler or no Hitler. But, even so, was not Briand right in having at least *attempted* this policy of Franco-German *rapprochement*, and of bringing Germany into the 'peace system'?

. . . .

1930 to 1932—years in which Tardieu and Laval played the dominant part in French affairs—were marked by a reaction against Briand's policy. Briand still remained at the Quai d'Orsay until January 1932; but his influence declined.

Unlike Briand, Tardieu always began by saying no; but, under British pressure, he nearly always finished by saying yes. It was he who negotiated the lamentable Young Plan, and agreed to evacuate the Rhineland—an evacuation which he surrounded with stern but purely theoretical safeguards. In 1930 he was offensive to Germany; this gave him a certain personal satisfaction, and it embarrassed Briand; but, in practice this changed manner amounted to little—except that it made England rabidly anti-French.

The Austro-German customs union which was revealed in March 1931 was a terrible blow to Briand. The nationalist Press, fulminating against the duplicity of Germany, declared the Customs Union to be the final proof of Briand's folly. In the end the Customs Union was condemned by the Hague Court by a majority of one; but the damage was done. Confidence was shaken; and the collapse of the Kreditanstalt marked the beginning of the tremendous financial crisis in Central Europe, which culminated in the Hoover Moratorium.

Briand, whose position was badly shaken by the Austro-German *coup*, tried to restore his authority by standing for the Presidency of the Republic. He was badly beaten by M. Doumer, the candidate supported by the Right of the Chamber and by the greater part of the Senate, of which he was president. It was another shattering blow to Briand. When he heard the result, he had a weeping fit, and fainted. He went to Geneva a few days later, and said he would become the 'pilgrim of peace.' The Press of the Right ridiculed the phrase, while the Left hoped that he would drop Laval, and become the leader of all the Left-Wing forces of the country. Feeling perhaps that death was near, he preferred to stay on at his beloved Quai d'Orsay. Laval was the real Foreign Minister.

When during the great financial crisis that summer Brüning came to

6

Paris, Laval refused him all help, though he promised to return the visit. He went to Berlin in August, trailing a doddering old Briand behind him. As they stood on the balcony of the Hotel Adlon the German crowd below cried: '*Retten Sie uns!*' The Right Press reported the words with much glee. But Laval did nothing to 'save' Germany. A Franco-German Economic Committee was set up; but it did nothing. During the Berlin visit, Laval and Briand also visited Hindenburg; Laval, rather obtusely, thought that by paying a visit to war criminal No. 2 he was making a great gesture of goodwill.

The Hoover Moratorium which, as the French said, 'was calculated to save American investments at the expense of reparations,' was badly received in France. Having failed to obtain the assurance that the United States recognized the legal interdependence of reparations and War debts —an interdependence that Poincaré had assumed in asking Parliament to ratify the Franco-British and Franco-American debt agreements, but which had never been formally recognized by the United States—the Radicals voted against the acceptance of the Hoover Moratorium. But Laval and the majority of the Chamber and Senate yielded to British and American pressure.

After the Hoover Moratorium Laval had few illusions left that reparations would again be paid, and he tried to make the best of a bad job. Leaving Briand behind, he travelled to Washington in the company of his daughter, José, and talked to President Hoover. But Hoover committed himself to nothing, and only said that the creditor powers must take the *initiative* in arriving at a settlement. That Mr. Hoover's phrase committed the United States to nothing became only too apparent after the Lausanne Conference in June 1932.

At the end of 1931 the Laval Government was blessed with a new problem: the Manchurian conflict. The League Council met in Paris on that occasion, for Briand, who was its president, was too ill to go to Geneva. Presiding over the League in the Clock Room at the Quai d'Orsay he cut a pathetic figure. He could hardly speak. He was overcome by a continuous fit of coughing and could continue his speech only by sipping Evian after every few words, and gasping for air. I still remember that bottle with the pink label standing in front of him, which he poured out with a trembling hand. He was like the dying symbol of forlorn hopes.

Shortly after the memorable Council Meeting at the Quai d'Orsay (the only international conversation from which Laval—how typical already of his attitude to the League!—had carefully kept aloof), Laval dismissed Briand, and took his place as Foreign Minister. Two months later—on March 7, 1932—Briand died.

One of the riddles of post-War history is whether or not Germany would still have gone Hitlerite *had the policy of Briand been allowed to continue beyond 1930*. The view held for a long time in England was that conciliation would have been achieved if only Briand had had his way, and if the concessions had been granted with less delay, and less hesitation, and with better grace. The opposite view, widely held in France and also by some Englishmen, is that the more Germany got, the more menacing and the more militarist she became; for was it not significant, they say, that the evacuation of the Rhineland should immediately have been followed in July 1930 by the first great election victory of the Nazis, and that the end of reparations should have been followed within scarcely a month—on July 20, 1932—by the 'eviction' of the Socialist Government of Prussia by Von Papen's 'Government of Barons'? Again, on December 11, 1932, the 'principle' of German equality was recognized at Geneva. Six weeks later, Hitler came into power.[2]

Shortly before Briand's death, Tardieu had again become Prime Minister. British opinion disliked him even more than Laval. England had developed a disarmament *mystique*—a feeling not unlike the peace ballot *mystique* of 1935; and the French view that security—that is, mutual assistance—must be organized first, and that only then could disarmament follow, was treated by most of the British Press as rank heresy, and by the British Government as a French attempt to drag Britain into Continental commitments—in other words (though these 'other words' were carefully avoided) to get Great Britain to recognize her obligations under Article Sixteen—the sanctions article—of the Covenant.

With the exception of the extreme Left—and M. Léon Blum was at that time the most prominent exponent of 'disarmament first'—French opinion found it difficult to be fired by this British disarmament *mystique*, and when the Disarmament Conference met in February 1932 Tardieu bluntly produced a plan for an international army.

The plan was, naturally, badly received in England, where it was said that under Tardieu France was carrying her clamour for security to altogether unheard-of lengths. Tardieu was annoyed, and when, in March, he was asked to come to Geneva to attend a Four-Power meeting

[2] There is another theory—not without foundation—that what contributed more than anything to the economic crisis in Germany—and so encouraged the rise of Hitlerism—was the super-protectionism of the Hoover Administration and the Ottawa agreements.

comprising Brüning and the British and American representatives, he gave full vent to his bad humour and developed an attack of laryngitis. It was Brüning's last chance of saving his government and the Weimar Republic in the face of a fiercely growing opposition.

$$\cdot \quad \cdot \quad \cdot \quad \cdot \quad \cdot \quad \cdot \quad \cdot$$

When Laval and Briand were in Berlin the Germans could well cry *'retten Sie uns!'* For at that time France was still financially (as well as militarily), the strongest power in Europe.

Yet, before the French public knew it, the rot had set in, and after the election of 1932, the new Herriot Government was again faced—as in 1924—with an alarming financial situation. For the prosperity under Tardieu and Laval was in reality—and as distinct from the Poincaré period—an artificial one. It was a period of financial scandals—the most important was the Oustric case, which contributed to the overthrow by the Senate of the first Tardieu Cabinet in December 1930—and sensational bank failures, and the Tardieu Government in particular, spent money without counting. Bankrupt shipping and air companies were refloated with public money, and the refloating of the Banque Nationale de Crédit alone cost the State two milliards. When the Herriot Government came into office after the 1932 election, the cupboard was bare. The economic depression which, Tardieu had foolishly boasted, would not affect France, was making itself felt.

II. THE ABORTIVE FRONT POPULAIRE OF 1932

FRANCE was tired of Tardieu and Laval; and the General Election of May 1932 resulted in a victory for the Left, with the Radicals as the main winners and the Centre parties as the main losers.

The Radicals and Socialists, though not agreed on any common programme, formed an election alliance, and agreed to withdraw their candidates in the second ballot for the benefit of the most favoured Left Candidate. The other Left-Wing groups also adhered to this arrangement, with the exception of the Communists (an important difference from 1936). The Socialist-Radical alliance worked, in the main, very

9

satisfactorily, though (and this again was different from 1936) more in favour of the Radicals than of the Socialists. The second ballot, on May 8, was held in a peculiar atmosphere. Two days before, a Russian maniac had assassinated President Doumer at an ex-servicemen's book sale in the Faubourg St. Honoré; and M. Tardieu, supported by M. Millerand, had tried to turn the affair into a Zinoviev Letter by maintaining (against all evidence) that Gorguloff, the assassin, was a Communist. The French electorate remained completely unaffected by this Red Scare, and voted just as they would have voted in any case.

The Socialists had expected a greater victory than their gain of seventeen seats; and at the Socialist Congress at the Salle Huyghens, on May 28, M. Léon Blum declared himself to be greatly disappointed.

But if the Socialist-Radical alliance worked well in the election itself, great difficulties started as soon as the question arose of forming a Left Coalition Government. Herriot, the premier-elect, was conservative in many ways, and he also greatly disliked the Socialists' insistence on disarming unilaterally to the 1928 level. He had the secret dossier about Germany's secret armaments on the brain. At their Congress, on May 28, the Socialists drew up a minimum Government programme—which, called after the Salle Huyghens where the Congress met, goes by the name of *Cahiers Huyghens*. It is interesting to look back on this programme; for, with its forty hour working week, nationalization of the manufacture of armaments, etc., it resembles—while going beyond it in certain respects—the Front Populaire programme of 1936.

But although all the items of the *Cahiers Huyghens* had figured in resolutions voted a few months earlier by the Radical Congress, M. Herriot refused to accept the *Cahiers Huyghens* as a basis for Government co-operation with the Socialists.

The divergence revealed on that occasion between Radical theory and Radical practice caused great discontent among the Left Wing of the Radical Party, and for a long time relations remained very strained between Herriot and young and bold Left-Wingers, like Cot and Bergery. *The discord between the two great Left parties—the victors of 1932— was the dominant note in French parliamentary life during the next two years, and was largely responsible for the great crisis of French democracy, which culminated in the riots of February 6, 1934.*

. . . .

The three principal events under the Herriot Government of June-December 1932 were the Lausanne Conference, where reparations were finally buried; the presentation to the Disarmament Conference in

November 1932, of the Herriot-Paul-Boncour Peace Plan providing for mutual assistance by means of national contingents earmarked for League Service, for the abolition of air bombing and the international control of civil aviation. Britain's 'sanctions' commitments under this plan were made fairly elastic. But Great Britain was still suffering from her disarmament *mystique*, and the Herriot-Paul-Boncour plan was little better received in England than the Tardieu plan earlier in the year. The third event was the War debts controversy, which ended in the overthrow of the Herriot Government on December 15. French public opinion was convinced that it would be iniquitous for France to pay another penny in War debts to the United States, now that reparations were dead—killed, in fact, by the Hoover Moratorium. Nevertheless, M. Herriot felt that it would be 'worth while' paying the War debt instalment of 19½ million dollars that fell due on December 15, for the sake of future Franco-American relations (for Herriot believed that America might still play a part in the organization of collective security) and also in order to keep in step with Great Britain who, on that first pay-day since the end of reparations, was still prepared to pay the United States the full instalment—and not merely a token ten per cent, as she did later. The Herriot Government was overthrown on December 15, 1932, and after a brief spell of a Paul-Boncour Cabinet, which on January 28 was overthrown over a small financial question, the Daladier Government came into office. The day it was formed Hitler was appointed German Chancellor.

· · · · · ·

This Daladier Government, which lasted nearly nine months—until October 23, 1933—was, in reality, the last normal and comparatively stable Government before the storm broke loose in January 1934. Mr. G. D. H. Cole, in his *Intelligent Man's Review of Europe To-day*, published in October 1933, wrote:

France, the traditional home of revolutionary movements since 1789, now seems by contrast the most stably organized of all nations of continental Europe. . . . Even to-day, while the French Socialists form a powerful party and Communism has a considerable following, the bourgeois Republic seems more stable in structure than any other continental state, and Socialism seems less likely in France than in Great Britain.

The danger of Fascism in France did not even occur to Mr. Cole.
Since its formation in January the Daladier Government had been supported by a large part of the Socialist party, but in the Autumn it

had to rely chiefly on its dissident Right Wing, that Right Wing which M. Blum in a famous speech in July 1933 had denounced as 'Fascist.' The *débâcle* of the German Social-Democrats, MM. Marquet, Déat and the other dissident leaders said, had shown that it was no longer any good to 'think internationally,' and that it was time for French Socialism to recognize this unpleasant truth. The class war was nonsense. The slogan they put forward was 'Order, Authority, Nation.' M. Blum declared himself 'horrified.'

The trouble started over the 1934 Budget, as soon as the Chamber met in October 1933 (a few days after Germany's departure from the League). Among the measures proposed by M. Daladier was a six per cent cut in state wages.

In spite of the numerous sops—such as the control of the armaments firms and the beginnings of a nationalization of the petrol trade—offered to them in the Daladier Bill, the Socialists (with the exception of twenty-nine members, who had already virtually split away from the Party at the July Congress, and who were to form, two months later, the Neo-Socialist Party[1]) refused, after lengthy negotiations, to support the Bill on a motion of confidence.

Blum's criticism of Daladier was precisely the kind of criticism that the Socialists were to address to every government between 1933 and 1936. Deflation was, in their view, not a remedy against the crisis, nor even a remedy against budget deficits, but, on the contrary, an aggravation of both the crisis, and, through the resulting diminution in purchasing power, of the financial difficulties of the State.

But justified as Blum's argument may have been in the abstract, he showed on October 23, 1933 that he lacked a certain sense of reality. For immediately after the overthrow of the Daladier Government, one did not need to be a prophet to say that the formation of a National Government, following the collapse of the Left-Wing majority, was now a matter of weeks. Everybody in the Chamber lobbies said so.

Less than a month later, the Socialists overthrew the Sarraut Government, and it was not until the Chautemps Government was formed that it began to dawn on the Socialists that this constant massacre of governments was beginning to irritate public opinion, and that Parliament was in danger of becoming totally discredited. So they resorted to a subterfuge. Instead of voting either for or against Chautemps's financial bill, they feigned indignation, and, walking in a body out of the debating hall,

[1] The Neo-Socialists then still included some good democrats like M. Renaudel, who were opposed to Blum's pedantic policy, and who foresaw its fatal effect on normal parliamentary government.

12

declared that they would have nothing to do with such disgraceful financial methods.

But this repentance came too late.

III. THE SIXTH OF FEBRUARY AND AFTER

SINCE the fall of the Daladier Government, on October 23, a large section of public opinion had been in a state of growing irritation against Parliament; the economic crisis was growing worse; the international outlook was depressing, and the Press of the Right, apparently frightened by the prospect of a belated reconciliation between the Socialists and Radicals, started a vigorous campaign in favour of a National Government.

And then, in the last days of the year, the papers began to speak of a great financial scandal at Bayonne engineered by a person called Stavisky. By the 5th of January the Stavisky scandal had risen from the *fait divers* status to the monumental front-page headline. In the Press of the Right the Stavisky scandal and Republican Government became synonyms.

Stavisky, in the meantime, had vanished, and it was not until January 8 that the police discovered him in a villa at Chamonix—with a bullet through his head. Nine-tenths of Paris were convinced—and even the Socialist Press said so—that Stavisky, who 'knew too much' had been 'suicided' by the police. But who had ordered his removal? Actually, the facts clearly suggest that he committed suicide—though very probably 'by persuasion'—while the police were encircling his villa.

However fantastic some of the stories published about Stavisky in the Press, they all agreed on the following points: that he was a jailbird who had been released *en liberté provisoire* in 1926; that his trial had been postponed nineteen times, and that he had been able, in the interval, to engineer one swindle after the other—the total amounting to some 200 million francs. It was also clear that he had had many influential friends in the police, in the judiciary, and in Parliament, without whom all this would not have been possible.

The Royalists of the *Action Française* fully exploited the situation. The first meeting of the Chamber was accompanied by noisy Royalist

13

demonstrations in the Boulevard St. Germain, with hundreds of young men shouting, '*à bas les voleurs!*'

Chautemps's attitude struck even many people of the Left as unfortunate: he appealed to the Chamber not to over-dramatize the *affaire*, and—worse still—refused to agree to the formation of a parliamentary committee of inquiry. The *Action Française*, which had published some 'revelations' about him even before the outbreak of the Stavisky case, intensified its campaign against Pressard, Chautemps's brother-in-law whom, in his capacity of *Procureur Général*, it declared to be directly responsible for the facilities Stavisky had received from the Parquet, the Public Prosecutor's office in charge of the conduct of prosecutions.

After many violent scenes in Parliament, the Chautemps Government resigned on January 25, before waiting to be overthrown by the Chamber.

The Royalist demonstrations in the streets had, in the meantime, become, not only more frequent, but more and more violent in character; they were popular with a large part of the public. The police, under M. Chiappe, treated the rioters with the utmost consideration.

. . . .

M. Daladier, the new Premier, had the reputation of a strong and honest man, and his appointment to the Premiership had a soothing effect on Paris. He thought that the Radicals had been discredited, and that another party government would be unpopular. He therefore began by trying to form an 'above-party government of strong men' belonging to almost every party, and including such respected members of the Right as M. Ybarnégaray—later a leading member of the Croix de Feu. In the process he treated the Radicals with some disdain, and they resented it. But the Right felt that Daladier was not the right man to form a National Government—they had their own plans, and waited until the situation had become still worse—and they let Daladier down. In short, by the time his government was formed, he had managed to make himself unpopular with everybody; and he felt that his chances were poor for surviving a motion of confidence at the Chamber.

Chiappe, the Prefect of Police, had behaved during the Royalist demonstrations in January, as no servant of the Republic should have behaved.[1] That, and the fact that he had always been hated by the Socialists and Communists, prompted Daladier to take a bold step, which would please the Left at the Chamber, and secure for him the sorely

[1] That, and not his alleged negligence in the Stavisky Affair, which Daladier later tried to prove, was the real Left 'case' against Chiappe.

14

needed Government majority. Three days before the meeting of Parliament he rang up Chiappe, and declared that the government wished to offer him the post of Governor-General of Morocco. Chiappe did not take long to understand that his presence was no longer wanted at the head of the Paris police. He refused. He declared that if he left Paris in the present circumstances, he would feel a dishonoured man. Daladier afterwards claimed that Chiappe was in a rage, and threatened to *descendre dans la rue*—to start a riot in the streets of Paris. Chiappe denied this and claimed that the Premier had misunderstood him; he had said: *je serai à la rue* and not *'dans la rue'*—I shall be in the street, a poor, homeless man.

Whatever may have been the exact words that Chiappe used on that occasion, Daladier had acted with great incoherence. Either Chiappe had played a discreditable part in the Stavisky affair or had shown by his behaviour that he was a menace to the Republic—and in either case it was absurd to appoint him Governor-General of Morocco—or else his conduct was impeccable, and there was no reason for removing him from Paris.

No less absurd was Daladier's dismissal of M. Fabre, the director of the *Comédie Française*, presumably because his production of Shakespeare's 'anti-democratic' *Coriolanus* had given rise, during the whole of January, to noisy Royalist demonstrations in and around the theatre, and his replacement by M. Thomé, the head of the Sûreté Générale. A policeman running the *House of Molière*!

. . . .

During the three days between the dismissal of Chiappe and the meeting of the Chamber, a great many things happened in Paris. The Right, naturally, decided that the treatment that their dear Chiappe had suffered could not be taken lying down. Rumours were, moreover, started on the Right that the real man behind it all was Frot, the ambitious Minister of the Interior, who, it was said, was planning a coup, and that Daladier was merely a tool in his hands. Stories were circulated about Senegalese troops having been called to Paris to shoot down anyone who opposed the government.

The facts have been distorted on both sides. February 6 was not, strictly speaking, a 'Fascist plot'; still less was it a 'massacre of patriots.' It is true that several ex-servicemen's organizations, the Royalists, the Jeunesses Patriotes, the Solidarité Française and other bodies hostile to the Government decided two or three days in advance to meet at various points of Paris in the afternoon and evening of the 6th of February, and to march across the Place de la Concorde towards the Chamber and to demonstrate against *les voleurs*. The Croix de Feu, who had already demonstrated in the Faubourg St. Honoré on the previous night, were to concentrate their forces on the left bank of the Seine, behind the Chamber. There is no doubt that there was some co-ordination between these various groups; and that one of the men behind the scenes was none other than M. Chiappe, still flaming with Corsican resentment over the loss of his job. But there is little to show that there was any clear plan to seize power, or even to capture the Chamber. It is true that on February 7, while the Daladier Government was still resisting the clamour for its immediate resignation, a plan was beginning to take shape for setting up a provisional Government at the Paris Town Hall; but on February 6, this plan had not yet been worked out; nor had any preliminary agreement been reached on the subject among the 'Fascist' leaders.

One has to remember that at that time the Croix de Feu, the Royalists, the Solidarité and the Jeunesses Patriotes had no more than a few thousand active members between them, and that they would have been incapable of a real armed uprising. What they reckoned on was the support of the Paris public as a whole; and the most that they could reasonably have aimed at was the resignation of the Daladier Government. When this happened, on February 7, Colonel de la Rocque announced that 'the first objective had been attained.' The 6th of February was less the work of Fascists than of an important section of public opinion, which had been worked up into a state of anger by a fierce anti-Parliamentary and particularly anti-Left campaign in the Press. The Press of the Right, and the people behind it, were alarmed by signs of a growing reconciliation between the Radicals and Socialists, and the possible restoration of a Left Cartel. They wanted a National Government dominated by the Right.

It is, unfortunately, only too true that, on February 6, Daladier had nobody *for* him in the whole of Paris, for even the best Republicans felt that the Daladier Government was not very well qualified to represent the Republic. Soon after four o'clock the Place de la Concorde was already crowded with people, many of them shouting '*à bas les voleurs.*' At five o'clock the first stones were thrown at a police lorry; and by six o'clock, after the closing of the shops and offices, the Place de la Concorde became a howling mob of about a hundred thousand people. All over the square, and in other parts of Paris, battles broke out between the rioters and police; the efforts made by parties of mobile guards and by mounted guards to disperse the crowds were in vain. A few of the mounted guards were dragged down from their horses and savagely beaten, until they were rescued by their comrades. Many of the horses were badly cut by razor-blades attached to the ends of walking-sticks— one of the weapons used by the 'peaceful demonstrators.' Other weapons and missiles included pieces of macadam broken up at the Tuileries end of the Concorde, and bits of iron railings and fragments of garden chairs brought down from the Tuileries gardens, which, like the Place de la Concorde, was crowded with rioters. But the main battle was in front of the bridge, where the cordon of police and mobile guards were pelted for hours with stones and pieces of iron. So many guards and policemen were injured during the evening that the cordon had to receive reinforcements every ten minutes or so. From time to time a party of guards would charge the crowd; but with no result. The rioters—mostly young men—had by this time made up their minds to break through the cordon, and to burst into the Chamber.

About seven o'clock a motor-bus was stopped by rioters (for strangely enough, the traffic had not been stopped in the Place de la Concorde) who, after several unsuccessful attempts, succeeded in setting fire to it. For two hours the bus burned, filling the air with the stench of burning rubber. Burning rags were also thrown through six of the windows of the Ministry of Marine, and it was only by fighting for their lives and with the greatest of difficulty—for the rioters persisted in cutting the hoses —that a fire brigade put out the flames by nine o'clock.

In the meantime the attacks upon the police cordon on the bridge had grown more and more fierce; and a few minutes before eight o'clock, when the cordon had been forced halfway across the bridge, the guards fired a first volley. Here is how I described that memorable episode in *France in Ferment*, written a few months after the riots:

> At 7.30 a procession of the Solidarité Française, numbering about 1,500 men, arrived in the Concorde from the Grands Boulevards. Their avowed intention was to break through the barrier on the bridge and to reach the Chamber. The fire-hoses which the police [in the Place de la Concorde] turned on them were captured by the rioters and turned against the police and guards. The mounted guards retreated almost in a state of panic, and added to the bewilderment of the *gardes mobiles* on the bridge. The rioters advanced shouting 'Come on to the Chamber! Throw the guards into the river!' Several of them pushed their way through the barrier of police vans [on the bridge], others ran along the parapets past the barrier. There was a moment of panic among the guards. The police and the guards, feeling their lives in danger, brought out their pistols. It was then that the

17

first shots were fired. Some were fired into the air, others at the rioters. M. Marchand and the officers tried to prevent the panic-stricken guards from firing any more, but before they could stop them there was another volley; many of the men who had been pelted with stones for hours had, by this time, lost all self-control. Six of the rioters were killed and forty injured. A stray bullet fired into the air killed a woman on the second floor of the Hotel Crillon.

During that onslaught many of the guards and police, including three of the men in command of the bridge, were injured—M. Marchand, struck on the head by stones and other missiles, had to be taken to the Chamber infirmary; Inspector Rotée had his ankle fractured; Captain Fabre, gravely wounded in the stomach by a piece of metal, was rushed to hospital. The rumour that he had been killed added to the exasperation of the guards.

Although the southern part of the Concorde was cleared almost as far as the obelisk (which was now no longer floodlit), the rioters on the northern side of the Square were frantic with rage. Thousands were now shouting, 'Assassins! Assassins!' at the guards on the bridge. The police forces in front of the bridge increased to nearly five hundred. Discouraged by the firing, the rioters kept for a time at a respectful distance.

Another volley was fired in similar circumstances shortly after eleven o'clock by the guards on the bridge; and this time six rioters were killed and seventeen wounded. It was the general opinion that if they had not done so, the rioters would have broken into the Chamber.

The rioters were a mixed crowd of people, many of them belonging to no particular organization; and, oddly enough, there were even some Communists among them. For among the organizations that demonstrated in the Champs-Elysées and the Concorde that night was the A.R.A.C., the Federation of Communist ex-servicemen. And when in his book on *France To-day and the People's Front* M. Thorez, the Communist leader, asserts that the Communists organized 'anti-Fascist' demonstrations on February 6, one cannot help wondering on what evidence the assertion is based.

The Croix de Feu were in reality less active during the riots than most of the other Royalist and 'Fascist' organizations. At that time they were still composed of ex-servicemen only; and instead of going into the Place de la Concorde, they gathered in the Esplanade des Invalides and its side-streets, at the back of the Chamber. Marching backward and forward, and singing the 'Marseillaise,' they created the impression that they *might* have broken into the Chamber (which was but poorly defended from that side) had they wished to do so, and had they been prepared to sacrifice a few lives.

With the Right, the 6th of February has become a heroic legend. I know many young Frenchmen who still point proudly to some little scar on their forehead. '*C'était le 6 Février, à la Concorde.*' If they had said: '*C'était à Verdun,*' they could scarcely have said it with greater pride.

.   .   .   .

On the following day the Daladier Government resigned. It thought at first of proclaiming martial law, and of resisting by every means. But the police could scarcely be relied upon any longer; and even the army was doubtful. And there was a loud public clamour in Paris for the immediate resignation of the government of *fusilleurs*.

Even the President of the Republic, pressed hard by Marshal Lyautey, who threatened that morning to march on the Chamber at the head of the Jeunesses Patriotes, was against the government, and threatened to resign, if the Daladier Government resisted. Early in the afternoon the Daladier Government hurriedly resigned. Immediately afterwards M. Lebrun called for M. Doumergue who, for several weeks past, had nursed his candidature for the Premiership—a candidature that was being advocated, more and more openly, by the Right Press.

February 7, with the police completely disorganized, was a day of lawlessness in Paris. Hundreds of sinister hooligans descended from heaven knows where upon the shopping centre; and between 8 and 10 p.m. the dark deserted streets resounded with the clatter of broken glass. When about ten o'clock police detachments began to patrol the streets most of the damage had been done.

The next morning M. Doumergue arrived at the Gare d'Orsay, and drove to the Hôtel Continental. He had dropped the smile that had made him so popular during his Presidency of 1924–31. He now looked grave and extremely self-important. He was like a grandfather who had come to restore order among a crowd of very naughty children. The following evening, February 9, his government was formed. The Radicals, who had got a serious fright on February 6, thought Doumergue the least of all possible evils, and readily authorized Herriot and four other Radicals to join the 'government of National Truce.'

.   .   .   .

The French working class had been taken by surprise. The Communists had actually taken part in the riots; and the *Humanité* of Febru-

19

ary 7 had treated the Daladier Cabinet as a 'government of murderers'; the Radicals were bewildered. On the night of the 6th, the Socialists had voted for the Daladier Government, but it was not, as M. Blum explained before the division, a 'vote of confidence' but *un vote de combat* —that is, a challenge to those who were trying to overthrow the government by unconstitutional methods. At that time the firing was already going on outside the Chamber of Deputies. The Socialist leaders took a serious view of the government's resignation under outside pressure, and urged Daladier to resist. But in vain.

Nevertheless, the overthrow of the Daladier Government by 'the street' could not remain unchallenged as far as the Socialists were concerned. On February 7 the Socialist Trade Union Federation (the C.G.T.) called a twenty-four-hour General Strike for the following Monday, February 12. The order was accompanied by a statement that this had been given in co-operation with the Ligue des Droits de l'Homme, the Socialist party, the Dissident Communist (*pupiste*) party, the Anarchist Union and others—but there was no mention of the Communists.

The Communists were keeping aloof. When, on the same day, the Socialist party called a protest meeting in the Place de la Bastille, for the following day (February 8), the Communists refused to associate themselves with it. Instead, they decided to hold a protest meeting of their own in the Place de la République on February 9. The Socialists thereupon called off their meeting at the Bastille, and decided to concentrate their efforts on the General Strike on the following Monday. The attitude of the Communists was curiously incoherent; yet feeling that their whole attitude on February 6 and 7 had been absurd, and that the working class was beginning to react sharply against the 'Fascists' (regardless of the faults of Daladier), the Communists suddenly decided to take the 'lead' in the anti-Fascist campaign by demonstrating in the Place de la République. It was perhaps a tactical mistake on the part of the Socialists to have called off their own protest demonstration the day before; for by doing so, they gave the Communists the chance to claim afterwards that they, and not the Socialists, were the first to have fought on the barricades 'against Fascism.'

The Place de la République had been cordoned off by mounted and mobile guards, and for four hours, in a cold fog, a guerrilla war went on in the narrow streets of the Faubourg St. Denis, and as far north as Belleville and the Gare du Nord, between the police and the Communists. After their ordeal of February 6 and 7 the police were in a state of 'nerves,' and fired indiscriminately at the Communists—who, needless to say, were a tough lot, and did not hesitate to manhandle a *flic* whenever they got a chance. I saw many of the workmen taken on stretchers to the Hôpital St. Louis. Four men were killed that night, and two more died of their wounds. In a way, it was an aimless 'demonstration,' and yet, there was a fine spirit of idealism among these men, who risked their lives simply in order to 'protest.' They were not the scum and rabble, as they were called in the Right Press on the following day : and although most of them were miserably poor people, not a single shop was looted during that night. Nor did they burn down any churches— which was another red scare story published in the British Press the next day. The 'demonstration' of February 9 was in the best revolutionary tradition of the Paris working class; and the death of the obscure workmen who sacrificed their lives fighting on the barricades that night, stirred in a strange way the imagination of the French working class as a whole. On February 9, 1936, not only red, but also tricolour wreaths were laid on the statue in the Place de la République.

It was not until February 10 that the C.G.T.U. (the Communist trade unions) decided to join in the General Strike, but making it clear, at the same time, that they had not been guided by Socialist initiative. The Socialists and the C.G.T. were greatly satisfied with the decision the Communists and their trade unions had taken. They felt that, in spite of themselves, the Communists were coming nearer a 'united front,' under the pressure of working-class opinion.

This General Strike was the first vast anti-Fascist demonstration in France. Except that the organizers of the strike had themselves decided not to make things too unpleasant for the ordinary citizen (they did not, for instance, stop the railways, water and lighting) the twenty-four hour strike was very nearly complete.

It was a warning, and a severe warning to the 'Fascists.' Though keeping formally apart, the Socialists and Communists in reality joined forces for the first time; and there were moments when the friendly Communist crowds would form a ring round the Socialist leaders, and when the Communist leaders were cheered by the Socialist rank and file, who shouted : '*La soudure !*'

It may reasonably be said that if in subsequent months the drift of the Communists towards the Front Commun was largely determined by Moscow's desire to build up an anti-Fascist front in France, it was determined, at least to the same extent, by the ardent desire of the rank and file—both Communist and Socialist—to join forces against the common enemy.

21

IV. PARLIAMENT BULLIED BY THE STREET— THE CROIX DE FEU

M. Doumergue, the new Premier, appeared to be well-intentioned at first.

On the face of it, his government was at first merely one of those National Governments that are formed in France in moments of crisis, when everything else fails. To the Radicals it was the 'lesser evil'; the greater evil would have been a non-parliamentary government arising straight from the February 6 riots. This government also was a product of the riots—but an indirect one. It was a Coalition Government stretching from the Right to the Neo-Socialists, and comprising a large number of old—and even very old—and experienced politicians. The aged Marshal Pétain—a national hero—was appointed Minister of War, and General Denain, Minister of Air; and the harmonious unity of the Cabinet was symbolized by its two Ministers of State—M. Herriot, the Radical leader, and M. Tardieu, the outstanding figure among the Nationalists.

With Barthou as Foreign Minister, Chéron as Finance Minister and Laval as Minister of Colonies, it looked a sound normal government such as had already been seen before. Alone, M. Marquet, the ex-dentist of Bordeaux, who had been so offensive to M. Léon Blum before leaving the Socialist Party, was believed by some to be a man of the future. With his abrupt manner and fierce look, and Hitler moustache, Marquet had—so it was believed—the makings of a Fascist leader. 'Order—Authority—Nation,' he had declared at the Socialist Congress.

In short, *la jeunesse* was not greatly impressed by the new government, and the Socialists would have nothing to do with it. As for the Communists, they succeeded admirably in depriving the first meeting of the Chamber under the new government of all its solemnity. They constantly interrupted Doumergue's Ministerial Declaration by calling him an assassin—and one Communist called him 'the new Joan of Arc.'

The man was mediocre and vain. He had lived for seventy-two years without striking anybody as being a great man. He owed everything to Parliament—and, one might say, to the seamy side of Parliament—that seamy side against which the rioters of February 6 had rebelled. For years he had belonged to the Radical Party; he had been a Freemason, and the art of parliamentary intrigue was no secret to him. At sixty-two he was elected President of the Senate, and when Millerand was forced to resign from the Presidency of the Republic, after the 1924 election, in the course of which he had been guilty of unconstitutional behaviour,

Doumergue became, almost automatically, by the pure force of circum-stances, President of the Republic. During his *septennat* (1924–31) he made himself superficially popular by always appearing on photographs and at public ceremonies with a broad grin on his face. During the finan-cial crisis of 1925–6 he intrigued against the Left, and made every effort to bring Poincaré back into power; but all that happened behind the scenes, and was not generally known. Later he also intrigued against Briand; but never very openly. No sooner had he retired from public life than he became a director of the Suez Canal Company with a salary of something like 600,000 francs a year. (The Communists never failed to rub it in, whenever Doumergue tried to impersonate a frugal Cin-cinnatus.)

But when, towards the end of 1933, the political crisis became acute, his name suddenly reappeared in the Right-Wing Press, which began to boost him, at first vaguely, and then openly, as a possible 'saviour' of France. The only ex-President of the Republic available in a great emergency requiring for the Premiership a prominent 'above-party' per-sonality with the air of a 'grand old man,' was Doumergue. Actually, he was old rather than grand; but his grandness was soon manufactured by the Press. He waited until the situation had become really dramatic —so that his reappearance in Paris could create the maximum effect. He wanted to be a national hero. And it was not a role that suited this old politician.

During the first half of 1934 the country was in an acute state of 'nerves,' and could hardly have stood the shock of a first-class political crisis that would have followed Doumergue's departure. The death of Prince, the Paris Magistrate, who was found dead on the railway line near Dijon on February 21, was exploited by the Press of the Right with an unscrupulousness that exceeded even the worst excesses of their Stavisky campaign. Prince had been at the head of the Parquet, the Public Prosecutor's office, which was responsible for the lenient treat-ment Stavisky had received during his seven years of *liberté provisoire*, in the course of which his trial was postponed nineteen times. Pressard, the Public Prosecutor, was the brother-in-law of Chautemps; and when Prince's dismembered body, with one leg tied to the rails, and a knife lying by his side, and a narcotic in his stomach, was discovered, the Press of the Right immediately declared that Prince had been murdered in this horrible manner by a gang in the service of Chautemps and Pressard, because Prince, they said, knew all about Pressard's role in the handling of the Stavisky Affair.

Subsequent inquiries not only proved conclusively that Prince was

23

anything but a *magistrat intègre* and that he had very good reasons to be afraid of being shown up; but they also left no doubt that the 'luring' to Dijon and his 'murder' had been staged by himself. In doing so he may have thought of saving his family from disgrace and from being deprived of a pension; he may also have wanted to clear his own name and play a trick on Pressard.

Yet at the end of February, before all the details of Prince's sudden departure for Dijon were known, it looked like a case of murder, and M. Sarraut, the Minister of the Interior, and M. Chéron, the Minister of Justice, both alleged that a *maffia* had murdered Prince. And even afterwards, when it was becoming clearer every day that Prince had committed suicide, the government still persisted in calling it murder. Léon Daudet said that there would have been a rebellion if they had *dared* to defy public opinion by calling it suicide. The 'blackmail of the street' was functioning to its full capacity.

Writers of detective stories were sent to Dijon and into the 'underworld' of Paris to outdo each other in sensational revelations about the *maffia*. But, oddly enough, whenever a paper hired a real detective, it never published his report. The *Matin* was the first to send a professional detective to Dijon, and he at once concluded that Prince had committed suicide. His report, though announced in advance, was not published. *Paris-Soir* went one better. Under headlines bigger than would be used if a world war broke out, it announced that it had engaged the three greatest detectives of Scotland Yard to make an independent investigation into the Prince murder—Sir Basil Thompson, Inspector Wensley and Inspector Collins. But, after nearly doubling its circulation as a result it finally failed to publish their report.

M. Doumergue did nothing to stop not only the *maffia* stories in the Press which were rapidly endangering the sanity of Paris, but also the savage campaigns in the Right-Wing Press against the Radical Ministers in his own Cabinet. The 'Party truce' was non-existent. But with public opinion in Paris in such a state, the Radicals could do nothing. The memories of February 6 were still fresh; the Croix de Feu were gaining in strength, and the Press missed no opportunity to suggest that if Doumergue went, there would be another and 'more decisive' 6th of February.

. . . .

During those first few months of the Doumergue régime the Croix de Feu were rapidly becoming a vital force in France. Many of the young men who joined it during those months were idealists. The 6th of February had a terribly seamy side to it—Chiappe, and the Banks, and the Press, who were determined to throw out the Radicals and Socialists. But it had its noble side—the youth who thought in all sincerity that they were fighting for a 'cleaner and better France.' And during the months that followed the 6th of February Colonel de la Rocque discovered a *mystique* that appealed to the best instincts of the Conservative youth of France—the *mystique ancien combattant*—the *mystique* of the disinterested man ready to sacrifice himself for his country, as against the low instincts of the 'parliamentary profiteers' who served themselves and not the country. Those Croix de Feu meetings in 1934 had a fine human quality. I take the following extracts from a description I gave of a Croix de Feu meeting in the Bal Buillier in June 1934.

None of them wore uniforms, but there was an unmistakable air of military discipline in the crowd. The people were neither rowdy nor stupid like the Solidarité Française. They were earnest, well-disciplined and, on the whole, decent-looking people. The elder men, the real Croix de Feu, wore tricolour armlets decorated with a fiery cross with a skull in the centre. The young men wore armlets with F.C.F.; these were the sons of the Croix de Feu.

What class did these people belong to? Except for a few ostentatiously proletarian-looking old men—some of them with wooden legs—stationed in front of the platform, nearly all these people were middle class and, I should say, upper middle class. The young people were of the *fils à papa* or University student type—a well-dressed and a well-washed crowd. . . .

And then there was a sudden commotion in the audience, 'La Rocque! La Rocque! La Rocque!' Pushing his way through the crowd La Rocque stepped briskly on to the platform. He greeted the audience with a charming smile and a wave of the hand. He was far less like Hitler than like a lieutenant in the *Ancien Régime*.

La Rocque spoke in a matter-of-fact, staccato, slightly raspy voice like a man giving orders to his soldiers.

'Before there is a new order of things, an end must be put to disorder, and the idea of authority must be restored. The men of the United Front who call us rioters, reason like Asiatics. We stand above little party combinations and electoral intrigues. We are patriots among patriots, *nous sommes des sociaux parmi les sociaux.*'

Those were the heroic days of the Croix de Feu; they were many young men there, who had their heads broken in the Place de la Concorde, fighting thoughtlessly and spontaneously 'against the deputies,' and who must have been disappointed—not that they knew exactly what they would have preferred instead—when the Daladier Government they had driven out, was replaced, two days later, by a government presided over by an old politician of seventy-two.

Colonel de la Rocque tried to console them. He treated the Doumergue Government as 'a poultice on a gangrenous leg'—as a temporary solution to be followed, before long, by a better and more complete solution. La Rocque's 'sixteen years of profiteering' was not unlike Hitler's 'fourteen years of Shame.' He had no clear programme, but said that there was no need for any.[1] A *mystique* was more important; and a *mystique* he had undoubtedly created. And there were some young men in the movement who scarcely hesitated to call themselves openly Fascists.[2]

During 1934 the Croix de Feu became the rallying-point for the Conservative youth of France. The old and select ex-servicemen's organization was enlarged by affiliated bodies, like the Volontaires Nationaux, which gave an opening to the young. The organization of the *dispos* (short for *disponsibles*)—young men ready at a moment's notice to carry out La Rocque's orders—laid the foundations for those 'lightning mobilizations' which became the regular practice of the Croix de Feu in 1935, and alarmed the Left so much.

V. DOUMERGUE'S PLOT AGAINST THE REPUBLIC

THE Stavisky Affair had shown that there was something far wrong in France. The parliamentary system seemed discredited, and appeared to call for drastic reforms, and, in taking office, the Doumergue Government had promised such reforms. In March, a Parliamentary Committee, including several Radicals, had approved, by a large majority, but hurriedly and thoughtlessly, certain constitutional reforms, including one strengthening the Prime Minister's powers. Doumergue was the first French Premier to adopt the wireless as a frequent means of

[1] Later he assembled his ideas in a book called *Service Public*—a collection of platitudes with a vaguely Fascist and 'Corporatist' tinge. A number of ideas like the 'family vote' had also been borrowed from the Royalists. La Rocque, whose brother is an A.D.C. to the Duc de Guise, was suspected by many of being Royalist rather than Fascist in sympathy.

[2] As distinct from certain definitely Fifth-Column elements, the Croix de Feu, despite all their admiration for Mussolini, remained anti-German in the main. (Author's note, 1942.)

doing propaganda for himself and his programme. They were called 'Addresses to the Nation.' This rather weakened the position of the Radicals in their subsequent conflict with Doumergue. But it should be emphasized that if the Radicals rebelled against Doumergue in October, after approving several of his reforms 'in principle' earlier in the year, it was not because they suddenly began to consider the principle of these reforms entirely wrong, but because, by that time, Doumergue and the people behind him (Tardieu and the Croix de Feu) had become definitely suspect in their eyes. They also realized on second thought that the Doumergue reforms had little bearing on the evils revealed by the Stavisky Affair; and that they aimed at something different.

At the time (if not to this day), the French Constitutional conflict of September-November, 1934, was grossly misunderstood abroad. Under the influence of the French Right-Wing Press, there was a widespread belief among foreign commentators that Doumergue was trying to improve French democratic methods; and even so excellent a journalist as Mr. Vernon Bartlett went so far as to proclaim Doumergue the Great Defender of French Democracy against the selfish, intriguing politicians.

Doumergue's first few broadcasts had merely amused 'the Nation,' who thought his grandfatherly ways absurd, but harmless.

The fifth 'Discourse to the Nation,' incorporating Doumergue's constitutional proposals, was, however, in a more poisonous vein: it contained all his stock arguments of how he had saved France in a spirit of self-sacrifice, and of how the Socialists and Communists had become *the* enemy. But it was not until the 7th Discourse—which he made a few days before his fall—that the Radicals also received their due share of his detestation.

The fifth Discourse began *moderato*, with the usual touches of communion between the great man and *his* people.

Here then were his proposals, the first of which was six weeks later, to break up the 'National' Government:

'Let us give the government authority,' he said, 'by inserting a few words in the Constitution, which would endow the head of the government with the title and rights of Prime Minister. Let us allow the Prime Minister, when the government is in disagreement with the majority of the Chamber, to appeal immediately to the country without having to go through the present formalities and procedure. You can be sure that Cabinet crises will become rare when the fear of immediate dissolution will put the brake on impatient and usually

27

unjustifiable ambitions, which are more frequently at the root of such crises than a conflict of principles and ideas.'

Further, M. Doumergue proposed that the government alone should have the initiative of proposing expenditure; that the new Budget, if not voted before December 31, should be passed by government decree (this 'decree' Budget of the following year being the same as that of the current year); and that the government officials who were 'a privileged class, protected against all economic uncertainty' be forbidden to belong to trade unions, to strike, or to indulge in any kind of political agitation against the State.

In his sixth Discourse to the Nation, on October 4, most of his speech was merely a harangue against the Front Commun. He (Doumergue) had offered the Socialist leader (Blum) a seat in the government.

> He refused my offer; and I regretted it; for I made my offer in all sincerity. But I concluded from his refusal that the Socialist-Communist alliance was close at hand. I was not mistaken.

After enumerating all the horrors of a Socialist-Communist Government, Doumergue concluded, almost hysterically: 'How can we avoid dictatorship and civil war? It is quite simple. The Union of all Frenchmen, except the Front Commun and its naive sympathizers, has become indispensable. Without such a union nothing can succeed.' The Fascists were not even mentioned, they were classed, by implication, among the defenders of freedom.

What roused the storm was the proposal concerning the Prime Minister's prerogatives. But what puzzled many people was Doumergue's (and also Tardieu's) claim that the plan had been borrowed from the British Constitution.

The most apt criticism on the subject came from England, and was extensively reproduced in the Left Press. It was a letter in the *Manchester Guardian* of September 29, 1934, by Mr. Ivor Jennings:

> M. Doumergue is asking for powers which no British Prime Minister has ever had.
>
> In the first place, it is the business of the Cabinet, not of the Prime Minister, to advise a dissolution. Moreover, where the Cabinet decides on dissolution the King can insist on a formal minute. . . . The question has not appeared important in England because normally the Cabinet is homogeneous, and the Prime Minister has either to agree with his Cabinet or break up his party. If we were as accustomed to coalitions as are the people of France we should recognize the importance of the distinction. For it is easy to imagine circumstances in

which a Prime Minister of a Coalition could, by a timely dissolution, strengthen his own party at the expense of the parties of his colleagues.

In the second place, the Prime Minister of the Cabinet has no *right* of dissolution. . . . The fact that the present King granted a dissolution to Mr. MacDonald in 1924 is no more proof of such a right than the fact that Queen Victoria granted a dissolution to Lord Derby in 1859. It would certainly be a dangerous doctrine that the Prime Minister of a Coalition Government could, without his colleagues' consent, demand and insist upon a dissolution. The justification for any action of his lies in the majority which he and his colleagues possess in the House of Commons. He has no personal authority except the support of the Cabinet. The justification of the King's discretion lies in his assumed impartiality in party questions.

The strength of the British Government, so far as it exists, does not lie, as M. Doumergue appears to think, in the powers of the Prime Minister, but in the support of a reasonably homogeneous party. That support is in part maintained by the prerogative of dissolution; but only because the existence of two or three large parties usually creates a strict alternative between a dissolution and the accession of the opposition. If the present party system were broken into fragments it is clear that the King would have to exercise his discretion with care.

I am not arguing, of course, that the power of dissolution is not necessary in France. I suggest only that it must be justified by French conditions and not by false analogies with the British constitution.

But the controversy that was let loose by the broadcast of September 24 was interrupted for about a fortnight by the assassination at Marseilles on October 9 of King Alexander of Jugoslavia and M. Barthou, the French Foreign Minister, and by the internal complications to which it gave rise.

The constitutional controversy broke out with renewed violence about October 20, a few days before the opening of the Radical Congress at Nantes. On October 22, M. Doumergue received M. Bienvenu Martin and other prominent representatives of the Left-Wing majority of the Senate, who had come to protest, in the name of France's republican liberties, against his proposed reforms. The meeting was a stormy one; and M. Doumergue lost his temper completely. The Senators argued that there was no valid reason for depriving the Senate of its privileges and for leaving the dissolution of the Chamber to the sole discretion of the Premier, or even of the Premier *and* the President of the Republic. They rightly observed that they had never been asked, since 1877, to sanction the dissolution of the Chamber, and that there was therefore no

29

reason why they should be considered an obstacle in the way of dissolution.

Apart from Doumergue's conflict with the Senate majority, the most important prelude to the Nantes Congress—a prelude which did perhaps more than anything else to give courage to the Radicals in their struggle against Doumergue—was a series of articles by M. Blum in the *Populaire* from October 19 to October 24. The Doumergue Government, he said, was in substance a Fascist Government. The Chamber had surrendered in February to the blackmail of the 'street.' Were Doumergue and Tardieu now going to try it out on the Senate?

'Many a deputy,' M. Blum said, *'would cease to be free*; for his arguments and feelings for and against the government might be outweighed by personal considerations, which will have no connection with his inner convictions or with his duty towards his constituents. And if individual deputies are no longer free, *Parliament will no longer be free either*. And if there is no free parliament to face a Government, there is no parliament. But let us further assume that there is a sufficient number of heroic deputies to overthrow the Government. What will the Government do in that case? In terms of Article 6 of the Constitutional Law of February 25, 1875, *the government that is overthrown by the Chamber has to resign. Not so if Doumergue's project is voted by the National Assembly. The government that has asked for the dissolution of the Chamber remains in power. In the past the Chamber dismissed a government; now a government will dismiss the Chamber.* I wonder what to call such a régime—I certainly cannot call it a Republic.

'Why,' M. Blum said in conclusion, 'is the adventure of May 16, 1877, described in history as a *coup d'état*? Was it because MacMahon dissolved the Chamber? Surely not. The dissolution procedure was perfectly legal. *The reason why it was deservedly called a* coup d'état *was that the Marshal dismissed a government—the Jules Simon Cabinet—with a majority at the Chamber, and because, after the dissolution, he maintained in office the Broglie-Fourtou Cabinet which had been condemned by the chosen representatives of the people. Further, he gave the subsequent election campaign the appearance of a plebiscite— in which the electorate was asked to choose between the majority of the Cabinet and himself.* In the "reformed State" of MM. Doumergue and Tardieu such a *coup de force* after the manner of May 16, 1877, would become the normal method of government. This government would cease to be parliamentary. Such a State would cease to be a Republic.'

At the Nantes Congress the majority of the Radicals, though hostile to Doumergue, were prepared to give the negotiations with the Premier another chance.

The motion that was carried almost unanimously said that 'the Radical Party is ready to associate itself with any reform tending to increase governmental stability and to improve the functioning of the State apparatus, but it cannot endorse any measure which would create personal prerogatives liable to endanger the republican liberties of the country.'

But during the next week the *chantage de la rue*—the blackmail of the street—came clearly into play. M. Jean Goy, one of the leaders of a reactionary ex-servicemen's association, and several other less well-known people went about the Chamber lobbies, whispering mysteriously to anyone who cared to listen, that 'their fellows' were 'itching to come out at any moment.' In short, if Doumergue fell, there would be another 6th of February. Meantime, the conflict between Doumergue and Parliament reached breaking point and on November 8 the Radicals sent in their resignation. They called the Fascist bluff. Nothing happened. There were no riots in Paris. Doumergue departed in a frenzy of rage. In a statement to the Press he declared that he had been driven out by 'the men whose policy had led to the riots of last February and to the death of unarmed ex-servicemen' who had demonstrated that day in the Place de la Concorde.

This was a provocation of the worst sort. So much so that even Doumergue felt obliged to issue another statement asking the country to 'keep calm.' Actually, the country was keeping calm, and had no intention of starting a revolution for M. Doumergue's benefit.

There were some young Croix de Feu men who afterwards claimed that November 8 was the greatest opportunity the Fascists had ever had to march on the Chamber and to seize power, an opportunity that La Rocque had missed.

I doubt whether it was an 'opportunity.' On November 8 a Fascist *coup* would not have had one-quarter of the popular support that was given to the riots of the 6th of February.

Democracy, as M. Blum wrote at the time, had won its first victory over Fascism.

VI. ENTER LAVAL

Six hours after the resignation of the Doumergue Government, the new Government was formed, with M. Pierre Etienne Flandin as Premier.

Flandin, six-foot-four, and forty-six years old (he was the Benjamin of the Chamber in 1914) is a *grand bourgeois* and looks like a prosperous business man—and English rather than French. He counts Press Lords, Members of Parliament, and other well-known Englishmen among his friends and likes to give himself English airs.

The adjective 'incomplete,' that has been applied to him, is rather apt. One always feels with Flandin that there is 'something lacking.' He has little personality; his speeches are sound and well delivered, but are incapable of stirring the imagination or arousing enthusiasm. Personally, he is courteous and amiable; but he leaves people indifferent. He is colourless.

In the days of Tardieu, M. Flandin, the Minister of Finance, was very unpopular with the Socialists and Communists. He had been legal adviser to the Aéropostale Company, which went into liquidation in rather unfortunate circumstances, and although M. Flandin was not guilty of anything very definite, his association with the company was exploited against him.

But in time they became more lenient towards him—especially since his open breach with Tardieu in 1932.

In taking office after Doumergue, he did not abandon the 'party truce' formula, and the construction and party composition of his government closely resembled the Doumergue Cabinet. The wily Mandel, joining any government for the first time, became Minister of Posts and Telegraphs, where, even at the risk of making himself unpopular with the officials, he was to do some useful work, especially in improving the French wireless. General Denain, in spite of his Croix de Feu sympathies, remained Minister of Air; but at the Ministry of War, Marshal Pétain, who had refused to continue, was replaced by his protégé, General Maurin. (It was not true, however, as was alleged in the Press of the Right, that he had branded Doumergue's forced resignation as 'a crime against France.')

The Flandin Government was received almost joyfully by the Chamber, which granted it an overwhelming vote of confidence. The Doumergue nightmare was over. As if to prove to M. Doumergue that Parliament was capable of doing good work even without his reforms, the Chamber voted the 1935 Budget in record time, and in the process agreed to abolish the individual deputy's right to propose expenditure.

In a speech on November 28, M. Flandin indicated the principal feature of his financial policy: neither deflation nor devaluation. 'Deflation in France,' he said, 'is practically at an end. Fortunately, world prices, in terms of gold, are definitely rising.'

But a great deal of adjustment in industrial production was also necessary, and such adjustment—including lower costs—would be difficult unless interest rates came down. He therefore advocated a revival of trade by means of cheaper money. This proved a stumbling-block. On January 1, M. Flandin replaced M. Moret, the orthodox Governor of the Bank of France by M. Tannery, who was believed to favour a more liberal credit policy.

Unfortunately, M. Flandin was soon to be disappointed. M. Tannery became an obedient tool, not in the hands of the Government, but of the Regency Council of the Bank. The latent conflict between M. Flandin and the Bank of France broke out a few months later; and his policy of cheap money was defeated.

Although, for a long time after the Doumergue fiasco, there was little street rioting, the membership of the Croix de Feu continued to increase, and their organization, aided by generous donations from financial and industrial magnates, was improving; but the old fervour was gone. The extremists in the movement could not forgive La Rocque the 'opportunity' he had missed, and were becoming restive. In April, 1935, there was a notable example of 'direct action' when a number of them raided the Socialist headquarters in the rue Feydeau in Paris; several of the men were arrested on the spot; and Colonel de la Rocque condemned and denounced them. His 'uncomrade-like' attitude on that occasion increased the discontent among the Fascist extremists in the movement; and it is about that time that several prominent Croix de Feu men (who had favoured a *putsch* on the day of Doumergue's resignation) resigned in disgust. But the Croix de Feu were not played out yet—as they were going to show in 1935, under the more sympathetic Premiership of M. Laval.

.   .   .   .

Internationally, Laval had become the dominant figure in French politics long before the formation of his own Cabinet in June 1935. He had succeeded M. Barthou after the Marseilles assassinations at the Quai d'Orsay; and, by refusing the Premiership after Doumergue's resignation, he had clearly shown his determination to remain master of France's foreign policy. The automatic pistol of the Croat terrorist killed not only King Alexander of Jugoslavia, but also M. Barthou, and with him, a definite French foreign policy.

The policy of Barthou, during his eight months in office, was to build up a vast defensive alliance against Germany which, in his opinion, was obviously and inevitably preparing for war. To keep up League appearances, he left the pacts open for Germany to join; but since she had no desire to join them he was quite prepared to do without her; and if his system amounted in practice to an encirclement of Germany, it would be, he said, her own fault. He thought that, whatever she signed, she would not keep her promises. Only a vast anti-German coalition could keep Germany quiet. He brought Russia into the League, and laid the foundations for the Franco-Soviet Pact; he prepared the plans for an Eastern Mutual Assistance Pact, and also hoped, by reconciling Italy and Jugoslavia, to 'organize security' in the Mediterranean and in Central Europe, and to settle in a permanent and satisfactory manner the problem of Austrian Independence.

His visits to the Little Entente capitals in May 1934 were a triumph: for the Czechs, Rumanians and Jugoslavs felt that the foreign policy of France had at last fallen into the strong hands of a man who knew his own mind, and who was not prepared to abandon Eastern Europe to German penetration. But Poland proved the stumbling-block. Beck and Pilsudski, who both received him rather coldly, resented his *rapprochement* with Russia, and would not enter the Eastern Pact unless Germany came in too (for which there was no hope). Nor was England very friendly to Barthou. His 'policy of encirclement' was denounced as dangerous and shortsighted—though, in principle, the British Government finally approved of the Eastern Pact. As for the Mediterranean, the conversations were cut short by the assassin's bullet. The encouragement Ante Pavelich and the other Croat terrorists had received from Italy infuriated Jugoslav opinion, and—for a time at least—it was no good resuming Barthou's attempts to 'reconcile' the two nations—a reconciliation to which he had attached the greatest importance.

Laval kept us guessing: would he, or would he not continue Barthou's policy?

The short meeting I had with Laval towards the end of November was something of a revelation. The Russians, the Little Entente and others, were getting worried. Rumours were current of direct conversations that Laval was hoping to start with Germany; and the probable visit to Paris of Von Ribbentrop was widely spoken of. Laval, wearing the usual white tie, sat at his desk in his study at the Quai d'Orsay, whose luxuriously gilded furniture contrasted strangely with the Minister's plebeian appearance. An envelope with a German stamp lying

34

in front of him, and addressed briefly to 'Aussen-minister Laval, Paris,' caught my eye. I referred to the worries of the Russians and the Little Entente and to the rumours about Von Ribbentrop. Laval stood up. 'Look at this,' he said, walking across the room and pointing to a map of Europe on the opposite wall. 'Do you see this big red patch right in the middle of Europe?' he said, pointing at Germany. 'Do you *really* imagine that we can have peace and collective security in Europe so long as we haven't brought *this* into our peace system?'

It was a flash that lit up everything, showing in one second the difference between Barthou's policy and the policy that Laval intended to pursue.

.   .   .   .

Laval is a 'man of the people' and is proud of it—not that this protects him against certain *parvenu* ambitions—such as the ambition to marry his daughter into an aristocratic family. He is also secretly proud of being a Papal Count; Mussolini, who arranged it beforehand with the Vatican, must have been aware of Laval's weakness for titles.

He was born at Chateldon, a small town in Auvergne, where his father kept a café and a butcher's shop, and was also in charge of taking mail-bags to the station. Laval's biographers suggest that young Pierre was not satisfied with the plebeian career his father had mapped out for him, and insisted on being sent first to a secondary school, and later to the Faculty of Law in Paris. For a time he was *pion* (supervisor) at a school at Lyons, where he served under Herriot who was *professeur agrégé*. Later he returned to Paris, where he became a 'poor man's' lawyer, and soon afterwards legal adviser to the C.G.T. The Socialist Party—of which he had become a member—held him in high esteem. On May 8, 1914, the *Humanité* wrote:

> In short, he is a young man come straight from the people, and as a *militant* he has done his duty valiantly, and has placed at the disposal of the Socialist Party his indefatigable energy and his pungent and convincing eloquence. His profound knowledge of labour problems, and his fine gifts as a speaker promise to render even greater services to the Party when he becomes a Deputy.

In May 1914, after an election campaign, in the course of which he thundered against 'Capitalism, the cause of all sufferings and all iniquity,' and against the 'folly of armaments,' and promised to 'liberate Labour of all oppression and exploitation,' he was elected deputy for the Paris suburb of Aubervilliers. He styled himself 'Revolutionary Socialist' and in the 1914 Chamber he was the youngest Socialist member. When the War broke out, he was one of the two deputies whose names were inscribed in the famous Carnet B.—the list of dangerous revolutionaries to be closely watched by the police. He did not serve in the War. In a particularly sickly biography of Laval, Mlle Odette Pannetier describes his distress at being turned down, for reasons of bad health, by the *conseil de révision* (though the same book contains in another connection, a rapturous description of his perfect health and marvellous endurance). Actually, one may doubt whether he had any great desire to go to the front. During the second half of the War he belonged to the minority of the Socialist Party in favour of peace negotiations with Germany through the Second International. 'Stockholm' (where the proposed meeting with the German Social Democrats was to take place), he exclaimed at the end of a pacifist speech at the secret meeting of the Chamber, on June 2, 1917, shortly after the diastrous Nivelle Offensive—Stockholm is our Polar Star!' He also spoke at length of the mutinies in the French Army, and was, in short, thoroughly 'defeatist.'

Towards the end of the War he began to evolve towards the Right. 'Democracy,' he said in a speech in 1919, 'will never fraternize with the Bolshevists.' He was defeated in the 1919 election, but re-elected in 1924 as a moderate Left-Wing independent on the *Cartel des Gauches* list. After holding a number of posts in Left Governments in 1925, he became Minister of Labour in Poincaré's National Government of 1926, and in 1930, having been, by this time, elected to the Senate, he joined Tardieu's Cabinet, also as Minister of Labour. It fell to his lot to elaborate the new Social Insurance system—a task which almost gave him the appearance of being a 'Left' Minister in an otherwise reactionary cabinet. Then, in 1931, he became Premier. He was much less disliked by the Left than Tardieu. He called himself an Independent, claimed to stand 'above party,' and it is certainly true that then, and even much later, he still had numerous personal friends on the Left; and even among the Communists. For it was Laval's first principle throughout his political career never to burn his bridges.

Laval is an Auvergnat, and like many Auvergnats he is dark-skinned and negroid—though the slant of his eyes is mongol rather than negroid. With his sallow skin, his thick but short lips, scarcely covering what looks like an excessive number of irregular and dirty teeth, and his thick boyish head of smooth black hair (only beginning to turn grey), and his dark impenetrable mongol eyes, he is unimpressive at first sight. But his physique is not without good points; he has a finely shaped, narrow nose, and his hands are small and expressive—so unlike the big paws of Herriot.

Although he is a rich man (and his enemies will tell you that he is worth 40 or 50 or 60 million francs) he takes, like Briand, little notice of his clothes, and even his famous white tie is not always perfectly tied— nor always perfectly white.

No, Pierre Laval is not impressive at first sight; and yet he has a personality which grows on you. He has an engaging smile and a charming voice which makes even new-comers perfectly comfortable; and even at the height of his power he never abandoned his old habits of *camaraderie* and tutoyage—a survival of his Socialist days.

'*C'est un malin,*' people would say about him; and he was proud of being *malin.* He never pretended to be a dreamer; nor could he ever be accused of being a doctrinaire. I remember the following dialogue in the Chamber Lobby one day:

A. (*indignantly*): Laval has never even read the Treaty of Versailles!
B. (*with sublime irony*): *C'est sa force!*

.   .   .   .

Laval's most immediate worry at the end of 1934 was the Saar plebiscite. Barthou was prepared to use the Saar plebiscite as a means of inflicting at least a moral defeat on Germany. He wished the status quo vote to be as large as possible, and he gave the status quo leaders financial support. Laval, on the contrary, was desperately anxious to see the Saar problem cleared out of the way: he hoped that, after that, an agreement with Germany would become easier. Barthou was fully prepared, if it was found necessary, to send French troops into the Saar to police the plebiscite. Laval shuddered at the thought of sending French troops into what he considered in advance to be German territory. If it came to the worst—that is, if no international police force could be found to go to the Saar—he was prepared to send some French police (preferably some German-speaking police from Alsace) to do the work; but certainly not French troops.

He was overjoyed when, at the Council Meeting at Geneva early in December, Mr. Eden agreed—in spite of all the previous opposition from Mr. Baldwin and the Beaverbrook and Rothermere Press—to send British troops into the Saar, and when Italy, Holland and Sweden agreed to send contingents as well.

In the meantime Herr von Ribbentrop, Herr Abetz and other official and semi-official representatives of the German Government were coming to, or staying in, Paris, and Laval had serious hopes that great progress would be made towards a Franco-German *rapprochement* once the Saar plebiscite was over.

Jean Goy, representing the reactionary ex-servicemen, went to Berlin and was well received by Hitler; and before a sceptical Chamber M. Montagnon, the Neo-Socialist Deputy, paid a tribute to the Hitler movement, which, he said, was being misunderstood and underrated in France. Young men like Bertrand de Jouvenel and Stanislas de la Rochefoucauld, fascinated by Hitlerite 'dynamics,' and believing more in the virtues of a Franco-German alliance than in the League, acted as go-betweens between the German official and semi-official emissaries and M. Laval. Whether M. Laval himself was—at that time—already prepared to talk to Germany in terms other than Geneva terms is uncertain; but, in any case, he was beginning to believe that he was 'the only man who could save France from war.'

The Saar plebiscite was fixed for January 13, and Hitler got 90 per cent of the votes.

But Laval was soon to be disillusioned.[1] For no sooner was the plebiscite over than the German Press became aggressively anti-French. Ribbentrop and other German emissaries who had been coming to Paris in December, had now vanished. The 'only territorial difference' (as Hitler called it) between France and Germany having been cleared out of the way, the German Press immediately proceeded to nurse Germany's other grievances. Two months later, on Saturday, March 16, Hitler solemnly tore up Part V of the Treaty of Versailles and reintroduced conscription in Germany. This opened a new phase in European relations.

VII. BUILDING ON SAND

I T WOULD scarcely be true to say that Laval was 'anti-League' from the outset. It is even probable that he was anxious at first to pursue a League policy, and to achieve the maximum of 'collective security,' Laval's efforts were directed, during his first phase at the Quai d'Orsay, towards bringing Germany into the 'peace system'—by persuading her

[1] Soon after the plebiscite a friend remarked to Laval: 'And those illusions you had about Germany?' 'Illusions,' Laval replied curtly, 'that were attributed to me.'

to adhere to the regional pacts. Perhaps he did not believe that these pacts were a solid guarantee against war; but he thought that Germany's formal adherence to them might at least postpone war for a time. He also felt that countries like Germany and Italy had legitimate grievances, and he constantly tried to suggest that he would do his best to satisfy these grievances; in the meantime he tried to keep them happy with little concessions. But during the early part of 1935, Laval had not yet come to the conclusion that only a free hand for Germany in the East would save France from war. Had he lost all faith in the 'collective system,' he would hardly have signed the Franco-Soviet Pact on May 2. Later, however, he did his best not to submit the Franco-Soviet Pact to the Chamber for ratification. 'Laval,' a Soviet diplomat observed, in commenting on his hesitations about the Soviet Pact, 'is a dustbin of conflicting desires.'

But he certainly had a strong predilection for coming to terms with the Great Powers, and Italy's friendship was infinitely more important to him than the Eastern alliances. To his rustic brain, the Little Entente countries were something far and outlandish.

. . . .

Whether during his Rome talks he gave Mussolini a free hand in Abyssinia may be a matter of some speculation; though he himself denied it very emphatically in the course of the ratification debate.

But what probably happened was that Laval was so delighted with the cordiality of his talks with Mussolini that when the latter mentioned Abyssinia, Laval showed a notable lack of interest in the subject.

The French Press sang pæans of praise to Laval—'the first French Foreign Minister who had visited Rome since the War'—for the Rome agreement which, it said, marked the final reconciliation between the 'two Latin sisters.' 'France and Italy,' Bertrand de Jouvenel was told by a high dignitary in Rome, 'will henceforth be the centre of cultural radiance in Europe.'[1]

The whole of France's foreign policy during 1935 was dominated by this widespread belief in the value of the Rome agreements and in the strength of Franco-Italian friendship. It was somehow taken for granted that, owing to Austria, and to Italy's natural reluctance to see 'the German flag flying on the Brenner' her friendship for France was sincere and—inevitable.

Mussolini's process of bamboozling Laval and a very important part of French opinion was a masterpiece of Machiavellian diplomacy. Later,

[1] *Le Petit Journal,* January 7, 1935.

at Stresa, he supported Laval's mutual assistance schemes, and joined in the 'Stresa Front' against Germany; and it was also at Stresa that the ground was prepared for the subsequent Gamelin-Badoglio agreement concerning the withdrawal of French and Italian troops from their common frontier. It was all bluff.

On March 22, the Chamber ratified the Rome agreements unanimously, less 9 Communist votes.

M. Blum declared himself satisfied with the assurance given by M. Laval that there was not a word of truth in the story that he had given Mussolini a free hand in Abyssinia.

The Duce had France at his mercy: for with Italy as her friend and with all her troops available for the Rhine frontier, she felt secure as seldom before. Was she to throw away her own security for the sake of Abyssinia? The blackmailing of France had been prepared with exquisite refinement—and without her even knowing that it was blackmail!

And even as late as May 1936, when Abyssinia was defeated and sanctions were about to be lifted, an important part of French opinion still hoped that Italy would now consent to return to the Stresa Front! Not until sanctions had been raised did Italy openly join forces with Germany.

. . . .

Between the Rome agreement and its ratification another development took place, which, at the time, was considered as being of the utmost importance. It was the Anglo-French declaration of February 3, the outcome of M. Flandin's and M. Laval's visit to London.

Here was the basis for a new peace settlement; and, in particular, the door had been left wide open for an armaments agreement with Germany and for a 'legalization' of German rearmament. But Hitler preferred not to discuss the matter.

A few weeks later, and before any conversations had begun (for owing to Hitler's 'cold' Sir John Simon's visit to Berlin was postponed) Germany found what she thought to be a good excuse for simply tearing up Part Five of the Treaty of Versailles. The excuse was the doubling of the period of military service in France.

. . . .

The 'lean years'—that is the years in which there would be a shortage of recruits owing to the low birth-rate during the War—had been, for some years past, a matter of grave concern to the successive French Governments, especially in view of the growing rearmament in Ger-

40

many. One had to face the fact that Germany was rearming night and day; and, as M. Flandin said, in defending the 'Two-Years Bill,' there would be, without it, a fall in the number of recruits from about 250,000 in 1934 to an average of 118,000 during the 'lean years' (1935-9); and in 1936, there would be only 208,000 men with the colours in France, unless one added to these the 72,000 colonial troops 'temporarily' stationed in France. But even 228,000 was little compared with German effectives, which he estimated at 600,000. With the two-year service, France could at least be certain of a standing army of 400,000 men.

At all events, the Chamber voted the 'two years' by 350 votes to 196, and 39 abstentions. The Radicals were divided; even those who voted for the Government had insisted that the two-year service should be limited only to the lean years and be subject to alteration in case of better international conditions; but the Socialists and Communists were deadly hostile.

> There was at the root of all this, M. Blum said, a campaign in favour of a militarist policy, and that precisely at a time when France was happily beginning to get rid of Fascist influences. [During those months the Croix de Feu were lying very low.] The alarmist campaign in the Press was in full swing. In fact, those who were clamouring for the two-year service were less concerned about effectives than about the quality of the army. It was argued that two-year recruits made better soldiers than one-year recruits, and this, M. Blum said, suggested that the General Staff were determined to turn what looked like an emergency measure into a permanent system. The General Staff had Napoleonic ambitions, and were anxious to create a shock army suitable for aggressive ends (cries of 'No!'). If Hitler's Germany were to attack France, he was certain that the working class would rise like one man to defend the country.[2]

The Communists became more rapidly reconciled to the 'two years' than the Socialists. Stalin's statement to Laval during the latter's visit to Moscow in May, that 'he welcomed the military policy of the French Government which consisted in maintaining the army at a level consistent with France's security' was of decisive importance. The French Communists dropped their campaign against the 'two years'; and even the Socialists, in spite of Blum's attack on Stalin's 'unfortunate and ill-considered statement,' did not persist—with the exception of the

[2] Appalling, in the light of what happened, this Socialist fear of an army of *quality*. De Gaulle's book had shortly before come out, but was treated by the Left as 'Fascist.' Marshal Pétain, about the same time, wrote a laudatory preface to General Chauvineau's book demonstrating *the ineffectiveness of tanks!!!* (Author's note, 1942.)

extreme Left Wing under Marceau Pivert, who, as late as 1936, advocated at the Socialist Congress, amidst loud cheers from the gallery, and much to the embarrassment of M. Léon Blum, the Premier-Elect, the abolition of the 'Two Years.'

. . . .

The Hitler *coup* of March 16, created more annoyance than surprise in France. In a military sense, it was of no great importance, for German rearmament had been an open secret for a long time. But, diplomatically, it was a serious matter. The purpose of the German Government's move was obviously to deprive the signatories of the Rome and London agreements of any bargaining weapon.

Both Right and Left in France began to feel that a close understanding with Russia had become more essential than ever, and it was decided that Laval would go to Moscow, not in June, but much earlier, if possible.

Mr. Eden was also preparing to go to Moscow and Warsaw; and there was no reason why his plans should be altered as a result of the Hitler *coup*.

Sir John Simon's visit to Berlin on March 25–6 and (to quote the *communiqué*) his 'frankest and friendliest talks' with Hitler did not in any way improve the chances of the London programme. But, apart from that, the visit was not unilluminating—especially if we accept the overwhelming story told by the *Daily Telegraph* that Hitler outlined to Sir John Simon a programme very much on the lines of *Mein Kampf*, complete with the annexation of the German-speaking parts of Czechoslovakia, etc. It has also been suggested that during Sir John's visit to Berlin the ground was prepared for the subsequent Anglo-German naval treaty.

At all events, Sir John Simon and Mr. Eden were much impressed by Hitler's grasp of foreign affairs—which was different from Arthur Henderson's experience two years earlier, when Hitler (as Henderson told me at the time) 'flew up in the air and bellowed platitudes for an hour on end.' But in two years Hitler had learned a great deal, and knew to perfection all the weak points of British and French diplomacy.

In spite of some British opposition to such a move, France had almost instantly appealed to the League Council against Germany's violation of the Treaty of Versailles; and the French protest was among the subjects to be discussed at the Three-Power Conference at Stresa, which met on April 11, five days before the meeting of the League Council.

In these talks with Mussolini, England was represented by MacDonald and Simon (but not Eden), and France by Flandin and Laval. The talks were conducted on Isola Bella, and the Conference abounded in comic sidelights. An agreement was reached about maintaining peace in Europe—and the British and French statesmen departed, thoroughly pleased with the Duce. On the last day, Ramsay MacDonald expressed great satisfaction with the result of the Conference, and said that *Britain, France and Italy had shown the greatest unity of purpose.* 'As for Germany—we have given her—I don't like to call it a warning—but we have indicated our feelings about it, and expressed regrets, and are still anxious to take up the work of consolidating peace that has been interrupted.'

'AND DID YOU NOT DISCUSS ABYSSINIA WITH MUSSOLINI?' somebody asked. Mr. MacDonald stared. 'MY FRIEND,' he replied sharply, 'YOUR QUESTION IS IRRELEVANT.'

.   .   .   .

And that at a time when 200,000 Blackshirts had already been dispatched to Eritrea, and when Mussolini's war preparations were already in full progress. But the question was 'irrelevant' to the British. In the circumstances it was naturally, equally 'irrelevant' to the French. They were greatly pleased with the formation of what they called the 'Stresa Front'; and preparations were made at Stresa for the subsequent military convention for the withdrawal of troops on either side of the Franco-Italian frontier.

.   .   .   .

After long and troublesome negotiations and much hesitation and resistance, Laval signed the Franco-Soviet Pact on May 2. It was a strictly 'League' pact:

'The provisions of the Treaty,' the Protocol that was attached to it said, 'shall not be carried out in any way which being inconsistent with the treaty obligations undertaken by one of the Contracting Parties, might expose the latter to sanctions of an international character.'

Lengthy consultations had gone on between M. Laval and the British Government; and before being signed, the final form of the treaty *had been approved by London.* It is important to emphasize this in view of the approval with which Hitler's arguments about the incompatibility of the Franco-Soviet Pact and Locarno were to meet in the British Press after Germany's repudiation of Locarno.

43

VIII. CHAMBER VERSUS BANK OF FRANCE

ON MAY 30, the Flandin Government—the eighth since the 1932 election—was overthrown. Like most French Governments, it fell on a financial issue; but in circumstances that had a graphic quality, and left a deep impression on public opinion.

But, about the beginning of April it was learned that a large number of bonds would mature for repayment on June 15, and that the Government could not pay—unless it made friends again with the Bank of France. Making friends with the Bank meant enforcing severe cuts on the Budget; and yet, M. Flandin had declared that he would not resort to further deflation; but the Premier's dilemma gave the devaluationists their chance. A part of the Press—particularly M. Patenôtre's *Petit Journal*—had become openly devaluationist; and among politicians M. Paul Reynaud, though without any official political following, began to be listened to more and more eagerly. M. Reynaud's constituency is the 2nd Arrondissement of Paris, a district depending largely on a *de-luxe* export trade, and on tourists; and this added some practical weight to M. Reynaud's theories.

The great sin that all critics of the Bank of France have laid at its doorstep is that the speculation on the probable devaluation of the franc during May 1935 was not checked in any way by the Bank. At last, on May 23, after a long struggle, Flandin surrendered, and agreed to ask the Chamber for plenary financial powers—with a view to carrying out the programme of deflation desired by the Bank. At once the Bank rate was put up.

To cut the story short, the Flandin Government was defeated on May 30, by a large majority, which would not consent to the plenary powers.

It was M. Bouisson, the President of the Chamber, who formed the new Government, with M. Caillaux as Minister of Finance. If there was a touch of tragedy in the fall of M. Flandin, who had made his last speech at the Chamber, with his arm in plaster and a temperature of 104, the one-day Cabinet of M. Bouisson was all comedy.

M. Bouisson had been for seven years President of the Chamber. He was a Marseillais, with a gruff manner, a shiny bald head, a pointed white beard, and a vast abdomen, which together with the evening dress the Speaker always wears, gave him a certain air of majesty.

After the fall of the Flandin Government, he assumed the airs of a minor Doumergue. His Government was, naturally, a 'National' Government, with Ministers of State and all that. But the most sensational

44

feature in his Cabinet was his Minister of Finance—M. Caillaux. This sudden reappearance in the front rank of the French political scene of the seventy-three-year-old man added another page to the thrilling Caillaux Legend. Actually, in French eyes, Caillaux is much less of a romantic and legendary character than in British and American eyes. He is personally disliked—in his own Radical Party even more than elsewhere. His brusque and superior airs, his lack of *camaraderie*, his claim to be a gentleman *'de la haute bourgeoisie, presque de la noblesse,'* as he himself wrote, offends their democratic susceptibilities.

For years, M. Caillaux, as President of the Finance Committee of the Senate, had preached orthodox finance and what he called 'penance'—penance for past extravagance. He was clearly a deflationist, and no sooner was the Bouisson Government formed than the Radicals realized that Caillaux's economy cuts would be ruthless.

M. Bouisson, who had been condemned to neutrality and moderation during his seven years in the Speaker's chair, suddenly burst out into a stream of home truths, and declared that he would not have any discussions with the Chamber until November, and if they insisted on asking him questions in the next few days, he would simply send them on holiday. In short, the Government had too much serious work to do to be bothered with Parliament.

How a man who had presided over the Chamber deliberations for so many years could suffer from such a lack of psychology was truly astounding.

When the vote was taken it was found that the Government was down by two votes.

The next morning M. Laval agreed to form the new Cabinet.

But before the end of the day Laval gave up the task. The Left-Wing Radicals, under Daladier, were playing with the idea of an anti-Fascist coalition, supported by the Communists, and were not inclined to surrender to the Bank of France after the Chamber had already scored two victories over it.

The next day M. Piétri—a very 'correct' gentleman, though a Corsican—who had been Minister in several Cabinets in the past, was asked to form the Cabinet.

Nevertheless, he failed to form the Cabinet—and this for a very interesting reason. What happened was this: the Radicals had persuaded M. Piétri not to insist on plenary powers after the Flandin and Bouisson model, but to be content with 'limited powers'—a system under which the Government would be able to bring into operation a number of laws 'each with a clearly specified object.' It was obvious that under this system Caillaux's programme of deflation would be greatly watered down, and the Bank of France held that unless the Budget was, more or less, put in order, it could not and would not grant greater facilities to the Treasury.

There was also another difficulty—this one of a political order. The Radicals wished Daladier to be given a post in the Cabinet. But the Right would not hear of it. Daladier was still *'le fusilleur'*—and Colonel de la Rocque afterwards claimed that, if only Daladier had been given a Cabinet post, the Croix de Feu would have started trouble in Paris.

A Bourse panic was feared; and although spokesmen of the Bank of France said in private that *they* had enough gold left to hold out against the Chamber, they continued to suggest in public that unless a Government with plenary powers was formed, the franc might go.

That night things had got 'bad enough'—so bad that Laval was able to form his Cabinet with comparatively little difficulty.

The Radicals and the Chamber were in the end obliged to climb down. But the Chamber's resistance to the Bank of France—a resistance that had brought down two Cabinets—did not pass unnoticed in the country; and encouraged the subsequent campaign against the Bank.

An all-round 10 per cent cut in budget expenditure was agreed to. In Paris, there were a few protest demonstrations and more serious disorders broke out among the arsenal workers at Brest and Toulon in the second week of August. There the 'protest' against the cuts degenerated into rioting, and three people were killed in the protest. Still, it was not so serious as to warrant the vast headline 'REVOLUTION IN FRANK-REICH' that caught my eye when, one evening in August, I arrived in Berlin.

There were many who afterwards wondered whether, in saving the franc in June 1935, France had not missed a good opportunity.

IX. THE RISE OF THE FRONT POPULAIRE

Can you seriously expect the French people, who made one great, one small, and two medium revolutions, to cry our joyfully: *'Vive Henri VI!'*—SALTYKOV.

THE beginning of the 'anti-Fascist rally' in France dates back to the days immediately following the riot of February 6, 1934. In the course of 1934 the Socialists and Communists drew closer together, and

46

on August 27 of that year they signed the United Action Pact, which marks the formal beginning of what came to be known as the Front Commun.

Its purpose was, among other things, to 'mobilize the entire working population against the Fascist organizations', and to 'defend democratic liberties.' Actually, the rank and file, much more than the leaders, wanted this 'united action.' The Communist leaders at first rejected the overtures made by the Socialists, and when, shortly afterwards, in February 1934, they suddenly went all out for co-operation, this *volte-face* aroused the Socialist's suspicions. M. Blum thought the directives from Moscow a little too nationalist, and inspired by Stalin's consideration that, from the point of view of Moscow, at any rate, a non-Fascist and militarily powerful France was preferable to any other.

As for the Radicals, the majority of them remained loyal to *bourgeois* democracy and to the National Government formula so long as the Flandin Government remained in power. But at the same time the idea of the Radical Anti-Fascist Front was making progress with the Radical rank-and-file. In May 1935, the victory in the 5th Arrondissement—the 'moderate' Latin quarter—of Paris of Professor Rivet, who was the 'anti-Fascist' candidate, over M. Lebecq, the National candidate, and one of the 'heroes' of the 6th of February, had the symbolic significance of a first resounding victory over 'Fascism.'

It was the Communists who, after the fall of the Bouisson Government, proposed the formation of an 'anti-Fascist' Government, 'stretching as far as M. Bonnevay.' M. Bonnevay, though a member of the Right Centre, had shown himself scrupulously fair as Chairman of the Committee of Inquiry into the 6th of February riots, and had so become the target of violent Fascist attacks.

Many Radicals were fascinated by the Communist proposal; but the Socialists would not hear of it.

In June 1935, the Socialist majority still held that they could not share power with any *bourgeois* party and that it must be 'everything or nothing.'

.   .   .   .

It so happened that June 1935 was marked by a sudden reappearance on the French political scene of the Croix de Feu. The Croix de Feu had lain very low during the Flandin period. They knew the Government to be hostile to them.

During the double Cabinet crisis of May–June, they were not in evidence. While the crisis was in progress, they held a great rally, which caused some talk at the time—only it was held not in Paris, but at Cambrai, some 150 miles north of the capital! It was not very dangerous.

The Croix de Feu leaders suddenly realized that there now sat at the head of the Government not a hostile Flandin, but Laval who, they had reason to believe, was not unsympathetic to the movement, and with whom friendly co-operation—like the old co-operation with Doumergue —might be possible. As time went on, and as the hostility between Laval and the Socialists and Communists grew, the relations between him and the Croix de Feu became more cordial. An intimate friend of his repeated to me—I think it was a little later, in October—the following reflection that Laval made to him in a moment of candour: 'Yes, I am on good terms with the Croix de Feu. *Ce sont des vrais Français.* They include some of the finest elements of the youth of France. They will become some day the backbone of a real big anti-capitalist, though non-Marxist, party. I like them. *Que voulez-vous que je fasse?*' he said wistfully. 'My old Socialist and Communist comrades will not have anything more to do with me. There is nobody else I can fall back on.'

As was to be expected, the Left became greatly alarmed by the sudden revival in the energies of the Croix de Feu. It was the Délégation des Gauches[1] who, on June 24—about a fortnight after the formation of the Laval Cabinet—asked the Premier what he was going to do about the Croix de Feu.

Laval, fingering his white tie, declared that he was greatly concerned about the situation. 'I shall defend the Republic,' he said, putting the maximum of warmth into his voice; '*Mes amis,* I owe everything to the Republic; how would I not be devoted to it?'

July 28, the day on which Parliament rose—was an important landmark in the history of the Front Populaire. A meeting took place that night at the Mutualité to celebrate the 'symbolic' victory of Professor Rivet, the anti-Fascist candidate in the recent municipal election. The three speakers at the meeting were MM. Daladier, Blum and Thorez.

M. Daladier received a tremendous ovation from the audience—for it was his presence at the meeting that symbolized the extension of the Front Commun to the proportions of a Front Populaire.

He proceeded to show that the greatest evil in France was the financial oligarchy. The Fascists merely represented this oligarchy. The Premier of the 6th of February was clearly rehabilitating himself in his new role.

M. Blum said he hoped the Front Populaire victory of the 5th Arrondissement would 'extend to the whole of France.'

---

[1] This standing committee of *all* the Left-Wing Parties, which was formed about that time, was to play an increasingly important part under the Laval and Sarraut Governments. Laval was to find it very troublesome.

M. Thorez, the young Communist leader, declared that the Communists also wished to join the Front Populaire, to defend the liberties of the working class. All three speakers agreed that their adherence to the Front Populaire did not imply any loss of independence.

The meeting created a sensation in France as the beginning of something very big. Meantime, a Committee (comprising members of all the Left parties, though not all of them officially accredited), drew up the '14th of July Oath' and organized a giant procession in the Place de la Bastille. The Radical leaders, without committing the Party to anything, agreed that Radicals could take part in the rally, but that they were to sing the Marseillaise, and carry tricolour, and not red flags.

. . . .

What were the Croix de Feu—the real creators of the Front Populaire—doing in the meantime? On July 7, Colonel de la Rocque made one of the most incendiary speeches in his life. He 'no longer cared a hang about legality,' and prophesied that the Croix de Feu would soon take power.

It was then—so it was said in Paris at the time—that Laval intervened. The next day an article by Colonel de la Rocque appeared in *Excelsior* which was a complete climb down. Moreover, the Colonel strongly protested against the allegation that the Croix de Feu were being subsidized by financial and industrial magnates. It was decided that the Croix de Feu would meet in the Champs Élysées on the 14th.

. . . .

At last the great day came. Some of the London papers were full of panic stories of how a civil war might break out in Paris that day. They were to be disappointed.

All the police did was to separate East from West, and to see that neither procession transgressed the limit fixed for them. And everything went off perfectly smoothly. The Bastille-Nation procession of the Left was the most impressive thing of its kind ever seen in Paris. Some 300,000 to 400,000 people took part in it. The police were absent, and everything was organized by the Front Populaire stewards themselves.

The anti-Fascist procession took place in a holiday mood. The slogans on the banners were confined to anti-Fascism, and were not directed against militarism or even capitalism—except for a few references to the 'financial bastilles' that would soon be captured.

The procession was mostly Socialist and Communist; and the Radicals were not in great evidence. Still, it was a beginning. M. Daladier was warmly cheered; and so were M. Pierre Cot and M. Guernut, perched on the roof of a taxi and displaying a large tricolour flag.[2] The union between radicalism and the United Front was effectively symbolized by the two cars—which drove down the Faubourg St. Antoine side by side—the old Faubourg St. Antoine of 1789—one car flying a red, and the other—M. Cot's—a tricolour flag. Paul Faure and young Maurice Thorez sat on top of the car with the red flag. *'Les Soviets partout! Les Soviets partout!'* the demonstrators shouted and the crowd, as usual, sang the 'Internationale.' Nobody sang the 'Marseillaise'; and the tricolour flags were few and far between—the Communists had not adopted them yet. Still, it was a beginning.

Later, at the opposite end of the town, the Croix de Feu lighted the flame on the tomb of the Unknown Warrior. There were some 30,000 of them in the procession. First came the older men with their War medals; and then the Volontaires Nationaux. A crowd of about 50,000, largely composed of young women in pretty summer frocks, lined the pavements, cheering frantically—*'Vive La Rocque! Vive La Rocque! La France aux Français!'* Numerically, it was insignificant, compared with the vast Bastille procession; but the military discipline of La Rocque's men was impressive. The 14th of July 1935 marked not only the beginning of the Front Populaire; it was also the apotheosis of the Croix de Feu. At no moment had La Rocque's prestige stood higher. The Left knew it; and were determined not to allow his prestige to grow any bigger.

X. FRANCE AND ABYSSINIA

MUSSOLINI had Laval, as well as M. de Chambrun, the French Ambassador in Rome, in his pocket from the start. He gratefully accepted the 'deserts' Laval presented to Italy in January; and held

[2] By some accident the blue and white portion of their flag was half ripped off, and the red part alone remained firmly attached to the staff. One can imagine the symbolic significance the hostile papers attached to this!

out the promise of a regular Franco-Italian alliance. Laval returned from Rome feeling a great statesman.

To salve his conscience in relation to the Little Entente, Laval at Stresa proposed a Danubian Conference; and Mussolini assented—but, naturally, the conference never took place. Laval did not really mind; for he was interested only in the independence of Austria, and by that time Mussolini had given him full assurances that if only France and Italy hung well together, the matter would be well looked after.

At the beginning of June, Laval still took a philosophic view of Abyssinia. It was about that time that the British Government suddenly woke up, having for months treated the matter as 'irrelevant.'

No sooner was the meeting of the League Council over, at which Mr. Eden first voiced the anti-Italian policy of the British Government, than the Italians began their long process of intimidating the French. Reports were published in the French Press that Herr von Hassel, the German Ambassador in Rome, had just proposed to the Duce a compromise on Austria. No *Anschluss* would be attempted even if a Nazi Government was established in Vienna.

M. Laval and many Frenchmen still believed that an attack on Abyssinia was, somehow, compatible with Italy's continued membership of the League, with her loyalty to the 'collective system' and even with the Stresa Front. And the purpose of Mussolini's alleged *rapprochement* with Germany was precisely to discourage the French from following Mr. Eden.

And then, a few days later, there happened something which played into the hands of the pro-Italian elements in France. It was the sudden conclusion of the Anglo-German naval agreement. Apart from being an 'act of disloyalty' and incompatible with the Anglo-French declaration of February 3, it was interpreted by not only the pro-Italians in France, but by everybody in France as a blow to the League policy of collective security and 'indivisible peace'.

The pro-League elements in France were extremely perturbed by the naval agreement, and by the manner in which it was concluded. But the pro-Italian elements were triumphant. Their first reaction to the Anglo-German agreement was highly significant. The *Echo de Paris*, the *Intransigeant* and some of the other papers suggested a subtle form of revenge on England. They said that in view of England's 'betrayal of League principles,' there was no longer any reason why France should in future oppose Italy's ambitions in Abyssinia in the name of these League principles which were so grossly ignored by England when it suited her.

51

Apart from that, Laval perhaps also had a suspicion that he had been duped by the Anglo-German naval agreement. One of his intimate friends told me that day: 'We have been duped by England. If she had not talked so much about "international co-operation" in the last few months, France might have got in first with a direct military agreement with Germany. Now that the Germans have got from England what they want, they will not bother. I am afraid we have missed the boat.'

A few days later, on June 21, Mr. Eden left for Rome. He stopped in Paris and had a long talk with Laval, whom he tried to convince that the naval agreement, though concluded in a somewhat unorthodox manner, was calculated to become an important element in the general system of security. Laval was not reassured, and felt obliged to repeat the 'reservations'—that is, the protest—of the French Government.

But, for a time, all these problems were relegated to the background. What mattered now was Abyssinia. French opinion suddenly found itself in the unpleasant dilemma of 'choosing between England and Italy.' This presented Italian propaganda with a great opportunity. In well-informed diplomatic quarters in Paris, where a great deal is known about such things, it was estimated that Italy had spent about sixty million francs on pro-Italian propaganda in the French Press during the second half of 1935. It was a good investment. Laval looked on encouragingly and complacently.

Abyssinian barbarism and savagery were one of the stock themes; the greatness of Mussolini was another, the terror of throwing Italy into the arms of Germany was a third; but the most popular theme of all was the duplicity and hypocrisy of England. Lake Tsana and the Blue Nile and the Sudan, and hegemony in the Mediterranean—these, we were told, were the things that mattered to England, and not League principles, which she had consistently ignored—as was only too apparent (to take the most recent example) from the Anglo-German naval agreement.

French official spokesmen, in the meantime, thought it monstrous that European security should be wrecked for the sake of Abyssinia; they urged a gentle handling of Mussolini, and claimed that he was simply 'bluffing,' and that he had no intention of starting any war in Abyssinia. The Left was perplexed, and found it difficult to uphold the pro-British case so soon after the naval agreement.

The turning-point came in September with Sir Samuel Hoare's speech on the 11th. France had now clearly to take a decision—for Britain and the League, or for Italy.

The speech created a sensation at Geneva, and Laval, and all the other delegates hastened to reaffirm their loyalty to the League. In France, Sir Samuel Hoare's speech appeared to facilitate the task of those who had always been sincere supporters of a League policy. True, Sir Samuel's speech was not devoid of loopholes. Its most important phrase—'collective resistance against unprovoked aggression'—contained two somewhat elastic adjectives; but, even so, it was important to take Britain at her word.

But four days later the Home Fleet was sent into the Mediterranean. At once the pro-Italian elements in France, who had been stunned by Hoare's speech, recovered their energies, and raised a loud outcry that the British Government was trying to drag France into a war. In spite of the Hoare speech, the earlier campaign against Britain's 'imperialistic interests' and her 'duplicity' immediately doubled in intensity.

When on October 3 the war actually broke out, and the question of sanctions arose things went from bad to worse. The Fascist *Solidarité Française* wrote, '*M—— pour l'Angleterre*'; and on October 11, Henri Béraud wrote in *Gringoire* an article which even created a diplomatic incident, for Sir George Clerk, the British Ambassador, found it necessary to lodge a protest against it at the Quai d'Orsay. It scarcely deserved that honour—it was full of the old nonsense about the Intelligence Service; it contained a 'rigorously authentic' account of the conversation in Berlin between Sir John Simon and Hitler on June 18, the anniversary of Waterloo (Sir John was by that time Home Secretary and was certainly not in Berlin that day); and it said: 'In France only hall-porters and M. Flandin are pro-British.' And, after dismissing England's dead in the last War as a mere trifle, compared with the Hundred Years' War, it concluded with the words:

I hate England in my own name and in the name of my ancestors. I hate her by instinct and by tradition. I say, and I repeat that England must be reduced to slavery. . . . The day will come when the world will have the strength and the wisdom to enslave the tyrant with his reputation for invincibility. Concord between the continental nations alone can save Europe and the world. Who knows? Perhaps the day is near.

It was the case of a Fascist mentality gone wild. And not even an honest Fascist mentality.

The Home Fleet entered the Mediterranean on the 15th. A few days earlier at Geneva, Laval had been approached by the British Government, who wished to know whether France would be 'with them' in the event of an armed conflict with Italy. It was at this point, according to Pertinax, that Laval missed the greatest chance in his career. For, at that moment, on the eve of Sir Samuel Hoare's speech, Laval could have obtained certain British assurances concerning German aggression which he would not have obtained on any other occasion. But he was so concerned about Italy, that he would commit himself to nothing, and let the great opportunity slip.

When the Home Fleet entered the Mediterranean, he pointed out (rightly, one may add) that the League Council had not asked the British Government to do so. When the war broke out, he very reluctantly agreed to sanctions. As for Franco-British naval co-operation in the Mediterranean, he formally agreed to it after long-drawn-out negotiations, and the exchange of several very sour notes, on October 26—but this time without receiving anything in return.

Sanctions—rather harmless financial and economic sanctions—were agreed upon at Geneva on October 19. A few weeks later, the British Government, which had fought so gallantly for the League, scored its great election victory. And then came the climb-down.

There are strong grounds for saying that the British Government, aware of the sentiment existing in the country, did not dare take any line other than a 'League line' during the weeks preceding the General Election. And while it was fighting 'the battle of the League' it continued to suggest through the Press that if sanctions were to prove a failure, it would be France's fault; and that, but for Laval's resistance, Britain would have gone to almost any length (whatever 'almost' meant) to enforce sanctions, strengthen the League, and safeguard Peace for years to come.

There is the French note of October 18, hitherto unpublished, which shows fairly conclusively that Sir Samuel Hoare's determination to make the League triumph was not very grim even in September. M. Laval recalled that on September 9, Sir Samuel Hoare had *spontaneously* informed him that *in no circumstances* would the British Government apply to Italy any sanctions other than financial and economic sanctions; *and that such measures as a naval blockade of Italy or the closing of the Suez Canal were out of the question.*

The Hoare-Laval Plan was formally agreed upon between its two signatories on Sunday, December 8. Sir Samuel Hoare had arrived in Paris on the Saturday, and it was afterwards alleged on the British side that his battle with Laval had been a very stiff one. Actually there was no battle at all. The plan had been virtually agreed upon between the

54

Quai d'Orsay and the Foreign Office several days in advance; and it was not until four o'clock on Sunday that Hoare and Laval began to examine the plan and add a few touches here and there. When Sir Samuel left for Paris on that Saturday, he must have known exactly what the position was (he probably had a draft of the plan in his pocket). For it is well to remember that for several days in advance the diplomatic correspondents of nearly all the leading English papers had published (with minor variations) summaries of the Hoare-Laval Plan. The 'dope' had been handed out to them in handfuls by the Foreign Office, which was trying to 'prepare' public opinion for the shock.

XI. THE FALL OF LAVAL

'Etes-vous pour la déflation ou pour la dévaluation?'
'Moi, dit Rappoport, se tordant comme une petite folle,
moi je suis plutôt pour la *délavaluation.*'
—*Le Canard Enchaîné.*

I. THE FASCIST 'MARCH ON PARIS'

THE Laval Government took a long time to die. The Chamber had many grievances against him; but it could not help admiring the little man's genius for manœuvring. The short session of November–December 1935 was one of the most exciting in French Parliamentary history—and it was Laval who made it exciting. He produced the rabbits out of his hat with an unperturbed air of a professional conjurer.

We have seen how, before Parliament rose in June, Laval assured the Left with his hand on his heart 'that he owed everything to the Republic.' But suddenly, on September 23, at their Meaux Rally, the Croix de Feu made a spectacular *rentrée.*

About the middle of 1935 a new Fascist movement had come into sudden prominence. This was the so-called 'Front Paysan,' led by a man of the name of Dorgères. In the summer of 1935 the agricultural slump was at its worst in France, and Dorgères tried to exploit the discontent for his own ends. He was a fiery demagogue, who did not hesitate to preach to the peasants the non-payment of taxes, and who conjured up visions of how he and his Greenshirts would one day march on the Chamber of Deputies and 'shoot down the whole damned lot.' Not that this prevented him, in April 1935, from standing for Parliament in the Blois by-election (a constituency left vacant by M. Chautemps's election to the Senate); and in that Radical stronghold Dorgères failed by only a very narrow margin to be returned. His alleged association with the landed nobility did much to discredit him in the eyes of his supporters; and the rise in agricultural prices, which began in the autumn of 1935, also helped to restore loyalty to the Republic among those whom Dorgères had, for a short time, led astray. Another blow to Dorgères was the decision taken by the Agrarian Party, of which the 'Peasant Front' was an emanation, to dissociate itself from Dorgères's violent methods.

But the Croix de Feu were of more lasting importance.

The official purpose of the Meaux Rally was to commemorate the anniversary of the battle of the Marne.

The Croix de Feu had numerous patrons among wealthy landed proprietors; and it was usually on some 'private' estate that the rallies were held—which, in the eyes of the Croix de Feu leaders, rendered them perfectly legal. Nevertheless, the Left considered them a provocation; especially when they were held in or near some 'proletarian' centre. Considering that they were being provoked, the Left decided to organize 'counter-demonstrations' whenever such a rally took place. On October 6, a thousand Croix de Feu men assembled on a large farm at Villepinte, near Paris. While they were there, a crowd of several hundred Socialists and Communists, led by the Maire of Villepinte in person, with the tricolour ribbon across his chest, assembled outside the farm, protesting vociferously against the rally. Some blows were exchanged, and a few shots were fired, and the *garde mobile* had to be called out to restore order. The Maire of Villepinte, who was largely responsible for the trouble, was thereupon suspended from his duties by the Minister of the Interior—which, naturally, annoyed the Left Press, which said that the Laval Government was taking sides with the Fascists.

On October 20, the *Populaire* came out with a tremendous story—a plan of the coming Croix de Feu occupation of Paris, complete with every detail. On the previous day, according to the same paper, the Ministry of the Interior had sent out an ultra-confidential circular to the Prefects asking them for information about the eventual concentration of the Croix de Feu troops in the Paris region 'planned for October 20.'

Yet, on the 20th, the day of the Senate Election, nothing happened. The *Populaire* claimed that, 'alarmed' by its revelations, La Rocque had called off the *putsch* 'this time.'

The Radical Congress at the Salle Wagram was completely dominated by the question of the 'Fascist Menace.' The Congress agreed not to send an ultimatum with a time limit to M. Laval, but only a warning that, unless adequate legislation against the Leagues was put before the Chamber as soon as it met, the Radicals would leave the Government.

That settled the most immediate problem with which the Congress was faced. As regards the adherence of the Radical Party to the Front Populaire, the Radical Party said it would gladly co-operate 'with all sincere republicans without exception.'

2. THE LEFT AND ABYSSINIA

When the Radical Congress met, the Abyssinian War had been in progress for three weeks. We have seen, in a previous chapter, how the entire Right-Wing Press in France had—in many cases under the influence of Italian bribery—gone rabidly pro-Italian.

The violence of the anti-League propaganda was equalled only by the open appeal in the *Action Française* to murder one hundred and forty Left-Wing deputies and senators 'the moment war with Italy broke out.'

When, in October, a manifesto protesting against Italy's aggression was published by Paul Claudel, François Mauriac, Jacques Maritain, André Thérive and other prominent Conservative Catholic intellectuals, the *Echo de Paris*, though calling itself a Catholic paper, refused to reproduce it.

The French Left, however, were feeling very uneasy. They were pro-League and pro-sanctions, yet in the matter of military sanctions the French Socialists were rather more reserved than their British brethren.

'To prevent Italian aggression,' Blum wrote on September 8, 'it is not necessary to make war on Italy. Of all the great powers Italy is the most vulnerable to economic sanctions.'

He was overjoyed by Sir Samuel Hoare's speech of September 11, and noted 'an irresistible movement of opinion at Geneva which may change the face of the world.' But, a few days later, when British battleships had been sent into the Mediterranean, his tone changed. In an article called 'England's Fault,' he wrote that the Admiralty had got out of hand; 'it is playing into the hands of the pro-Mussolini Press by suggesting that sanctions are inevitably military.' When the war actually broke out, Blum no longer maintained that economic sanctions would be sufficient. 'Eventually, however, Peace may require the application of armed force. A defensive war is just as atrocious as a war of aggression; but it is still better than if the world made a cowardly surrender to wars of aggression.' But there was not much more enthusiasm for sanctions among the Socialists than among the Radicals. They all at heart regretted that the League should be put to the test over—Abyssinia.

At the Radical Congress, Herriot made a long and heartfelt speech about the League and Anglo-French co-operation, and about the necessity of applying the Covenant. For all that, M. Pierre Cot, one of the few men in France who were prepared to go the whole length of military sanctions, was specially asked by M. Herriot not to make a speech at the Congress.

3. THE CROIX DE FEU 'GO TORY'

On December 6, exactly twenty-two months after the Sixth of February, an extraordinary thing happened. M. Ybarnégaray suddenly mounted the tribune. A distinguished ex-soldier, and always a fair opponent, he is one of the few members of the Right for whom the Opposition have a personal regard. The Chamber heard, not without surprise, that M. Ybarnégaray had come to speak on behalf of the Croix de Feu, with its 712,000 members, and of his friend, Colonel de la Rocque. But he made the announcement with such an air of sincerity that it caused no uproar. He said that a legend had been woven round the Croix de Feu and their leader. The Colonel had been described as a conspirator, as a budding dictator, as an enemy of the Republic. 'Those of you who know him know that this is not the case.' A Communist intervened and asked why several members of the Croix de Feu had recently left the organization.

M. Ybarnégaray (alluding to M. Doriot): 'Has such a thing never happened in your Party?' (Laughter.) 'If you want to know the truth, Colonel de la Rocque got rid of these people precisely because they were tending to drag the movement into a dangerous adventure.'

The dissolution of the Leagues, he said, was not an effective solution. The solution lay in disarmament. 'I swear upon my honour,' he said, 'that the Croix de Feu have no munition stores. But the disarmament must apply to individuals.' (Loud cheers.) He thereupon read the text of two Bills which he asked the Government to adopt:

(1) Any person found carrying arms shall be punished with one to three years' imprisonment.[1]

(2) Any foreigner guilty of the same offence shall be immediately expelled from France as well as his family.

Suddenly, Blum rose. 'This,' he said, 'is what I wish to say to M. Ybarnégaray. We are prepared to dissolve our organizations in so far as they are semi-military in nature. But are you prepared to do the same?'

M. Thorez, for the Communists, declared that he identified himself with M. Blum's words—the Communist Party would also dissolve its self-defence formations. And then, in tense silence, M. Ybarnégaray replied: 'Yes; in the name of the Croix de Feu, I declare that we also are prepared to dissolve our association in so far as it is semi-military in character—and I use the word "semi-military" in the sense that you, Mr. Blum, have given it.' The whole scene, and M. Ybarnégaray's undertaking, created a tremendous sensation. And M. Laval, who had been watching the scene with a contented air, declared that 'the Government would draw the necessary conclusions from what it had heard.' Ybarnégaray's spectacular offer had got Laval out of a serious difficulty, though the League's dissolution bills passed by Parliament some days later went much further than the Croix de Feu or Laval had anticipated.

4. LAVAL'S SWAN-SONG

Frankly, the Hoare-Laval Plan did not at first arouse anything like the indignation it caused in England. People on the Right chuckled joyfully over the cynical *volte-face* of the British Government, and said that the British General Election was just as good a swindle as the Stavisky Affair.

The Left, on the other hand, were taken aback. Most of them did not mind very much about Abyssinia *per se*; but they were disturbed by this sudden change in British foreign policy. Did it mean, they said, that Abyssinia was a nuisance that had to be disposed of as quickly as possible, and that Britain would *then* return to a real League policy; or did it, on the contrary, mean that Britain had never had any serious intention of supporting the League? In this connection, the reports from London that the British Government was proposing

[1] Asked in 1934 before the Parliamentary Committee inquiring into the February riots, whether the Croix de Feu were armed, Colonel de la Rocque said: 'No, they are not armed, except that three Frenchmen in four carry a revolver, and the proportion must be about the same in the Croix de Feu.' One of the great difficulties in France is the almost unrestricted sale of firearms.

to revise and 'sterilize' the League Covenant, by taking the sanctions mechanism out of it, were rather disquieting.

On December 18, Sir Samuel Hoare resigned, and, that same night, M. Herriot, unwilling to break up the Laval Government at that particular moment, resigned from the Presidency of the Radical Party.

The resignation of Sir Samuel Hoare was a terrible blow to Laval— but although he told Hoare on December 8 that they would 'stand or fall together,' he changed his mind and did not resign. Instead, he carefully prepared his own defence in the great foreign debate that was to take place on December 27 and 28.

Two-thirds of the Chamber had been worked up into a state of righteous indignation by the time Laval began his second speech—at the end of the debate on December 28. It was, in a way, the best speech he had ever made. This time he spoke for over an hour. The speech was, at times, of high rhetorical quality with touches of pathos, which one scarcely expected from a 'realist' like Laval.

'Peace is fragile, and I can assure you that I was capable of measuring the consequences that even a distant war would have on European peace, and on France's security.'

As for Germany, was it being suggested that he was conducting suspect negotiations with that country? Stressing his words, M. Laval said: 'In my opinion there can be no solid peace in Europe without a Franco-German *rapprochement*. But I must add that I do not wish such an agreement except as part of the organization of European security. "What wonderful horizons would open before us if this were possible," I said to Sir Samuel Hoare. "Our two countries could then bring Germany into the system of collective security." '

As the speech progressed, the hostility of the Chamber gradually melted. The cheers which came at first only from the Right spread to the Centre, and even some members of the Left cheered at one or two points.

But there was one very paradoxical thing about this speech. It was a perfect League speech; and yet it was cheered, not by the defenders of the League, but only by those who are hostile towards it or lukewarm. *Neither the Right nor the Left believed in Laval's sincerity.* He got a majority of twenty votes. It was touch and go.

Thanks to this speech, Laval—the central figure in French affairs in 1935—had steered his way by hook and by crook into 1936, still premier and still Foreign Minister. But not for long. In the middle of January, the Radicals, led by Herriot, broke into open revolt against Laval. The Budget and the anti-Fascist laws had been passed; as Foreign Minister

Laval was played out; somebody was needed who would make a better match for Mr. Eden; and the election was only three months ahead. Laval was too wily to be allowed to 'make the elections'—for there is still an old (and mistaken) belief among Radicals that the Government, with Prefects and secret funds at its command, can influence an election.

The Laval Government, without meeting the Chamber again, was disrupted from within.

He departed from the Quai d'Orsay with an unperturbed air; not like an evicted tenant, but like a man going away for a holiday. And yet, looking back on it all, and especially on the Duce's failure to respond immediately to the Hoare-Laval Plan, he said to a friend that day: *'Mussolini, quel salaud tout de même!'*

Two days later the Sarraut Government was formed—in good time for King George's funeral.

XII. FRANCE A SECOND-CLASS POWER?

THE FRANCO-SOVIET PACT AND HITLER'S LOCARNO COUP

THE unfortunate Sarraut Government, which scarcely six weeks after its formation was to face the worst international crisis since the War, was regarded at first as being merely a stop-gap Cabinet which would 'carry on' until the General Election, and do nothing of any importance, except get the Franco-Soviet Pact ratified. The Premier, M. Sarraut, was an old man of sixty-four, looking sometimes like a village *curé*, and sometimes like Mr. Pickwick, with an unfortunate platform manner, and a verbose, florid style of oratory. But he was a Sarraut, the brother of Maurice Sarraut, the Editor of the *Dépêche* of Toulouse, the most influential Radical paper in the country, and was himself one of the owners of the paper.

His Government was not, however, a purely Left Government, still less a Front Populaire Government. It included some of the most determined enemies of Laval, such as M. Delbos, the Minister of Justice, who had made a slashing attack on the foreign policy of Laval and M. Guernut, Minister of Education. It also included Déat, who became Minister of Air. M. Flandin was Foreign Minister, and in taking office he assured his party, the Alliance Démocratique, who disliked the Sarraut Government, that 'he agreed with the foreign policy of M. Laval, except in some details'—which was not quite what one would have expected from the Foreign Minister of a Government that had been formed as a reaction against Laval.

M. Sarraut soon discovered that in this history-making epoch of ours, it was no fun to rule a great country for even a day. No sooner did Sarraut and Flandin settle down to a short rest after obtaining a big majority at the Chamber than Paris was overrun by Kings and Prime Ministers from all over Europe (they had been at King George's funeral in London) and there were ten days of luncheons and dinners and receptions and diplomatic conversations.

The first important step that the Sarraut Government took, soon after the foreign kings and statesmen had departed, was to submit the Franco-Soviet Pact to the Chamber for ratification. Laval, though its original signatory, had deliberately delayed its ratification. For one thing, he feared to offend Germany. The German Press had, for some weeks past, conducted a violent campaign against the pact. In spite of this Press campaign Herr von Neurath had, at the end of January, assured the British Government that Germany had no intention of taking action 'about the demilitarized zone' in the near future; and it was, somehow, not believed that Germany would *really* go so far as to violate Locarno. The German Press campaign was simply regarded as an attempt to persuade France not to ratify the Franco-Soviet Pact, which, of course, went contrary to Hitler's doctrine of 'localized' war, and to his desire for a free hand in the East.

The ratification debate, which began on February 13, was a long one. At the first meeting M. Torrès, the Rapporteur of the Bill, who is also a leading French jurist, explained why exactly the pact was perfectly compatible with Locarno. It was, he said, strictly a League Pact, compatible in every detail with the League Covenant.

In the past many people on the Right, who regarded Germany as Public Enemy No. 1, had been in favour of the pact and had warmly encouraged M. Barthou's successful work for a Franco-Russian *rapprochement*. In 1934 Henri de Kerillis had written enthusiastic articles about the Red Army and Air Force; and Pertinax (who was more consistent than de Kerillis) had maintained ever since 1933 that France and Russia must be 'on the same side.' Without having any exaggerated notions about the Red Army, he felt, none the less, that it was important, in case of war, to prevent Germany from using Russia, if not as an ally, at least as a source of raw materials. In this he agreed with most of the French Army leaders, including General Weygand. But, regardless of what the generals thought and of what many of them had recently felt themselves, the deputies of the Right were now determined to vote against the ratification of the pact.

Anti-Communist arguments against the pact received vigorous support from M. Jacques Doriot, the former Communist leader, who had now become violently anti-Soviet. Talking like a man with 'inside knowledge' (his former Communist pals listened to him in contemptuous silence), Doriot claimed that the French Communist leaders regarded war as a means of achieving world revolution. If a war broke out the Soviets would abandon their French allies in the middle of it, and try to bring about a revolution in France. The ex-Communist's speech was loudly cheered by the Right and Centre. And M. Xavier Vallat, in protesting against the pact said that it was no good using the old argument that François I had allied himself with Soliman the Magnificent. After all, the Sultan did not keep a Moslem Party in France, expecting it to overthrow the Monarchy and replace the Bible by the Koran.

The pact was defended with much vigour by the Left—above all, by the Communists and the Radicals. The Socialists, who in the recent past had openly criticized the pact, were still rather lukewarm. With his *in so fars* M. Spinasse was not wildly enthusiastic; and there were no doubt many Socialists who voted for the ratification largely for the sake of the Front Populaire and the unity of the Left parties.

.   .   .   .   .   .

Two days after the Chamber vote, a 'sensational' interview with Hitler was published simultaneously in *Paris-Midi* and the *Daily Mirror*. It had been given to Bertrand de Jouvenel, the son of the late Henry de Jouvenel, of Four-Power Pact fame—a young man with strong Fascist leanings, a youthful admiration for Hitlerian 'dynamics,' and a great contempt for Geneva. 'The Leader of this Germany,' Hitler said to him, 'has nine-tenths of the people behind him. . . . I know what you think. You are saying to yourself: "Hitler is offering us peace. But is he doing so in good faith? Is he sincere?" Now, think! Would it not be ruinous for both our countries if they clashed again on a new battlefield? . . . I want to show my people that the idea of eternal enmity between France and Germany is absurd; I want to show them that we are not hereditary enemies. The German people know it. The reconciliation between Germany and Poland was far more difficult. But they followed me. . . .'

And then came the usual tirade about Bolshevism as a world menace; and particularly a menace 'to certain countries' less immune against the poison than Germany. 'Don't you realize what you are doing? You are allowing yourselves to be dragged into the diplomatic game of a Power, whose only aim is to work havoc among the great European nations. . . . Russia is an explosive force, and her armaments are gigantic. As a German I must take account of such a situation. In the life of a nation there are decisive moments. To-day, if she wishes, France can put an end for all time to the "German menace." '

The interview was a warning. It is said that it was orignally intended for publication before the final ratification debate, but that it was held up for two days by the Quai d'Orsay.

The interview made a certain impression on the man-in-the-street in Paris; and one or two members of the Right even claimed that Hitler had at last provided the Right with 'a splendid election platform.' They little knew what was in store.

It was the French Government who decided to ask Hitler the questions that Jouvenel had failed to ask—and that was, on what terms he was offering France Germany's friendship. The Press of the Left, though critical to the interview, was almost unanimous in saying: 'Let's speak to him—let's ask him what he wants.'

That was the week in the course of which the League Council, taking up the question of the oil embargo once again, sent an appeal to Italy to consider a new offer. Flandin had insisted on this being done; and would not hear of Mr. Eden's proposal to apply the oil embargo.

While the Powers were waiting for the Italian reply, and while the French were becoming more and more worried, the news came from Germany that Hitler had called the Reichstag for the following day, and that a repudiation of Locarno and an occupation of the demilitarized Rhineland zone were to be expected.

.   .   .   .

The demilitarized Rhineland zone was not a unique phenomenon. Many international treaties of the past had provided for 'demilitarized zones.' The Treaty of Vienna provided for a small French demilitarized zone north of Basle; and Savoy had been demilitarized for years—and both these treaty provisions were observed by the French. So demilitarized zones do not necessarily mean 'national humiliation.'

The demilitarized Rhineland zone, which comprised the left bank of the Rhine and a fifty-kilometre strip of the right bank, and which included such centres as Aix-la-Chapelle, Cologne, Trier, Frankfort, the great armament city of Essen and—since 1935—the Saar territory, had a distant origin. French and German military authorities have always agreed that the Rhine is the 'natural and military' frontier of France and Germany.

When Germany was defeated in 1918 the question of 'neutralizing' the Rhine and of preventing another German invasion was foremost in the minds of French statesmen and military experts. As early as November 27, 1918, Marshal Foch presented a memorandum to Clemenceau in which he wrote:

> Henceforth the Rhine must become the Western military frontier of Germany; Germany must be deprived of all political and military claims on the left bank of the Rhine—she must, in short, be deprived of all the facilities for rapidly invading (as she did in 1914) Belgium, France, and Luxembourg, and for reaching the North Sea coast, and so threatening England. . . . In view of the moral and material situation of Germany, and in view of her numerical superiority over the democratic States of Western Europe, this is an indispensable guarantee for the maintenance of peace.

Foch advocated the creation of a buffer State on the German left bank of the Rhine under permanent inter-allied occupation.

Mr. Lloyd George and Mr. Philip Kerr (later Lord Lothian), while admitting the justice of France's aims, disagreed with the method she proposed. They could not agree with the French argument that the German left bank 'could easily become another Belgium' (that is, a new State with a national consciousness of its own); they felt that the establishment of such a State would create insuperable technical difficulties, exasperate German nationalism, and create a pro-German movement in England. Nor were they prepared to commit Britain to a share in the 'permanent' occupation of the buffer territory—though Clemenceau explained that 'one British flag was all he wanted,' and that the French would take care of the rest. The British proposed a number of alternatives.

The British and American counter proposal was sensational—'an unprecedented proposal of vast importance,' M. Tardieu, Clemenceau's henchman, wrote. It was none other than the offer of a pact promising France immediate military help against all unprovoked aggression on the part of Germany. In exchange the French were to abandon all ideas of an independent Rhineland under permanent inter-allied occupation.

Between March 1919 and the following June, when the Versailles

65

Treaty was signed, the French Government took this Anglo-American Pact for granted, and, while refusing to abandon altogether their idea of a Rhineland occupation, they agreed to its being limited to fifteen years as a guarantee that Germany would carry out her obligations under the Peace Treaty. In addition to the fifteen-year occupation the Allies agreed on the necessity of demilitarizing the Rhineland zone, which was to comprise not only the left bank but also a fifty-kilometre strip of the right bank. Demilitarization means no fortifications, either old or new; no troops of any kind; and no facilities for mobilization.

The Anglo-American guarantee came to nothing, and in the years that followed the only guarantee left to France was the fifteen years' occupation of the Rhineland. The great opportunity had been missed and France had been 'let down.' The French did not share Mr. Lloyd George's view that Germany was 'out' for at least sixty years. It was this feeling of grievance and disappointment that explains the last desperate attempts made by the French to recover lost ground 'while there was still time,' such as the Ruhr occupation and the encouragement they gave to the Rhineland Separatists—an abortive movement that they themselves had largely created.

In 1925 came Locarno. The Poincarists and Clemencists were disappointed, and said it would prove as worthless as the old Anglo-American guarantee; but the bulk of French opinion, led by Briand, welcomed it.

The Germans were even more pleased with it than the French. 'We obtained at Locarno one hundred per cent of what we desired,' Stresemann wrote. 'It preserves the Rhineland for us and allows us to recuperate the German territories in the East.'

It was automatic alliances that Stresemann feared most; and he was not greatly embarrassed by any 'League' treaty, such as the Franco-Polish or Franco-Czech Locarno agreements. The great mistake that Germany made in 1914, he wrote, was to be *too obviously* the aggressor.

.   .   .   .

I was in the rue Royale, at the Madeleine, about eleven o'clock on the 7th of March. *Paris-Midi* had just come out, and the kiosks were taken by storm. In great agitation people read the vast headlines: 'LES TROUPES ALLEMANDES ENTRENT EN RHÉNANIE.' There was great consternation. '*Alors, c'est la guerre?*' '*C'est la mobilisation?*' By a natural reflex, people looked at the sky, wondering if 'something' would not suddenly appear. '*Et que fera l'Angleterre?*' That was the first, or rather the second reaction—the first was 'War?' I was soon able to tell the French what *l'Angleterre* would do about it. At the British Embassy they shrugged their shoulders. 'No, you won't move England because the Germans have marched into Germany.' And the 'British reaction' was illustrated by the pleasant little incident that had happened that very morning. Mr. —— was dictating a dispatch to the typist: 'The German troops have entered Cologne.' 'Cologne?' said the typist. 'But I thought Cologne was in Germany.'

After lunch I went to the Chamber; it was a Saturday, but the lobby was crowded with deputies and journalists. *'Qu'en pensez-vous?'* I asked. Reply: *'Et les Anglais?'* It did not matter what *they* thought; what mattered was what the English thought. 'Well, there's one thing to be thankful for,' young Piétri said, 'and that is that Laval would not let us quarrel with Italy. A nice mess we should have been in.'

'Are you going to mobilize?'

Young Alfred Silbert, just back from the Croix de Feu headquarters: 'Our young fellows are in an excellent frame of mind. It's the same with the Communists—I've just seen some. Everybody's ready to march—if it has to be done.'

M. Montagnon, Neo-Socialist deputy: 'No, I don't think we'll mobilize. We may be more easily beaten in two years' time—but, after all, it means two extra years of life; and something may turn up in the meantime. *Est-ce qu'on sait jamais?'*

Even so, it was a terrible shock. It brought war much nearer. It was a blow to all the security planning, apart from being a direct threat to France. *'Les troupes allemandes entrent en Rhénanie'* was not, from the French point of view 'Germans marching into Germany'—it was the capture of France's first line of defence. There was the Maginot Line behind—God bless Maginot—but how long would the Maginot Line hold out against heavy guns?

The Cabinet and the Generals met that afternoon. Mandel, Clemenceau's realistic disciple, advocated immediate mobilization. It was now or never. Hitler must be forced to withdraw his troops; it might mean the end of the Hitler régime. Sarraut and Delbos and several of the other Ministers were in favour of some kind of prompt reaction that would make the world, and particularly England, sit up. England might back the French, and force Hitler to withdraw his troops, with the French Army ready to march in. But they weren't quite sure.

General Gamelin was consulted. 'You can mobilize two classes, or else have a general mobilization, but there's nothing in between,' he said. Two classes were useless and a general mobilization was a tremendous adventure. and what if the Government were not prepared to march into the Rhineland, and if Hitler were to call the bluff? How was the vast demobilization to be explained away? It would be worse than useless upsetting the whole life of the country, unless one was prepared to make the great plunge. Besides, the General did not seem very confident. And some of the other ministers asked: 'What will England say? And what about the League? And where is the money to come from?' M. Flandin seemed particularly bewildered. As for Déat he seems to have dwelt on the weakness of the French Air Force.

In the end it was decided to reinforce the frontier garrisons, to man the Maginot Line, to concentrate the Air Force near the frontier, and— to appeal to the League Council.[1]

That day, in Warsaw, the French Ambassador was informed that the Polish Army would march if the French Army marched. But the answer was 'No.' The last opportunity was lost.[2]

That evening Flandin announced France's appeal to the League Council. He also disclosed the highly significant fact that on the day following the publication of the *Paris-Midi* interview the French Government instructed its Ambassador in Berlin to ask Hitler at once on what terms he proposed to re-establish Franco-German friendship. M. Francois-Poncet saw Hitler, who asked for a few days' reflection. At the same time he specially asked that the Ambassador's visit should not be made public, and then on Saturday morning the Ambassador was informed that the repudiation of Locarno was Germany's reply to the French question. This showed that Hitler had deliberately wished to conceal France's request for negotiations, so that he could attribute his repudiation of Locarno to the 'irresponsiveness of France.' Yet, had he agreed to negotiate, a compromise on the zone would no doubt have been reached.

Hitler's proposals for a new agreement after he had just violated Locarno, were rejected by the French. Particularly, his proposal for a French demilitarized zone, was unacceptable on practical grounds—the Maginot Line had been built at a heavy cost, and, obviously, could not be scrapped and rebuilt so many miles further back.

---

[1] I have no documentary evidence to support my account of what happened in the course of those Government deliberations on March 7; and I have compiled it from the more reliable fragments of information, some given to me by the people directly concerned. I believe my account of what happened is roughly correct. Many of the stories told about those critical deliberations are obviously untrue.

[2] There was another thing that had added to the hesitation of the French—and that was the news that although the German Army was still weaker than the combined Franco-Polish Armies, Goering might, in a fit of recklessness, send over Paris the 2,000 aeroplanes he had assembled that day. Many of them were ramshackle old 'planes, but still——.

Moreover, the Hitler plan ignored from the outset the strategic inequality of France and Germany; and if his proposal sounded 'only fair' to most readers of English Sunday newspapers, it was grossly unfair to anyone who had studied the map and compared French and German effectives.

. . . .

On Sunday, March 8, M. Sarraut, in a broadcast, declared that France would not negotiate under threat of violence, and that she would not allow Strasbourg to be exposed to German guns.

It would have been all right if it had meant anything, but the phrase meant nothing. The German Press seized upon it—'and what about Karlsruhe? and what about Freiburg? and what about ——?'

On Monday Mr. Eden declared that Britain would abide by the Locarno Guarantee as far as France and Belgium were concerned. It was the least thing he could decently do.

And then there started the dismal comedy of the League Council meeting in London. Flandin threatened to leave London; on another occasion he burst into tears. It ended in a complete French *dégonflage*. No economic sanctions; no 'symbolic' evacuation—nothing. Indeed, why should there have been any such 'symbolic' gesture? In the majority of the British papers Hitler's 'generous offer' was welcomed with loud cries of approval. The majority of the British public did not understand or did not wish to understand the meaning of the Locarno *coup*. The 'Locarno spirit'—that British-made phrase—was not even mentioned. Hundreds of cranks[3] rushed into print with their Letters to the Editor, raking up stories of the ill-treatment of British soldiers *by the French population* during the War; the Ruhr was raked up (but never Belgium or concentration camps); George Robey recalled the horror of the black troops on German soil; France was the villain, and Hitler the hero of the Locarno *coup*; others announced sanctimoniously that they had always been opposed to Locarno; and would not have England committed to 'anything beyond the League Covenant' (as if the League Covenant was not a vastly greater 'commitment' than Locarno); and we were also told that 'seventy per cent of Clubland is definitely pro-German.' Here and there, a few sane voices ventured to ask timidly 'whether we were not throwing in our weight on the wrong side'; but Winston Churchill, Sir Walter Citrine, the Duchess of Atholl, the *Yorkshire Post*, the Diplomatic correspondent of the *Manchester Guardian*, the writer of

[3] Many of whom, e.g. Prof. A. P. Lawrie, later turned out to be members of The Link. (Author's note, 1942.)

one 'Letter to the Editor' in five (if that) were like voices crying in the wilderness. General Smuts from South Africa joined in the Heil Hitler chorus.

It did not matter if Gauleiter Wagner, speaking at the Munich election meeting on March 14, just before Hitler's arrival there, declared: 'We have not broken any treaties. But even if we have, we deny others the right to condemn us. What Hitler declares to be right is and will remain right for all time. What Hitler did on March 7, benefited the German people. Anything that benefits the German people is right; anything that harms the German people is wrong.'

And so Germany got away with it. The League, built on the principle that treaties must be observed, became a byword of futility. With the blessing of the majority of 'British public opinion' (as reflected in the 'Letters to the Editor') Europe entered, in March 1936, into a jungle of lawlessness.

And France, who had sought strength and security in scraps of paper called 'Pacts,' became, as a Croix de Feu man remarked to me one day, a second-class power. For after the destruction of Locarno, the most gilt-edged of all the scraps of paper, the value of all international treaties slumped heavily. The League Covenant more even than the rest.

A few weeks later I had occasion to discuss the Locarno *coup* with a responsible public man in England. 'The French were bloody fools,' he said. 'Their first thought was to ask our advice. Of course we couldn't give them "permission" to mobilize. If you want to kiss a girl you don't ask her permission. But if they *had* mobilized, without our permission, then we, with our genius for compromise, would have come forward with a beautiful compromise proposal. Hitler would have had to climb down —and think of the effect in Germany!—the Rhine frontier would have been saved, the League would have been put on its feet again, and England—good old England!—would have "saved European peace." For there would have been *no* war. The Germans were not ready to fight. We knew that Hitler carried out his *coup* against the advice of the Reichswehr. The French should have known that England will always accept a well-managed *fait accompli*, whether it comes from Germany— or from France. Damned fools!'

XIII. THE ELECTION OF 1936 AND THE FRONT POPULAIRE PROGRAMME

THE French election campaign opened in a rather subdued atmosphere. France was still under the impression of the Locarno *coup*.

Later, however, as polling day approached, these national apprehensions, common to all, receded somewhat into the background: for the Locarno *coup*, however serious in itself, was scarcely an election issue. In Alsace, 'Franco-German *rapprochement* at any price,' and 'down with the Soviet Pact' were, clearly, election slogans; while in Lorraine, on the contrary, an important part of the population could not forgive the 'Left' Government of M. Sarraut its failure to march into the Rhineland on March 7.

It may be said that the entire 'programme' of the Right and Centre Parties consisted in their hostility to the Front Populaire, which they declared, 'must not pass,' as it would mean civil strife, revolution, the fall of the franc, ruin, desolation, and war—the idea being that a weakened France would soon fall an easy victim to foreign aggression. The villainy, duplicity and hypocrisy of Moscow were loudly denounced. But the Right knew from the start—and Henri de Kerillis proclaimed it as early as February—that they were fighting a losing battle.

The anti-Front Populaire candidates were an incoherent crowd of people, with little or nothing to unite them, except their opposition to the Front Populaire. They represented, in the eyes of only too many voters, the 'spirit of the Sixth of February'—and did not even represent it effectively. The Croix de Feu, who might have given some 'dynamic' vigour to the election campaign of the Right, had decided not to run candidates (as de Kerillis had proposed); and declared that they would be simply the 'arbiters' in the election—a role in which they were to fail utterly and completely.

This is the kind of gibberish Colonel de la Rocque wrote:

We shall keep vigil so that the election of 1936 does not throw France into a state of mutiny and decay—which would be inevitable but for our great work of French Revival. Having thus avoided the worst, and in a clearer atmosphere, all men of good faith, and wherever they may come from, will recognize each other. And there shall then be the great arbitration which will cast aside all the harmful causes; and will destroy and remedy their effects.

The items in the Front Populaire programme which played the most important part in the election campaign were the measures against the

'200 families' and against the *marchands de canons*—the armaments manufacturers; the dissolution of the Fascist Leagues; the (albeit partial) abolition of the Laval economy decrees; and (in industrial constituencies) full trade union rights, holidays with pay, and a shorter working week.

Of the three Parties of the Front Populaire, the most spectacular campaign of all was conducted by the Communists. They used pictorial posters more than any other party—and they found that it paid. Their slogan was POUR UNE FRANCE LIBRE FORTE ET HEUREUSE. Moscow themes and Moscow terminology were carefully excluded from them; they breathed, if anything, the romantic revolutionary spirit of Paris, with reminiscences of the Great French Revolution, 1848, and all that. (Even the Commune was put aside as something suspect in the eyes of the *bourgeois*.) Rude's statue of the *Marseillaise* at Napoleon's Arc de Triomphe was the subject of one of their dazzling tricolour compositions; they all but missed adapting to their own uses the Napoleonic myth of Béranger and the *Mémorial de Sainte-Hélène*; and as for Joan of Arc, they started a discussion in the *Humanité* which tended to show that the peasant girl of Domrémy would have been much more in sympathy with the People's Front than with the Royalists, who had proclaimed her *la Sainte de la Patrie*, but whose forebears had betrayed her and burnt her alive. '*Liberté, liberté chérie*' the Communist posters wailed. It was clever propaganda in its own way; but just a little surprising, coming as it did from the Communists. It tended to reconcile the revolutionary spirit with the national spirit; it touched the sentimental strain of *quarante-huitard* revolutionism dormant in many a Parisian's heart—be he a workman or a little *bourgeois*. Many a French patriot, feeling that the Communists had put something 'dynamic' into the somewhat moth-eaten *jacobinism* of the Radicals, was tempted to vote for them. Needless to say, the enemies of the Communists explained only too readily that all this sublime poster sentiment about *notre grande révolution*, and the soldiers of Valmy, as well as Maurice Thorez's election broadcast, with his brotherly appeal to the rank and file Croix de Feu 'who feel and suffer all that we feel and suffer' were simply intended to serve the purposes of Moscow—which, with an eye on the balance of power in Europe, was only too glad to stir up French patriotism and militarism, and national solidarity.[1]

[1] We touch here on one of the great contradictions of communist policy: for Stalin's desire for a *strong* France was, later, very poorly served by the encouragement the French Communists gave to the stay-in strikes and the 40-hour week. Local considerations and competition with other 'extremists' played a part in this. Sometimes, when things went very far, the Communists would say they were

Yet, whatever may have been the precise intentions of the Communist leaders, the rank and file were rather pleasantly impressed by this new slogan, '*Pour une France libre, forte et heureuse,*' by the romantic recollections of not merely 1789, but of Valmy and the Marseillaise, and by such brilliant anti-Fascist propaganda as their picture of Hitler with a blood-stained knife (marked Krupp-Wendel) between his teeth—a replica of the old anti-Bolshevik poster—*le couteau entre les dents.*

And as for those voters who sang the Internationale, and desired a Soviet Republic, the Communist leaders told them, as Thorez told the British public in his book, *France To-day and the People's Front:*

> Only a minority of the French working class now enters the fight with the resolute determination to establish Soviets in France. . . . That is why the setting up of Soviets cannot be the immediate aim. Nevertheless, the Communists must lead the majority of the people who are determined to repel Fascism. And in the course of this struggle they will be able to convince the masses of the necessity for a Soviet Republic in France.

The Communists made tremendous headway in the urban constituencies, and, above all, in Paris and the Paris suburbs, where the 'Fascist menace' had made itself felt more directly than in other parts of France.

XIV. INFORMAL NOTES ON A TOUR THROUGH VARIOUS PARTS OF FRANCE IN APRIL 1936

LENS, *April* 5.

HERE at Lens, which was, as it were, the capital of No-Man's-Land, though nominally 'under German occupation until October 14, 1918,' there is not a single pre-War house. The entire town was wiped out; though a few people managed to live here among the ruins right through the War. And to say that the French care less than the English for 'home'! A clean neat new station built in concrete; new churches, a new town hall, a large and ugly war memorial in the spacious boulevard

---

'*débordés*' by 'Trotzkyists' and 'Anarchists,'—a theory at least partly borne out by Trotzky's pamphlet on the French crisis of June 1936. I discuss the matter in some detail in *Moscow* '41. (Author's note, 1942.)

lined with rickety-looking young trees. Numerous Polish shop signs; *bureau dla naturalizacji* opposite the very station.

In this part of the country, where memories of war are still fresh, people do not like to talk about the 'next war.' But beneath the surface of provincial calm, there is, and has been, especially since March 7, a real undercurrent of anxiety. Last month there was something of a run on the savings banks, and shopkeepers will tell you that business has dropped considerably within the last four weeks, with people, not knowing what will happen, putting their money aside and frightened to spend it.

LILLERS, *April 7.*

There was a good Communist poster of the graves and ossuary of Douaumont at Verdun, with words to the effect that the Communists would prevent 'this' from happening again. At Bruay, an important mining village, I saw the Socialist Mayor who said that the German *coup* of March 7 had been 'specially arranged between Hitler and the French reactionaries, with a view to preventing a "Left" election in France. But for Hitler,' he said, 'the Left would win a tremendous victory, but the *bourgeois* papers—which are the only papers read in the villages—exaggerate the menace, and some of the village people think that the Right can come to terms with Hitler, and so save us from war.'

The only bus I could find to get out of Division last night took me to Lillers, on the main Dunkirk-Arras line. The hotel proprietor here is a fair-haired Englishman from Newcastle. He got married to a French girl during the War; had taken her to England; but last year he learned from her parents that the station hotel was for sale. 'They are queer chaps, the French are,' he said. 'They nearly had a fight in this hotel the other day, and since then the Left chaps and the Right chaps come here on different nights. It's not safe to have them together . . . and, Lor', don't they just love us. "*Sacrés Anglais,*" they say to me, "will you or won't you come over in the next war?" '

MONTLUÇON, *April 11.*

This is the Bourbonnais, 'the sweetest part of France,' as Sterne calls it in his *Sentimental Journey.* How different from the Pas-de-Calais!

Montluçon, with a population of 42,000, is in the very heart of rural France. Montluçon itself is a rare phenomenon; an industrial town without any unemployed—very different in this respect from Limoges. It has a big factory of motor tyres, munition works and chemical works specializing in fertilizers.

74

This afternoon I went to see M. Dormoy,[1] the Socialist Mayor of the town. M. Dormoy is an imposing man with a black beard, and is considered to be the 'big boss' of Montluçon—for although he is a Socialist, he owns a great deal of house property in the town. Rural Socialism, as I soon discovered, is something different from urban Socialism. I got my first glimpse of it at a small election meeting M. Dormoy held at the Mairie of Lignerolles, a small village five miles outside Montluçon.

His attacks on the '200 families,' on the *marchands de canons* and on the Press 'paid by Hitler and Mussolini' were loudly cheered by the farmers. His speech was a rather colourless performance—the kind of speech one hears only too often at the Chamber. He attacked Laval, but also spoke with much bitterness of England who had 'let down' France on March 7.

After completing his political speech M. Dormoy recalled all that he had done in the last four years for the commune of Lignerolles. He had secured a 10,000 francs subsidy for the water-works; two of the roads had been classified as 'national' roads, and henceforth the State and no longer the commune was responsible for their upkeep; and he had been promised an extension of the automatic telephone to Lignerolles. At this point the audience became extremely lively and even aggressive. Why, one of them asked, were the octroi (municipal customs) duties on butter and vegetables so high at Montluçon? 'I am here as your Parliamentary candidate,' M. Dormoy replied, 'I am not here as Mayor of Montluçon.' But the farmers persisted. Why were the Montluçon hospitals buying their milk from one particular source and none of it at Lignerolles? And so on, and so on.

One realized what a dog's life a French deputy has to lead with his constituents bothering him all the year round with constant requests for little services and favours (and M. Dormoy had fifty-one communes to look after!). For to render such services is, in the eyes of most of his constituents, the main function of a deputy—even a Socialist deputy.

The farmers hate the '200 families'; and if they vote for the Socialists, it is because they expect to be protected against the big trusts—the big milling concerns, and the manufacturers of fertilizers.

GUERET, CREUSE, *April* 13.

No one in this part of the world is taking Fascism too seriously. To the people, who seldom see anybody who is not either a Socialist or a

---

[1] Later a member of the Blum Government, and, after the death of Salengro, Minister of the Interior. Murdered by Cagoulards in 1941.

Radical, the Republic is eternal. The 'fussiness' of Paris is treated with a touch of contempt.

The Radical Mayor of the town, an old man with a drooping white moustache and looking a little like Clemenceau, who received me with old-time courtesy, spoke with some melancholy of the progress the Socialists are making in rural France at the expense of the Radicals. He expressed the view that Paris might still be the intellectual centre of France, but with its irresponsible fussiness it could no longer be regarded as its political centre. 'The gulf between Paris and the provinces,' he said, 'has been steadily growing.' He was not sure whether the peasants had given serious thought to the League of Nations and the right policy to be adopted. All he knew was that they wanted peace, peace, and peace.

I spent Easter Sunday at Evaux-les-Bains, in the Creuse, where I was regally entertained by the local baker, M. Maneyraud, who happens to be the son-in-law of old Thiébault, my Paris concierge.

The evening we spent in the local café at Evaux in the company of the leading Republicans of the town—my host, the tailor, and the postman. The tailor, a young man of about thirty-two, was a passionate Republican, who had wept with rage when Daladier had allowed himself to be driven out by the February riots. 'Provincial France,' he said, 'was taken by surprise. But now we have been warned. If the Fascists start any nonsense again,' he cried, thumping the marble table with his fist, 'provincial France will march on Paris like one man.'

He and the postman and my friend the baker all proclaimed their passionate devotion to the Republic and to the League of Nations. They were surprisingly firm on this point, and held that collective security alone could save France from war. They also denounced with much violence the '200 families' and the armaments manufacturers, and were enthusiastic readers of Bergery's *Flèche* and of the *Canard Enchaîné*, the satirical Left-Wing weekly, whose influence in the district they declared to be 'tremendous.'

LYONS, *April* 15.

Lyons and Herriot—the two names are inseparable. M. Herriot has been the Maire of Lyons for thirty-one years and is widely regarded as the greatest municipal administrator in France. His local efficiency is a matter of amazement to those who regard M. Herriot as a statesman with more failures than achievements to his credit, and who are apt to talk only too glibly of his weakness and 'sloppiness.' And he has managed, through his political influence, to get a lot of subsidies from the State. Lyons puts this to his credit.

At the Town Hall at Lyons I gained access to the holy of holies— *le Cabinet du Maire*—without great difficulty.

M. Herriot looked rather weary and a little sad. What were the prospects after the elections? I asked. M. Herriot threw up one hand in a weary gesture of indifference. 'I don't know,' he said briefly. 'And the Front Populaire?' I asked. He shrugged his shoulders. '*Que voulez-vous mon petit, que je vous dise?*' He had obviously no great liking for the Socialists, least of all the Socialists at Lyons.

'How,' I said, 'would you define the position of Lyons on the political map of France?'

M. Herriot reflected for a moment. 'Do you not know the saying,' he said, 'that "Paris is the capital of France, but Lyons is the capital of the Republic"? It is still true.'

He had two election meetings in his constituency that night, and offered to take me with him in his car if I came back in an hour.

The first meeting was in a small café in a shabby working-class district. It was packed with little shopkeepers, workmen, and a few postmen and railwaymen. M. Herriot said he would not make a speech, but simply answer any questions the audience cared to put to him. 'I am not much of a novelty,' he said. 'And if you want somebody fresh and new you can do better than vote for me. But such as I am,' he smiled, 'I shall be glad to represent you again. I am getting old. I am like a bottle of wine. It's for you to say whether it is getting better or worse with age. I am not hankering after reactionary votes. I appeal only to democrats. I am now probably standing for the last time,' he said sadly. '*Eh, oui.* Time passes. I am nearly sixty-four.'

An unemployed man asked some question about the family allowance he was—or was not—receiving. M. Herriot dismissed the matter by telling him to come to the Mairie. Another young man asked how Fascism should be fought. M. Herriot was now in his element. 'Vote against it!' he cried. 'Vote against it. That's the first thing to do.' He then told the distressful story of the savage Fascist campaign against him. 'I have been threatened with death. I have been slandered and libelled. The first thing the new Chamber must do is to pass a new libel law. We have among us to-night an English journalist who knows how much it costs in his country to libel people.' 'Monsieur le Président,' I said, 'it sometimes costs even *too* much.' 'Maybe,' Herriot smiled, 'but in France it costs nothing at all.' He was obviously feeling strongly on the subject.

77

There was an unemployed fellow with a broad grin, who asked him what he thought of the Franco-Soviet Pact. 'Ah,' said M. Herriot, 'now *there* is a sensible question. I went to Russia for the first time in 1922, and I wrote a little book about it in which, I am proud to say, I spoke of the future friendship between our two countries. . . .'

'*Vive la Russie!*' the unemployed fellow cried. The audience chuckled and M. Herriot laughed. '*Eh, oui,*' he went on. 'In 1932 I went to Russia again, and I said to them—' There followed an account of how he had persuaded the Russians to 'drop Germany' and to drop the 'world revolution'—for 'peace was not solid enough to stand it,' and to come to Geneva to organize European peace. And since they had come to Geneva the Russians had always been on France's side and their conduct had been irreproachable.

Amid loud cheers M. Herriot drove off to the other meeting. This also took place in a poor-looking café, with rows of bottles on the shelves and people sitting on the zinc counter. M. Herriot squeezed himself into a corner at the end of the long tables, and asked for a cup of coffee.

One heckler was an exquisitely polite young man, who, 'in the name of sixty-nine newsvendors,' wished to ask le citoyen Herriot why the sale of newspapers had been prohibited in the rue de la République on Saturday nights. M. Herriot recalled that the sale of certain Fascist papers by pugnacious propagandists had given rise last year to street clashes, and while he sympathized with the professional newsvendors— for to them it was a question affecting their livelihood—it was difficult to discriminate between different kinds of newspapers. 'But come and see me at the Mairie. Never in my thirty-one years at the Mairie have I refused to receive a delegation of workers.'

Some good fun was provided by a retired railwayman—old, doddering, and slightly tipsy—who persisted in asking M. Herriot why the Radicals had brought into power '*le fameux Doumergue*, the man of the decree laws, who had not even been elected by the people.' M. Herriot proceeded to explain at some length how the Doumergue Government was formed after the February riots. But the old man continued to interrupt: 'The Radicals were no good. And they called for *le fameux Doumergue*. Now, I want to know why you had to bring back *le fameux Doumergue*?' By this time everybody was roaring with laughter, including M. Herriot himself. 'But the Radicals didn't bring him back,' he said. 'The President of the Republic brought him back.' 'No, it was you who brought him back,' the old man cried. 'And he was not even elected by the people.' He was visibly enjoying his own success. Still, after some further protests against *le fameux Doumergue*, he at last gave way.

M. Herriot spoke again of the slander and libel to which he had been subjected by the Reactionary Press, and explained why he had been forced to break up both the Doumergue Government and the Laval Government. Poincaré, he said, was loyal; 'but not these two.' He had disagreed with Laval's foreign policy, and, moreover, the attitude of the Reactionary Press had rendered their further co-operation impossible. 'When Laval went to Russia they all cried, "*Bravo! Bravo! Vive Laval!*" Yet, when I attended a meeting organized by the Friends of the Soviet Union I was branded as a traitor and a Russian agent.'

STRASBOURG, *April* 19.

'We cannot allow Strasbourg to be exposed to the German guns,' M. Sarraut, the Premier, said on March 8, the day after Hitler's occupation of the Rhineland. The bridge of Kehl is only a mile away from Strasbourg, and, as Hitler has refused to make the required 'gesture,' Strasbourg is, and will probably remain, exposed to the fire of German guns. There was something of a panic here in the second week of March. The shops dealing in trunks and suitcases did—as one of their owners told me—some 'golden business' during those days, and there was a run on the banks and savings banks. In a few days several hundred million francs were withdrawn. But the people no longer consider war as an immediate probability, though here—as elsewhere in France—the danger of a German adventure in Austria is considered very real.

This morning Jean Knittel, the best-informed journalist in Alsace and most hospitable and most entertaining of hosts, took me in his car 'down the Maginot Line.' It was a perfect spring day as we drove north along the main road, three miles west of the Rhine, lined with pear-trees in full blossom. On the left were the wooded Vosges mountains, on the right, the dark-blue silhouette of the Black Forest. Looking back, we could see the high spire of Strasbourg cathedral. 'You know the passage in Heine,' Knittel said: ' "I should like to stand on the top of Strasbourg cathedral, and spread out a tricolour flag, large enough to cover the whole of Germany!" '

．　　．　　．　　．　　．　　．　　．

They don't speak German in Alsace, but a dialect as incomprehensible as Norwegian. Last night I went to a big election meeting at Strasbourg held by the Dissident Communists (though there is little Communism about them) who now style themselves the *Heimatsfront* or the *Arbeiter und Bauren Partei*. It is an extraordinarily incoherent combination of various Alsatian tendencies. A witty American who was in Strasbourg

79

some time ago described it as a combination of Trotzky, Goering and the Pope. It produces two papers—the *ELZ—the Elsass-Lvthringische Zeitung*—and the Dissident Communist *Neue Welt*, both with only very small circulations. These papers are not openly pro-German, but contain such propaganda as: 'What have they [the French] made of Alsace? An armed camp, in which the workers cry in vain for bread.' (Actually the economic depression is not much worse here than anywhere else.) These two papers are quoted extensively in the German Press as the representative expression of Alsatian opinion.

The two principal speakers at the *Heimatsfront* meeting were Herr Hüber, the former Mayor of Strasbourg (who spoke in dialect) and who is standing in the election, and Herr Mourer, the present Deputy for Strasbourg 2. Mourer, who has not distinguished himself in any way at the Chamber, is a young man of thirty-eight, and a former officer in the German Air Force. He spoke in German, for he comes from Metz, where people speak either French or German, but not dialect.

Herr Mourer spoke with great admiration of Hitler, and said that he could 'fully appreciate Germany's point of view,' when she denounced Locarno. Alsace, he said, would be the first to suffer from a Franco-German war, and it was absolutely essential that France and Germany made friends. All obstacles like the Franco-Soviet Pact must be cleared out of the way. The Jewish emigrants who had been driven out of Germany, were now trying to take their revenge on Hitler by provoking France into attacking Germany; but if they succeeded, they would have a heavy price to pay. This outburst against the Jews was loudly cheered —for in Strasbourg, where most of the trade is in Jewish hands, there is strong anti-Jewish feeling, which is now being thoroughly exploited by the *Heimatsfront*—much more loudly, indeed, than Mourer's defence of Hitler and the Locarno *coup*, which was received with visible coolness and scepticism. Even so, this pro-Nazi propaganda—supported by Germany—seems to be making some headway in Alsace, and words like 'make friends with Germany at any price for Alsace's sake' do not seem to be without effect.[2]

The Dissident Communists of Alsace are the most important autonomist group with pro-German and pro-Nazi leanings. Among the autonomists, they represent the 'Left,' and their main object is to capture votes

[2] Mourer was re-elected in the 1936 election and Hüber beat Weill. Under the Front Populaire Government with Blum, a Jew, at its head, this pro-Nazi propaganda tended, for a time, to increase, and 'Berlin rather than Moscow' became a fairly popular slogan in certain Alsatian quarters. The great military parade that accompanied M. Lebrun's visit to Strasbourg in September did, however, a great deal to check this propaganda.

which would normally go to the regular Socialists and Communists. But while more virulently autonomist than the Catholic autonomism of a Stürmel or Rossé, even the autonomism of the Dissident Communists is not Separatist.

Alsatian autonomism in its most prevalent sense is therefore simply a movement in favour of the status quo, and against any change. 'Autonomism,' an Alsatian told me, 'is simply a revolver we keep in our drawer. We shall bring it out when the burglar comes'—the eventual burglar being, for instance, a French Left-Wing Government.

It may safely be said that if only a negligible part of the Alsatians would welcome a return to Germany, and perhaps fifteen or twenty per cent are autonomist in a more than sentimental way, all the rest are, at heart, perfectly content to be French citizens—provided their privileges are left intact. Only the Alsatians are, by nature, professional grumblers; and the French are not unduly disturbed by their grumbling. For under German rule they grumbled a hundred times more. And many of them still remember the reign of terror during the War, when French was not allowed to be spoken in the streets of Strasbourg and 20,000 Alsatians were deported to Germany.

Of the sixteen deputies elected in 1932, one may say that ten were fully pro-French—which does not mean that they are not Alsatians—far from it.

The ten 'purely French' deputies include two Socialists. Of the six deputies who are not 'one hundred per cent' French, one is a Dissident Communist; three, M. Dahlet, M. Rossé, the Mayor of Colmar, and M. Stürmel (this one officially an autonomist), have been rather troublesome from the French point of view and have been apt, under various influences, to denounce the 'forced assimilation' practised in the schools; and the remaining two are simply Catholics with strong regionalist, but not autonomist, sentiments.

NANCY, *April 23.*

Lorraine—or rather this part of Lorraine, which was not annexed by Germany in 1871—has been, and still is, the stronghold of French nationalism. The population of Nancy, which was 40,000 in 1870, nearly doubled after Germany's annexation of Alsace-Lorraine, many of the Alsatians who would not stay under German rule settling at Nancy, the capital of the old Duchy of Lorraine. It had a profound effect on Nancy. The Lorrainers—much more than the Alsatians—have in their blood this feeling of an ever-present German menace—and it is probably stronger now than ever. Many of the peasants here have been blaming

81

the Government for not having 'marched into Germany' on March 7. These Lorrainers, who have never forgotten 1914 and 1870, would that day have welcomed a preventive war.

Here at Nancy one is a million miles away from the cheerful and optimistic republicanism of the country south of the Loire. This nationalism has been fruitful soil for all kinds of anti-Republican movements, and nearly all the deputies for Lorraine are men of the Right. They include M. Louis Marin, the G.O.M. of the French Conservatives. But M. Marin, at least, is a good Republican. Rather different are such representatives of Lorraine as M. de Wendel, the steel magnate, who was until recently a deputy for Nancy, and M. Désiré Ferry, the editor of the *Liberté*, the most Chauvinist paper in France, and an avowed member of the Croix de Feu. The Royalist organization at Nancy, with 1,000 active members, is one of the strongest outside Paris; stronger still is the local organization of the Croix de Feu, and there are also groups of Jeunesses Patriotes, Francistes, and so on.

The Front Populaire has been putting up a strong fight at Nancy— and it is an uphill fight. In 1932 M. Marin had a majority of 6,000 and M. Désiré Ferry one of 10,000. Yet it is chiefly M. Ferry whom the Front Populaire has been 'after.' It is this member of the Croix de Feu who glorified in his paper the 'spirit of the Sixth of February,' who conducted the most savage campaign of all against the Radical leaders, and supported all the anti-Parliamentary movements in the country.

I went to a meeting held in a café by a Left-Wing candidate, a young Paris barrister called M. Lapie, who turned out to be the private secretary of M. Paul-Boncour.

The next day he took me in his car to a village some five miles from Nancy. The village, with its stone cottages and dung-heaps and its hens and pigs wandering about the road, was more primitive than the Alsatian villages. At the Mairie, with its fly-stained patriotic pictures and a portrait of President Carnot, we were received by a distrustful old *garde champêtre*, who, after receiving a tip, volunteered to announce the meeting by beating his drum round the village. This he did, calling out at the same time that a candidate was waiting at the Mairie for '*Messieurs les électeurs.*' After a long wait ten or twelve yokels arrived at the Mairie, wearing caps and rough country clothes. Some of them wore wooden shoes, others carpet slippers, for it was Saturday afternoon.

The Socialist candidate had, by coincidence, also arrived in the same village, and the Radical and Socialist decided to hold a joint meeting. The Socialist, who emphasized the fact that he was a War veteran (the young barrister, on the other hand, could only say that he was a reserve officer),[3] went on to talk about the armaments manufacturers, who were working hand in hand with Germany; about the Office du Blé, the Socialist remedy for the agricultural crisis; and about the big land-owners, 'who in 1792, came from Coblence at the head of the Prussian regiments, in the hope of killing the Front Populaire of those days.' The peasants listened silently and ironically to both the Socialist's and the Radical's speeches. They treated the young Paris barrister with particular distrust. 'We don't want any young people here,' one of them said. 'But, surely,' the Socialist replied, 'M. Ferry has never done anything for you but come here once in four years to ask you for your votes.' 'That's enough!' an old peasant said. 'We don't want to listen to you any more. You have done nothing but attack M. Ferry.'

We then drove off to another village. 'Such fine people,' M. Lapie complained, 'but so irresponsive.' The other meetings were little better. The peasants obviously disliked the young Paris barrister; 'he is not even a chap from Lorraine,' one of them declared.

In the evening we drove to a large meeting in an industrial suburb of Nancy. There the Front Populaire enthusiasm was in full swing, and, far from contradicting M. Lapie when he denounced the Comité des Forges and the Fascist propaganda of M. Ferry's paper, the people cheered lustily. There is just a chance he may get in.[4]

XV. ENTER LÉON BLUM

THE first ballot was held on April 26, and the second on May 3. In the first, only in less than half the constituencies was a candidate—who had secured an absolute majority—returned.

On both Sundays the polling was calm and orderly; but this was not a sign of indifference—the poll was eighty-five per cent—higher even than in 1932.

There have seldom been any 'landslides' in France; and if one keeps to this rough division between Left and Right, one will find that even in

[3] M. Lapie has since had a distinguished career in the Foreign Legion and is Free French Governor of Chad.

[4] Thanks to the close co-operation between the Left-Wing forces, M. Ferry with his 10,000 majority, was beaten by M. Lapie by 300 votes.

the 1936 election the 'landslide' was not as important as was suggested by the number of deputies returned for the Right and Left parties.

But the Left won, because they adhered closely and loyally to the Front Populaire Pact—the electorate even more so than the candidates themselves. When Marcel Déat, the Neo-Socialist Minister of Air in the Sarraut Government, refused to withdraw in favour of the Communist who had scored a few votes more than he, the electorate punished him for this breach of the Front Populaire Pact. But Déat was one of the few Left candidates who did not observe the rules of the game.

Perhaps the most notable eve-of-the-Poll episode was an appeal by Marshal Pétain for 'National Reconciliation.' The appeal was full of Croix de Feu terminology, and the Right hoped that this intervention in their favour by the eighty-year-old Hero of Verdun would create an impression. But it was of no importance. Neither was Colonel de la Rocque's final eve-of-the-Poll statement—the most openly Fascist statement he had made for a long time.

Though there are always some doubtful and shifty elements at the Chamber—particularly along the Centre-Left border—the Left had, nominally, 379 seats, as against the 239 seats of the Opposition. In the old Chamber the figures were, respectively, 342 and 269.

The number of votes cast was as follows:

	1936	1932
Right	2,254,000	2,262,000
Radicals	1,461,000	1,805,000
Centre	1,938,000	2,225,000
Small Left Groups	518,000	511,000
Socialists	1,922,000	1,931,000
Dissident Communists	95,000	85,000
Communists	1,503,000	794,000

The victory of the Front Populaire was complete; and it was a clear verdict against Fascism, against deflation, against the '200 families,' against the *marchands de canons*, and against 'National Government.' The support (albeit grudging support) they had given to deflation and to the National Governments of MM. Doumergue and Laval, had cost the Radicals over forty seats. France was going to turn over a new leaf.

M. Léon Blum, the leader of now the largest party in the Chamber, was the most obvious candidate for the Premiership. Two days after the election, it was officially announced that Blum was prepared to form the new Government. For three weeks M. Blum was in a peculiar position. The powers of the old Chamber did not expire until May 31; and, according to the Constitution (or so at least it had been traditionally interpreted), the old Government had to remain in power until the new Chamber met. In May 1936, this proved a particularly unfortunate arrangement. It has been, though not necessarily rightly, observed that the impatience caused by three weeks' waiting had at least something to do with the great stay-in strike movement, which broke out towards the end of the May interregnum; and that effective action by the new Government immediately after the election victory might have discouraged such a movement.

Moreover, a serious financial crisis had started after the first ballot on April 26; and during the first week in May, the flight from the franc and the export of gold again took on alarming proportions. Instead of M. Sarraut, the French Premier, plain M. Blum, without any official Government position, was expected to do something about it. Almost equally serious was the international situation. Addis-Ababa had been captured by the Italians, and the question arose of raising or continuing sanctions. M. Flandin was not in a position to take any decision—and neither was M. Blum.

Léon Blum is so complex a character that he cannot be fairly described in a few words. It is agreed that his mind is a sophisticated one, and the words 'esprit subtil' have often been applied to him, both in a laudatory and in a derogatory sense. He has also been called a doctrinaire—though never a demagogue; but even the word doctrinaire suggests a mind more rigid than Blum's. He has also been described as a refined intellectual—and, indeed, when you see Blum, you sometimes imagine that Marcel Proust's Swann would have looked rather like him in his old age. At the same time, this esthète and salonnard is also the successor of Jaurès, and a leader of the French working class.

Léon Blum was born in 1872, one of the five sons of a wealthy Jewish ribbon manufacturer who had moved to Paris from Alsace. 'Before going to the Lycée Charlemagne,' he wrote, 'I frequented the elementary schools around the rue Granéta where I got to know the children of small Republican artisans.' He used to pester his father with questions as to why he sold his goods dearer than he had bought them. The most important influence of his early years was his maternal grandmother, known in the family as la Communarde because of her fiery sympathy for the Commune of 1871. She was a woman of strong character, who converted young Léon to Socialism at the age of six, and trained him in the cult of revolutionary heroes.

He became a well-known social figure, the author of a good book on Stendhal, a successful civil servant, and one of the three or four most famous theatre critics in Paris. But 'for a man of his position he was singularly persistent in very radical opinions. His book on marriage scandalized orthodox moralists.'[1]

On July 31, 1914, Jaurès was assassinated, and the Socialist Party was left without a head. Perhaps Blum was aware of this when, soon after Jaurès's death, he became, for the first time in his life, actively connected with politics. At the age of forty-two he became *chef de Cabinet* to Marcel Sembat, Minister of Public Works. During those years he made a careful study of the Parliamentary system, and assembled his views in a series of articles published anonymously in 1918 (they have since been reprinted in book form).

In 1919 he stood for Parliament for the first time. It was the *bleu horizon* Chamber with its vast Nationalist majority. During the War the Socialists had been divided, and, after the overwhelming victory of the Right, were suffering from a certain inferiority complex. It was Léon Blum who, a few months after his election, succeeded in convincing the Majority that the small Socialist group was capable of not only systematic, but also articulate opposition. This sore necessity of creating and maintaining an opposition in the smug Chamber of 1919—an opposition which would miss no opportunity of criticizing the Government—had a far-reaching effect on Blum's Parliamentary career. To be leader of the Opposition became almost second nature with him—and in later years, when his target was no longer an all-power Poincaré, but some poor Radical Premier, sorely in need of indulgence, he sometimes overdid his 'oppositionism.'

It has often been said that if only Blum had had the physique and the voice of Jaurès, he would have been a great political leader in France. But he is not a great orator. His voice—to use Jules Renard's phrase—is a girl's voice—and is sometimes scarcely audible in the Press gallery of the Chamber. The gesture he makes with his long arms are not always devoid of a touch of comedy; to stress a point, his long forefingers suddenly start revolving in front of his face, 'like a mouse cleaning its whiskers,' as David Scott once remarked. But one really has to read his speeches, to realize fully the alertness and clarity of his mind.

He was a Marxist, and believed in the international solidarity of the working class; he believed that the Socialists could be strong only by 'being themselves.' He deplored the attacks made on the Socialists by the Communists, and felt that, of all the Socialists, the French Socialists deserved least of all to be treated as flunkeys of the *bourgeoisie*; and

[1] Quoted from the excellent sketch of Blum in the *Morning Post* of May 22, 1936, by its Paris correspondent, Darsie R. Gillie.

he continued to hope that the two working-class parties would some day be reunited.

His relations with the French working class were rather peculiar. He represented in their eyes, as it were, the Centre of the Party; the Left militants, like Zyromski and Marceau Pivert (each from his own point of view), did not think him sufficiently revolutionary[2]; as for the Right Wing, they considered him too uncompromising as a Parliamentary leader, and too internationalist in temperament.

The Socialist rank and file had a great personal regard for Blum; but it would be untrue to say that he was popular. He was not 'one of ours'; and they usually called him 'Monsieur Blum'; for 'camarade' didn't quite suit him, somehow. Blum is always a little distant except with people he knows very well; and he can—quite involuntarily—make many a new-comer feel shy and uneasy.

There was, for a long time, a legend in France that Blum was enormously rich; and even the Socialist rank and file believed it—though they never held it against him. Actually, he was well off until a few years ago; but since 1934 he has been almost on the verge of financial difficulties. Since the Sixth of February many French dressmaking and milliners' firms have been boycotting Blum ribbons, from which he received the bulk of his income.

For Blum was detested by the Right as few men are. In 1934 and 1935 the *Action Française* and the *Solidarité Française* and certain other pro-Fascist papers did not hesitate to advocate, more or less openly, the murder of Blum. At the time of the Abyssinian conflict, the *Action Française* warned Blum and one hundred and forty other public men of the Left that they would be massacred the day France was dragged into war with Italy. This incitement to murder was not in vain. On February 13, 1936, a crowd of Royalists had gathered near the house of Jacques Bainville, off the Boulevard St. Germain, waiting for his funeral procession to begin. By an unfortunate coincidence Blum, M. Monnet, the future Minister of Agriculture, and Mme Monnet happened at that moment to drive from the Chamber down the Boulevard St. Germain. The Royalists rushed at the car and stopped it; and, dragging Blum out of it, proceeded to beat him savagely, striking him on the head and neck with a number-plate. He would probably have been battered to death, but for the timely intervention of a few brave police-

---

[2] There was—and subsequent events like the Spanish war were to confirm it—a sharp difference between Zyromski and Pivert. Roughly speaking, Zyromski was a pro-Stalinite, and Pivert a Trotzkyist pacifist, closely resembling the Spanish POUM. (Author's note, 1942.)

men assisted by a number of house-painters, working close by, who had witnessed the scene. Streaming with blood Blum was taken to hospital and took several weeks to recover.

That afternoon M. Sarraut made the most vigorous speech in his life, and a few hours later the Royalist leagues were dissolved. Three men were later arrested and identified as Blum's aggressors.[3] Three days later a vast protest demonstration of the Front Populaire marched from the Panthéon to the Place de la Nation. That day the French working class felt a greater personal devotion to Blum than ever before. He had become 'one of ours.'

Such is the complex personality of this tall, grey-haired, shortsighted man, with a drooping moustache who, in May 1936, was on the point of becoming Premier of France. How would this merciless critic of all Governments behave once in office himself? He was watched with great curiosity, and except for the indefatigable Charles Maurras, who shrieked hysterically '*à bas les juifs! à bas les juifs!*,' most of the Press reserved judgment. Among other things, it was no good quarrelling in advance with a man who would shortly be in control of the secret funds.

As already said, there was something of a financial panic during the first week in May, in the course of which the Bank of France lost two and a half milliard francs of gold. On May 10, before the National Council of the Socialist Party, who cheered Blum with a depth of feeling that had never been observed before, the Premier-Elect sought to reassure the Bourse. The franc—even though he did not consider it the most important question of all—would not, he said, be devalued; there was no mystery about the future Government's programme—which was simply the programme of the Front Populaire—(and this did not provide for the capital levy demanded by the Communists) ; and while M. Blum was aware of the courage with which the policy of deflation had been pursued—this was a little bouquet for M. Régnier, who was still Finance Minister—there was no doubt that this policy had proved a failure.

The Bourse was reassured. The more 'dynamic' forces of the Left, on the other hand, were a little disappointed; and it was perhaps since that day that the conviction began to grow among the working class that the Front Populaire Government might require a little 'pushing' from outside. This feeling was clearly reflected in the stay-in strikes, which broke out a fortnight later, and thanks to which a number of important labour reforms were to be pushed through Parliament with unexpected speed.

[3] Subsequently, Charles Maurras was sentenced to eight months' imprisonment for incitement to murder.

On the day after his speech, Blum formally asked the Communists and the C.G.T. to enter his Government. The Communists refused. Though supporting the Front Populaire Government, they would exercise control over it through a 'ministry of the masses,' with the most ardent and disciplined elements of the Front Populaire assembled in it.

This rather suggested that while the Socialists were going to bear the brunt of the battle in office, the Communists would try to play the leading part in the constituencies, and to secure a sort of 'moral leadership' over the Left-Wing forces of the country.

As for the C.G.T., it also decided not to be represented in the Government. M. Jouhaux, the Secretary-General of the C.G.T., who had been very 'reformist' for many years, but who had regained something of the revolutionary syndicalism of his younger days, since the recent amalgamation of the C.G.T. and the C.G.T.U. (the Communist trade unions), put forward, about the middle of May, a scheme for three-month Labour Bonds with which to finance a vast plan of public works. The proposal was badly received by M. Blum, who thought it as unsound as anything conceived by the financiers of Nazi Germany—whose example had, indeed, suggested the plan to M. Jouhaux. Moreover, M. Racamond and other Communists in the C.G.T. were hostile to joining the Government. Blum regretted the refusal of the C.G.T. to enter his Cabinet; as for the Communist refusal, he was perhaps relieved—though he never openly admitted it; he knew them to be troublesome customers; and he also knew that even a partly Communist Government would make a bad impression abroad—especially in England; and the first principle of Blum's foreign policy was to keep on good terms with England.

Nevertheless, the aloofness of the Communists had immense disadvantages, as their future conduct was to show.

Blum's first speech on foreign policy during that intermediary period was made at a luncheon at the American Club on May 15. The most important passage in his speech concerned France's future relations with the Fascist countries (which, for years, Blum had unceasingly cursed in his articles and speeches):

'With all nations of the world,' he said, 'whatever may be their internal policy, we wish to co-operate in eliminating the causes of conflict which might, some day, lead to war. We wish to work with all nations and for all nations, provided they sincerely desire to work with us in building up peace.'

Thorez was at the height of his popularity during those days. A burly fellow with healthy red cheeks, curly fair hair, a beautiful voice, and a cruel little mouth, Thorez was like the ideal proletarian of old Marxist posters strangling the snake of capitalism with a muscular arm. The young ladies of the upper *bourgeoisie* thought him quite delightful— they were thrilled to see a 'real Bolshevik' give a lecture in the West End, and never thought he would be so nice and well behaved, and such a *joli garçon*.

.   .   .   .

But their enthusiasm did not last long. For on May 26 the first stay-in strike both out at the Usines Nieuport at Issy-les-Moulineaux, where these aeroplane works were 'occupied' by eight hundred workers. It was the beginning of the most formidable strike movement that France had ever known.

Four days later, when the strikes seemed to be 'definitely' subsiding —in reality they had subsided only temporarily on account of the Whitsun week-end—Léon Blum made his most important pre-Premier speech at the Socialist Congress then meeting at the Salle Huyghens. The galleries were packed with the *militants* of the Seine Federation— many of them Left-Wing extremists—who loudly cheered Zyromski's defence of stay-in strikes, and Pivert's demand that the new Government reduce the term of military service. Many of them were teachers. But the great event of the day was Blum's speech.

Several times in the course of it the whole congress rose like one man and cheered frantically, and when the speech was over, dozens of militants rushed to the tribune to shake his hand and to embrace him. This speech defined exactly the view Blum took of the functions of the Front Populaire Government, and has often been quoted on later occasions. This is what he said:

> The Front Populaire Government is a new thing. It represents not merely a combination of parties but a powerful mass movement. It will be new by its methods and by the character of its action.
>
> Our mission as a party is to build up a new society, but I shall tell you frankly that the task of the Front Populaire Government is different. Neither the Socialists alone nor the Socialists together with the other proletarian parties have a majority. Our duty is simply to carry out the Front Populaire programme.
>
> We are going to act within the framework of the present régime, whose very vices we have denounced.
>
> The question is whether there is a possibility of at least securing within the present régime relief for those who suffer, and of creating a peaceful transition from this Society to the Society which remains

our aim? Are a small ration of justice and well-being and a large ration of hope possible in the present society?

Alluding to the failure of the Communists to enter the government and, on the other hand, to the Fascist menace, M. Blum said:

> I am spoken of as a Kerensky who is preparing the way for a Lenin. I can assure you that this is not going to be a Kerensky Government; and it is equally certain that if we fail we shall be succeeded not by a Lenin.

Three days later, on Thursday, June 4, the Sarraut Government resigned, and a few hours afterwards the formation of the new Cabinet was announced. This was one of the largest Cabinets in the records of the Third Republic, and M. Blum had built it up on a somewhat new basis, by grouping the members of his Cabinet into seven main departments, with numerous under-secretaries, in accordance with the principles he had laid down in his book on government reform.

It was a presentable team; with a great deal of new blood—which was a pleasant change from the everlasting Bonnets and Queuilles and William Bertrands. It included many young men—M. Monnet, the Minister of Agriculture was only thirty-five; M. Zay, the Minister of Education thirty-three; and many of the under-secretaries were in their early thirties. There were—a complete novelty—three women under-secretaries.

XVI. THE GREAT STRIKES OF JUNE 1936

Three things run through the life of the Paris worker—work, enjoyment and—from time to time—revolution. He manages all three with speed, enthusiasm, and a very considerable degree of competence. That is why a stranger constantly feels (even the late Mr. Pogodin noticed it) as though something in Paris were always on the point of breaking out.—SALTYKOV, *Beyond the Border*.

THERE were two big strike waves: first a very short one, before the Whitsun week-end of May 30–1; and then, a much vaster one, which reached its climax on June 7, but took weeks and months to subside. The great strike started, as already said, on May 26, at the Nieuport Works at Issy-les-Moulineaux, near Paris.

During the next three days, the movement rapidly spread, especially in the engineering industry of the Paris region, which came almost completely to a standstill; and also spread to the building trade, including the men employed in demolishing the Trocadero for the 1937 Exhibition. Nearly everywhere the works were occupied by the strikers.

Although the Communists afterwards claimed the credit for this strike movement, it probably was, in the main, largely spontaneous. It was started by the rank and file; and if many men in this rank and file were, nominally, Communists, they acted in most, if not all, cases, without any previous consultation with the Communist leaders. It seems that the leaders—whether Socialist, Communist, or C.G.T.—were taken by surprise.

Trotzky, in his significant little book, *Whither France,* pays a tribute to 'the unequalled political instinct the Paris working class displayed in starting the ball rolling during that last week in May.' 'During those days,' he writes with his usual sarcasm, 'when Blum was looking at himself in the mirror from every angle, making pre-governmental gestures and uttering pre-governmental sentences, and commenting upon them in articles which were always concerned with Blum, but never with the proletariat—during those very days a magnificent, truly spring-like wave of strikes rolled over France.'

. . . .

On Friday, May 29, about 70,000 men were on strike in the Paris area alone—the strike had not yet spread to any appreciable extent to the provinces. The workers' demands varied from place to place; in many small factories the demands were scribbled in pencil on a scrap of paper by an improvised strikers' committee—and, while in some works the demands (concerning wages, working hours, or such things as 'a litre of milk a day to metal polishers doing work injurious to their health') were of a local character, in most of the works the demands related to wider issues—collective bargaining, the forty-hour week, holidays with pay, recognition of workers' delegates chosen by the men themselves.

By June 3, the number of strikers in the Paris area was estimated at 350,000. The extent of the strike was shown by the number and the different types of trade affected. The drivers of the Black Marias struck and prison-vans had to be driven by police inspectors. The C.G.T. in a helpless-sounding note stated that 'it did not forget the duties of the working class as far as the provisioning of children, old people, and the sick was concerned.' In a number of factories, the strikers 'imprisoned' the directors and managers.

On June 4 the strike continued to spread like an epidemic. It was obvious that, in spite of some occasional interference by Communist deputies here and there, the strike was spontaneous and was simply spreading by contagion.

Nevertheless, Paris lived through some anxious moments on June 4 and the following days. On June 4 the ordinary citizen began to experience the first effects of the strike when, in the morning, he found that his newsagent had only a very limited supply of newspapers to sell. Later, he also learned that the Halles had got into a state of complete disorder during the night, the lorry-drivers having refused to take delivery of the goods at the Paris railway termini. Hundreds of tons of fish and vegetables remained piled up for hours at the stations until the railway companies themselves decided to transport the goods to the Halles. But, at any rate, Paris did not go hungry that day.

Even so, the developments at the Halles had caused something of a panic among housewives, especially in the *bourgeois* quarters, who began to buy up large quantities of flour, macaroni, tinned milk and other tinned food. A strike also broke out in the petrol trade. Taxi-drivers doubted whether they would have enough petrol to carry on the next day.

The strike of the Messageries Hachette became general. Most of the copies of *Paris-Midi* remained unsold that day.

That afternoon, the negotiations between the workers and the employers of the engineering industry, where a provisional agreement had been reached during the previous week, were broken off by the employers, and that very evening the Renault works were 'reoccupied.' At the same time it was reported—which was reassuring—that the petrol and food transport strikes were on the point of being settled. That was the night on which the Blum Government took office.

Alas! there were no papers on the following day to announce the formation of the new Government—except the *Populaire*, the *Humanité* and the indefatigable *Action Française*.

The Government was also working hard to settle the strike at the abattoirs that had broken out that morning. The most spectacular new development was the extension of the strikes to the Grands Magasins. At the Galeries Lafayette a notice was displayed in the windows with a large title: 'Prostitution or Hospital for Consumptives?'

The young girls were visibly enjoying the strike as a novel experience; but declared, with a touch of grimness, that it was high time they got better food and better wages. Some of them were earning no more than 400 francs a month. One of the assistants produced a note-book and proceeded to explain, with much excitement, that he had earned only

512 francs last month. 'And in addition to it all, the management expect you to be well dressed and to have a clean shirt and collar.'

I also drove that day to the Renault works at Billancourt, where I was allowed into the offices of the strike committee, but not into the works. There were two women and four men in the committee-room. These people had a grim, determined and revolutionary air—rather like a Jacobin club, I thought—or a Soviet. The employers' Syndicate, they said, had broken off negotiations the day before; and it did not matter any more what this Syndicate did. So the strikers' committee had made up its mind to get an agreement out of M. Renault personally. It was no good relying on a Syndicate, or even on an act of Parliament, such as Blum had promised; for 'such laws are not always observed anyway.' The strike at Renault's last week, they said, had begun in 'anarchical conditions,' but now everything was being managed by the strikers' delegates. Half the strikers were now sent home for twenty-four hours, and the change-over took place at noon; and no women were allowed to stay in the works overnight. The property was being treated with the utmost care, and it was strictly forbidden to sleep in new motor-cars.

This is what Jacques, a young fellow at the Renault works, whom I had known for some time told me about the first stay-in strike. This lasted only three days, but was soon followed by another that went on for a fortnight.

JACQUES' STORY

Jacques is a young mechanic on the Renault works. He is not a Communist, but mildly Socialist, and does not belong to any trade union. (Indeed, almost all the labour in the French engineering industry is non-union.) He has been only a few months at Renault's. Like all the 32,000 other workers and employees of Renault, he took part in the 'stay-in' strike. He is employed in the artillery section; for it would be wrong to imagine that 'Renault' means motor-cars. At the Billancourt works, cars are now only a secondary product; but full time—and indeed, more than full time—is done in the sections producing war material—tanks, aeroplane engines, armoured-cars, and so on. Here is the simple account he gave me of how it all happened.

'I arrived at the works at 7.30, on Thursday morning, as usual,' Jacques began, 'and knew nothing about the coming strike. At 7.50 I still knew nothing. But at eight o'clock one of the chaps in my team said: "At nine o'clock we stop." The chap is a Communist and must have been told in advance. At five minutes past nine the strike started in the riveting-room, in the left wing of workshop No. 32. Half an hour later work had stopped in the whole building. The current was being cut off bit by bit. At eleven the current was cut off at the power-station. In my particular section there are eight hundred chaps. At nine o'clock one of the Communists went round saying to us: "Comrades, we must join forces to get the forty-hour working week and a paid fortnight's holiday. There is no reason why we shouldn't get holidays just like the office employees, who don't work nearly as hard as we do. We must also see that we get our wages increased by fifty to seventy-five centimes an hour." The other demands included the dismissal of married women whose husbands worked in the factory; no reprisals against the strikers; shower-baths and better lavatories. And, naturally, we must also insist on getting a collective contract.

'Now I must say that between nine and eleven many of us did not know what to do. The young chaps were specially nervous: what if we were to go on strike, and then be the first to get the sack? We waited to see if anybody would not follow the strike movement. But as everybody stopped work we naturally did the same.

'At eleven o'clock it was agreed that every team—there are thirty to forty workers in each—appoint two delegates. These delegates went that day to the meeting at the Labour Exchange. But nothing was settled that day.

'The rest of us stayed in the works, with the exception of three or four men in each team who were sent out to get wine and beer, and bread and sausage;—for there was, naturally, no food on the premises. They had their cards taken away by the pickets, who gave them back when they returned with the provisions. Apart from these chaps, no worker could get out of the factory. It was quite a job to get permission even to go across the street to telephone—for I had to tell them at home I might not get back for the night.

'The real fun at the factory started about one o'clock, after we'd got our helpings of bread and wine and sausage. I must say that the strike had come quite unexpectedly, and it was a terrible blow to the restaurants around the works, who had prepared, as usual, the thousands of lunches for the workers. In this weather much of the food was wasted. Nearly all the people at the works lunch at these restaurants. The four-course lunch for seven francs is quite good. But after our improvised lunch inside the factory that day we had nothing to do, and to while the time away, we arranged dances in several parts of the works. There were among us a concert player and a violin player, and another chap had brought a concertina. We built up a platform with packing-cases for the "orchestra." In other parts of the works they put on the wireless, or had a gramophone to play dance music. Couples of men and women, and couples of men (for there weren't enough girls to go round) danced all over the place, among the vans, and among the piles of scrap-iron. At two o'clock we held a grand procession from the works down to the island on the Seine. This island, which is part of the Renault works, is over a kilometre long, has railway-lines on it and a track for testing cars. It is connected with the mainland by a bridge and an underground tunnel. The workers that day felt very much at home. Many of us kept saying: "To-day, at any rate, we are the masters." We had found a lot of red signalling-flags among the railway material on the island; and we helped ourselves to them, and the Communists drew the hammer and sickle on them in chalk. We used them in the procession. Twelve thousand of us must have marched in the procession, roaring and screaming (for the women were the most vociferous of all)—*"Les Soviets partout!"* and *"Vacances payées!"* and *"A bas le Seigneur!"*—meaning M. Renault and singing the Internationale and the Carmagnole and the Marseillaise. Women and everybody else wore their blue overalls. It was a tremendous procession, and went on for about four hours. When I got back to my own workshop there was still no reply; and it was obvious that we would have to stay the night. Nobody could get away, except, as I already said, to telephone; and even the foremen and engineers were not allowed to leave. They all looked very glum, and whispered to each other in corners. The chief engineer looked particularly fed up, for he is held responsible for the timely delivery of the army orders. He kept scratching his head and telephoning in great agitation all day long. Still, there was no trouble anywhere. The strikers' watchword was "Calm," a word written in chalk all over the place—over the walls and doors and motor-vans and machinery.

'It got rather rowdier as time went on, but it was not very serious either. In the evening the factory was invaded by men selling the *Paris-Soir*, in which we were able to read all about the strike; and at the entrance any number of local tradesmen had assembled with baskets of food and cases of wine and beer. The strikers' delegates bought up all the stuff in no time. There was no bread left in the bakeries at Billancourt, and no cigarettes in the tobacco-shops—and the "delegates" had to be sent to Paris in taxis to get both bread and cigarettes. That day M. Renault's "no-smoking" regulations were overlooked with a vengeance. We were the masters.

'At night the dancing started again all over the place. Many of the fellows had got extremely drunk by this time; and there were many fights—not political fights, but about the girls. There was also one drunkard who fell off a ladder, and had to be carried to the infirmary. "He is spitting blood!" somebody cried in alarm. But it was only red wine. We spent the evening dancing and singing, and reading newspapers, and playing cards and discussing the "situation"—and drinking a great deal. Some of the couples went off to the island for some quiet fun.

'It was not easy to find a comfortable place to sleep in. Many lay down simply on the ground. None of us, of course, had any blanket

or pillow or anything. Others got into the army vans and lorries, and
railway-carriages on the island; one of our chaps slept in the open air
inside a tank; and although we had received strict orders not to
damage any property, we could not resist the temptation—in spite of
our dirty overalls—of getting into the brand new touring-cars. A few
drunks who had got into the cars for the night were sick all over them
—it was unfortunate. I lay in my car, more comfortable than many
others, but not very happy. I was shivering with cold, and I could
not sleep; for every other moment somebody would burst into song—
the Internationale or *Tout va très bien Madame la Marquise*. Still, I
had the pleasant feeling of being one of the lords and masters of
Renault's.

'We did not feel very well the next morning. At six o'clock we were
allowed to go out to have coffee in a neighboring café; or, if we
preferred, we could help ourselves to the large cans of free coffee and
bread the Communist municipality of Boulogne had sent to the works.
We felt bored and tired that morning. We sat in the sun trying to get
some heat into us. At noon we again went out for lunch, going through
the usual control by the pickets. In the afternoon we again danced,
though without the same gusto. In the meantime, the workmen's wives
had brought them their wireless sets, as well as blankets for the next
night, and thermos flasks and bedroom slippers and what not. We had
no idea how long the "stay-in" strike would last. One of our chaps
had two whole joints brought to him—enough to last him a fortnight.
Women carrying babies, and crowds of children came into the works,
which they had never seen before, and inspected everything with a
landlordly air.

'In the meantime negotiations were continuing somewhere. But at
five still nothing was known. By six, many of the people were getting
impatient—especially as we were on the eve of the Whitsun holiday.
Many said they would go home to-night. The three days' Whitsun
holiday was perhaps decisive; many said that Renault wouldn't have
"got off so easily" otherwise. Otherwise they would "have hung on
for a month." The same chap who announced the beginning of the
strike, also told us at seven that the strike was over. Renault had
promised that there would be no reprisals; he had promised to
increase the wages of the women earning less than four francs an hour;
part of the strike time would be paid for; and he also promised to
examine the strikers' other demands in a broad-minded spirit, and
would give a reply as soon as possible. The strike, he said, "must
stop, or else the works will be evacuated by force."

'Fortunately,' Jacques said, 'it didn't come to that. If the police had
come in to drive us out, there would have been murder let loose; and
the plant would have been smashed to pieces.

'As soon as the agreement was reached, the bosses recovered their

97

authority, and one of them ordered me to sweep up the banana skins and other rubbish. The result of the strike was really negligible, and most of us wouldn't have yielded but for the Whitsun week-end. There are some Croix de Feu chaps among us, but they supported the strikers, and said La Rocque considered their demands perfectly just and legitimate.

'We have lost money over this strike,' Jacques concluded, 'but so also has Renault. He must have lost several millions. If nothing happens in a fortnight, the strike may start again. Our people are determined to get the forty-hour working week. They want to get for forty hours what they now get for forty-eight hours. In principle they are also opposed to overtime. In the armaments section some of us work up to fourteen hours a day; the qualified workers make anything up to 2,000 francs a month; and perhaps even more; but it's tiring and the principle is wrong. In the other sections—such as motor-cars—they work perhaps only five hours a day. Many of the workers agree that the demands made by the strikers were really excessive— you can't ask for everything all at once. But everybody agrees that, as an experiment, the strike was well worth trying out. And if Renault tries to cheat, we'll start again—in a fortnight, or perhaps even sooner.'

On June 5, Léon Blum, the new Premier, made his first broadcast speech. He appealed to the workers to observe discipline and to the employers to treat the dispute in a broad-minded spirit.

But this broadcast (naturally) did not put an end to the strikes, and when the Blum Government appeared for the first time before the Chamber on the following day, Saturday, June 6, over a million people were on strike in France.

The industrial districts of Paris and of the *banlieue* were an extraordinary sight during those days. Building after building—small factories and large factories, and even comparatively small workshops—were flying red, or red and tricolour flags—with pickets in front of the closed gates. Many of them had collection boxes ('For the Strikers') outside, some with tricolour ribbons round them.

A picket outside a small factory in the rue Broca said to me one day: 'We've been occupying the factory for ten days now. Our boss said to us this morning: "This is getting a bit thick. You are behaving like a lot of dictators." So I said to him: "We'd rather have this sort of dictatorship in the framework of the Republic—*dans le cadre républicain*—than Hitler or Mussolini." ' The phrase was a little illogical; but it reflected a curious belief in the creation of a new planned economy and of an authoritative form of government—with a preponderant influence of the working class.

The claims of the railwaymen and bank clerks were among the few to be settled without a strike; and, with a sound instinct, the public services never ceased work. It was important not to antagonize the general public—though some writers of the Right later claimed that Moscow had given special instructions to the Government employees and municipal workers of France.[1]

.   .   .   .

It was about June 12 that the strikes definitely began to subside, after reaching a record of over a million simultaneous strikers. The Matignon Agreement on June 7 had, if not an immediate, still a decisive effect on the strikes. It was hailed by the C.G.T. as the greatest victory in the History of French Trade Unionism—though the fact that the strike continued on a large scale, even after the Matignon Agreement, showed that the C.G.T.—in spite of its membership which had increased, in a fortnight, from one and a half to nearly three million—had not yet achieved anything resembling full control of the strike movement.

The truth is that about June 7 the Communist leaders themselves were becoming greatly alarmed by the extent of the strikes. Communist deputies could be heard complaining: '*Nous sommes débordés.*' Others blamed the Trotzkyists for it—though as a Socialist deputy from Marseilles remarked, in attacking the Communists some days later, 'there aren't ten Trotzkyists in the whole of Marseilles.' And on June 10 M. Maurice Thorez, the Communist leader, himself proclaimed that 'it is important to know when to stop a strike; for otherwise one is apt to play into the hands of the reactionaries.'

Still, when, about the middle of June, the great strike wave was over— the Communist leaders assumed the role of the Great Victors. Maurice Thorez, referring to the stay-in method, proclaimed 'a new legality,' and said that if the workers took good care of the plant during the stay-in strikes, it was because 'the factories would soon be the property of the workers, anyway.'

On Sunday, June 14—a day when the slightly-reassured *bourgeoisie* went to the great race-meeting at Chantilly—the Communists held a *Fête de la Victoire* in the Stade Buffalo at Montrouge. It was, in its own way, the most impressive thing I had ever seen in Paris. The vast Front Populaire processions of the past had been impressive enough; but their pageantry, if pageantry it may be called, had been left to individual

[1] *Revue Politique et Parlementaire*, July 10, 1936, p. 20.

initiative, and there was a notable lack of organization in the arrangement of banners and other colour effects. But at Montrouge that day
there was an organizing hand behind everything. For everything had
obviously been thought out in advance. The method of it all was
reminiscent of Moscow, not to say Berlin.

The greatest enthusiasm was aroused by the appearance on the gangway of the strike committee of Renault's[2] carrying a banner combining
the Socialist, Communist, and Republican emblems and saying, 'We won
because we were united.' At the head of them marched M. Costes, the
Communist deputy for Boulogne, with a tricolour ribbon across his chest.
The women wore red scarves.

And then suddenly a dramatic thing happened. Four immense flags
in the middle of the stadium were hoisted up the flagpoles, and as they
unfurled in the wind one realized that each of them was the newly
devised national flag of Soviet France—a red flag with the tricolour in
a top corner and a golden R.F. (*République Française*) on the red
field, with the Communist hammer and sickle between the two letters.
With these flags fluttering in the sun, and these banners, and these
processions of the Communist leaders and militants, and the surging
crowd of over 100,000 people, one suddenly had a strange vision of a
new France in the making.

And looking back on the great strike, old Charles Rappoport, the
little Marxist gnome, could be heard growling in the Chamber lobbies—
'Blum, Thorez, Jouhaux—pouf! *Mais le peuple—le peuple a toujours
raison.*'

XVII. WHAT THE WORKERS GAINED

THE Blum Government made its first appearance before the Chamber
on Saturday, June 6, in an atmosphere that was heavy with anxiety.

On the all-important monetary question M. Blum said that it was
necessary to adopt a new policy which, instead of contracting consump-

[2] *The Destiny of France* contains Jacques's story about the second stay-in strike
at Renault's. It was more disciplined than the first, but the recreations included
football matches, cycle races, theatrical entertainments by well-known actors and
a mock-trial and funeral of La Rocque.

tion, would increase it. But this would not be done by means of devaluation; *there would be no monetary coup d'état.*

This pledge not to resort to a 'monetary *coup d'état'* was one of the most extraordinary statements made by M. Blum that day. M. Paul Reynaud sharply criticized the statement, and warned the Government that if it did not devalue at once, it would have to do so later 'in much less favourable circumstances.'

Turning to the question of the stay-in strikes, M. Blum said:

I have been asked whether I regarded these factory occupations as legal. *No, I do not consider them legal. These occupations are not in agreement with the rules and principles of French civil law.* But what conclusion do you expect me to draw from this statement?

The employers, the factory owners, have not asked that the factories be cleared by force. Far from it! In the first letters they addressed to the government they formally excluded such a possibility. [Turning to the Opposition.] Do you wish me to evacuate the factories by armed force? Is that what you mean? [Loud cheers on the Left.]

He declared that three Bills—concerning the forty-hour working week, collective contracts, and holidays with pay—would be immediately tabled by the Government, and he asked the Chamber to discuss them by an extra-rapid procedure.

That was the first effect the strikes had on Parliament. In May, even M. Jouhaux, the Secretary-General of the C.G.T., spoke of the forty-hour week in terms of international agreements to be reached at the I.L.O. at Geneva. The strikers were right—Parliament and the Government needed 'pushing.'

In the course of the debate the Opposition had harped, above all, on the illegality of the stay-in strikes; and M. Xavier Vallat[1] of the Croix de Feu, had attacked M. Blum personally by saying that—

For the first time in her history is this Gallo-Roman country of ours ruled by a Jew. . . . I would prefer to see, at the head of the government, a man with deeper roots in the national soil.

Blum went white with anger, and there was a terrible uproar.

The whole of the following day was taken up by negotiations at the Hotel Matignon, the Premier's office, between the representatives of the C.G.T. and the representatives of the Confédération Générale de la Production Française. The meeting was presided over by M. Blum in person. The outcome of this interminable meeting was the famous 'Matignon Agreement,' on trade union rights and collective bargaining.

[1] Now (1941) in charge of enforcing the anti-Jewish laws adopted by Vichy.

It should be said from the outset that the manner in which the agreement was negotiated had its weak points. On the one hand, the C.G.T. represented legally only a fairly small proportion of the workers; on the other hand, the Confédération Générale de la Production Française, though the largest employers' federation, with a national membership, nevertheless represented chiefly the larger industrial employers (and not even all of them); and the smaller employers afterwards accused the C.G.P.F. of having betrayed them by signing the Matignon Agreement. Their argument was that the Comité des Forges and other large employers could well afford to grant to their workers all the concessions provided in the Matignon Agreement; and it was even suggested that, in signing it, the large employers were deliberately trying to ruin their smaller and weaker competitors.

Many Englishmen, who thought that the position of the trades unions was more or less the same in France as in England, found all this great enthusiasm over the Matignon Agreement rather puzzling. Had there been no collective bargaining in France before? they asked.

Let us look back for a minute. The pre-War syndicalists, who were revolutionary in temper, regarded collective bargaining as an intolerable restriction on the right to strike. But, in time, it came to be valued as 'an absolute negation of the principle of authority and domination';[2] and in 1920, M. Jouhaux himself, who had ceased to scorn orderly relations with employers, complained that the big employers refused to recognize collective bargaining.

It was in 1920 and 1921 that the C.G.T. suffered two terrible blows. One was the failure of the general and railway strikes of 1920—a failure which was followed by ruthless reprisals by the Government and the employers—25,000 railwaymen were dismissed outright, and the larger employers made it a rule to boycott union labour. Trade union membership dropped at a catastrophic rate. The second blow to French trade unionism was the split in the C.G.T. in 1921, when the more extreme elements broke away and formed the C.G.T.U. The more extreme syndicalist elements went over to the C.G.T.U., and although this new organization had a psychological atmosphere that was akin to the revolutionary syndicalism of pre-War years, the C.G.T.U. nevertheless came under the close control of the Communist Party and the Profintern, the Red Trade Union International. It was not until the formation of the Front Commun in 1934 that a parallel tendency towards amalgamation manifested itself in the C.G.T. and the C.G.T.U.; and this amalga-

[2] See the excellent and detailed *Labour Movement in post-War France*, by D. J. Saposs, Columbia University Press, New York, 1931.

mation was formally agreed upon in January 1936. Since then there has been a struggle for supremacy in the new C.G.T. between the extremists (and M. Jouhaux had by this time regained some of his pre-War extremism) and the moderates—with M. Belin as their principal spokesman.

But the most extraordinary feature of French trade unionism was the high proportion of members not employed in private industry. Thus, in the C.G.T. in 1927, sixty per cent of the members were state employees, or the employees of public or semi-public services. The Government officials' right to strike was a moot point; and MM. Doumergue and Tardieu, as we have seen, wished to make it perfectly clear—through a constitutional law—that they had no such right.

In the C.G.T.U. the 'private' trades were more adequately represented than in the C.G.T., but there also the public and semi-public services accounted for thirty-five per cent of the total membership of 450,000.

The great strike movement of June 1936 broke out in circumstances more favourable than any that had existed for years. The Matignon Agreement was confirmed and completed by the Collective Contracts Act of June 24, providing for the procedure by which collective contracts were to be drawn up, and the points which they must cover: trade union freedom, freedom of opinion, workers' delegates, minimum wage, conditions of dismissal, organization of apprenticeship, procedure to be adopted in cases of dispute, etc. It laid down much firmer rules for the contents of the contracts than the law of May 1919.

The collective contracts had the effect of giving the workers greater stability and security ('he knew where he stood'); though in certain branches of the building trades, where a worker could be dismissed at one hour's notice before, the time was increased, under the collective contract, to only five hours. In certain trades flourishing on sweated labour, such as the Paris Department Stores—where the stay-in strike continued for three weeks—some of the wages were increased in actual practice, by fifty and seventy-five per cent, under the arbitration (accepted by both sides) of M. Salengro, the Minister of the Interior. Many employers, who felt that these agreements had been 'forced' upon them, declined to sign them for more than a year.

As a result of the strikes and the Matignon Agreement the membership of the C.G.T. rose from 1,300,000 in May to nearly 5,000,000 in September.

Another equally popular law voted by Parliament on June 20 introduced compulsory holidays with pay—fifteen days for all who had been employed with their firm for not less than a year and shorter holidays for others.

In the summer of 1936 this law proved a godsend to holiday resorts. M. Lagrange, the Under-Secretary for the organization of Sports and Leisure, who had got the railways to issue no fewer than 500,000 'Lagrange' tickets to wage-earners, claimed that this law had created almost a 'social' revolution.

With the Bills for collective contracts and holidays with pay, it was comparatively plain sailing. With the Bill introducing the forty-hour week the government was on more dangerous ground. The Bill met with furious opposition in the Senate—but the Senate voted it none the less—again under the pressure of the strikes.

A Communist deputy remarked to me about that time: 'Of course the Senators are going to vote it; they are haunted by the vision of a Front Populaire demonstration of 500,000 people trampling down the flower-beds in the Luxembourg garden' [outside the Senate]. He was right; they voted it—though not without many murmurs about 'outside pressure'; and they continued to bear the Blum Government a grudge.

This law was, naturally, severely criticized as being, in the absence of an international agreement, economically unsound; some even said 'suicidal.'[3] The Government was not in a hurry to apply this law; its first application—to coal-mining—was, indeed, decided upon on September 25 —the very day the Government also decided to devalue the franc.[4] It was not a simple coincidence; for by passing the labour reforms (which were bound to increase very considerably costs of production) before devaluing the franc, the Blum Government had, in the opinion of even its friendly critics, put the cart before the horse. The over-valued currency, they said, had handicapped France for years; by increasing costs on top of this handicap, the Government was placing France in an altogether impossible position.

.   .   .   .

The labour reforms of June 1936, combined with the financial policy of the Blum Government, have gone—especially in the British and American Press—by the name of France's 'New Deal.'

That the policy of deflation was not a success was easy to show; the

[3] Particularly with reference to the international situation and French Armaments. But it is remarkable how few people in France in 1936 thought in international terms. (Author's note, 1942.)

[4] Before the end of the year the forty-hour week was extended to certain other mines, to the textile and engineering trades, and to bakeries in certain parts of the country.

trade recovery that could be observed in most countries since 1934 was conspicuously absent in France; exports continued to drop from one low record to another; and the tourist trade, owing to the high cost of living, was dead.

Ever since 1934 M. Paul Reynaud had urged the government to devalue the franc, as this 'could not go on.' For a long time he was a voice calling in the wilderness. It was not until after the General Election of 1936 that such inveterate 'defenders of the franc' as M. Germain Martin came forward in the financial Press with articles in favour of an 'alignment of currencies'—for the word 'devaluation' was still taboo.

Many members of the Blum Government were privately convinced that the Government was wrong in committing itself to a defence of the franc. I remember one of them telling me, a few days before the formation of the Government: 'If we devalue at once, we'll be able to carry on for four years; *sans ça, nous sommes foutus.*' But the Communists were, officially, hostile; they declared it to be robbery of the poor; and said instead that 'the rich must pay.' The C.G.T. leaders were less uncompromising.

The Senate voted all the Bills—but, it must be admitted, with very bad grace. And M. Caillaux, who, for years, had preached the unimaginative doctrine of penance to the French, dismissed the Blum-Auriol New Deal as 'Rooseveltism for Lilliputians.' France was up to her ears in debt; interest rates were high; and the increased costs of production would only aggravate her handicaps as an exporter—handicaps caused by the divergence between home and world prices. Such was the orthodox criticism of the French 'New Deal.'

The assurances that there would be no 'monetary *coup d'état*,' and M. Vincent Auriol's cautious management, even tended for a time to improve the Bourse quotations of Government loans, and the repatriation of capital that the Government attempted to force upon investors, as well as the restrictions the banks had placed, at the Government's request, on foreign exchange transactions, resulted, for a time, in a net increase in the gold reserve. Unfortunately, exports had fallen, for various reasons (strikes, higher costs, etc.), to new low levels; the Spanish Civil War created a new atmosphere of nervousness, and the new German *coup* of August 31, doubling the term of military service, obliged the French Government to adopt a new programme of additional military expenditure—sixteen milliards in the next four years. Where was the money to come from?

In spite of restrictions, gold began to run out again, and by September 23, the gold reserve had sunk below fifty milliard francs.

At the Ministerial Council on Friday, September 25, devaluation was decided upon. That night, M. Vincent Auriol was in telephonic communication with London and Washington until the final text of the Three-Power Declaration in favour of monetary co-operation and the maintenance of world prices was agreed upon. When at 1 a.m. he finally received the Press, he looked completely exhausted. He even forgot to say that the Bank of France had decided to stop gold exports from the following day.

The devaluation of the franc was received with considerable resignation by the general public. What most people said (not without a touch of scepticism) was: 'Well, let's see if things improve a bit at last.' The Government, naturally, did not call it devaluation; it preferred to call it an 'alignment of currencies.'

The *Temps* said that the Three-Power Declaration was largely a put-up show, of small practical value. Actually, the Declaration was of some importance, both practical and moral. It eliminated the danger of a currency war, and of tariff reprisals against devaluation; and the lead taken by the three Democracies against autarchy had its moral significance.

The Communists were dissatisfied—or at least said that they were dissatisfied—with the devaluation; but the *Peuple*, the paper of the C.G.T., treated it in a fair spirit, and with undisguised approval.

M. Belin was right, the operation had been carried out in a cool and level-headed manner. Unfortunately, it had come rather late.

A member of the Blum Government told me a few days later: 'It didn't hurt, did it? If only it had been done sooner! say in May 1935, when there were still seventy milliards of gold in the Bank. Still, better late than never.'

The four-day devaluation debate at the Chamber and Senate, which were reassembled for the occasion, was stormy and disagreeable.

All that the Senate agreed to was to restore certain earlier cuts in War pensions, and to give some compensation to small bondholders, and particularly to the holders of 'Auriol Bonds.' But the Government servants received no compensation, and, instead of the sliding scale for wages, M. Blum could only get the Senate to agree to a procedure of Government arbitration in labour disputes to be caused by a notable rise in the cost of living—but even this procedure was limited to three months.

Ever since June, the Senate had treated the Blum Government with great distrust, and had accused it of 'condoning illegality'—of which the stay-in strikes were the most glaring example. One day in June, at the instigation of M. Caillaux, M. Bienvenu-Martin, the ninety-year-old 'father of the house,' asked M. Salengro whether, yes or no, the government would tolerate any more stay-in strikes. M. Salengro, not being a great parliamentary debater, and feeling the Government to be in danger, could think of nothing better than to utter a categorical 'no.'

Afterwards, he (and other members of the Government) tried to explain this away by saying that force would be used, but only as a very last resort, after every effort at a peaceful settlement had failed.

In October, to please the Senate, the Government actually used the police against stay-in strikers. When, on October 3, a stay-in strike broke out in a number of Paris hotels and restaurants (it was a particularly unpopular strike; devaluation had just been passed, and many foreigners had come to Paris to take advantage of it, and the motor show had just opened) the staff were, in several cases, 'invited' by the police to clear the premises. A few days later a chocolate factory in Paris was evacuated by the police; this was a more difficult operation; and in the process a number of strikers and policemen were injured.

XVIII. '200 FAMILIES' AND 'MERCHANTS OF DEATH'

IN THE General Election there was no more popular war-cry on the Left than 'Down with the 200 families.' For months before the election, several papers, like *La Lumière*, Bergery's *Flèche*, and others, spent ninety per cent of their polemical vigour in denouncing the Regents of the Bank of France, and the '200 families'—the two hundred largest shareholders of the Bank with voting powers, who came to be identified in the popular mind with the financial oligarchy.

Without dwelling on the spectacular denunciations of the '200 families,' I shall summarize the grievances against the Bank of France by quoting the sober report of the Finance Committee of the Chamber, published on July 16, 1936, when the Bank of France Reorganization Bill first came up for discussion. What were the anomalies of the Bank of France before its transformation?

The Regency Council of the Bank consisted of the Governor, the two Assistant-Governors, three auditors (*censeurs*) and fifteen Regents. The Governor and Assistant-Governors were appointed by the Government, but the Regents and Auditors were chosen by the two hundred largest shareholders. Now, the Governor, though appointed by the Government, was apt—as past experience had shown—to come under the influence of the Regents. The Governor must hold no fewer than one hundred shares —which, a few years ago represented the large capital of nearly two million francs—and the Regents usually helped the newly-appointed Governor by providing him, in one way or another, with his one hundred shares. Moreover, it was within the power of the Regents to promise the Governor dazzling posts on the boards on the biggest companies, after his duties at the Bank of France were at an end. Several ex-Governors of the Bank of France still hold such posts. In short, more often than not, the Regents had the Governor in their pocket.

In the General Election speakers of the Left frequently said that the *Banque de France* must be transformed into the *Banque de la France*, that is, France's Bank. What is the new system?

First of all, the '200 families'—that is the two hundred largest shareholders—have been 'democratized' down to the level of the 40,000 other shareholders, and each shareholder, regardless of his holdings, has now only one vote. The powers of the shareholders have been diminished. They elect the three Auditors (*censeurs*)—(who, it is true, are not powerless; for they can, if they are unanimous, veto the issue of banknotes; though, apart from that, they cannot vote on the Regency Council)—and also two of the Councillors. The General Council, taking the place of the old Regency Council—and here we are at the heart of the reform—now consists of twenty-three members with voting powers: the Governor, the two Assistant-Governors and the twenty Councillors. Of these twenty Councillors, seven represent the Finance Ministry and various other financial government offices and organization. Two represent the ministries of National Economy and Colonies. Of the remaining eleven Councillors, six are chosen by the Minister of Finance from lists submitted to him by the Artisans' Federation, the Co-operative Societies, the Chambers of Commerce, the C.G.T. (the trade unions), and representative bodies in trade and agriculture. One member is elected by the Staff of the Bank, one appointed by the National Economic Council and the remaining two, as already said, by the shareholders. The Governor is made independent of outside influence. He is no longer required to be a shareholder; and is paid a full salary for three years after leaving the Bank. During this period he cannot enter any private employment. (In the original Bill he was to receive a life pension and never work again.)

Thus, both the General Council and the Governor have come under the effective control of the State. 'Apart from the share capital,' says M. Jenny, an expert of very orthodox financial views, 'the Bank of France has to all intents and purposes been nationalized.'[1]

· · · · · · ·

Second only in unpopularity to the '200 families' were the *marchands de canons*, the 'Merchants of Death.'

At Geneva, one French Government after another urged an international convention for stopping the private manufacture of and trade in armaments. It was a question on which French opinion (as the election campaign showed) felt very strongly. Much as the French people would have preferred an international agreement to precede a purely 'national solution,' they decided, in the absence of greater keenness elsewhere, to lead the way. Again France had put herself at the head of human progress.

The French people felt the scandal so keenly, that the Nationalization Bill was voted almost without opposition. The law of August 11, 1936, provides that the Government may, before March 31, 1937, decide, by decree, on the total or partial expropriation by the State of any concern engaged in the manufacture or trade in armaments, including anti-gas equipment.

But the most startling progress of all was made, soon after the law was passed, in that part of the French armament industry which concerns aeroplanes.

To show how this nationalization works in practice, I can do no better than quote the statement made to me in November 1936 by M. Pierre Cot, the Minister of Air in the Front Populaire Government, when he received me in the dazzlingly modern Air Ministry.

'In principle,' he said, 'every firm in this country manufacturing aeroplanes and aeroplane engines will be nationalized. You see that the whole problem is not only one of morality, but, especially in the case of aeroplanes, of efficient production and ultimately of National Defence. Financially, we cannot fail; for fortunately—or, I might say unfortunately—we can always be certain of one thing: orders. In the case of areoplanes the money spent on expropriation is a good investment; we shall spend, say, 400 million francs on the plant (the manufacturers will be only too

[1] *Revue Politique et Parlementaire*, August 1936, pp. 230-1.

glad to get all this ready cash) ; but our orders in a year will amount to 800 million.'[2]

The statement shows that the problem is a relatively simple one, and by no means impracticable, as some people in Britain and America have tried to show, in an effort to silence the public outcry against the 'Merchants of Death.'[3]

XIX. LA ROCQUE AND DORIOT

AFTER the Election the Croix de Feu were in low spirits; and feeling was running high, among the rank and file, against Colonel de la Rocque, who had failed so completely in his election 'arbitration.'

Taking advantage of this feeling of defeat among the Croix de Feu and the other Fascist Leagues, the Blum Government issued, on June 18, a decree dissolving the Croix de Feu, the Solidarité Française, the Jeunesses Patriotes and the Francistes. The moment was a propitious one for taking action against the Leagues; and, in any case, Left opinion in France was expecting the Government to do something about it at once.

I went to see La Rocque that night. The poor man looked bewildered. Drawing up a communiqué he fumbled interminably with his fountain-pen. 'What do you think of the future of France, *mon Colonel?*' I said. 'Not rosy,' he replied, 'but not red either,' and laughed in his best drawing-room manner.

In practice the dissolution did not really amount to very much; though its moral effect was considerable, and many thousand members resigned from the Croix de Feu—a few going over to the Communists—'the only dynamic force in the country,' and a certain number going over to the newly-formed French Popular Party of M. Doriot; but many left without joining anything else.

During the second half of June and the first half of July, members of

[2] Interview in *Manchester Guardian*, November 9, 1936.

[3] The nationalization of the armaments firms was not to be carried out to any real extent in the years that followed; and if the nationalization of the aircraft works did not produce any satisfactory results, it was not the fault of the nationalization, but of the worthlessness of the plants concerned. (Author's note, 1942.)

the dissolved Leagues got into the habit of holding sporadic demonstrations in the Champs Élysées every Saturday and Sunday night. On American Independence Day on Saturday, July 4, these young men had the good taste to greet a delegation of American War veterans, who had laid a wreath on the Unknown Soldier's grave, with cries of 'France for the French!'

The Fascists claimed that there would be some real fun on July 14. For, as distinct from the previous year, only the Front Populaire demonstration was authorized; and there was to be no counter-demonstration from the Right.

Hundreds of thousands of Parisians had swarmed to the Esplanade des Invalides and the the Champs Élysées to see the traditional military review. After days of rain, the day was marked by glorious summer weather. Infantry, cavalry, motorized units, heavy artillery, tanks and armoured cars marched or drove past in rapid succession from the Invalides across the Pont Alexandre III, whose high equestrian statues glittered in the sun, and, after passing Clemenceau's statue, turned into the Champs Élysées down to the Place de la Concorde.

The sky was perfectly blue, and after the review was over, military planes engaged in 'sky-writing' the words 'Liberté, égalité, fraternité,' much to the delight of the people.

It was the most impressive military parade Paris had seen for years, and in the diplomatic tribune it was generally agreed that it left no doubt about France's military efficiency. One of the objects of the parade was to prove that the Front Populaire Government was fully as capable as any other of looking after the national defence of the country.

In past years the working class had not taken much interest in the military parade, and the public which cheered the army was mostly composed of conservative West End elements. But on this occasion the Left-Wing papers had urged their readers to hail the 'Republican Army' on the morning of the 14th, and the crowd was an extremely mixed one.

As the troops marched past the young men in front shouted '*La France aux Français!*' and those behind in exactly the same rhythm, '*Le Front Populaire!*' Sometimes the Right cry drowned that of the Left and sometimes it was the other way round. 'Long live the Republican Army!' the Left shouted as the troops marched past. 'Long live the French Army!' the Right shouted, while an elderly man remarked, 'Let it be both French and Republican'—a remark which met with approval from both sides.

The afternoon was taken up with the Front Populaire procession, the most immense procession Paris had ever seen. The Colonne de Juillet in the Place de la Bastille, marking the spot where the old prison had stood, was gaily decorated with national flags, and with flags of the French provinces, and the large tribune and bandstand in front of it were surrounded by large panels with portraits of Robespierre, Marat, Voltaire, Diderot, Rousseau, Victor Hugo, Barbusse and the obscure little workman from Lille who had composed the Internationale.

Tricolour flags, or flags combining the red and the tricolour, were far more numerous than in 1935, when the plain red flags were still in the overwhelming majority.

. . . .

Little more was heard of the 'dissolved ones' for several weeks to come, except that the leaders of the Croix de Feu had formed a new Party, called the French Social Party.

The Colonel and the faithful Ybarnégaray toured the country in the hope of reviving the faltering spirits of the ex-Croix de Feu and the ex-Volontaires Nationaux.

As in 1935, so also in 1936, the Croix de Feu made a sudden *rentrée* about the 1st of October. This time the *rentrée* took a peculiar form. On Friday, the 2nd of October, the French Social Party called a mass-meeting at the Vélodrome d'Hiver in Paris, but at the last moment M. Salengro, the Minister of the Interior, prohibited it. Unfortunately, it so happened that the Communists were going to hold a meeting of their own in the Parc des Princes, the west-end stadium at the Porte de St. Cloud, two days later.

This meeting was not prohibited; and, after the prohibition of the Vélodrome meeting, the Colonel raised a loud protest against this unfair discrimination. The French Social Party was a legally constituted body; and he decided that M. Salengro's challenge could not remain unanswered.

On Saturday night the rumour went round that the Croix de Feu were proposing to occupy overnight the Parc des Princes, the stadium where the Communist meeting was to take place. To prevent this, the Communists themselves occupied the stadium during the night.

On Sunday afternoon, October 4, 20,000 police and Mobile Guards were concentrated in the south-west quarter of Paris, where the Conservative quarter of Auteuil meets the working-class suburbs of Boulogne and Billancourt. Police aeroplanes continued to circle over that part of Paris all the afternoon.

This did not, however, prevent numerous clashes between Communists and small groups of Croix de Feu who appeared in the neighbourhood.

Numerous ambulances were rushing all over the district and a policeman told me, shaking his head, that some of the injured he had seen were 'in a mighty queer state.' Others were injured in truncheon charges. In numerous places the Croix de Feu had set up dressing-stations of their own, marked with tricolour flags.

While these sporadic fights were going on over a large part of Auteuil and the police were manœuvring with great skill to prevent any major clashes, the Communist meeting in the Parc des Princes went on as usual. From time to time the crowd of 50,000 which had assembled in the stadium would sing the Internationale. The stadium was decorated with red flags and also with the flags of 'Soviet France,' a red-flag with a small tricolour in the top left-hand corner. They closed the meeting by singing the Marseillaise. By that time the roads round the stadium had been cordoned off and the Communists dispersed without any serious trouble.

. . . .

While the Croix de Feu—or rather, the Parti Social Français—were at their lowest, a rival organization appeared on the scene in the summer of 1936. It was the Parti Populaire Français, founded by Jacques Doriot, the former Communist leader and Mayor of St. Denis.

Doriot, a solidly built man with a strong chin, curly back hair and tortoise-shell glasses—a black-haired Danton his admirers call him—began as a workman and became in time the parliamentary leader of the Communist Party. Then, in 1934, he put forward a proposal for something on the lines of the Front Populaire—a coalition between the Communist Socialist and Radical elements of the country; for (said he) France being only one-fifth proletarian, nothing can be achieved without the support of the *petite bourgeoisie*. He was expelled from the Communist Party as a heretic. In the Senate elections in October 1935, he joined forces with Laval; and during the discussion of the Franco-Soviet Pact in February 1936, he denounced his former comrades with extraordinary violence. About the same time he gave a number of interviews to German papers in which he advocated a French *rapprochement* with Germany against Russia. In the 1936 election, he was returned for St. Denis, for years his stronghold, by only a narrow majority of 500 votes over his Communist competitor.

Unlike La Rocque, Doriot is not handicapped by being an aristocrat. He is personally a brave man, as he showed during the Communist riots of February 9, 1934. But he suffers deeply from thwarted ambition. Many of the people who supported the Leagues and the Royalists financially and otherwise took, at first, a fancy to the new party. Its paper, *L'Eman-*

113

cipation Nationale, was sold on the boulevards and read by much the same public as the Royalist *Action Française.* The text was provided by people like Pierre Dominique and Bertrand de Jouvenel. Dominique, though nominally a man of the Left, is a great admirer of Mussolinian 'dynamics,' and was violently pro-Italian and anti-British during the Abyssinian conflict. Paul Marion,[1] an amateur economist, who has gone through half a dozen newly formed parties in the last two years, joined the group.

In November 1936, the first National Congress of the Parti Populaire Français was held at St. Denis, that strange city ten miles north of Paris, where the tombs of the French Kings are surrounded by some of the grimiest slums of the industrial *banlieue.*

There were 800 delegates at the Congress, and most of them lunched in the big hall of the famous Hôtel du Grand Cerf. The largest number of the tables had been reserved for 'Marseille.' Around these sat M. Sabiani, and his *nervi*—a tough-looking crowd of gangsters. There were several negroes among them. At my table—which happened to be the table of the 'Lyons Federation'—I was seated next to a commercial traveller, who had never belonged to any party before, and who declared the Blum Government to have failed in its labour reforms. 'It has done some good only to the labourers; but it has harmed the skilled worker, whose economic status has been lowered by all this trade union tendency towards "equality" and human standardization.' Opposite me sat an elderly shopkeeper from Cannes. He had belonged to the Croix de Feu, but had felt that La Rocque had not been 'energetic enough.' As for Doriot, he confessed that he wasn't greatly interested in his programme; but he *did* feel that Doriot was right to fight against Communism.

I joined, in the theatre bar, the young aristocrats and intellectuals of the party: Bertrand de Jouvenel, Bertrand de Maud'huy, and others. They were obviously enjoying themselves in this 'dynamic' atmosphere—though I am not sure that they were taking it all very seriously. The party had, obviously, not 'caught on' as much as the curiosity it aroused at first had suggested.

'Why,' I asked, 'did Doriot want to have such disreputable people as the Marseilles *nervi* in his party?' 'Every dynamic party,' I was frankly told, 'has got to have its thugs.' 'Do you propose to run candidates, or do you believe in direct action?' 'No, old parliamentary methods are not much good; as for direct action—everything will depend on the circumstances. Suppose there is a Communist uprising—that's when we'll come forward and stamp out the Communists.'

[1] Now (1942), Minister of Information at Vichy.

There is just a remote possibility that Doriot may some day be pushed into the limelight by some entirely new international situation when his greatly advertised pro-Germanism and anti-Sovietism would be of use.[2]

XX. 'AEROPLANES FOR SPAIN!'

ROBERT DELL (*ringing up from Geneva, and very indignantly*) ; 'I say, there is no need for a Fascist Government in France; the Fascists will always find a Government of the Left to carry out their policy.'

AT ANY other time, the arrival in power of the Front Populaire Government would have been hailed as the beginning of a new era in international affairs. The Government would have been expected to bring about a *redressement* in French foreign policy, as remarkable as the *redressement* of 1924, when the Cartel des Gauches reversed the Ruhr policy of Poincaré and devised the Geneva Protocol.

The policy of the Blum Government may be summed up in a few words : caution; and *rapprochement* with England. For the rest, time would show whether the restoration of anything resembling a League order could still be achieved.

.   .   .   .   .

The first international problem with which the Blum Government was faced were the economic sanctions against Italy, which were still going on, although Italy had won the war.

When, on June 16, the British Cabinet decided to stop sanctions against Italy, the French Government did not protest. By saying that it would do 'anything' that Britain proposed, it prevented the British Government from placing on France the blame for this surrender to Italy.

But at the same time, certain members of the French Government—and particularly M. Delbos—believed that once sanctions were cleared out of the way it would again be possible to make friends with Italy ; and several papers spoke of the 'reconstruction of the Stresa Front' !

[2] Written in 1937—The 'remote possibility' has materialized beyond Doriot's brightest hopes. (Author's note, 1942.)

At the Chamber on June 23, Delbos, the Foreign Minister, expressed the humble conviction that 'Italy would co-operate.' He deplored Germany's failure to reply to the British questionnaire of May 6; but said that Herr Hitler had often proclaimed his wish to be friends with France. 'We have no intention of doubting the words of a man who, during four years, knew the horrors of the trenches.'

Coming so soon after the Locarno *coup*, such compliments must have convinced Herr Hitler that there was not much to fear from the French Government. He was right.

The basis of Blum's foreign policy was co-operation with England. Some of M. Blum's and M. Delbos' critics felt that this dependence on England was going to unnecessary extremes; that, to please England, France was visibly neglecting Russia and the Little Entente, and was being almost unduly polite to Germany. These criticisms were to gain in strength in connection with Dr. Schacht's visit to Paris at the end of August, and, still more in connection with the Spanish Civil War. The severest critics of Blum were the Communists. They were greatly offended by the polite reception M. Blum had given to Dr. Schacht. Hitler's Minister had arrived in Paris two days after the doubling of the term of service in the German Army; and he had come to assure the French that this measure was 'not directed against them.' 'Against whom then?' the Communists asked.

.   .   .   .

During the second half of 1936 the international situation was dominated by the Spanish Civil War. It broke out about the middle of July, and, almost immediately, the question arose: what shall the French Government do?

On the face of it, the answer was clear; there was no reason why the legal Government of Spain should not have a right to *buy* armaments abroad, even if, for one reason or another, these could not be supplied to it free of charge by sympathetic Governments.

But it became clear, before long, that the civil war in Spain was not a purely internal affair; for the Rebels were being supported by the Fascist Governments of Germany and Italy. A victory for the Rebels would obviously be a disaster for France. 'And it would be the last straw,' a Frenchman told me at the end of July, 'if, in addition to all our worries, we were obliged in future to maintain an army along the Pyrénées!'

Already the French Government was issuing one denial after another of the allegations that armaments and munitions were being, or had been, sent to the Spanish Government, and, in the Chamber lobbies on July 30, when I asked a member of the Government what the fuss was all about, and why the Spanish Government could not at least *buy* what it wanted in France, he raised his arms to heaven and whispered mysteriously: *'Vous comprenez, c'est très délicat, TRES DELICAT!'*

It was *délicat* for a number of reasons. First, because, in a speech earlier in the week, Sir Samuel Hoare had treated the Spanish Government and the Rebels as 'rival factions.' Secondly, because the French Press of the Right had started a furious campaign in favour of the Rebels, and against the 'Reds.' Since the Rebels were the avowed enemies of France, the campaign was, on the face of it, a thousand times more monstrous than even the campaign, a year earlier, in favour of Italy and against Abyssinia and the League.

The 'Fascist International' was working at full blast; and was threatening to work up a part of French opinion into a state of frenzy with its stories of how Blum was trying to drag France into war for the benefit of his Spanish friends. It was *très délicat*: for there was a danger that any French intervention in Spain might plunge France into a war with Italy and Germany, or into a civil war.

Before long, the Blum Government gave way.

Already on August 2, Delbos warned the French supporters of the Spanish Government against an 'ideological crusade.'

On August 8, the Cabinet met, and after a stormy sitting, decided to prohibit the export of all war material to Spain, though 'reserving the right eventually to authorize the delivery of unarmed planes by private industry. . . . The Government firmly expects that its attitude will facilitate the conclusion as speedily as possible of the definite agreement which is proposed in the interests of international peace.'

There is, of course, not the slightest doubt that, about August 1, the British Government clearly intimated to the French Government that if, as a result of her 'competition' with Italy and Germany in sending arms to Spain, France were attacked by the Fascist countries, Britain would not consider the attack an unprovoked one, and *the Locarno guarantee would not come into operation.*

Sir George Clerk, the British Ambassador, encouraged by his pro-Franco adviser, Sir Charles Mendl, had, indeed, given a strong warning to that effect to M. Blum. On September 16, this was publicly stated by Zyromski, one of the Socialist leaders.

This British pressure is undeniable; but it seems that on that occasion the Blum Government displayed an even more than usual eagerness to please the British Government.

The truth is, as it was already on March 7, when Sarraut and Flandin refused to call the German bluff: fear, and the determination to avoid the risk of war at *any* price.

．　　．　　．　　．　　．　　．

Although the 'blockade' that was officially enforced by France on the Spanish Government on August 8 was not perhaps completely water-tight, there is not the slightest doubt that anything that may have crossed from France into Spain since July 25, and especially since August 8 was mere driblets, compared with the enormous amount of war material sent to the Rebels.

Feeling ran high among the French working class, not only against Italy and Germany, but also against the Blum Government. Already on July 30, at a Socialist ceremony in memory of Jaurès, Blum's pious recollections of Jaurès had been drowned in a chorus of cries: *'Des avions pour l'Espagne!'*

After the frightful massacre of 2,000 people at Badajoz—a genuine 'atrocity,' which had nothing to equal it even among the unverified 'Red' atrocities of the reactionary Press in France and England—the outcry became louder and louder.

On September 3, a vast meeting was held at the Vélodrome d'Hiver, where thousands had come to hear La Pasionaria, the Communist woman deputy for Oviedo, and the idol of the Spanish working class.

'Aeroplanes for Spain!' Twenty times in the evening the cry went up from thousands of people, and echoed through the vast Vélodrome d'Hiver. Thirty thousand people—many of whom had lined up in the queues two hours before the beginning of the meeting—had come to hear her.

There were at first several French speakers—M. Belin, representing the trade unions; M. Marty, the Communist Deputy, and several others, as well as a young man representing the Catalan militia.

The arrival of La Pasionaria at the meeting was greeted with frantic cheering. She was a tall woman, wearing a plain black dress, with a calm sad face—one of the finest faces one had ever seen. This miner's wife, with her hair turning grey, had all the noble beauty of the Basque race. When she smiled, she smiled sadly and with some bitterness. How absurdly unlike the female ogre of the *Action Française*!

She then spoke. She spoke in Spanish. Few people in the audience understood exactly what she said, but the effect of her speech was over-whelming. It was the most beautiful voice ever heard on any French public platform. It had the mellow tone of a viola. She never screamed; her modulations and her transitions from soft to loud were gentle and scarcely perceptible; but the anguish in her voice when she spoke of the men now dying in Irun, the bitter irony when she spoke of the generals, the anger when she mentioned Hitler and Mussolini, the pathos when she appealed to France and the French people, whose battle was being fought by the Spanish Republicans—all these emotions communicated themselves to the spellbound audience.

.　　.　　.　　.　　.　　.

It was two days later, on September 6, while the French working class was feeling more bitter against its Government than ever before, that M. Blum made his famous speech at a Socialist gathering at the Luna Park. The speech was to become something of a turning-point in the attitude of the French people towards the Spanish Civil War.

It was a strange speech, and stranger still were the reactions of the audience. At the beginning, a large part of the audience—though mostly Socialist—was hostile to Blum. In the end, Blum received an ovation, and a great demonstration of loyalty and devotion.

How did he manage it?

For one thing, he represented it all as though it were a personal tragedy and he used the *vox humana* stop with greater effect than ever before.

It was in the national interests of France, Blum said, that the Republican Government of Spain should remain in power. With such a government the Pyrénées frontier of France, and her communications with North Africa were secure. With Spain under a military government, one could not be sure of anything.

'Alas! during a long time, during a much much longer time than we had anticipated,' he said, '*we had, owing to our perhaps all-too-confident offer,* to remain with our hands tied, while the other Powers had still full political and juridical (?) freedom of action.

And yet, think what would have happened if we had not made our offer of August 8. Remember that one of the Rebel chiefs declared that, rather than suffer defeat, he would plunge Europe into war. Do you not think, that we have, after all, saved Europe from war at a particularly critical moment?'

And then came the boldest statement of all, and one on which the whole argument hinged:

As you know, all the Powers have subscribed to our proposal. And as far as I know, there is not a single piece of direct or circumstantial evidence to show that the agreement has been violated so far.

At best it was a quibble.

'My friends, my friends,' M. Blum exclaimed, 'I am a Frenchman—for

I am one—proud of France's history, and reared in her tradition. I shall leave no stone unturned to assure her security and her defence. And to my last breath, I shall do everything to avert war for this country. I cannot accept the idea of preventive war even when some think war inevitable. War is possible only the moment it is admitted to be possible.'

The audience rose, singing the Internationale, and crying, 'Vive Blum.'

The speech had a curious effect on the French people. The clamour for 'Aeroplanes for Spain' subsided very noticeably. Blum had touched the most vulnerable spot in any Frenchman's heart—the fear of another war.

XXI. 'GRINGOIRE' AND THE SUICIDE OF ROGER SALENGRO

'Les réactionnaires sont des méchantes gens.'—ANATOLE FRANCE.

A T NINE o'clock at night, on November 17, after a hard day's work, M. Roger Salengro, the Minister of the Interior of the Blum Government, and Socialist Mayor of Lille, came home, sat down in an armchair in the kitchen and turned on the gas.

The first news that reached Paris was that Salengro had died of heart failure; but soon the truth came out.

In his note to Blum he wrote:

My wife died eighteen months ago, slandered and feeling the slander deeply.[1] My mother has not recovered from her operation and slander is eating into her. I am neither a deserter nor a traitor. My party [the Socialist party] has been my life and my joy.

Salengro was a man of great personal simplicity. With his round face and turned-up nose, and broad grin, he looked like a big boy, except that he was nearly bald, with funny little tufts of fair curly hair carefully parted in the middle. He was a hard worker, an able administrator, and, as Minister of the Interior—an office he took when the great strikes were in full swing—he handled the situation with skill and tact and 'settled' (as Blum said) 'the greatest social upheaval in France's recent history without the loss of a single drop of blood.'

[1] This was a reference to the attacks made on him and his wife by the local Communist Press.

A campaign was started against him in *Gringoire*—*'la feuille infâme,'* as Blum was to call it—about the beginning of August. This campaign consisted in showing that Salengro, who served as a dispatch-rider during the War, had deserted to the enemy on April 7, 1915. Apart from producing the 'evidence' of six ex-soldiers who claimed to have witnessed this 'shameful scene' (though none of them, oddly enough, had figured as a witness at Salengro's trial), *Gringoire* also alleged that *le cycliste* had been sentenced to death by a court martial, and that the 'second' court martial which acquitted him *in absentia* in 1916 had been 'wangled' by Salengro's political friends.

The absence of any record of this first court martial was attributed by *Gringoire* to the 'fact' that the records had been tampered with. The campaign was taken up by several other papers of the Right.

At first Salengro ignored these attacks—and his silence was interpreted by *Gringoire* as new evidence of his guilt—but, as the campaign increased in violence, the Government was obliged to intervene. General Gamelin, the head of the French Army, and two representatives of the most important ex-servicemen's organizations, were asked to inquire into the case, and they reported that there was no evidence of Salengro having been sentenced to death for desertion. Actually, he was sentenced only once—and that was by a German court, which condemned him to two years' imprisonment for insubordination and for his refusal to 'work against France' in a German munition factory. The evidence produced by his French fellow-prisoners showed that he had displayed great personal courage in defying the Germans. For all that, the *feuille infâme* continued its campaign.

The Chamber took up the 'Salengro case' on November 13, and, with the exception of sixty pro-Fascists (including several friends of Chiappe), it again 'acquitted' Salengro.

Since 1934 *Gringoire* specialized in slander as a political weapon more than any other paper. This paper, which had started its career as an ordinary gossip weekly, with a great deal of magazine matter, had developed, since 1934, into an important organ of 'public opinion' with a circulation of over half a million. For there is a section of 'public opinion' in France which is extremely gullible, and likes nothing better than dirt about public men. There was a Sixth of February public which was prepared to swallow the most abominable stories about any man of the Left —the more abominable the better. *Gringoire* was owned by the Carbuccia gang—and 'gang' is the only right word. Carbuccia is the son-in-law of Chiappe, the notorious ex-prefect of the Paris police; and Chiappe is the man behind this 'journalism.' Henri Béraud—the author of the famous

'Reduce England to Slavery'—is the obedient tool in the hands of these people.

Papers like *Gringoire, Candide, Le Jour,* and a few others, have done more than anything else to stir up hatred in France, and to keep France divided, as far as possible, into two camps. A well-known journalist of Left-Wing sympathies said to me a few days before Salengro's death: 'In the past I used to lunch and dine with all sorts of people. Now I can be on friendly terms only with people who have more or less the same political convictions as I have. With the others one is scarcely on speaking terms.'

It may be argued that the Press of the Left has not always been fair to its opponents either. This is true in a sense. It has pulled Laval's leg about his 'sixty millions,' it has pulled Tardieu's leg about the N'goka Sangha case; but it has never been either as persistent or as sadistic in its 'persecutions' as are the pro-Fascist papers. Nor has it ever (with the possible exception of the Communist Press in the past) specialized in manufacturing 'revelations.' And of sheer sadism even the *Humanité* was never guilty.

Anatole France was right: *'Les réactionnaires sont des méchantes gens.'* And the *méchanceté* of the pro-Fascist Press has, in actual practice, been a much more disturbing psychological factor in France than the existence of the Croix de Feu.

The Press Bill that the Blum Government introduced at the Chamber a week after Salengro's death filled a long-needed want. The jurisdiction of the *Cour d'Assizes*, with its unwieldy and costly machinery was, in cases of libel, 'largely theoretical,' as the preamble to the Blum Bill said. Under the new system libel actions go before the *Correctionnelle*, that is, a Court without a Jury, and one endowed with a rapid procedure. Critics of the Bill have observed that the elimination of the jury is an undemocratic measure; and this is true in a sense—though, as past experience has shown, French juries can be extremely unreliable in a libel action of a political or semi-political nature.

The clause concerning damages, however, brought the Bill dangerously near the British law, and met with some opposition. On the other hand the clauses obliging newspapers to show to whom they belong and to declare any money received from abroad—an important measure when one remembers the Italian subsidies of 1935—were more than justifiable. Only, was the clause concerning foreign subsidies also practicable? How could the money be traced? There is the well-known case of a distinguished 'diplomatic correspondent' of a certain Paris paper, who was dismissed after his refusal to share with the proprietor a *pourboire* he had received from King Alfonso's government.

BOOK II: 1937–39

I. 1937

(DEALING MAINLY WITH THE DECLINE OF THE FRONT POPULAIRE AND
OTHER FRENCH INTERNAL MATTERS)

ALL things considered, 1937 was not a very eventful year—at least
not in Europe. It was, as it were, a year of transition, in which
nothing really decisive happened. Germany was proceeding with her
rearmament, but the Nazi extremists were still being kept in check by
General von Fritsch and other cautious people. In Spain, by the end
of the summer, the Government had lost the northern provinces of
Bilbao and Santander; but the rest of Government Spain was holding
out.

During the year Britain and France rendered at least one service to
the Spanish Government—it was when they signed the Nyon Agreement.
For although it did not completely end piracy in the Mediterranean, it
at least prevented a regular Italo-German blockade of Spain's Mediterranean coast. It also had the psychological value of showing that, when
it came to the point, France and Britain were capable of acting independently of the Dictators. The moving spirit of the Nyon Conference
was Mr. Litvinov; but much credit is also due to Mr. Eden, who acted
at Nyon as he had not acted for a long time. For at Nyon his style was not
cramped by the proximity of Downing Street. And this gave M. Delbos
some courage, too.

. . . .

And France? France muddled along. The apprehensions of the finan-
cial difficulties confronting her were fully justified. Already, in February,
M. Blum realized that 'this could not go on.' In a memorable speech at
St. Nazaire on February 24 he proclaimed that the time had come for a
halt, for a *pause*, as he called it—a pause in the application of the Front
Populaire programme, in the increase of public expenditure, in the rise
of prices—'so that we may consolidate the ground we have conquered.'
In the financial debate at the Chamber that followed the St. Nazaire
speech, the Opposition behaved, for the first time since June 1936, with
an air of extraordinary self-assurance. For a week or more there had
been heavy pressure on the franc, and when, waving a cutting from

123

The Times, M. Fernand-Laurent, a member of the Right, claimed that a milliard francs of gold a day had been leaving Paris for London for some days past, M. Vincent Auriol, Blum's unimpressive Finance Minister, became very angry, shouted that the affairs of the Exchange Equalization Fund were nobody's business, and then mumbled in conclusion an awkward and ambiguous denial.

Again, as in October 1936, Blum was in a dilemma. Would he order exchange control, adopt a more or less autarkist system, and so abandon the Tripartite Agreement of September 25; or would he save 'financial liberalism' at the price of making some important concessions to the orthodox financiers, who were obviously not fully satisfied with the announcement of the 'pause'? The 'coercive' way was advocated not only by Vincent Auriol who, poor man, had his style constantly cramped by Blum's international considerations, but also by M. Labeyrie, the Governor of the Bank of France. But Blum still preferred to choose the 'liberal' way. With the 'coercive' way he might have gone boldly ahead with the Front Populaire programme: only—it would have meant much less harmonious relations with England, and a suspension in the work of *rapprochement* with the United States which, for the first time since the War, was showing signs of becoming an important, perhaps decisive, factor in international affairs. Moreover, about that time, the British Treasury gave him a polite but firm warning; and on March 5 the Blum Government made its climb-down.

A committee of highly orthodox experts, including M. Rist and M. Baudouin, were placed in charge of the Exchange Equalization Fund. This was perhaps most unwise, for the Committee in question had the Government well on the leash, but 'confidence' had to be restored; and that was the price High Finance demanded from M. Blum. He gave way. The Bourse went up; and the first $8\frac{1}{2}$ milliards of the Defence loan (which, with its *garantie de change* clause, was as safe a bet as one could desire and was almost an admission that a new devaluation was coming) was bought up by the banks in no time. Blum, though feeling a little uneasy at heart, looked like a happy man, and said that France had never in the last ten years been stronger, and never had the outlook been so hopeful.

.   .   .   .

His joyful mood did not last long. On the night of March 16 the Premier, wearing full evening-dress, was at the opera listening to a concert of British music, conducted by Sir Thomas Beecham, when the news reached him of bloody rioting at Clichy, the Paris suburb. The workers had arranged there a mass demonstration against the 'provocation of the Croix de Feu,' two hundred of whom, complete with wives and children, were attending a private show at the local cinema. M. Dormoy, the Minister of the Interior, had not considered the Croix de Feu meeting illegal, and had refused to prohibit it; in the circumstances the meeting had to be protected by police cordons; and there was a clash between the police and the workers' demonstration in the Place de la Mairie; six workers were killed, and a couple of hundred injured; among the injured was M. Blumel, M. Blum's secretary, who had rushed to Clichy as soon as he heard that trouble had broken out. At midnight Blum drove to the hospital at Clichy, where his white tie and top-hat contrasted strangely with the bloodstained caps of the Clichy rioters. His first reaction was to resign. He felt as though he had been stabbed in the back.

Clichy had a disastrous effect. Confidence was immediately shaken. The Trade Unions—who had been hostile to the 'pause,' which they considered incompatible with the Front Populaire programme—arranged a six hours' general strike two days after Clichy; it was hardly a demonstration of friendship for the Government. Whoever was mainly responsible for Clichy (and it is hard to believe that it was all the work of *agents provocateurs*) it was clear that certain extremist working-class elements were in a vicious mood, and were taking Blum's 'surrender to the 200 families' very badly. It seems that the Clichy 'demonstration' was organized by two local leaders—one Socialist, the other Communist—who were competing among themselves in 'extremism.' Extremism was the fashion of the time. Playing up to the extremists, Thorez, the Communist leader, thundered at a protest meeting at the Vel d'Hiv against 'Governments of the Left who pursue a policy of the Right' and against the police. And the *Libertaire*, the Anarchist paper, appeared with a headline:

LE SANG OUVRIER A COULÉ

and it compared Blum to 'bloody Noske.'

Clichy was not soon forgotten. For weeks afterwards there was serious labour trouble—especially at the Exhibition. It was officially to open on May 1; at the end of April only the German, Russian, Italian and Belgian pavilions (employing their own labour) were finished. The rest promised to be two, or even three, months late. The workers would not hear of overtime, and strikes were frequent.

Strikes continued to break out in various trades. M. Jouhaux, afraid of losing his grip on the rank-and-file, sent a sort of ultimatum to the

Government demanding, among other things, a loan of ten milliard francs for a vast public works programme—an amount which could, obviously, not be found without exchange control or some other forms of coercion.

The Government firmly rejected M. Jouhaux's demands, and in May there was a notable improvement in the general outlook. M. Blum succeeded in bringing about an 'exhibition truce'; the collective agreements, which were about to expire, were automatically extended for six months; and it looked as though the Blum Government would last at least until the autumn. The Exhibition, though far from ready, and with large flags hiding from M. Lebrun's sight so many skeletons of unbuilt pavilions, was nevertheless officially opened on May 24.

.   .   .   .

But suddenly, in the first week in June, fresh trouble started. The Bourse went crashing downhill, the three per cent Rentes falling far below sixty francs—a level to which they had never sunk since the panic days of 1926. The flight from the franc started again with renewed vigour. 'A bankers' ramp,' the Left-Wing Press complained. The resignation of Horace Finaly from the post of managing-director of the Banque de Paris et des Pays Bas looked particularly sinister. Finaly was a modern and 'liberal' banker, with many personal contacts with the politicians of the Left, and, on the whole, friendly to the Blum Government. He was replaced at the head of the Banque de Paris by M. Moreau, the ultra-reactionary financier who shortly before, had boasted in an article in the *Revue des Deux Mondes* of how he had done his best to turn out one Left Government after another when he was Governor of the Bank of France in 1925. This change in the management of one of the most influential of the Paris banks was generally regarded as a sign that the 'City' had sentenced the Blum Government to death. The Blum Government felt that the time had come to act. But without the goodwill of the banks, what could it do? Where could it borrow money—even short-term money—to bridge the gulf? In the meantime the Senate had already declared war on the Government. On June 10 a resolution concerning the forty-hour week in the hotel trade, and openly hostile to the Government, was passed by a large majority of the Senate. And then came what looked like the *coup de grâce*: on June 12, M. Rist and M. Baudouin resigned, saying they could not defend the franc any longer unless Blum accepted all their suggestions. It looked like part of the bankers' conspiracy.

Unable to agree with his colleagues on a detailed programme of financial reform, M. Blum made, on June 15, a bold move: he decided to ask Parliament for plenary powers. It was an unusual course to take; for in the election campaign no one had attacked legislation by decree more severely than the Socialists and Radicals.

The Chamber did not like the Plenary Powers Bill; but voted it none the less after a stormy debate. It was believed at first that the Communists would vote against the Government, or at least abstain, in which case the Government would be defeated. In the end they voted for it, 'for the sake of preserving the Front Populaire.' Paul Faure, the Socialist Minister of State, jokingly explained as follows the sudden change in the Communists' intentions:

At five o'clock they rang up Moscow, and the fellow who spoke to them said they were not to vote for the Government. At midnight they rang up Moscow again to make quite sure. Another person answered the 'phone. 'You are to vote for the Government.' 'But you told us at five o'clock we were to vote against.' 'Yes, but the comrade who told you that has since been shot. You are to vote *for* the Government; do you understand?'

But the Senate was a different proposition. Ever since June 1936 the Senators had borne Blum and the Front Populaire a savage grudge. The day of reckoning had come. But now the real fun started. M. Caillaux, the most influential man at the Senate, had the time of his life.

If, in the past, the Government was hostile to plenary powers, and is now asking for them, what guarantee have we that M. Blum, who is favourable to parliamentary government to-day, will still be favourable to it to-morrow?

He referred to the 'non-parliamentary outlook' of the C.G.T. Wagging his bald head, and moving his arms stiffly from side to side, the old man looked like a tragic puppet. He spoke in an ironical Punch-and-Judy voice, which at times rose to the high pitch of an angry scream. His conclusion was that the Government was unworthy of the confidence it was asking for; in the words of Richepin, he said, the Government was:

Comme une femme soûle
Qui dans l'infini roule
Sans savoir pourquoi, ni comment!

True, he apologized for the adjective, but that was only *pro forma*. Vincent Auriol, speaking like a crucified martyr, became almost hysterical, and although Blum treated the Senate to some home truths, and

127

told them, in effect, that they were not the true representatives of the French people, he gave it up in the end, and the Cabinet resigned.

The truth perhaps is that Blum was riding for a fall. He would probably have been most embarrassed if the Senate had granted him plenary powers—especially the 'limited plenary powers' that some of the Senators were, at one moment, ready to grant him. As for real plenary powers, there was a danger—and the Senate was fully aware of it—that the C.G.T. might drive him much further than he, with his *not* very revolutionary temperament, would like to go.

. . . .

Chautemps, suave and polite, was asked to form the new Government. He had been on good terms with Blum, and had often helped him in settling labour disputes. Blum went before the National Council of the Socialist Party, and implored them to let him enter the Chautemps Government. The Socialists, he said, must be loyal to the Radicals, as the Radicals had been loyal to them. If they refused to enter the Chautemps Government it would mean the end of the Front Populaire. And he spoke gravely of the *Leipzig* incident; and said that the most important thing of all was to provide France with a normal Government at once. The belief that France was going to pieces could only encourage Hitler. The Socialists grumbled, and were very angry with the Senate, but, in the end, agreed. Needless to say, they also deplored the proposed appointment of Georges Bonnet to the post of Finance Minister.

If ever there was a Radical who had no love for the Front Populaire, it was Bonnet. Bonnet, whom, some months earlier, Blum had appointed Ambassador in Washington largely in order to get him out of the way —for he was constantly conspiring against the Front Populaire, and was doing his best to demoralize the Radicals—now returned from Washington with a triumphant little smirk on his face. But the Banks liked Bonnet, and so did the Senate; and it granted Chautemps plenary powers with the greatest of ease, and even with a touch of cordiality. The first thing Bonnet did was to devaluate the franc once again. He made it a 'floating franc,' but hoped to maintain it in the neighbourhood of 130 to the £. A fortnight after that M. Bonnet submitted to the Cabinet a number of decrees increasing taxation or reducing expenditure by nearly ten milliard francs. As a sop to the Left, M. Bonnet agreed to the semi-nationalization of the railways. The working class were disillusioned, and rather embittered. The Front Populaire procession of July 14 was a sad spectacle. The enthusiasm and vigour of 1935 and 1936 were gone. It was a big procession; but all the little shopkeepers of the Faubourg

Saint-Antoine who had crowded the pavements a year before to cheer the procession had now stayed at home, or had gone to the Bois de Vincennes to lie on the grass. The workers were not even very sorry for M. Blum, and not even very angry with the Senate. For one thing, the cost of living had gone up a lot, and their wives grumbled—and some even blamed Blum for it. At the Socialist Congress at Marseilles that week Blum was howled down by the revolutionary extremists of the Marceau Pivert group. Marceau Pivert, the elementary schoolmaster with the ascetic's face, who combined revolutionary fanaticism with a gentle and slightly crazy smile, was going to gain in importance in the months that followed. He had already rebelled against Blum's 'pause.'[1]

· · · · · · ·

The Paris Exhibition created a general holiday mood. No doubt, Picasso's panel of Gernika in the Spanish pavilion was a terrifying thing, and the German pavilion was ominously heavy and overpowering; but the aggressively nude Teutons in front of it were an object of loud mirth, especially to the young people who would photograph each other in the shadow of those formidable—loins; and the proletariat took a certain joy in scribbling in the visitors' book in the Soviet pavilion: *'Les Soviets partout. A bas Bonnet!'*

Front Populaire Government No. 2 continued its unexciting existence until the middle of January. Unexciting—that is perhaps an exaggeration. There was the whole international situation over which M. Delbos tried not to become too excited; but which was exciting for all that. And then there was the Cagoulard affair which was perhaps less funny than it sounded. A number of queer and, in some cases, tragic, things had happened in France during the year. One was the horrible murder, on a quiet country road in Normandy, of Carlo Rosselli, the brilliant Italian anti-Fascist journalist, and of his brother Nello. That was in June. And then, one Saturday evening in September, something that sounded like a couple of rockets went off in the neighbourhood of the Etoile. As a result, the headquarters of the Employers' Federation in the rue de Presbourg collapsed, and killed two policemen in the process; and another house belonging to another employers' organization was wrecked in the rue Boissière, a few hundred yards away.

[1] Officially, the Pivertists did not break away from the Socialist Party until the Royan Congress in June 1938. Being left to themselves, without the authority of the Socialist Party behind them, they later lost in influence. Even so, their 'trotzkyism' continued to encourage all forms of labour unrest. The Communists, when charged with causing serious unrest in France at a time when internationally this was most undesirable, liked to blame the Pivertists and others for it. Not *entirely* without reason.

It was a complete mystery at first. The Press of the Right claimed that the Anarchists were at it again—after thirty or forty years of inactivity. Others accused Moscow: Employers' Federation—obviously the outrage had come from the Left. The Press of the Left spoke of an act of provocation organized by the employers themselves. But about the same time the word *cagoulard* was first mentioned. Cagoulards, the hooded men; a French Ku-Klux-Klan! It sounded both funny and intriguing. But it took several weeks before the word came to mean something more than a joke. It was when several large private arsenals in Paris and other towns were discovered by the police, as well as the existence of an organization known as the C.S.A.R. (*Comités secrets d'action révolutionnaire*). A number of prominent business men—among them M. Deloncle—and men like M. Pozzo di Borgo, who in the past had played a leading part in the Croix de Feu and other Fascist and semi-Fascist organizations, before their dissolution, were arrested. The police claimed that the C.S.A.R. numbered about 6,000 members.

The dissolution of the Fascist leagues and also their failure to achieve anything by more or less legal means had inevitably sent some of their wilder members underground. They were prepared to fight the Republic by every means, and the financial support given to the C.S.A.R. by Germany and Italy did not put them off. 'Hitler rather than the Front Populaire' was a genuine reflection of a state of mind existing among these people. Most of the arms came from Italy, Germany and Rebel Spain and there were strange contacts existing between the C.S.A.R. and certain agents of General Franco. The attempt to capture the *C2*, a Spanish Government submarine anchored at Brest was made by the notorious Major Troncoso, the military governor of Irun, with the assistance of several Frenchmen, including former Croix de Feu men. M. Chautemps in a speech at the Chamber in November referred to the extreme gravity of the C.S.A.R. affair, 'especially in view of the origin of the arms.' In Government quarters it was openly said that the show was run from Italy, and the name of Baron Aloisi was freely mentioned. No doubt, some French money had also been spent on the arms dumps; at the time of the first Blum Government there were any number of panicky and *bient pensant* people who were ready to contribute to any organization calling itself anti-Red. As the police inquiry proceeded, and more arrests were made, the suspicions were confirmed that there was a link between the murder of the Rosellis, the rue de Presbourg explosion, and a number of other outrages; and that the link was none other than the C.S.A.R. The purpose of an outrage like the rue de Presbourg explosion was obviously to create bewilderment and internal tension in France—such outrages might prove extremely useful in the midst of an acute international crisis.

If the C.S.A.R. did not revive the Front Populaire in a governmental sense, it certainly made an enormous impression on the country, and contributed to the success of the Left-Wing parties in the municipal elections in October. Though on a smaller scale, it acted on French minds much as La Rocque had acted on them in 1935 and perhaps delayed by a few weeks the final breakdown of the Front Populaire even in an ideological sense.

But in December, more trouble started.

·　·　·　·　·　·　·

The stay-in strike at the Goodrich tyre works at Colombes was the most unpleasant business of all; the Government thought at first of clearing the works with the help of the police, but the strikers were so defiant that, to prevent bloodshed, the police had to be withdrawn. The Right-Wing Press accused the Government of 'lack of authority.' In Paris, the lorry-drivers struck, and the Christmas food supply had to be brought to the Halles in army lorries. The *Libertaire*, the Anarchist paper,[2] chuckled over this 'strike-breaking by the Front Populaire Government.' Other strikes broke out, and on December 29, just as Paris was getting ready for the New Year *réveillon*, the buses and metros went on strike. The strike was fortunately settled twenty-four hours later. But it was a mischievous strike, and it created much ill-feeling; and it showed that the C.G.T. included certain unruly and irresponsible elements capable of taking grave decisions without asking the advice of the trade union leaders. M. Jouhaux was as displeased with the strike as anybody else, and so were the Communists—or, at any rate, their leaders.

If this strike was largely due to a lack of trade union discipline, there were other strikes where the strikers had genuine grievances against the employers. M. Chautemps therefore decided, early in January, to call together a conference of the Trade Unions and Employers' Federations with a view to agreeing on the terms of a Labour Code, which would subsequently be approved by Parliament, and so become law. The employers unfortunately boycotted the conference; and this placed the Chautemps Government in a difficult position. This boycott was accompanied by a new attack on the franc.

The behaviour of M. Chautemps in the days that followed was truly

[2] Certain Anarchist writers, notably Henri Jeanson, came into prominence as writers under German patronage in 1940. (Author's note, 1942.)

bewildering. On January 13, at the instigation of M. Bonnet, his Finance Minister, who said that he could not 'go on like this,' he called a meeting of Parliament and demanded a vote explicitly rejecting exchange control. This was asking a lot from the Socialists, many of whom had, since the fall of the Blum Government, come to the conclusion that only with exchange control could the Front Populaire programme be carried on. M. Chautemps's strange move looked like a deliberate attempt to break up the Front Populaire majority. What strengthened this impression was that in the speech he made that afternoon he violently attacked the working class, and scarcely said anything of the sabotage of the Employers' Federation who had just wrecked his Industrial Peace Conference.

The Socialists, nevertheless, gave way, and agreed to vote his motion against exchange control; but this did not suit M. Chautemps. So, in order to break up the Government, he violently attacked the Communists saying that 'he did not desire their votes.' This was too much for the Socialists to swallow; they declared that M. Chautemps had broken up the Front Populaire majority, and the Socialist Ministers resigned from the Cabinet. It was whispered that M. Chautemps was bullied into this manœuvre by certain financial interests, who had threatened to continue their offensive against the franc: they (like M. Bonnet) were determined to break up the Front Populaire majority, and also to turn M. Dormoy, the Socialist Minister of the Interior, out of office; for they felt that he was showing an excess of zeal in conducting his inquiry into the Cagoulard case.

. . . .

Be that as it may, it was the end of the Front Populaire Government No. 2. Front Populaire Government No. 3, which was not formed until nearly a week later—on January 18—was a plain Radical Government under the same M. Chautemps, but no longer with Socialist participation. Parliamentary wits declared that if this went on much longer the 'Front Populaire Government No. 6' would be composed of M. Tardieu, M. Laval and the Cagoulards. During the Cabinet crisis, M. Blum, who was first asked to form the new Government, launched the idea of a 'National Government around the Front Populaire—from Reynaud to Thorez'— that is, a National Government comprising all the 'truly democratic elements of the country.' He felt that if a National Government *must* come, it should at least be a predominantly Left Government. His idea was not accepted; but he hoped that it would make headway, and would materialize sooner or later.

And so, M. Chautemps was back in office again at the head of a much weaker combination. As expected, this Government stayed in office only a short time. It had part of the Labour Code passed by Parliament, but when on March 5 M. Chautemps asked the Socialists if they would support his request for plenary powers and they said no, he suddenly resigned three days later, without waiting for a Chamber vote. He said he did not wish to 'break up the Front Populaire majority'—for one ought to add that, since the formation of his second Government, he had been all honey to the Left, even though he had driven the Socialists out of his previous Government. The subtleties of M. Chautemps during these two months took one's breath away.

As will be shown later, there were some who wondered whether his real reason for resigning on March 8 was not a strong suspicion in his mind that something serious was about to happen in Austria. Chautemps, of course, denied this. The fact remains that, on the day Hitler's troops marched into Austria, France was without a Government. But the time has come to see how French foreign policy had fared during all these months.

II. FRANCO-CZECH IDYLL

ON DECEMBER 19, 1937, a train steamed into the Gare de l'Est. It was bringing back to Paris M. Yvon Delbos, France's Foreign Minister, after his three weeks' 'tour of friendship' in Central and Eastern Europe.

M. Delbos, smiling his gentle smile, came out of the train and said: *'J'ai fait un excellent voyage.'* That was for the afternoon papers. A few days later, before the Foreign Affairs Committee of the Chamber, M. Delbos, as an honest man, admitted that the *voyage* had not been as *excellent* as all that. No doubt, the ordinary people in Poland and Jugoslavia and Rumania still felt deeply attached to France and all that France stood for; but the Governments—no. The Czechoslovak Government alone was as wholeheartedly pro-French as were the Czech people.

France, absorbed in her domestic problems during eighteen months, had almost forgotten the Rhineland *coup* of March 7, 1936. The re-militarization of the Rhineland had been a savage blow to collective security, and to the whole structure of France's Eastern alliances. It had weakened France strategically in relation to Central Europe; and if the Czechs continued to place absolute confidence in the French alliance, it was partly because they had no other choice, and partly because the French assurances were eloquent in the extreme. But, after all (they reflected), the 'Bohemian bastion' was as essential to France as the French alliance was indispensable to the integrity of Czechoslovakia.

But in Warsaw, in Belgrade, and in Bucharest they regarded the Rhineland *coup* as a turning-point in the post-War history of Europe. And there were also other reasons why the Jugoslavs and the Rumanians and the Poles were dissatisfied with France. About the middle of 1936, Blum had turned a deaf ear to the proposals for a mutual assistance pact made to Paris by Belgrade and Bucharest. Blum had said that before France could commit herself to defending Jugoslavia and Rumania, she desired the three Little Entente countries to sign a mutual assistance pact among themselves. Aware of Germany's designs on Czechoslovakia, Rumania and Jugoslavia said they would rather not. Moreover, Nazi propaganda had been active in these countries, and their ruling classes were in any case prejudiced against the Front Populaire. The stay-in strikes of 1936 and the labour unrest generally had given them the idea that if France was not exactly 'Communist,' the 'Reds' were playing too important a part in her internal affairs. . . .

In Jugoslavia there was also an influential set around Prince Paul who, largely owing to its past associations with Tsarist Russia, was strongly prejudiced against the Soviets, and so against the Franco-Soviet Pact—whatever it was worth in a military sense.

Shortly before leaving Paris, M. Delbos had, together with M. Chautemps, the Premier, gone to London; and there had been much talk of a 'general settlement' with Germany. Lord Halifax had returned from Germany, where he had seen Hitler at Berchtesgaden—only it is doubtful whether Lord Halifax fully reported to the French Ministers all that Hitler had said to him about Austria and Czechoslovakia.

A surprise was awaiting M. Delbos. In passing through Berlin the Nord Express stops at three different stations. At Bahnhof Zoo M. Delbos was welcomed by M. François-Poncet, the French Ambassador; at the Bahnhof Friedrichstrasse, the Polish Ambassador and Czech Minister in Berlin welcomed him; then came the Schlesischer Bahnhof. And here was Herr von Neurath in person! He entered M. Delbos's compartment and there, in the presence of M. François-Poncet they talked for over ten minutes.

This extraordinary display of German courtesy and goodwill is curious when one thinks that the Austrian tragedy was to start barely two months later—when the unfortunate Schuschnigg was summoned to Berchtesgaden. However, it is only fair to say that Von Neurath was to be replaced by Ribbentrop in the interval.

In Warsaw M. Delbos was met by Colonel Beck and other personalities, and outside the station there were large crowds who waved flags and shouted *'Vive la France!'*

Words, words?—no. France, that source of generous ideas. France with her immense cultural heritage still meant a great deal to these people—to liberals, intellectuals and to all civilized human beings generally, in all those countries east of Germany. The Polish Government, however, was less enthusiastic. Beck, no doubt, referred to the Franco-Polish alliance, but in his speech at the Foreign Office banquet he defined the nature of friendship as follows:

> The peculiarity of friendship is that while each of the friends pursues his own aims and defends his own interests, he is able to consider with the greatest benevolence all the problems concerning the other.

The Poles showed much interest in the prospect of a return of colonies to Germany, and said that Poland ought to be given some too. Colonel Beck also attached great importance to Neurath's 'gesture.' The League of Nations was not mentioned in his speech; but at the same time he said that Poland had no intention of adhering to the Anti-Comintern Pact. But the chief object of Delbos's visit to Warsaw—his proposal to mediate a friendly settlement between Poland and Czechoslovakia—was completely unsuccessful. Beck said in effect that the Polish Government preferred 'bilateral' talks to any kind of mediation.

The correspondent of the *Deutsche Allgemeine Zeitung* claimed that he had asked M. Delbos:

> whether the Polish Government had shown any interest in the Czech problems.
>
> M. Delbos made an evasive gesture, which was greeted by an outburst of hilarity from those present.[1]

And so M. Delbos went off to Bucharest. Rumania was, just then, on the eve of a general election, and in a state of great agitation. Shortly afterwards the Goga Government was to come into office. But at that

[1] *Deutsche Allgemeine Zeitung*, December 7.

time M. Tatarescu was still Premier and M. Antonescu Foreign Minister. They were friendly—friendlier than Beck—and the Rumanian people were enthusiastic about M. Delbos.

The intellectuals were equally friendly. 'In the realm of culture,' the *Temps* wrote, 'it seems certain that the Rumanian *élite* has remained faithful to the French language and to French culture.'[2]

Only 'hostile propaganda' had made much headway in the last year. The leaders of the opposition parties boycotted all the official receptions given in M. Delbos's honour—which was all the more deplorable when one remembered how three years earlier M. Barthou, during his visit to Bucharest, received an unanimous ovation from the Rumania Parliament.

King Carol was friendly and so were M. Tatarescu, and M. Antonescu. Trade relations—oil against armaments—were discussed, and so was the mechanization of the Rumania Army, on the development of which General Gamelin, during his visit a few months earlier, had insisted. But there was an undercurrent of uncertainty in all the talks.

'Collective security,' M. Antonescu said, 'can exist only if the security of Central and Eastern Europe is not detached from the security of Western Europe.'

M. Antonescu was looking far ahead. And there was one thing that was disturbing him, as it was disturbing many other people in that part of the world. France had tied herself to the apron-strings of England; she had allowed England to force upon her the policy of non-intervention (even before anybody else had agreed to it) ; owing to the British Government's dislike of Russia, France had consistently cold-shouldered the Soviets, and had refused to enter into staff talks with them ; and although M. Blum and M. Delbos had sworn a hundred times that nothing was more sacred than the Franco-Czech alliance, M. Antonescu (and many others) wondered how it would really work if it ever came to the test. Would not France again ask England's permission to mobilize, as she had already done on the fateful day of March 7, 1936, when the Reichswehr reoccupied the Rhineland?

The most dramatic episode during the 'tour of friendship' occurred at Belgrade. As M. Delbos, accompanied by M. Stoyadinovitch, was leaving the station, he was greeted by an incredible chorus of cheering from the enormous crowds who had gathered in the vast square outside. They were waving frantically innumerable French flags, large flags and small flags, and they had also brought with them a huge panel with a portrait of M. Delbos.

[2] *Le Temps,* December 11.

This cordial—perhaps too cordial—demonstration (the *Temps* correspondent wrote) had a deplorable sequel as soon as the official carriages had driven past on their way to the French legation. Four or five thousand demonstrators formed themselves into a procession, and breaking through the police cordons, marched through the town shouting *'Vive la France!' 'Vive la Démocratie française!' 'Vive Delbos!'* They were charged by mounted gendarmes who tried in vain to disperse the crowds. In one place the rioters barricaded themselves against the gendarmes and threw stones at them. The gendarmes fired. At the moment of writing there is one dead and several wounded.

Granted that it was tactless and all that; granted also that the demonstration was essentially an anti-Stoyadinovitch demonstration, the eloquent fact remained that in the minds of the Jugoslav students the notion of liberty was associated with their idea of France, and Stoyadinovitch was both 'against France' and 'against liberty.'

Delbos and Stoyadinovitch—the latter had just returned from a visit to Rome—had hardly anything to say to each other except some courteous platitudes.

Pro-French rioting was, however, spreading right through Jugoslavia.

'Everywhere,' 'the *Sud-Est* Agency cabled on December 13, 'the population is organizing pro-French demonstrations in honour of M. Delbos.'[3]

In the great naval harbour of Split large crowds assembled outside the French consulate singing the 'Marseillaise.'

Through the whole of Jugoslavia they were singing the 'Marseillaise.' The Serbian *intelligentsia* were passionately pro-French.

But Stoyadinovitch did not feel like that, and was only too glad to see the last of Delbos.

.　　.　　.　　.　　.　　.　　.

As the train on its way to Prague was crossing the Hungarian plain, Delbos remarked wistfully to one of the journalists in his carriage: 'At last we are going to see some real friends.'

At Prague, richly decorated with French and Czech flags, the popular enthusiasm was as great as in Belgrade, but this time with the full approval of the Government. It was to be the last French State visit to that Czechoslovakia which France had, in 1919, done so much to create. Beneš, Krofta, Hodza—here at last were real friends. Masaryk was mentioned affectionately in all the speeches, and M. Delbos travelled out into the country to lay a wreath on the old man's grave.

[3] *Le Temps,* December 14.

And in a speech, which was going to cause great annoyance to the German Press, he declared:

'Fraternity' is a word which is often used in after-dinner toasts; and it sometimes means little. But in the case of France and Czechoslovakia it defines perfectly their relations. While casting aside every idea of domination, I may say that Czechoslovakia is like an extension (*un prolongement*) of France. We are united by so many ties, we feel things in such a similar way, and our régimes are so similar that a Frenchman in Czechoslovakia feels as though he were in France, and a Czechoslovak in France feels as though he were in Czechoslovakia.

In the course of one of the official receptions, M. Delbos met two of the Sudeten leaders, Herr Kundt and Senator Pfrogner. They told him that they did not wish to be treated as a minority any longer, but emphasized their loyalty to the Czechoslovak State. It seems certain that the Czech Government easily persuaded M. Delbos not to worry about the matter; and leave it for them to settle. They would do the best they could; but territorial autonomy would be a menace to the integrity of Czechoslovakia, and could not possibly be agreed to. M. Delbos did not 'insist.' According to another report, M. Delbos hardly discussed the Sudeten question at all.

Czechoslovakia gave France's Foreign Minister an affectionate send off.

Here is a Havas message from Cheb describing M. Delbos's homeward journey:

At Cheb, on the German frontier, M. Delbos was greeted with the playing of the 'Marseillaise' and of the Czech national anthem. Once more he expressed his gratitude for the reception given him in Czechoslovakia and emphasized the indissoluble bonds uniting the two countries.[4]

It was through Eger (or Cheb as the Czechs called it) that Hitler made his triumphant entry into the Sudetenland in October 1938.

[4] *Le Temps,* December 20.

III. THE TROUBLE STARTS

THE tragic year of 1938, which was to see the end of Austria and the dismemberment of Czechoslovakia, began with a setback for the Fascist cause. After a deadly battle that had lasted nearly a fortnight—part of it was fought in a blinding snowstorm—the Government troops entered Teruel. Never had the outlook for the Spanish Government looked better than during those first weeks of 1938. But during the month of January, France took little interest in foreign affairs. She was stewing in her own juice.

There had been a wave of strikes at the end of December; and the first half of January saw an abortive 'industrial peace conference'; the resignation of the Chautemps Cabinet; a Cabinet crisis that lasted nearly a week—in the course of which M. Blum, aware of the grave international situation, first proposed a National Government 'around the Front Populaire,' and M. Bonnet tried for the first time his hand at Cabinet-making—and, in the end, the formation of a new Chautemps Government, only without the Socialists in it any longer. It was a very weak and unrepresentative Government. It was one of those stop-gap Cabinets which have often proved unlucky internationally.

The Chautemps Government was anything but impressive. It, nevertheless, received from the Chamber, not exactly a vote of confidence, but the benefit of the doubt. The vote was an unusual one—501 for the Government—and one (the irrepressible M. Bergery) against. There were about 100 abstentions on the Right. The Government meant, above all, a further step in the disintegration of the Front Populaire. Looked at from the international point of view, the whole Cabinet crisis—*de Chautemps à Chautemps*—was something wretchedly frivolous. So also was the overwhelming 'vote of confidence' given to the new Chautemps Cabinet. André Albert, the youngest deputy at the Chamber, and something of an *enfant terrible*, remarked before the vote: 'The bigger the Government's majority, the less time will it last.'

The Ministerial Declaration included some promises which were calculated to sweeten the temper of the Left, as well as some passages in praise of the Front Populaire:

> The Front Populaire, that spontaneous outburst of the democratic instincts of the people—an outburst which followed the bloody incidents [the riots of February 6, 1934] which revealed a threat to the régime—a régime to which the nation is profoundly attached, has the double significance of a powerful will to defend the Republic and of an ardent desire for social justice.

And M. Chautemps actually promised to introduce 'within the shortest time' a Bill providing Old Age Pensions for needy workers—a substantial sop to the Left, but a promise that was actually never going to be carried out.

The League Council met on January 27. It was the hundredth Session of the League Council. It was perhaps the last meeting where some faint illusions were still entertained on the future of the League.

The main task M. Delbos and Mr. Eden had undertaken was to prevent the League Covenant from being wrecked. The discussion on the Committee of Twenty-eight on an eventual revision of the Covenant resulted in the dossier on the revision being sent to the Assembly, which would in due course give the Committee further instructions. Until then, the Committee would suspend its labours.

In the opinion of the British and French Governments, the best that could be done was to postpone and avoid all important decisions, in the hope that conditions *might* improve in the next few months. In view of a revival of piracy in the Mediterranean, the British and French Governments decided to reinforce the Nyon patrol, and to attack all submerged submarines. With the Chamberlain régime establishing itself in England, the most Mussolini and Franco had to fear was a British inquiry, or—in very bad cases—British 'representations' at Burgos! When one looks back on February 1938, that Anglo-French decision of February 2, to 'attack all submerged submarines' seems like the last action taken by France and Britain without any regard to the feelings of the Dictator countries.

It was during the first week in February that reports came from Germany which gave England and France something of a shock. There was no longer much doubt of what had happened, especially when it was learned that Ribbentrop had been appointed Foreign Minister in place of Von Neurath. The Nazi extremists had gained the upper hand. It is true that Paris was to remain puzzled for a day or two longer than any other capital; for on February 7, an 'occasional correspondent' claiming to write from Bâle, gave an entirely different version in the *Temps* of what had happened.

The theory that the appointment of Von Ribbentrop to the post of Foreign Minister meant the beginning of a 'wild' foreign policy was dismissed by the 'occasional correspondent' at Bâle with the remark that 'perhaps it was, above all, necessary to clear the German Embassy in London of Ribbentrop's presence.'

This article in the *Temps* of February 7 aroused comment in Paris.

Partly because its authorship was widely attributed to a high official at the Quai d'Orsay. Why did he write this article? The only plausible explanation was that the Government—or certain members of the Government—were anxious that French opinion should not become too worried about the developments in Germany. Schuschnigg's visit to Berchtesgaden produced the same irresponsible optimism. The *Intransigeant* claimed that Schuschnigg had stuck to his guns, and had pretty well told Hitler where he got off. It was not until several days later that the ugly truth of the Berchtesgaden meeting began to leak out.

But certain people in France had nevertheless smelt a rat; among them was M. Flandin, who was in close contact with certain London Press lords; and these kept him informed.

It was about February 10 that M. Flandin came out, with renewed vigour, in favour of a 'retrenchment' policy. He blamed everything on the Communists and on the Franco-Soviet Pact. But for the Communists, he said, France could live in happy harmony with Germany and Italy. In Germany, too, the Government must have been informed of the way the wind was blowing in London; for it is otherwise inconceivable how Hitler could have attacked the British Foreign Secretary with such personal violence on the afternoon of February 20. Flandin in France and Hitler in Germany seemed to know more about the doings of the British Cabinet than almost anybody in England.

Hitler's speech was the most violent he had ever made.

And, on the night of the same day, after an interminable Cabinet meeting at 10 Downing Street, the B.B.C. announced with laconic brevity that Mr. Eden had resigned.

Every editor in Paris that night was puzzled as to which of the two items of news was the more important—Hitler's speech or Eden's resignation. In the end most of them decided in favour of Eden's resignation.

The reactions in Paris were described as follows in a Paris message in the *Manchester Guardian*:

Mr. Eden's resignation has caused the deepest commotion in Paris, deeper even than is outwardly shown in French Government quarters. In the view of many observers it is perhaps the final blow to all the beliefs and political principles the majority of the British and French people upheld together for so many years.

For all this places France in a singularly delicate position. No doubt she will have to co-operate with Britain whatever its Government, just as Britain will have to co-operate with France whatever hopes Lord Halifax may have of gaining Germany's friendship. But what, it is asked, about France's allies, Poland and Czechoslovakia? And what about the League? . . .

The repercussions of such a state of affairs, were it ever to come about, are incalculable. But the instinct of the great majority of French public opinion is that a Four-Power Pact policy, or anything like it, would be suicidal. And is Spain, it is also asked, to be handed over to German and Italian domination?[1]

It was a fearful blow to M. Delbos. It looked as though his policy to which he had clung in spite of everything, was finally crumbling. On February 16, a few days after the Berchtesgaden ultimatum, he had remarked to a number of French journalists—'How can we interfere in a quarrel between a country of 70,000,000 and a country of 7,000,000, and with all the guns on the side of the former?' With Mr. Eden in office, Hitler was still kept guessing. But Mr. Chamberlain's speech of February 22 gave him a completely free hand.

The speech was as bad as anyone in France could have anticipated. For Mr. Chamberlain said:

If I am right, as I am confident I am, in saying that the League as constituted to-day is unable to provide collective security for anybody, then I say we must try not to delude small weak nations into thinking that they will be protected by the League against aggression—and acting accordingly when we know that nothing of the kind can be expected.

And on the previous day Mr. Chamberlain had expounded a theory which, for all his friendly references to France, disturbed many Frenchmen—for it looked exactly like a return to the Four-Power Pact of unholy memory:

The peace of Europe must depend upon the attitude of the four major Powers—Germany, Italy, France and ourselves. For ourselves, we are linked to France by common ideals of democracy, of liberty, and Parliamentary government. France need not fear that the resignation of my right honourable friend upon this issue signifies any departure from the policy of the closest friendship with France of which he has been such a distinguished exponent.

On the other side we find Italy and Germany also linked by affinities of outlook and in the form of their government. The question that we have to think of is this: Are we to allow these two pairs of nations to go on glowering at one another across the frontier, allowing the feeling between the two sides to become more and more embittered, until at last the barriers are broken down and the conflict begins which many

[1] *Manchester Guardian,* February 22.

think would mark the end of civilization? Or can we bring them to an understanding of one another's aims and objects and to such discussion as may lead to their final settlement?

.   .   .   .   .   .

When one looks back on it, one realizes that it was this Chamberlain speech which acted like a signal in France for letting loose all the defeatist propaganda which was to have such a profound effect in the months that followed.

.   .   .   .   .   .

The great foreign affairs debate at the Chamber that began five days after Mr. Eden's resignation is of particular interest; for it shows that French opinion was still, on the face of it, almost unanimous in reaffirming France's 'traditional' policy. But only on the face of it.

.   .   .   .   .   .

Under the Front Populaire Governments of 1936–7 Flandin became one of the principal leaders of the Opposition; and it was towards the end of 1937, after a visit to Berlin, that he began to preach openly his New Policy of 'retrenchment.' Flandin, who had never succeeded in impressing himself upon the public's attention, had now discovered a way of being 'taked about.' The reactionary Press eagerly published his articles, and, thanks to important connections in London, he was also given a great deal of publicity in England. Though at first seemingly hostile to the Daladier Government—for the Premier had a certain distrust of him—he was going to be on increasingly good terms with M. Bonnet, the Foreign Minister. If in the February debate M. Flandin acted as Mr. Chamberlain's whipping boy, in the year that followed he was to go a good deal beyond Mr. Chamberlain's 'appeasement' policy.

The debate opened with a speech by M. Pezet, a member of the Catholic *Démocrates Populaires*, a vice-president of the Foreign Affairs Committee, and a personal friend of Schuschnigg's. Large sections of the French Catholics were deeply concerned about the fate of Catholic Austria.

Pezet, who had, clearly, given much thought to the international situation, plunged straight into the subject; and sounded in the very first sentence the Chamberlain-*versus*-anti-Chamberlain *motif*; though Mr. Chamberlain was disguised as M. Flandin.

'Mr. Winston Churchill,' Mr. Pezet said, 'has highly praised the valour and the power of the French Army; while M. Flandin [Mr.

Chamberlain] is basing his policy on the temporary abdication of France and on our present helplessness. . . . The French Government is speaking well and firmly; but it is acting without authority; and it has had bad luck.'

This was obviously an allusion to Mr. Eden's resignation.

M. Pezet recalled how M. Delbos had said: 'It would be tragic if France were in the dilemma of abandoning to their fate the States of Central Europe, in spite of our agreements, and of coming into conflict with England in our determination to be faithful to our allies.'

M. Pezet then came to the Austrian problem and to the Berchtesgaden ultimatum of a fortnight before.

But suppose the Government is unable to give a clear answer, suppose it feels obliged to cover up the truth behind a screen of pious words, and suppose that in reality we are going to be compelled to change completely our foreign policy—then, I think, it is only right that I should say to you: this change will in reality have come about as a result of Lord Halifax's visit to Berlin, of M. Stoyadinovitch's visit to Berlin, and of M. Flandin's visit to Berlin—what a succession of journeys to the banks of the Spree! Before these journeys and before M. Delbos's tour in Central Europe the successive Governments of France always spoke a different language.

M. Pezet added that there were plans which had gone far beyond the Anschluss; M. Beck, he said, had already talked to M. de Kanya about a common Polish-Hungarian frontier in sub-Carpathic Russia! In short, *the dismemberment of Czechoslovakia was already being planned.*
And Austria?
Mussolini, M. Pezet said, had informed M. Stoyadinovitch in December: 'I am still against the Anschluss, but I have my hands tied.'
There followed the familiar argument about the road to India; a road on which Austria was the first and most essential obstacle. 'How blind England is!' M. Pezet cried, and, after recalling all the guarantees given by England to support Austrian independence, he said:

I cannot recall without some melancholy and a touch of irony the words used by Sir John Simon when in announcing the results of the Anglo-French talks of February 3, 1935, on the necessity of guaranteeing as well as possible the independence of Austria: 'We have the reputation' (he then said) '—and I trust it is a well-deserved reputation—for keeping our word.' . . . Are France and England to turn a deaf ear to the appeal Chancellor Schuschnigg addressed to them yesterday? Oh, I know only too well that certain members of this

House will say to me: 'Read Mr. Chamberlain's speech. Does it sound as if we could expect any help from England if we tried to save Austria and Czechoslovakia?'

I only say that these small nations have been deluded for nineteen years; they have been told to hold out, and resist and organize themselves; they have been told that they would be helped if the occasion arose. And now when the moment has come, are we to drop them? That is what I call 'deluding' them.

If the same technique of pressure and interference that Germany is now applying to Austria is also applied to Czechoslovakia—will France carry out her obligations under the Franco-Czech treaties of January 25, 1924 and October 16, 1925? What advice did M. Delbos give the Czechs? Did he advise them to resist or to yield and resign themselves?

His remark produced what the *Journal Officiel* called *mouvements divers*. If I remember rightly, the main reaction was to say that 'the Czechs would naturally be expected to resist.'

M. Pezet's speech created a deep impression at the Chamber. It left an undercurrent of anxiety.

The suggestion of France's helplessness in the face of the Berchtesgaden ultimatum was very apparent. Peaceful pressure *might* have worked—but no longer with Mr. Chamberlain in charge of British foreign policy.

M. Marcel Boucher and other speakers of the Right took a more partisan line. If France was unable to help Austria it was because she had lost Mussolini's friendship. If only France had stuck to Stresa, and had not associated herself with the folly of sanctions!

These French illusions about Stresa were pathetic; and almost to this day it is impossible to convince many Frenchmen that Stresa was nothing but a piece of Italian trickery; for, whether he was later to get a free hand in Abyssinia or not, there is nothing to show that the Duce had the slightest intention of sticking to the 'Stresa Front'.

The Socialists were poorly represented in that debate. M. Blum's wife had died at the end of January (a reason, by the way, why M. Blum had not persisted in his Cabinet-making shortly before), and the Socialist speaker was M. Salomon Grumbach, a man of great ability, but one whose rather unfortunate music-hall manner irritated the Right, who on several occasions broke out into loud anti-Jewish abuse.

M. Grumbach quoted large chunks of *Mein Kampf* and attacked M. Flandin.

'For some days past,' M. Grumbach said, 'a big campaign is being

145

conducted by a former Premier. Being a former Premier his responsibility is three times heavier than if he were an ordinary mortal like myself. . . . I can hear his words in every language on the wireless, and see them in every foreign paper I can read. And I am profoundly convinced that if the world is left with the impression that the statements of M. Pierre-Etienne Flandin are of considerable importance, the danger to peace would be enormous, for it would be an encouragement to all the enemies of peace, and to those who wish to demoralize the French nation.' (Cheers on extreme Left. Protests on Right and Centre.)

Not that the Right and Centre were unanimous. The next speaker was M. Ybarnégaray, of the P.S.F. (the former Croix de Feu), and the chief representative in the Chamber of Colonel de la Rocque; and he joined in the attack on M. Flandin—and on Mr. Chamberlain for that matter. For M. Flandin—in himself a person of no great importance—acted at the Chamber as though he were the representative of Mr. Chamberlain.

'There is no lack of people,' M. Ybarnégaray said, 'who will crowd the waiting-rooms of Ribbentrop, Goebbels and Goering, and who, without any mandate, and without any authority from the Government, go there, like so many pilgrims, to collect promises and assurances. Peace? Yes. There is not a Frenchman who does not want peace passionately. But peace at any price—No!'

The Croix de Feu man, who was also one of the most respected men at the Chamber, was cheered by the entire Left and 'on various benches of the Right and Centre.'

M. Ybarnégaray then spoke of Austria and of Hitler's ultimatum to Schuschnigg:

He was given three days. And during these three days not a word of moral support came to him from London or Paris, or anywhere. It is a regrettable silence, but one that Hitler anticipated when, at Berchtesgaden, he said sneeringly to Schuschnigg: 'Are you counting on France and England? You are wrong. When I occupied the Rhineland in March 1936, they didn't budge. Do you imagine they are going to budge for you?'

If I ask this question about Austria, it is because *you are now in a far better position than you may be very shortly, when Czechoslovakia is, in turn, involved.*

The Anschluss has not yet been achieved. And I persist in believing that an energetic reaction by France and Britain could yet prevent it. *To threaten Chancellor Schuschnigg is one thing, to decide on a mili-*

tary invasion of Austria is quite another, and I am not sure that Hitler would risk it. Are France and England ready to unite on the Danube, as they have united on the Rhine and to defend nations whose independence they have guaranteed?

If so, let them say so openly; *everything may yet be saved. If not, let them say so just as openly. But in that case, it will be a different policy, a policy of weakness and abdication—a policy of retrenchment behind the Maginot Line.* If that is your policy, say so, M. Delbos!

All that, as it would be called to-day, was good anti-Munich stuff; and M. Ybarnégaray stated the dilemma very clearly. Only, like many other men of the Right, he continued to entertain illusions about Italy: 'If we had not helped the Negus,' he said in effect, 'there would have been no Berchtesgaden ultimatum.'

The debate continued. M. Mistler, the young president of the Foreign Affairs Committee, who was later to be among the most ardent defenders of a Munich policy, spoke. On the whole, he agreed with M. Ybarnégaray; but there was a difference in tone, a difference in emphasis. The speech was, somehow, more philosophical; M. Mistler dwelt on the unfortunate fact that the democracies lacked both the organization and the dynamic vigour of Germany; and said that France ought to pull herself together. And he added cautiously:

But, there are certain vital areas—the Rhine, the Mediterranean and Central Europe—where, after consulting our allies, we must say that there is a point at which great risks begin, and beyond which this country must throw in her whole weight.

'Only'—and here M. Mistler became even more cautious—'we cannot pursue such a policy alone, and we must be sure to act in close agreement with Great Britain.'

And still more cautiously he added:

But I think it would be a mistake to be in too great a hurry in adopting an attitude which would not be without danger.

M. Péri, the Communist speaker, quoted Mr. Churchill on several occasions, complained that the Government had neglected the Soviet Pact, and spoke scathingly of the City of London and 'those who advise you to adopt the theories of the grouse-shooting pro-German Press lords of Great Britain.' He was loudly cheered by the Left, while several members of the Right shouted: *'Sac au dos!'*

M. de Monzie, who was to be another ardent protagonist of a Munich policy later in the year, spoke quite differently in February.

147

He admitted that Austria had always striven to unite with Germany; and the Austrian Socialists were in 1931 among the strongest supporters of the Anschluss. But now the position was different.

And it was particularly sinister, that at such a moment, M. de Monzie said, Hitler should have proclaimed his intention to 'protect' his racial brethren. An astonishing pretension. It was as if France suddenly claimed a right to exercise control over the French Canadians!

I shall not be childish enough to imagine that this revival of the national sentiment in Austria is sufficient to resist violence coming from outside. But what shall we do? Shall we do nothing? I do not think that is M. Flandin's intention. Yet M. Flandin has been talking of 'retrenchment.' And he has expressed these views in a dangerous way; especially *because his views reflect the feelings of many people in this country who see in every diplomatic démarche a risk of war.*

M. Flandin tells us: France will become more Imperial than European. I reply to this that there can be no Empire without a head. What would be the British Commonwealth without the greatness of England, without these forces of cohesion that exist in the City and in English life, without that head which rules the body?

A French Empire run by a Little France—a France without European prestige? No, it's out of the question.

And M. de Monzie's remedy was simple. Apart from the Franco-Soviet Pact, which, he said, ought to be developed into real military alliance,[2] he said that Mr. Chamberlain's England had entered into negotiations with Italy; it was for France to join in. And he quoted with approval Mr. Churchill's phrase: 'Oh, if Italy will consent to return to the Brenner, I'll forgive her everything.'

M. Marin, the Right-Wing leader, and once an ardent supporter of the Ruhr policy, and a man who had ceaselessly warned France against Germany when Germany was still disarmed, also saw the last hope in an attempt to 'return to Stresa.'

The two speakers who in that February debate came nearest to the 'Munich' outlook were M. Montigny—who is, as it were, M. Caillaux's representative in the Chamber—and, naturally, M. Flandin.

M. Montigny said:

Since, rightly or wrongly, we have not created an army fitted for our foreign policy, and since it would take years to create one, we must—unless we are mad—adopt a foreign policy compatible with our military possibilities.

[2] Turning to M. Péri, M. de Monzie remarked that although the Communists were now lamenting the departure of Mr. Eden, it was Mr. Eden who had always opposed a regular Franco-Russian alliance.

He refrained, however, from revealing the enormous implications of his phrase.

The biggest uproar during the debate occurred when towards the end of the second day M. Herriot, the Speaker, announced:

'*La parole est à M. Flandin.*'

The Left, and particularly the Communists, rose to their feet and greeted M. Flandin with the Nazi salute, shouting: 'Heil Hitler!' 'Heil Flandin!' and '*A Berlin!*' and 'Seyss-Inquart!' The Right and part of the Centre cheered.

At last silence was restored and M. Flandin spoke.

This debate, he said, was the gravest that had been conducted at the Chamber since the War. One had to get down to fundamentals. Events in Europe were developing in such a way that France was faced with the choice between war and peace.

'For some weeks past,' he continued, 'I have been treated as the mouthpiece of pro-German Press lords; I am called pro-Nazi, and pro-Fascist; and that reminds me of the time when I was treated as an agent of the Soviets.'[3]

After saying, with his hand on his heart, that he had never cared for anything but the interest of his country (loud cries from the Left of '*Aéropostale! Aéropostale!*'),[4] M. Flandin gave a long quotation from 'the noble speech of Sir (*sic*) Neville Chamberlain.'

Sir Neville Chamberlain knows that the time has come to act. Because peace—the Peace of Versailles—is on its deathbed.'

France, M. Flandin said, had concluded a number of pacts. All these pacts and alliances were concluded within the framework of the League Covenant. What was the value of these pacts when the League Covenant was dead? France, as he had said some time ago, could not accept the risk of acting single-handedly the policeman of Europe.

'When Mr. Baldwin proclaimed that Great Britain's frontier was on the Rhine, he entered into a serious obligation.

Some of you gentlemen complain because British opinion is rather reserved about intervening in Europe. But remember that Britain is rearming, while our armaments works, our economy, our finances and our morale, all need adjusting. It is not until these are adjusted that you can try, together with England, to practise a policy of intervention.

In the circumstances, let us, for heaven's sake, stop striking heroic

[3] M. Flandin was Foreign Minister in February 1936 when the Soviet Pact was ratified.

[4] A reference to a financial scandal in which he was alleged to have been involved.

attitudes because Austria is being *gleichgeschaltet*. When the question of peace and war arises, nothing can be worse than not to look the facts in the face.'

After that M. Flandin spoke about Italy. In January 1935 M. Laval had signed an agreement, which included a Franco-Italian convention for the defence of Austrian independence. The Abyssinian affair had ruined everything, and since then France had done nothing to restore friendly relations with Italy.

What, then, was M. Flandin's attitude to, say, a German attack on Czechoslovakia? He was cautious, very cautious on this point—even though he had already questioned the value of pacts 'within the framework of the League Covenant' at a time when this Covenant no longer meant anything.

> '*Messieurs*,' he said, 'far be it from me to suggest that we should repudiate our obligations; but we ought to make sure whether we are able to observe them.'

M. Flandin admitted that Germany was 'a nation of conquerors; but France also was a nation of soldiers.' And he tried to console himself with the following thought:

> 'European hegemony may be the dream of an ambitious dictator; but it was also the dream of Napoleon, and his imperialist attempt failed when it was faced with a coalition. No attempt at European hegemony can succeed any more than it did under Napoleon.'

And then he came to the Maginot Line.

> 'To-day we are sheltered behind the Maginot Line. If ever we are attacked, we shall be strong enough to hold out until the freedom-loving countries of Europe come to our aid as they did in 1914.'

M. Flandin, aware of the hostility of the Chamber, was more cautious in his choice of words than he had been in speaking before the Foreign Affairs Committee in December. His weakest argument, of course, was the argument about the Maginot Line and about the coalition that would inevitably come to France's aid were she attacked. For in 1914 France was supported from the very outset by a coalition, and Germany had to fight on two fronts—which might not be the same next time.

M. Reynaud undertook the task of smashing M. Flandin's arguments:

> 'We all want peace,' M. Reynaud said, 'and it is only a question of method; and let no one come and tell me that I represent the "War Party."'

The abdication of France in Central Europe would be fatal. For,

'having, without firing a single shot, gained control of Rumanian oil, Hungarian wheat, and the Czechoslovak war industry, and having established a common frontier with Italy, what would Germany do next?

You say: there is the Maginot Line. Quite right, and no one knows better than I do how precious it is in our national defence. *But there is not a single expert who will claim that any line of fortifications can resist indefinitely against an indefinite accumulation of tanks and artillery.*

Are we then to yield without war in the name of 'fairness'? The Germans will say that it is only fair that they should have colonies, and the iron ore of Lorraine, and that they should be handed over Alsace.

And then the day will come when our colossal neighbour will make things so unbearable to the pride of a noble people that we will be thrown into war, without friends, without honour.'

M. Reynaud deplored the departure of Mr. Eden, but believed that England would not stand aside if France defended her vital interest in Europe. 'England cannot afford to see France crushed, whatever may be the personal feelings of the men in charge of her public affairs. *Only we must remember that in the matter of Central Europe it is France who must take the initiative and take her responsibilities.*'

M. Flandin fidgeted uneasily on his bench.

M. Reynaud then added:

'Between the movements of opinion in the United States and the admirable spirit of the working class of Vienna there is a powerful moral link. What the false realists do not see is the greatest of all realities— the moral reality.'

One of these 'moral realities' was the moral unity of the French people. Alluding to the probable formation in the near future of a large National Government, M. Reynaud said:

'The world will soon be startled to see that it is impossible either internally or internationally to speculate on France's lack of unity.'

A large part of the Chamber rose and cheered.

Though M. Reynaud was not in the Government, this was the best 'government' speech.

M. Delbos, a tired and disappointed man, was less dazzling—though his arguments were of the same order.

M. Delbos spoke respectfully of Mr. Chamberlain, but preferred not to dwell on the implications of Mr. Eden's departure.

And while—significantly enough—he refrained from saying much about Austria—he was completely categorical about Czechoslovakia:

'And I desire to say once again that our obligations to Czechoslovakia will, if it comes to the point, be faithfully observed.'

And, later in the debate, M. Chautemps, the Premier, reaffirmed M. Delbos's pledge to Czechoslovakia and attacked the defeatists.

M. Chautemps, who, in the Spanish affair, had been all along a 'non-interventionist at any price,' was also going to be one of the principal supporters of a Munich policy in September.

The motion on which the Chamber voted said:

The Chamber approves the statements of the Government and trusts that it will safeguard national dignity, assure the maintenance of peace, and the respect of treaties within the framework of collective security and the League of Nations.

This motion was adopted by 439 votes to two. But—there were about 150 abstentions. And these abstentions—though they also included simply opponents of the Government, such as M. Ybarnégaray of the P.S.F. —also included a great many people who were already *Munichois* at heart. Openly, at any rate, the 'defeatism' on the Left was not going to develop until later. It is true that nobody was openly against the repudiation of treaties—a point M. Paul Reynaud emphasized; and yet— M. Flandin was cheered by a large part of the Right and Centre. And what they were cheering was not so much his cautious platitudes as their grim implications.

But below the surface there was a feeling of deep uncertainty in France; and, when, a fortnight later, the Anschluss came, France did not budge. During the Chamber debate no answer was given by the Government to the question: 'How are you going to help Austria?'

March 11 provided the answer: 'We cannot help Austria.'

IV. FRANCE AFTER THE ANSCHLUSS

THE SHORT-LIVED BLUM GOVERNMENT

NEWS, more alarming every day, had been coming from Austria since the Berchtesgaden ultimatum.

And yet, somehow, nobody believed that Germany would *invade* Austria. Austria might be placed under Nazi control; Seyss-Inquart might play an increasingly large part; but the semblance of Austrian independence would somehow be observed. Hitler, it was believed, would be afraid of offending Mussolini too much if he invaded Austria. A *putsch*, perhaps; but not an invasion.

Almost every day I used to see at the Chamber a well-known liberal Austrian journalist. 'Austria has still a lot of life in her,' he would say, 'just you wait and see.' And on that dramatic day when Schuschnigg announced the Freedom Plebiscite for the following Sunday, my Austrian friend was triumphant—'Didn't I tell you! Didn't I tell you!' he cried, almost weeping. 'You'll see, we'll get a seventy per cent majority against the Nazis on Sunday! Monarchists, Catholics, Jews, Socialists, Communists—everybody is behind Schuschnigg. The Socialist trade unions are being revived—after the plebiscite we'll have a real Democratic Austria! *Es ist ja wunderschön!*'

Two days before the plebiscite, while Schuschnigg had become a national hero in Vienna, the German troops moved across the frontier. It created a fearful shock in France—even among the people who had as good as accepted the Anschluss as inevitable. People somehow continued to think of Central Europe in terms of German 'claims' and 'rights'; they did not visualize armies crossing frontiers. It was something new and fearful. The brutality of the whole thing, the cynical reasons given by Germany for invading Austria, the atrocities that closely followed upon the invasion—all this was deeply disturbing to the French.

But while French opinion was shocked, and the French Press was unanimous in proclaiming its indignation, the invasion of Austria had, at the same time, a strange psychological effect on the country. War, which had been an abstraction in most Frenchmen's minds, had now become a reality. France lost nearly one and a half million men in the last war; and rural and provincial France especially, which is not accustomed to reasoning in big international terms, was tired of war, and sick at the thought of war. The invasion of Austria aroused indignation at first, but also gave many 'that sinking feeling.' Was war becoming a tangible reality once again? There had been Spain, of course—but that was, after all, a 'civil war.'

And it was this 'sinking feeling' which was going to be exploited to the full by the disciples of M. Flandin, and—by Fascist and German propaganda. On February 21 and 22 Mr. Chamberlain proclaimed his lack of interest in Central Europe; but the effect of the Anschluss was to make not only England, but even the Chamberlain Government more Europe-minded. In France, significantly enough, the Anschluss had rather the opposite effect. It is extremely curious that it was after the Anschluss, and not before, that France witnessed the first explosions of that defeatist campaign which was to gather such impetus during September.

The campaign was at its height in March and April. It was conducted at that time almost solely by the Right-Wing Press.

'Will you fight for the Czechs?' *Gringoire* wrote on April 9—the very *Gringoire* which had exclaimed three years earlier: 'Will you fight for the Negus?' Czechoslovakia was described as being 'not a country at all'; as 'the worst abortion that had come out of Woodrow Wilson's brain' (the writer of the article, incidentally, forgot that at the Peace Conference it was the French who insisted upon the 'strategic' Sudeten frontier, and that they were doing so against the advice of the Americans); the anti-Czech campaign conducted by *Candide* and *Gringoire* was also supported by the *Action Française*, by the *Jour*, and by a number of provincial papers like the *Petit Provençal*, the *Eclaireur de Nice* and others.

Why the League, which could have become the best safeguard of French security if properly handled, had always been an object of aversion and hostility to the French Right is something of a mystery—except that its basis was democratic, and so, distasteful. And although the *Action Française* was not so emphatic about 'dropping' Czechoslovakia as, say, *Gringoire*, and was inclined to say that France could do nothing because she had gone all mouldy with Republicanism, it was still clear that Charles Maurras had made up his mind not to raise a finger for the Czechs. Such *nationalisme intégral* was surprising—except that in reality the *Action Française* had long ago ceased to be a Nationalist paper, still less a Royalist paper, and had become completely Fascist in mentality—an interesting point strongly emphasized by Georges Bidault, the Catholic writer, in the *Europe Nouvelle*.

The anti-Czech campaign, though still limited to only a relatively small number of papers in March and April, was sufficiently violent to prompt M. de Kerillis in the *Epoque* to sound the alarm. *'Monsieur Hitler, ne vous gênez pas, prenez Prague!'* he wrote on April 17.

'Dear Mr. Hitler,' he wrote, 'France is the ally of Czechoslovakia, but she is determined not to keep her promise and her solemn undertaking to defend her. So don't worry about us!'

Here, for instance, is a Company, with headquarters in Marseilles, who have just sent me a sumptuous illustrated tract, and who tell me that they have sent this work to all the notables of the 2,800 communes of the nine departments of South Eastern France—'to all the mayors, assistant mayors, village councillors, priests, teachers, doctors, veterinary surgeons, hairdressers, stationmasters and tradesmen.' This tract has only one object; and that is to explain to the French that Czechoslovakia is an artificial country, unfit to live, and unfit to be defended, and which Germany can grab at a moment's notice.

And there followed the usual Kerillis tableau of Europe after the fall of Czechoslovakia:

Bohemia and Slovakia are a bastion, a great junction that commands all the roads of Europe. With Czechoslovakia under her rule, Germany will be able to encircle Poland and Hungary, and gain an outlet to the reserves of oil and wheat in Rumania and Russia. If Hitler takes Prague, he will, in fact, have become master of Europe.

Is it to be a bad Frenchman, or a 'friend of Moscow' to remember that for the last thousand years our ancestors have struggled in order to prevent German hegemony over Europe—a hegemony which would mean the end of France?

M. de Kerillis, since 1936 Nationalist Deputy for Neuilly, a youngish-looking man with a peaky little face, was going to become the chief 'warmonger' of the Right during the September crisis. Kerillis was also the only deputy of the Right who, on October 4, 1938, refused to vote for Munich. The only others who voted 'against Munich' were—the Communists.

.   .   .   .

That respectable organ of old-fashioned Radicalism, the *Dépêche* of Toulouse, the organ of the Sarraut family, wrote one day in April:

We are literally encircled and reduced to the bare possibility of strategic defence. We are on the defensive on our Continental frontier, on sea, and in our colonies. We are not professional pessimists; but it is no use denying facts.

155

And in a technical article in the *Journal des Débats*, General Duval used arguments of the same sort.

But the greatest windfall of all came to the anti-Czechs from the *Temps*, in the form of an article signed by Professor Joseph Barthelémy, the leading authority on French constitutional law.

Professor Barthelémy argued that since the Franco-Czech alliance was linked with the League Covenant, and formed part of the Locarno system of treaties, and that since the Locarno system had been repudiated by Germany, France was no longer under any legal obligation to go to the aid of Czechoslovakia.

> Is it necessary that three million Frenchmen, all the youth of our universities, of our schools, our countryside, and our factories should be sacrificed in order to maintain three million Germans under Czech sovereignty?[1]

Coming from so responsible a writer and so responsible a paper, the article created an uproar not unlike the row that was caused in London by the famous *Times* leader at the beginning of September, advocating the cession of the Sudetenland to Germany. The Barthelémy article caused great alarm in Czechoslovakia; for thousands of copies of it, translated into German or bad Czech, were distributed in pamphlet form throughout Czechoslovakia under the title: *Czechs! France says: 'Nothing Doing!'*

The day the article appeared, M. Osusky, the dapper Czech Minister, dashed in great agitation to the Quai d'Orsay, and a few days later the *Temps*, presumably at the urgent request of M. Bonnet, the new Foreign Minister, published an editorial in which it flatly contradicted all M. Barthelémy's legal arguments.

And, alluding to M. Barthelémy's reference to the Locarno Pact, the *Temps* went on to say that this was irrelevant for two reasons:

> First, because France has never considered her agreement with Czechoslovakia as being simply a little screw in the Locarno machine. Secondly, because the violation by Germany of the Locarno agreement on March 7, 1936 does not mean that the other signatories of the agreement are thereby freed of their obligations; and this point of view was definitely accepted in London on March 22, 1936, when the relations between France and Great Britain were rebuilt on the basis of Locarno.

However, by the end of April the campaign began to subside—partly as a result of the Anglo-French meeting in London on April 29. Even

[1] *Le Temps*, April 12. The author is now Minister of Justice at Vichy.

Gringoire published a strong article by M. Tardieu upholding Czechoslovakia and expressing strong disapproval of the anti-Czech line taken by the paper during the previous weeks.

The great part of the Press—particularly the Left Press—had continued to uphold Czechoslovakia throughout March and April; the only important exception among the papers of the Left being *Syndicats*, the trade union weekly of strong pacifist tendencies, edited by M. René Belin, one of the 'moderate' leaders of the C.G.T.

    .   .   .   .

There was something tragic and slightly absurd about the second Blum Government. The Chautemps Government resigned with great suddenness a few days before the German march into Austria. While this march was in progress, France was without a Government. The task of forming a Government was entrusted by the President to M. Léon Blum, who, as leader of the Socialist Party, was nominally responsible for the fall of the last Cabinet. In January, with an eye on the international situation, he had already attempted to form a national Government 'around the Front Populaire' stretching 'from Reynaud to Thorez,' that is, from the democratically minded elements of the Centre to the Communist Party who, though not strictly democratic, had on innumerable occasions proclaimed their loyalty to democracy 'in the present circumstances.' One of M. Blum's motives in proposing such a National Government was to show that, if in emergencies in the past, a 'National Government' invariably meant a National Government controlled by the Right, it was possible, for once, to form a 'National Government,' two years after the election, which would not be in contradiction with the verdict of the Electorate. It would, for once, be a predominantly Left 'National Government,' and could still claim direct descent from the Front Populaire. The plan failed; partly because the entry of M. Reynaud into such a Government was vetoed by the Alliance Démocratique, the party to which he belonged, but in which M. Flandin pulled the strings; and partly also because many of the Radicals were reluctant to be associated with the Communists; they thought it would not look respectable; their Front Populaire ardour had been damped by eighteen months of Front Populaire Government. Instead, M. Chautemps formed his short-lived second Cabinet, which was to resign on the eve of the Anschluss.

French opinion had been deeply stirred by events in Austria, and M. Blum thought that the time was now *really* ripe for a National Government. While the German troops were marching into Austria, he called a meeting of the National Council of the Socialist Party, and implored them to authorize him to form a Government on an even wider basis than that which he had proposed in January. It was no longer to be limited to the 'sincerely democratic' parties; it would include everybody. Instead of *'de Reynaud à Thorez,'* it would now be *'de Marin à Thorez,'* and would so include even the die-hard Conservatives. Only the outspoken Fascists would be left out.

The Socialists are the largest party in this country. And M. Blum asked that he be given a 'wider mandate, an unlimited mandate.' He was asking for it, 'in the interests of the party, of Socialism, of the country, and of peace.' If he dwelt so much on 'Socialism' and the 'Front Populaire,' etc., it was because he was, after all, speaking to a Socialist audience.

He received full support from everybody—from Paul Faure, the Secretary General of the Party, and from the impetuous Zyromski, from the outset an enemy of Blum's non-intervention policy in Spain.

Only the revolutionary Pivertistes—a group closely akin to the Trotzkyists, and who were to leave the Socialist Party a few months later—refused to accede to Blum's request.

But it came to nothing. On March 12, M. Blum called together the representatives of the Right Parties and addressed a warm appeal to them.

> Let me say this: in case of war you are going to mobilize the Communists as anybody else. The Communists, after all, represent 1,500,000 workers, peasants and small tradesmen. You have no right to throw them out. You will be in need of them when you will want to speed up armaments production. You will need their help as you will need the help of the C.G.T. What are you afraid of? Are you afraid that they will weigh heavily on foreign policy? But remember that, as the head of the Government, I preserved my complete independence on the question of Spain. Some of you have said that the presence of Communists in the French Government would have a bad effect abroad. It is an impious and abominable argument, for France cannot accept any veto from a foreign Power.[2]

M. Blum admitted that it would be impossible for such a National Government to be in agreement on everything. But he was prepared to make the widest concessions. He said that the Right would choose the Finance Minister.

Many members of the Opposition were, in spite of themselves, moved

[2] An interesting remark in the light of Hitler's veto against Mr. Churchill, Mr. Eden and Mr. Duff Cooper in his Saarbrücken speech ten days after Munich.

and impressed. M. Paul Reynaud warmly supported M. Blum. The impetuous Henri de Kerillis rushed up to M. Blum, shook him by the hand and said: *'Monsieur Blum, vous êtes un grand Français.'* The Catholic *Démocrates Populaires*, profoundly shocked by events in Austria, passed a resolution saying that they would do nothing to hinder M. Blum in his task. But M. Marin, M. Flandin and M. Fabry carried the day. M. Flandin was particularly critical. No, the entry of the Communists into the French Government, however 'National', would deeply shock Mr. Chamberlain, and cause a breach with England. Germany and Italy would become openly hostile. He dwelt particularly on the deplorable impression it would create in England.

If the Right sabotaged Blum's plan it was largely for internal reasons. They knew that the Front Populaire, left to itself, would soon die a natural death, and that by agreeing to Blum's National Government they would prolong the presence of the Left Wing parties on the Government bench.

Having failed in his 'National Government', Blum formed a Government which was obviously unsuitable for the occasion. It was a plain Socialist-Radical Government, almost the very image of the first Front Populaire Government of June 1936. It lived only three weeks—and an unhappy life it was. Encouraged by the presence of a Socialist at the head of the Government, and provoked by the deliberately uncompromising attitude of the big employers (who had their own fingers in the political pie), the men in the Paris engineering industry went on strike; and for the first time since 1936 stay-in strikes broke out again on a very extensive scale. At one moment 150,000 men were on strike, and the unfortunate French aeroplane industry was brought to a complete standstill.

Blum, though supported loyally by Daladier, the War Minister, was in a desperate plight. The Senate, which had already thrown out his last Government, was determined to turn this one out without delay. Blum was determined to die fighting—or rather, his Socialist colleagues insisted that the Senate's challenge be accepted. They had the mistaken idea that the overthrow of yet another Left Government by the Senate could become the basis for a great anti-Senate campaign in the country.

Blum's plenary powers bill was a bold enterprise, and was intended, among other things, as a great financial sermon to the country. It went on the assumption that France could not go on living from hand to mouth as she had done for the last seven years—with a little inflation here, and a little borrowing here, there and everywhere. In the process her public debt had accumulated sky-high, and she was rolling down the slippery slope towards complete bankruptcy. The reliance on 'confidence' had been overdone; Blum argued that even in the most favourable conditions 'confidence'—that is, the repatriation of exported capital estimated at eighty milliard francs and the 'unfreezing' of the hoarded capital—could meet only a small part of the Treasury's borrowing needs. France, he said, would still have to continue borrowing forty or fifty milliard francs a year, with immense rearmament bills accumulating. In fact, he was proposing to put France on what might be called a semi-war basis, complete with a small capital levy, a camouflaged form of exchange control (if it meant a breach of the Tripartite agreement— one of the main causes of the collapse of the Front Populaire programme —it couldn't be helped), a large variety of taxes, and—this was to be Labour's share in the 'all-round sacrifices'—a readjustment of the forty-hour week. Trade and production would be revived by a wide expansion of credit. Here was planned economy, an economy reminiscent in some ways of German and Italian methods.

The plan was accepted by a small majority of the Chamber, but rejected by an enormous majority of the Senate. As in June 1937, M. Caillaux made another scathing attack on M. Blum and the Front Populaire, and accused M. Blum of wanting to ruin the French peasantry with his capital levy. M. Blum argued in vain that T. G. Barman in *The Times* had described his plan as the first constructive financial programme France had produced since Poincaré. M. Caillaux merely snorted *'Diable!'* which might be translated 'like hell it is!'

That day—it was April 8—outside the Luxembourg Gardens, two or three thousand workmen—most of them Pivertistes, who were distributing leaflets in favour of the Spanish POUM—demonstrated against the Senate; but it was a tame demonstration; it was too obvious that Blum was doomed to defeat. With the strike movement in full swing, the country was not behind Blum, and was waiting anxiously for more stable conditions.

M. Paul-Boncour was M. Blum's Foreign Minister, and his policy was intended to be a brake on 'Chamberlainism.' M. Paul-Boncour was a devotee of the League of Nations, and although he had always been considered rather a light-weight, the Left watched this resistance to Chamberlain with approval. As John Whitaker rather unkindly remarked at the time: 'Europe must have fallen pretty low if we have to pin our last hopes on Paul-Boncour!'

The foreign policy of the Government was outlined in the Ministerial Declaration and in the speech M. Blum made immediately after it.

France is unanimous in her passionate desire for peace.

We shall increase France's armaments . . . and endeavour to strengthen our friendships and alliances. Our slogan is: peace with honour and liberty. International morality and solidarity are our principle. The *rapprochement* of all forces of peace for the sake of collective security continues to be France's aim.

M. Paul-Boncour was keenly aware of the menace to Czechoslovakia. He did not think of Czechoslovakia in 'Runciman' terms; Czechoslovakia, to him, was still the Island of Democracy in the totalitarian sea of Central Europe, and a supremely valuable military ally of France. In the first week in April he summoned to Paris the French Ambassadors and Ministers in Bucharest, Warsaw, Moscow, Belgrade, Prague and Budapest, and instructed them to find out what military assistance, if any, could be obtained from the Governments to which they were accredited in the event of a German attack on Czechoslovakia. He was making a last desperate attempt to revive mutual assistance and collective security in Central and Eastern Europe, and was ready to guarantee France's leadership in this revived collective security. This in itself was enough to infuriate the Press of the Right and to give impetus to the anti-Czech campaign.

M. Paul-Boncour took little notice of Mr. Chamberlain; and rather went on the assumption that England needed France as much as France needed England, and that, if it came to the worst, England could not stay out. But, if collective security could be achieved it would *not* come to the 'worst'. At the same time he was not above making advances to Italy, and as good as promised to recognize the Abyssinian conquest, and to send an Ambassador to Rome.

Apart from Central Europe, M. Paul-Boncour's great concern was Spain. The outlook for the Spanish Government was grimmer than it had ever been.

Paul-Boncour 'relaxed' the frontier control of armaments, and large quantities of guns and machine guns and munitions were sent across the Pyrenees. Paul-Boncour hardly made a secret of it; he considered it to be a matter of life and death for France. It was alleged in the Press of the Right that he was actually proposing to send several thousand French troops to Catalonia to stop the Franco advance; it was said that the French General Staff had turned the scheme down. Whether the proposal was actually made is difficult to discover; but Paul-Boncour almost certainly considered it. He also considered the occupation of certain vital strategic points on the French sea route to North Africa—notably Cartagena and Minorca; but the British Government would not hear of it.

For it was at that time that Mr. Chamberlain was busy preparing his famous Anglo-Italian agreement, and support for the Spanish Government was the last thing he wanted. What he was hoping for was an early Franco victory.

There is good reason for saying that when the Blum Government fell on April 8, the British Government made it very plain to M. Daladier, the prospective new Premier, that it would consider the reappointment of M. Paul-Boncour to the Quai d'Orsay as eminently undesirable.

V. ENTER DALADIER AND BONNET

ON SUNDAY, April 10, the Daladier Government was formed. Daladier! The name has been on everybody's lips for weeks. Not only people on the Right, but also many people on the Left wanted Daladier—though for a different reason. It was felt that the man who had been War Minister for two years was the most desirable man to have at the head of the Government in the existing international situation. The 'strong-man' legend, the *'taureau de Vaucluse'* legend was being revived—and the most abject flattery was being poured down M. Daladier's throat by *Gringoire, Candide* and other pro-Fascist papers which in the past had treated him as *le fusilleur*. Such flattery must have sickened M. Daladier himself. Why *Gringoire* and the rest were rejoicing so much was, of course, because the formation of the Daladier Government marked the end of 'Front Populaire' Government, and finally killed the prospect of a National Government after the model advocated by M. Blum. They thought that the Government would soon lose the parliamentary support of the Left, and be obliged to depend on the support of the Right.

It would be idle to pretend that the satisfaction caused by the formation of the Daladier Government was confined to the Right-Wing extremists; the Radicals, and, in fact, the man-in-the-street, who had been profoundly disturbed by the strikes under the Blum Government, felt at heart that the Front Populaire experiment had come to an end. They were inclined to say that it was 'nice to be back to normal at last.'

The Daladier Government—the Government which was destined to deal with the Czech crisis—was a predominantly Radical Government. In spite of M. Blum's desire that the Socialists should participate, the Socialist rank and file, embittered by the indignities the last Blum Government had suffered at the hands of the Senate, would not hear of it. Instead, a number of men belonging nominally to the Opposition were included, among them M. Reynaud, M. Mandel and M. Champetier de Ribes. It is worth noting that it was these 'Right Wing' members of the Government who, at the height of the Czech crisis, were to prove much more 'anti-Munich' than the Radicals; and that it was they, and not any Radicals, who were, on one memorable occasion in September, to rebel against the foreign policy of M. Bonnet.

M. Frossard and M. Ramadier, belonging to the small party, the Union Socialiste, half-way between the Socialists and Radicals, were to drop out in August as a protest against M. Daladier's broadcast attacking the forty-hour week—an attack which they considered ill-tempered, and liable to annoy the working-class unnecessarily. They were replaced by M. de Monzie and M. Pomaret, nominally members of the same Party, though in reality much more 'capitalist' in their labour policy. A question asked in April was why so brilliant a man as M. Reynaud was relegated to the relatively unimportant post of Minister of Justice, when he was obviously cut out to be either Finance Minister or Foreign Minister. It seems that his financial remedies were a little too harsh for the Left; and M. Daladier still wanted their parliamentary support— at least for a time; why he was not made Foreign Minister is simply because he was too great a believer in collective security and other old-fashioned remedies to suit Mr. Chamberlain's taste.

.   .   .   .

But the two men who were to be the most in the public eye during 1938 were M. Daladier and M. Bonnet.[1]

At the end of April I went over to London to report the important Anglo-French talks, which established the first direct contact between Mr. Chamberlain and Lord Halifax and the two 'new men' of France. One day, during the Conference, I was lunching at the Hyde Park Hotel —the headquarters of the French journalists—with Paul Nizan, and we were discussing Daladier and Bonnet. Nizan remarked: 'Daladier is made all of one piece—he is a bit of a rustic, and quite simple to under-

[1] The following passages on Bonnet were written in 1938 and early 1939—with the maximum of tact. Bonnet was itching for a good excuse to have me expelled from France. I am told that he bought six copies of *France and Munich* and got his secretaries to read it in the hope that he might trip me up over a misstatement. Good business for me and Hamish! (Author's note, 1942.)

163

stand. Bonnet is a much more intricate character, full of funny "complexes." *Il est caricatural*, and perhaps his physical appearance, with that enormous nose of his, accounts for a lot of these "complexes". He is extremely vain, extremely ambitious, very touchy, very susceptible to flattery; and can be very spiteful and resentful if you rub him the wrong way. He is a man who wants to be loved, and who suffers at the thought that he is not lovable. Laval who, politically, resembles him in many ways, was, with all his faults, a likeable kind of chap. Bonnet has very few friends and no end of enemies. Instead of friends, he has "contacts"; he is very intelligent, very ambitious—and thoroughly hard-boiled. His ambition is to be Prime Minister—and he may get there yet. It is also his wife's ambition, and Odette, who is a pretty woman, very well dressed, a piece of Camille Pelletan, and so a lady with great political "contacts," has been a great help to Georges in his political career. She is known as *soutien-Georges*,' Nizan laughed.

Many months later I heard a strange story about Georges Bonnet from a man who did not like him. During the War Bonnet acted as counsel for the defence in the court-martial of a German officer. Bonnet considered the man to be innocent. He was nevertheless sentenced to death. And before the execution Bonnet stayed the whole night with him in his cell; and after the German had been shot, Bonnet smuggled his belongings to his old mother in Germany.[2]

Bonnet, who started his Government career on the Conseil d'Etat, was one of the young politicians whom the Cartel des Gauches brought into prominence in 1924. With his Radical contacts, with his intelligence and ambition, he climbed the ladder that many Radical politicians have climbed. By 1932—after another election victory of the Left—Bonnet had become one of the shining lights of the Radical Party, and was recognized to be one of the few able financial experts the Left had produced. He was Finance Minister in the Daladier Cabinet of 1933, and, in that capacity went to the World Economic Conference in London, where for the first time he met his British opposite number, Mr. Neville Chamberlain, Chancellor of the Exchequer. Mr. Chamberlain was not, however, impressed by the French Finance Minister, whom, it was said at the time, he found cagey and lacking in frankness. M. Bonnet was then one of the founders of the 'gold bloc.'

And then, in 1934, Bonnet's political progress, like the progress of several other Radical politicians, was savagely checked by the *Affaire Stavisky*. Like Dalimier, who died soon afterwards a broken man, like

---

[2] Poor Paul Nizan was killed in the Battle of France in June 1940. I last saw him when he was on leave in Paris in December 1939. (Author's note, 1942.)

Chautemps, and his brother-in-law Pressard, Bonnet was selected as an object for an outrageous Press campaign. *Gringoire, Candide,* and the rest, which in 1938 were to treat him as a great statesman, and as their favourite Minister, drowned Bonnet in buckets of foul abuse. The Stavisky Affair seems to have had a profound effect on M. Bonnet's character. Like many Radical victims of the Stavisky Affair and the 6th of February riots, Bonnet was restored to political life by the victory of the Front Populaire. In spite of it, he was one of its bitterest enemies from the start.

After a speech in which he severely criticized—and with some reason —M. Vincent Auriol's finance, Blum got him out of the way by appointing him Ambassador to Washington. During the decline of the Front Populaire in 1937 Chautemps brought him back in rather spectacular fashion from Washington, and appointed him Finance Minister. He arrived in Paris beaming with self-satisfaction, conscious of his indispensability and personal importance. His return marked the end of the Front Populaire in the financial and economic sense. On the night of his return a French journalist remarked: '*Ça ira mieux maintenant. C'est un malin. Et il a de belles relations dans la haute banque.*' At the Little Radical Congress in October 1937 he tried to force the Socialists out of the Government, and continued to plot against them; and it was also he who, indirectly, provoked the resignation of the Chautemps Cabinet in January 1938, which marked the end of Socialist participation.

.   .   .   .   .   .

Daladier is a different kind of man. He is not the typical 'politician' that Bonnet is. A man of simple origin, the son of a baker in a small town in Provence, he is proud of his plebeian, but healthy, rural origin —and is, in fact, rather snobbish about it. An unkind critic of Daladier once remarked: 'He always says, "Je suis *sorti* du peuple": meaning that he is proud not to be there any longer.' Like many French Ministers, he rose from the small tradesman class to be an 'intellectual,' and became shortly before the War a teacher of history. He fought at Verdun and had a good War record. Like Bonnet, he was brought into prominence by the Cartel des Gauches election victory of 1924, and before very long he became a leading light of the Radical Party—and, in fact, the leader of its Left Wing. He led the anti-Government Opposition in the Radical Party in the days when M. Herriot was co-operating loyally in M. Poincaré's National Government of 1926–8. The two Edouards were for some years (1928–32) in sharp competition for the real, if not nominal leadership of the Radical Party. Daladier, cultivating the strong silent manner—and silence is reckoned to be a sign of wisdom in Provence, his exuberant native land—soon acquired the reputation of a true Jacobin, a man of steadfast democratic, republican and anti-clerical principles—harder and more uncompromising than Herriot. On a public platform Daladier looked grim and a trifle Napoleonic. In private, he could be very charming, with a fund of quiet, almost English humour—very different from the imaginative, almost Gargantuan exuberance of the other Edouard. He was War Minister in 1932, and was popular at the War Office; and was Premier for the first time during nearly the whole of 1933—until October when that parliamentary disintegration started, which three months later was to culminate in the Stavisky Affair and the February riots.

This Daladier Government was in office during the first year of the Hitler régime. The international atmosphere was strained and Daladier dealt with the situation with commendable calm and level-headedness—though perhaps without any profound understanding of what was happening in Germany.

There was, however, already then an empirical strain in Daladier's character. Unlike Paul-Boncour, he did not reason according to certain set rules and principles; and although he was nominally a 'League' supporter, he did not, in May 1933, completely reject the Four-Power Pact, which Ramsay MacDonald had brought back from Rome; and when, in October, Germany left the League, Daladier did not consider it wicked to attempt direct conversations with her. It was with his approval that M. Fernand de Brinon published in the *Matin* in November 1933, the sensational interview with a peace-loving and Francophil Hitler—an interview which was presumably intended as a preliminary to a possible Franco-German *rapprochement*.

The day of the February riots, in the course of which Daladier rather lost his head, must have been the blackest day in his life. Overwhelmed by the tragic events, for which he was not responsible, but for which he had provided a pretext by sacking Chiappe, Daladier promptly resigned on the following day. But Daladier was a broken man, and retired into obscurity, only to see himself for months portrayed in the Press as *le fusilleur*, who had ordered 'unarmed ex-servicemen' to be shot down. The *Temps* boycotted his very name, and referred to him as *le député d'Orange*.

He did not make his *grande rentrée* into public life until the summer of 1935 as one of the leaders of the great Front Populaire movement. It was he who led the Radicals into the Front Populaire fold—rather against the wishes of the more cautious Herriot. But it was not until the Left Election victory of 1936 that Daladier found his way back to the Government bench. Daladier became War Minister and Vice-Premier; and on the face of it he remained loyal to Blum and to the Front Populaire until April 1938—though at heart he deeply resented the stay-in strikes and other excesses of the urban proletariat. He was very much the peasant.

．　．　．　．　．　．　．

In becoming Premier for the third time, he was received with enthusiasm by the men of the Right, and with much satisfaction by large sections of public opinion. For several days the Bourse soared, and funds which had been leaving France at a disastrous rate during the previous Blum Government, began to rush back.

The Ministerial declaration was certainly well drafted, except for the extreme caution that marked the passages on foreign policy. It opened with the words, 'A great and free country can only be saved by itself.'

'All problems, economic, financial, social, and political, are part of the single problem of security. France needs a healthy currency and a healthy rhythm of production, above all in the war industries. The Government therefore makes a patriotic appeal to both employers and workers. The workers must realize that stay-in strikes can create in France only a feeling of anxiety which may become a menace to the democratic régime. The employers, on the other hand, must apply loyally the labour code, which will, moreover, be completed by new provisions.'

Then came the important passage in which the Government said that

'thinking only of the national interest, it would assure without delay the resumption of the manufacture of armaments indispensable to national security'

—a promise which was loudly cheered on most benches except on the extreme Left.

As regards foreign policy, the Government said that it was determined to defend France's interests everywhere, as well as the integrity of her Empire. Without referring to Spain, the declaration added that 'the Government would not tolerate any threat to France's frontiers, to her sea routes, or her colonies and would deal firmly with all foreign agitators.'

'In all cases—in the case of strengthening our bonds with our friends *or in the case of proving our loyalty to all pacts and treaties we have*
167

signed, or in the case of entering into equitable negotiations, it is indispensable that all the national energies be united.'

Never had a Ministerial declaration been so uncategorical in its statement on foreign policy—except in its references to France's own interests. It contained no reference to the League of Nations. This omission may be easy to understand, but deserves to be noted all the same. In short it was felt that M. Bonnet, the Foreign Minister, did not wish to have anything said which would alarm Mr. Chamberlain and Lord Halifax.

On the whole, however, the declaration created a good impression, and was approved almost unanimously—by 576 votes to four. Both the Communists and the Socialists (the latter rather reluctantly, it is true) voted for the Government—chiefly for the sake of preserving the semblance of the Front Populaire majority. About one hundred members of the Right abstained. What added to the good impression made by the Government was the settlement, on the very day of the Ministerial declaration, of the strike in the aeroplane industry, and the prospect of an early settlement in the engineering industry. The Government had no difficulty in securing from both the Chamber and the Senate 'limited' financial powers.

As regards foreign policy, it was known that M. Bonnet's first official act in becoming Foreign Minister was to invite M. Osusky, the Czechoslovak Minister, and to say to him:

'Contrary to certain rumours spread by a hostile newspaper campaign, the position of the French Government in relation to Central Europe has not undergone any change.'

That was plain enough. And, as already said, it was M. Bonnet himself who was believed to have rapped the *Temps* over the knuckles for the Barthelémy article and to have insisted on the publication of an editorial contradicting the Professor's arguments in favour of abandoning Czechoslovakia.

. . . .

One of M. Bonnet's first tasks, in arriving at the Quai d'Orsay, was to try to make friends with Italy.

Since the withdrawal of M. de Chambrun a year earlier, there had been no French Ambassador in Rome; for the Italian Government demanded that the credentials of M. de St. Quentin, M. de Chambrun's successor, be addressed to the 'King of Italy and Emperor of Ethiopia'; and since the League Council had not 'recognized' the conquest of Abyssinia, France had her hands tied. The Italian Ambassador in Paris had, in turn, been withdrawn on October 29, 1937. It is true to say that the greater part of French opinion was entirely favourable to a *rapprochement* with Italy. It continued to be assumed that the Anschluss had greatly shocked Italy and that the Berlin-Rome axis had already cracked; and it is certainly true that public feeling in Italy was in the main hostile to Germany. A joke current in Rome at the time was that Mussolini had exchanged the *Passo Brennero* for the *Passo Romano* (the newly adopted goose-step).

One wonders when the idea first came to M. Bonnet that the *rapprochement* with Italy might be 'worked' through Spain. March and April were the blackest months for the Spanish Government. In March the Italian and German aeroplanes had performed their most hideous air raids on Barcelona and on April 15, supported by Italian troops and a large Italo-German air force, Franco's army reached Viñaroz on the Mediterranean, south of the Ebro, and so cut Government Spain in two.

It was at this time that the Anglo-Italian agreement was signed. This agreement was, on the whole, well received by the French Government, which thought that it was not without direct interest to France. It accepted the *status quo* in the Mediterranean (and the French naturally thought that this applied to their possessions in the Mediterranean, as well as to the British possessions—a belief the Italians were later to contradict), and it promised to leave Spain to itself. But although in principle everything between France and Italy had already been settled by the 1935 agreement, it is certain that M. Bonnet was willing to pay a 'supplement,' if Italy's friendship, or, at any rate, neutrality in case of war, could be firmly secured.

At any rate, two days after the signing of the Anglo-Italian agreement, M. Blondel, the French Chargé d'Affaires in Rome, had his first meetings with Count Ciano. The Italian Press, anticipating an early *de jure* recognition of the 'Emperor of Ethiopia,' sounded very friendly. This friendliness may also perhaps have been dictated by Mussolini's desire to put himself in a stronger bargaining position in relation to Hitler during the latter's coming visit to Rome.

.   .   .   .

A week later—on April 27—M. Daladier and M. Bonnet went to London to discuss the whole situation with Mr. Chamberlain and Lord Halifax. This French visit to London was the first since Lord Halifax had succeeded Mr. Eden at the Foreign Office. Since the last French visit Austria had disappeared; relations with Italy had greatly changed; the situation in Central Europe was infinitely more menacing; and in the Spanish civil war the position of the Government was now, thanks to 'non-intervention,' incomparably worse than it was in November.

When I recently looked up my 'forecasts' of the Anglo-French conversation, I could not help chuckling—all the more so as I was then gently charged with cynicism by a friend at the French Foreign Office, who also said that I was very wrong to say that Daladier, like Chamberlain, 'would be only too pleased if the Czechs came to terms with Germany at any price.'

'The watchword of the present British Ministers,' I wrote at the time, 'appears to be "realism," and they no doubt trust that their French guests will be equally "realistic." On the whole they may be certain that they will find in M. Daladier and in M. Bonnet men who will answer "Yes" rather more readily than "No." '

The French Ministers, while not known—like their Socialist predecessors—to have any brotherly sympathies for the Spanish Government, are nevertheless alarmed for purely military and naval reasons by the recent developments in Spain. They will want to know the reasons for the extraordinary equanimity with which Mr. Chamberlain and other members of the British Cabinet appear to view a rebel victory, in spite of repeated threats to Gibraltar in the rebel Press, extravagant declarations of friendship to Germany, German activities along the Straits of Gibraltar, and the uncertainty as to the ultimate departure of the Italians from Spain.

Great concern is naturally also felt about Czechoslovakia, but one has the impression that *while M. Daladier is prepared to take military action in the event of a direct German aggression against Czechoslovakia, he would, like the British Government, be only too pleased if the Czechs came to terms with Germany at any price,* and that the latest French assurances to Czechoslovakia do not cover the contingency of 'internal aggression' covered by the assurances given to Czechoslovakia by the Blum Government a year ago.

One suggestion is that *Great Britain and France may propose some form of mediation in the conflict between Czechoslovakia and the Sudeten Germans (in reality Germany).*

Partly with the help of German propaganda, *French opinion is becoming seriously divided on the necessity of 'fighting for the Czechs.'* A full-page article in *Gringoire* last week attacking Czechoslovakia— an article which was joyfully reproduced under immense headlines in all the German papers—is an extreme but not altogether insignificant example of the state of mind existing among wide sections of French opinion. By way of apology many Frenchmen to-day say that

Spain is of infinitely more vital importance to France than Czechoslovakia (not that they seriously propose to do anything about that either); while others say that instead of propping up Czechoslovakia, which is a 'hybrid' country, it would be better to prop up Jugoslav and Hungarian resistance to the German advance.

A common policy as far as possible in relation to Italy will be agreed upon, *though what the exact prospects of a Franco-Italian understanding are is still uncertain. It seems probable that Italy is less in a hurry to come to terms with France than she was with England.*

In particular Italy seems at the present stage reluctant to give France any promises about Spain and the Balearics in addition to those already given to Britain.[3]

It was not too bad as a forecast, though a long-term, rather than short-term forecast; for in London, a lot of unpleasant points—particularly about Czechoslovakia—were nicely camouflaged. On the face of it, Britain had 'never yet taken such a firm stand in Central Europe'; *in reality, it was during these Anglo-French talks of April 29–30 that Lord Runciman was, if not born, at any rate, conceived.* And in return for this British 'firmness' in Central Europe, the French agreed to be as weak as they could possibly be about Spain.

The Anglo-French talks lasted nearly two whole days.

The most tangible result of the first day's talks—or so it seemed at the time—was an Anglo-French agreement to pool their resources'—which meant not only a close co-ordination between the armed forces of the two countries, but also various common arrangements for making purchases of aircraft and of the basic raw materials for purposes of rearmament, and also for accumulating food supplies.

But at that time Mr. Chamberlain and Lord Halifax did not wish the impression to gain ground that they had concluded an alliance with France.

While M. Daladier was rejoicing, the British Ministers were, on the following day, a little taken aback by the use of the word 'alliance' and of phrases like 'virtual alliance' and 'defensive alliance,' not only in the French Press but also in a great many British papers, and it was strongly emphasized on the British side that the coming 'Staff contacts' were only a continuation of the contacts agreed upon in 1936 and that they did not constitute any new commitments or any change of British policy. On the Friday afternoon Lord Halifax actually hastened to give assurances to that effect to the German and Italian Ambassadors.

[3] *Manchester Guardian,* April 26, 1938.

Apart from that, the three main subjects were Spain, Czechoslovakia and Italy. As I wrote at the time:

'The French Ministers, aware of the response they would receive, do not even seem to have proposed any joint Anglo-French action which would tend to 'neutralize' the Balearics and so protect the French sea route to North Africa, and it appears *that they were satisfied with the British agreement that the Italians had pledged themselves to withdraw their troops from Spain and that they would 'almost certainly do so,' since it was in Italy's interest to remain on good terms with Britain!*

Any danger, it was thought, might be counteracted by France from her newly constructed military aerodrome in Corsica. In the circumstances both the French and British Ministers cheerfully agreed on the full maintenance of non-intervention, and the French even agreed to restore the international frontier control along the Pyrenees as soon as the British plan providing for the proportional withdrawal of foreign troops began to be applied.

Control apparently will come into force as soon as the international inspectors in charge of counting the volunteers have entered Spain, and may be terminated only if by the end of forty-five days the inspectors find that they cannot, owing to bad faith on either of the sides, succeed in their task. Considering Italy's avowed determination not to withdraw her troops before the end of the war, the whole scheme, with frontier control as its only effective measure, is another blow to the Spanish Government. Spain has again been betrayed.

As for the activities of Germany in Spain—which M. Daladier stressed as hard as he could—it appears to have been agreed that nothing special could be done about it just now, *but that there would be no harm when the time came—and perhaps even sooner—in cultivating the good graces of General Franco. Britain (Mr. Chamberlain said) was looking forward to friendly relations with Franco after his victory.*

It almost looks as though the whole proposal were calculated to hasten a rebel victory and to give pleasure to the Italians. M. Daladier was not at all keen on the scheme; but the British Ministers thought that if France hastened to make friends with Italy things would go better in Spain.[4]

It is hardly necessary to explain that Mr. Chamberlain was caring little for fair play in Spain, and that he was hoping desperately for an early Franco victory, which (so he thought) would completely 'normalize' relations with Italy. The French had similar illusions about Italy:

[4] *Manchester Guardian,* April 30.

172

a Havas note from London painted rosy pictures of a 'return to the Stresa Front.'

But the most urgent subject was Czechoslovakia. In the midst of the London meeting a Note came from the Czechoslovak Government indicating the extent to which Prague was prepared to go to meet Henlein's demands; and the document spoke of a very serious danger of war. It was earlier in the month that Henlein had formulated the eight points and the 'Karlsbad programme'—and this the Czech Government regarded as completely unacceptable. They were in principle prepared to grant the Sudetens a limited form of autonomy, but neither territorial, nor juridical, nor 'philosophical' autonomy, which would be contrary to the constitution, as well as the safety, of the Czechoslovak State.

The only way out of the difficulty was to bring pressure to bear on the Czechs. And that is what was in reality decided on April 29; and the pressure was already then called 'mediation.'

Although France and Britain agreed that a solution must be found compatible with the security and the constitution of the Czechoslovak State, they more or less openly agreed that the phrase 'within the limits of the Czechoslovak Constitution' should be stretched to its utmost capacity. It was clear that what Hitler wanted was the Czech 'Maginot Line' much more than his three million fellow Germans (for what did he care for his Tyrolese brethren whom the Italians were treating very much worse than the Czechs were treating the Sudetens?); but this was difficult to explain to the general public. Hitler's and Henlein's case was perhaps a bad and dishonest case—but it was a case for all that; and that is why Czechoslovakia was difficult to handle as a technical question independently of its psychological implications. It was not enough to say that Hitler and Henlein were using democratic principles for undemocratic ends!

.   .   .   .

France, at that moment, was passing through another of her periodic financial crises. The formation of the Daladier Government had been well received by the business world; but a few days later the boom on the Bourse came to an end, and there was again heavy pressure on the franc. There were continuous rumours that M. Reynaud was advocating a new devaluation—with the franc pegged to the £ at about 175. The rumours were not unfounded, and on the night of May 3— a day on which the franc had slipped to 170 in the £, M. Daladier made the sudden announcement on the wireless that it was necessary for France to make a fresh start; and that her anæmic economy must be placed on a solid financial basis at last—and he announced that the franc would be pegged to the £ and would not be allowed to fall below the rate of 179. This was the third devaluation since September 1936.

Although the first set of M. Daladier's decrees, which was published during the same week, was very unimpressive, and consisted of so many odds and ends, the effect of the devaluation was to bring in a short time about £100,000,000 of exported capital back to France. The motive behind this repatriation was profit-taking, rather than 'confidence,' but it all looked good, and the devaluation was of great help to the Government. The defence loan of five milliard francs was subscribed without the least difficulty, and in the first half of May there was a wave of optimism in France.

.   .   .   .

In Czechoslovakia the prospects for 'mediation' looked bad from the outset. On May Day Henlein made a violent speech in which, referring to his Karlsbad programme, he bluntly declared: 'I take nothing back.'

'No one,' he cried, 'has the right to call my recent speech a call to war. Our goal is equality of rights. This new order is of vital importance not for us alone but for the State and for all Europe. Every country which thinks that support of the Czech claim to overlordship serves the peace of Europe should note this. We will not accept the position of a minority.'

It was also on May Day that President Beneš sent a telegram to Hitler, which caused much interest, for it suggested that he was trying to improve the international atmosphere on the eve of the coming negotiations.

'On the occasion of the German national holiday I express to your Excellency my most sincere good wishes.'

I have not seen any record of Hitler's reply—if there was one.

The British and French 'mediation' began on May 7—ten days after the London meeting.

The British and French Ministers expressed the expectations of their Governments that the Czechslovak Government would go to the utmost possible limits within the framework indicated for a solution of the above question.

At the same time

the German Government was informed in the friendliest way of this action and was asked to invite Herr Henlein to negotiate with the Government at Prague on this matter.[5]

The British and French Governments were trying to square the circle; for they knew that neither Hitler nor Henlein wanted 'concessions' which would be 'compatible with the safety of the State,' as the French Minister in Prague had put it.

But the French and British Governments did not see, or did not like to see, this fundamental fact. It was hoped that, rather than go to war, Hitler would, *at least for a time*, accept some kind of home rule which would still keep Czechoslovakia intact. And then, with much suddenness, came the crisis of May 21.

During the previous days there had been rumours of German troop movements along the Czech frontier—rumours similar to those which has preceded the invasion of Austria. On May 20, Sir Neville Henderson, the British Ambassador in Berlin, made his first inquiry at the German Foreign Office about the alleged troop movements. He was informed by Herr von Weissaecker that the troop movements were a matter of routine and had nothing to do with the Czech elections. At three o'clock on the following morning, a grave incident occurred at Eger, where two Sudeten motor-cyclists, Hoffmann and Bohm, on their way to Germany, refused to stop at the Czech frontier, and were shot dead by Czech frontier guards. Large quantities of anti-Czech leaflets—mostly reprints from the French Press—were found in their possession. Early that morning, the Czech War Minister called up several thousand reservists, 'specialists,' etc. Prague declared that this was not a mobilization—a step that could not have been taken by the War Minister alone—but only a precautionary measure for preventing any disturbances in the election areas.

In any case, nothing serious happened. Germany, it was said, climbed down; partly perhaps because she realized that the Czech semi-mobilization had rendered a surprise attack on Czechoslovakia impossible, and partly because she was impressed by Britain's firmness. Such was the interpretation currently given to the events of 'May 21.'

In the days that followed the crisis of May 21, France was full of praise for the British Government, and for its Ambassador in Berlin whose firmness had averted war. May 21, it was said, was a lesson: if France and England were firm on all similar occasions, war could be averted. Except that in certain circumstances, the combined firmness of the Powers might not be sufficient; and Pertinax, for example, wrote that in order to 'make May 21 work again' it was necessary to rebuild

[5] Reuter, quoted in *Manchester Guardian*, May 9, 1938.

the 'French system,' and, in the first place, to assure in advance the support of Russia in any future emergency of the same kind—a precaution the British and French Governments had deliberately failed to take, despite repeated Russian offers of staff talks.

It must, however, be said, that certain members of the French Government—notably M. Bonnet—later claimed that the 'threatened invasion' of Czechoslovakia by Germany on May 21 was largely a show put up by the Czechs, for the purpose of testing the British and French reaction. And a man in close touch with M. Bonnet and M. Daladier later told me that the French Ministers 'could never quite forgive the Czechs their stunt of May 21.'

Even if Germany was not preparing to attack Czechoslovakia, it is still too simple to attribute the whole crisis of May 21 to a 'Czech stunt.' Whatever may have been the exact intentions of the Germans on May 20 and 21—perhaps *they also* were curious to know what not only the British and French, but also the Czech reactions would be to their 'troop movements.'

But apart from that, there was the genuine danger of a Sudeten *putsch* which might have been supported from outside—but for the occupation of the Sudeten area by the newly called-up Czech troops.

．　．　．　．　．　．　．

The optimism in Paris actually lasted longer than was justified by the facts. It is true that M. Bonnet was not fully reassured by the 'happy ending' of the 'May 21' crisis. It is curious that at that time M. Bonnet still appeared to support—at least in speaking to the Chamber Committee—the Czechs against excessive German claims. He thought it would be 'inadvisable for the Czech Government to grant minority rights to the Sudeten Germans which would be out of all proportion with their numerical importance.'[6] Nor did he *at that time* suggest that May 21 was only a 'Czech stunt.'

．　．　．　．　．　．　．

Most typical of the attitude of the greater part of the French Press was this headline in the *Intransigeant* of June 15:

> *Les négociations Hodza-Henlein qui vont s'ouvrir demain pourraient se prolonger jusqu'à l'automne.*

It is true that lower down there was the sub-title, '*Peu de chances*

[6] *Manchester Guardian*, June 4.

d'aboutir' ; but what mattered to the ordinary reader was the *jusqu'à l'automne.*

The negotiations between the Czechs and the Sudetens muddled along until July 20 or thereabout—and it was then that the British Government produced Lord Runciman.

VI. THE STRANGLING OF THE SPANISH REPUBLIC STARTS IN EARNEST

I F ON the Czech 'diplomatic front' France scored, on May 21, something that looked like a victory, there were no victories on either the Italian or Spanish fronts.

The French Ministers returned from London with the illusion that the road was clear for a Franco-Italian *rapprochement.*

On May 12 the League Council met, and although M. Bonnet and Lord Halifax knew that they could not obtain any unanimous vote on the acceptance of the Italian conquest, they got nine members of the Council to declare that 'in their opinion each member of the League is free to decide for himself whether or not to recognize the Italian conquest of Abyssinia.'

The Emperor of Abyssinia was at Geneva, and had just paid part of Abyssinia's contribution to the League—it was all very awkward. Still, the declarations made by the nine members of the Council were exactly what the French and British Governments had been longing for. It was a little trick that M. Avenol had invented. Abyssinia officially remained a member of the League; but the damage was done. However, M. Bonnet returned to Paris, feeling very pleased that the corpse of Abyssinia should have been cleared out of the way. There was nothing, he thought, to prevent a *rapprochement* with Italy at last.

And he was anxious to make friends with Italy, especially as the situation in Czechoslovakia was threatening to become nasty.

Unfortunately—and there was nothing new in this Italian technique— no sooner had France helped to dispose of the corpse of Abyssinia at Geneva than Mussolini made his savage attack on France in his famous speech at Genoa on May 15. The speech was very polite to England,

and was an obvious attempt either to drive a wedge between France and England, or else to compel France to yield on the question of Spain.

At that time the Spanish Government had, largely with the help of the French armaments, which had been sent there in the two previous months, succeeded in stopping the Aragon Offensive; and Mussolini and Mr. Chamberlain were both furious.

The speech was a bitter disappointment to the French Right, for in the course of it Mussolini also said that Stresa was 'dead and buried.' For these people had always refused to realize that Stresa had never been an Italo-Franco-British alliance, and was only an Italian manœuvre calculated to silence in advance any Anglo-French protests against the invasion of Abyssinia.

And the Genoa speech shattered another pleasant French illusion—namely that it was, as it were, by accident, that Mussolini had failed to counteract the Anschluss in 1938, as he had checked a Nazi advance on Vienna in 1934.

'Italy could not allow herself the luxury of mobilizing regularly at the end of every four years to prevent the inevitable conclusion of a national revolution.'

M. Daladier treated the speech as a piece of insolence. M. Bonnet, on the other hand, was much impressed by the phrase about the 'opposite sides of the barricade in Spain'; and felt that, especially with war threatening in Czechoslovakia, Italy must be bought off at any price. And he argued in favour of closing the Catalan frontier to armaments. He thought that that was also Mr. Chamberlain's desire. The Cabinet did not follow his advice, and he left the meeting in rather a bad mood.[1] At the end of the week came the Czech crisis; and for a time little more was heard of Franco-Italian relations.

.   .   .   .

How anxious Mr. Chamberlain was to speed up a Franco victory could also be observed from the view he took of the bombing of British ships in Spanish waters.

The Nyon patrol set up in the autumn of 1937 had been of great help to the Spanish Government; for it put an end to the blockade. The 'unknown submarines' guilty of this piracy were the great joke of

[1] In fact, he was in a filthy temper. I saw him, immediately after that Cabinet meeting, at Mme Tabouis's private lunch, at which he was the guest of honour. (Author's note, 1942.)

178

the year; it was suggested in Paris that the Boulevard des Italiens be rechristened the Boulevard des Inconnus.

But Italy and Germany overcame the difficulties placed in their way by the Nyon agreement. Instead of a naval blockade, they, and particularly Italy—gradually established a sort of air blockade over the Spanish Government ports.

The bombing was usually done while the ships—mostly British ships—were in harbour, that is, technically in territorial waters. In January four ships were attacked, one by a submarine, and three from the air.

This new outbreak of piracy, however, led to new measures to stop it. Mr. Eden, in the House of Commons, had said that if the attacks were repeated *the British Government reserved the right, without further notice, to take appropriate retaliatory action.*

For a time the warning had some effect, but once Mr. Eden had gone, the piracy started again, and in May and June, after the signing of the Anglo-Italian agreement it became almost a daily occurrence.

In little less than a month 'Franco' had sunk eight British ships, and had damaged several others.

Feeling was beginning to run high in England, and on June 13 Mr. Chamberlain at last spoke. He announced in the House of Commons that no action would be taken to prevent the bombing.

'I do not think any action we can take is practicable in stopping these attacks if they persist.'

The Government, he added, *had rejected any plan of retaliatory action.*

The speech, duly reported in Italy and Spain, had an immediate effect. On the following day two French ships were sunk and three British ships damaged.

But it left Mr. Chamberlain undeterred, except that, on June 23, he went so far as to say that the Government 'took a serious view of these attacks, and had instructed Sir Robert Hodgson, the British agent at Burgos, to ask the Burgos authorities to give an explanation of their action which on the face of it was entirely inconsistent with the assurances and promises they had made.'

For the rest, he repeated the old story—no protection for British ships could be afforded without risk of war, and ships must trade with Spain at their own risk.

The questions put to him by Mr. Attlee and Sir Archibald Sinclair may be summarized thus. Since British ships are trading legitimately with Spain according to the rules approved by the Non-Intervention Committee, why should they not be protected? For fear of what Franco might do? For fear of what another country might do? If so, what could be said for the merits of the Anglo-Italian agreement?

Mr. Chamberlain would not answer that question. He admitted that the risks were greater than merely a conflict with Franco.

'If you start a war-like action against Franco,' said Mr. Chamberlain, 'or against some objective of which the ownership is doubtful, who can tell if you can stop your operations there without beginning another major war?'

Finally, following a suggestion made in the House by Mr. Churchill, Mr. Chamberlain instructed Lord Perth to go and see Ciano and ask him to use his influence with Franco against further air attacks on British ships. The fiction that they were 'Franco' planes was politely observed.

It did a little good, but not much. On the day of Lord Perth's visit two more British ships were bombed by Franco—one at Valencia, the other at Alicante—and three British seamen were killed.

However, on the following day, Virginio Gayda announced in the *Giornale d'Italia* (with a nice ironical touch) that General Franco would not bomb British ships on the high seas, and would avoid bombing them in Spanish ports, as far as possible. 'Emphasis is placed in Rome,' Reuter added, 'on the exceptional treatment which is being offered to British shipping.'[2]

Everything tends to show that the British Government were extremely anxious for a rapid 'settlement' in Spain—that is, a Franco victory—without which the benefits of the Anglo-Italian agreement remained only theoretical.

.   .   .   .

What also suggests that Mr. Chamberlain was only too pleased to condone the air blockade of the Government ports was the 'suggestion' he made to France early in June, that she close the Pyrenees frontier completely. No such 'suggestion,' be it noted, was made to Portugal; it was hoped in London that a 'generous' French gesture would put Mussolini in a better mood for withdrawing his 'volunteers.' The frontier was effectively closed on June 13. Whether Mr. Chamberlain had any illusions that the Italian 'volunteers' would be withdrawn may be seriously doubted.

Mr. George Strauss asked the Prime Minister whether the British Government had made any representations to the French Government suggesting the desirability of closing the Franco-Spanish frontier.

[2] *Manchester Guardian,* June 30.

Mr. Strauss: 'May we take it that the action taken by the French Government was quite independent and under no pressure or representation from the British Government?'

Mr. Chamberlain: 'Yes, it was an independent decision of the French Government.'

As the Paris correspondent of *The Times* pointed out at the time, Mr. Chamberlain's reply was a quibble. The decision was, naturally, an 'independent' one, in so far as France is an independent and sovereign State; but the French certainly would not have closed the frontier without British pressure.

In the French Press of the Right there was at that time much quibbling over the phrase 'closing the frontier.' If the Left were protesting against the closing of the frontier on June 13, it meant that the frontier had been open until then. France, therefore, had been violating the non-intervention agreement, and nobody had the right to complain that Italy and Germany were violating it, too.

That was not the point. The French Pyrenees frontier was absolutely closed during the greater part of 1937. Until July, international observers were in charge of the control, and no armaments entered Spain. A great number of these observers—some of whom I happened to know personally —were violent 'anti-Reds,' and certainly did their job well; and Captain Lunn, their chief, paid a warm tribute to 'the most loyal co-operation' of the Gardes Mobiles. I am not so sure about the British control (for it was exclusively British and not international) on the Portuguese frontier; most of the inspectors were British residents from Lisbon, and were certainly on good terms with the Portuguese authorities, who themselves were working hand-in-hand with General Franco.

During 1937 the Spanish Government were certainly saved by the Russian armaments that reached them by sea; for hardly anything reached them by land, except during the last few months of the year— and not very much at that. The French frontier control was not properly 'relaxed' until March, when M. Blum became Premier and M. Paul-Boncour Foreign Minister; and under the Daladier Government the control remained 'relaxed'—until June 13. M. Daladier himself was much perturbed by the developments in Spain, and considered a Franco victory a menace to France; and although—as I already explained before —M. Bonnet considered about the middle of May the possibility of 'securing Italian neutrality' (for the situation in Central Europe was becoming dangerous) by closing the French frontier into Spain completely, M. Daladier would not have it. It took Mr. Chamberlain to persuade him to do so on June 13. The difference between 'control' and 'relaxed control,' or between a 'closed' frontier and a 'hermetically sealed' frontier was explained by M. Blum in the *Populaire* on June 18 (before he knew of the decision of June 13—which was kept very secret for a time).

'Since the open admission of intervention made last September by Italy and Germany, and since the failure of the negotiations regarding the withdrawal of "volunteers," France has suspended the international frontier control and has ceased to play the gendarme on her own frontiers.'

M. Blum regretted that the Communists should be clamouring for an official opening of the Spanish frontier, which he said, could do the Spanish Government more harm than good.

The Communists, in reality, had good reason to be dissatisfied; for unlike M. Blum, they knew that the frontier had already been closed. *Humanité* suggested that this French move constituted part of a new arrangement that Mr. Chamberlain might attempt to reach with Italy.

Already at that time Mr. Chamberlain had a valuable ally in M. Bonnet, not to mention M. Flandin.

M. Flandin, who since February had been, as it were, impersonating the 'New Policy' of Mr. Chamberlain, made, very significantly, a violent speech against the Spanish Government on June 11, that is, two days before the frontier was closed at Mr. Chamberlain's request. 'After the experience one had of M. Flandin just before the Eden crisis,' said a Paris message in the *Manchester Guardian* of June 13, 'one cannot but wonder whether he has not again been "tipped off" in London and is not trying once again to anticipate British policy.' He said:

Official France has not been neutral. She has been constantly sympathetic to the Reds and hostile to the Spanish Nationalists. The successive Front Populaire Governments have not ceased to tolerate an important transit of arms to Barcelona. Scandalous fortunes have been piled up through this traffic in the instruments of death.[3]

From what followed, it was clear that M. Flandin included the Daladier Government among the Front Populaire Governments and that he was trying to dictate a new Spanish policy to it.

It was a very significant speech, which was loudly applauded in the Right Press, and which could almost have been dictated to M. Flandin from London.

M. Bonnet's greatest ambition was to come to terms with Italy, and

[3] *Paris-Soir,* July 7.

it was necessary that Mussolini should no longer be able to say that France and Italy were fighting 'on opposite sides of the barricade.'

. . . . . .

In Milan, on June 2, Ciano made a speech which, from the French point of view, was no better than Mussolini's Genoa speech, and from the British point of view, considerably worse, for, unlike Mussolini's, Ciano's praise of the Anglo-Italian agreement was rather ambiguous.

Ciano gave what might be called his interpretation of the Spanish clauses of the Anglo-Italian agreement. It was clear that in his view Spain was a matter that concerned the Berlin-Rome axis far more than it concerned England.

In the end there was a glowing reference to 'the strong and noble Japanese people' who were fighting Bolshevism—'with which the Chinese Government have so unwisely associated themselves.' France was not even mentioned, except when Ciano spoke of Italo-Jugoslav relations, which, he said, were developing favourably 'without any unnecessary intermediaries.'

Even the most pro-Italian papers in France were much dissatisfied with Ciano's speech.

The *Temps* remarked that Count Ciano seemed to have overlooked two things—namely, that the Anglo-Italian agreement would remain meaningless so long as the conditions relating to Spain were not loyally fulfilled and so long as the agreement with England was not supplemented by one with France. In the view of French commentators Count Ciano's references to Spain clearly showed that no help whatsoever was to be expected from Italy in any attempt to mediate a peaceful settlement in the Spanish war.

M. Bonnet, speaking before the Foreign Affairs Committee of the Chamber on the same day, indicated that the Government would willingly appoint an Ambassador at Rome, but that it was anxious to see first whether anything good was likely to come out of the talks between Count Ciano and M. Blondel, the French Chargé d'Affaires in Rome.

Of course, no good whatsoever came out of the talks between Blondel and Ciano.

The French Government, for its part, did not wish Spain to be publicly discussed. On June 16 M. Cornavin, one of the Communist deputies, twice attempted to force upon the Chamber a discussion on Spain and on 'the criminal scandal of non-intervention.' But on both occasions the Government evaded the discussion, and a few days later the Chamber was hastily sent on holiday. It is curious that M. Daladier should, on

June 15, have made the following statement on Spain in his speech to the Executive Committee of the Radical Party:

'We remain faithful to the policy of non-intervention, but like all other international agreements it must be carried out loyally, reciprocally, and simultaneously. . . . We shall keep to the method of non-intervention, for we are determined that the destiny of Spain shall be settled by the Spaniards themselves.'

It is curious that he should have spoken of the 'loyal, reciprocal and simultaneous' respect for the non-intervention agreement three days after his Government had agreed at the request of Mr. Chamberlain and at the instigation of M. Bonnet to the *unilateral* closing of the Catalan frontier. A unilateral action to which M. Daladier had firmly refused to agree a month earlier.

The trouble is, that, throughout 1938, Daladier was swayed by contradictory influences. There were moments when he spoke with grim energy and warlike determination; but these moments were followed by other moments when he meekly followed Bonnet.

But Bonnet, like Mr. Chamberlain, was perfectly consistent. His Spanish policy—closely dependent on his Italian policy—did not vary for a moment between May 1938 and the bitter end; and although it is difficult to say exactly at what moment he made up his mind to abandon Czechoslovakia, from that moment onwards he was perfectly consistent —in spite of his public utterances and his assurances to the Czech Minister—assurances which he *had* to give.

As regards Spain, it is not perhaps without significance that it was very soon after the closing of the Catalan frontier to armaments and while the bombing of British ships was in full swing that the Bank of France refused to hand over to the Bank of Spain the £7,500,000 of gold it had held for it since 1931, on the ground that if the insurgents won, the Bank of France 'might have to pay twice.' The Spanish Government's claim was rejected by the first Chamber of the Paris Court of Appeal on July 6.

Feeling that the matter was not within its competence and was too delicate to be judged summarily, the Court decided that the civil tribunal in Paris must settle the action. This meant a year's delay.[4]

A year's delay! That is precisely what suited the enemies of the Spanish Government perfectly. The judgment was described in the Press of the Left as iniquitous, and was attributed to political wire-pulling.

[4] Reuter.

184

VII. ROYAL INTERLUDE

DURING that summer of 1938 there were days, and even weeks when France seemed to be living in a fool's paradise. Or was it that everybody was, more or less, practising a *carpe diem* philosophy? For, there were moments when France was reminded of the danger surrounding her.

But people forgot about it, and continued their preparations—for the *Fête Nationale* and for the British royal visit.

The political importance of the royal visit was obvious: it was to be a glowing demonstration of the Franco-British *entente*, 'the greatest safeguard of world peace.' It was somehow assumed that such a demonstration would even discourage Germany against doing anything very rash to Czechoslovakia.

The French like royalty, and above all, British royalty; some because they like royalty as such, others because the British Royal Family represents the head of a great democracy. Regarding those numerous Parisians who like royalty 'as such,' La Fouchardière was scarcely exaggerating when he wrote:

> It has been suggested that the public should be admitted to the royal apartments in the Quai d'Orsay after the royal visit; that ten francs should be charged at the door and the money be devoted to a charitable cause. I am sure it's a good idea, for our Parisians will pay ten francs to see empty royal apartments, even if they will not pay fifty centimes to see the President's apartments, complete with the President inside them.

Needless to add, the British royal visit was altogether more important than any other royal visits. The union of Britain and France was the best and the only solid hope in Europe, that peace might yet be saved. Not that many people in France were uncritical of the way the two great democracies had been 'saving peace.' Thus, while it is true that thousands and thousands of British flags were being bought by Parisians with complete spontaneity and without any official coaxing or compulsion, the *Canard Enchaîné* could not resist the temptation of producing a cartoon in which a Frenchman was shown putting up a Union Jack outside his window while another was seen looking at the sky and saying to him, 'The British flag—why, you are crazy! Do you want Franco to come and bomb you?'

．　　．　　．　　．　　．　　．　　．

Here are a few extracts from notes written at the time.

On July 19, punctually at ten minutes to five, the royal train, drawn by its blue and gold stream-lined engine and with the Union Jack painted on its sides, steamed into the Bois de Boulogne station.

The platform was crowded. Here were M. and Mme. Lebrun, M. Herriot and M. Jeanneney, the presidents of the Chamber and of the Senate, and nearly all the members of the Government and members of the British Embassy in their full-dress Diplomatic, Army, Navy, and Air Force uniforms.

The door of the fourth carriage opened and the King and Queen stepped out. The President then presented to the King and Queen M. Herriot and M. Jeanneney and the members of the Government.

What an excellent first contact with Paris! French art—old and new. The station was decorated with fine tapestries, delicately floodlit, and outside, Bourdelle's statue, standing on its high white pedestal and decorated with tricoloured streamers, looked dazzlingly bright when looked at from the dark hall. Moreover, after a dull morning and afternoon the sun had suddenly come out. At the foot of the statue large crowds of schoolchildren, many in pretty pale blue frocks and white bonnets, were waving British flags, and as the King and Queen came out into the open from the Gobelins Hall the military band struck up 'God Save the King.' At that moment the Union Jack was hoisted up the high mast beside Bourdelle's statue, and when a minute later the band struck up the 'Marseillaise,' ten thousand white pigeons, concealed behind the statue, were suddenly released, and rising in a wonderful fan-like movement, disappeared into the trees of the Bois de Boulogne.

On this funny afternoon the royal cavalcade sped down the Avenue Foch and past the Etoile and down the Champs-Elysées. What a reception Paris gave them! The enthusiasm was enormous—and spontaneous. Over the three and a half miles of the royal route, like an ocean wave the cry of '*Vive le Roi!*' sped down Paris. Paris was welcoming the King and Queen and the head of the great sister democracy.

By half-past five the great entry into Paris was over. And everybody said what a pity it was that the little Princesses had not come. 'They would have enjoyed it so much.'

.   .   .   .

The enthusiasm is general and is not confined to the 'West End' by any means. A large part of the public in the Champs-Elysées had come from the working-class districts. M. Blum, in the *Populaire*, warmly welcomed to-day the head of 'British democracy,' and the Communist *Humanité* was altogether enthusiastic about the King and Queen.

. . . .

On July 21 the King left by train for Versailles, to attend the great military review.

In spite of the dull weather the review, which lasted no less than seventy minutes, was a brilliant affair, and not only brilliant but strikingly competent in every detail. Salutes were fired, and after a bugle-call, battalion after battalion marched or rode past in perfect step to the sound of military music. First came several cavalry battalions; then, in their stiff, black, gold-embroidered uniforms and with their swords drawn, came the studious-looking cadets of the Polytechnique, many of them with spectacles on their noses; these were closely followed by the St. Cyriens with their picturesque tricolour plumes and carrying bayonets. Next came the sprightly Chasseurs Alpins—first a battalion wearing field helmets and then other battalions wearing the familiar large blue beret and carrying with their rifles either alpenstocks or pairs of skis.

And then, in the distance, far down the Avenue de Paris, one saw from the royal stand a whole forest of bayonets approaching. Though less colourful than the rest, these thousands and thousands of 'ordinary' French infantry, dressed in khaki, were deeply impressive as they marched in brisk and perfect step past the King. There were some twenty to twenty-five thousand of them, a fraction of France's conscript army—the successors of the *poilus* of Verdun, the flesh and blood of the people of France. Thousands and more thousands marched past—each man with his own mind and his own personality, but perfectly disciplined when performing his soldier's duty.

The *poilus* were followed by another ten minutes of 'pageantry.' Zouaves, wearing tall red fezzes, rode past, then some black Senegalese warriors, their band beating drums and twirling trumpets and trombones in the air; Algerian Fusiliers in broad blue plus-four-like breeches and blue tunics with splashes of yellow; and several battalions of the Algerian and Moroccan Spahis, in their white fluttering cloaks.

All this looked romantic; what followed was less so. It was the motorized and mechanized units, ordinary armoured cars, and armoured cars on caterpillar wheels drawing 75-millimetre field guns; then some specimens of long anti-aircraft guns followed by larger six-inch guns, their carriages inscribed with a useful motto: 'A well-kept gun is worth two.'

187

Next came a whole swarm of motor-cycles with armoured side-cars carrying automatic rifles, and more armoured cars carrying the famous Hotchkiss machine-gun, which can fire some five hundred rounds a minute.

The review closed with a great display of tanks—whole crowds of small ones looking like monstrous little brothers of the Baby Austin and running almost as fast; then larger and larger and larger tanks, the largest of all being the fifty-ton tanks which, like battleships, are not numbered but known by their names—mostly names of French towns and provinces. The largest of all the French tanks—those weighing eighty tons—were not shown, as they would have damaged the street.

Several hundred aeroplanes, in group formation, and mostly flying very low, droned over the city of the French kings. Here were the Dewoitine bombers and the beautiful (for in spite of grim associations they were beautiful) Bloch bombers, looking like so many giant dragon-flies, and most remarkable of all, the new Morane pursuit planes, flying at over three hundred and sixty miles an hour. The Morane planes are among the first mass-produced planes, and the French Government is making every effort to increase their production.

But most memorable of all were the artisitc functions—the sail down the Seine with its dragons at the Pont-Neuf, the *féte champétre* at Versailles, and the garden party at Bagatelle.

.   .   .   .

There was only one flaw in the otherwise perfect atmosphere of the royal visit, and that was the absence of any really direct contact between the King and Queen and the ordinary people of Paris. And this flaw was corrected on their own initiative by the King and Queen when, shortly before midnight, they appeared on the floodlit balcony of their apart-ments of the Quai d'Orsay and waved to the thousands of people who had been waiting all evening outside and calling for the King and Queen. The enthusiasm of the crowd was such that several people who witnessed the scene said they had never seen anything like it in Paris since Armistice Day in 1918.

.   .   .   .

It was during the royal visit that a decision of the utmost importance was taken. It was when Lord Halifax informed the French Ministers of the British Government's proposal to send Lord Runciman to Prague. The French agreed. Captain Wiedemann had, during the previous week, visited London.

The decision to send Lord Runciman to Prague was kept dark for several days. At the reception at the Quai d'Orsay on the last night of the royal visit to Paris, while Lord Halifax was talking at great length to M. Flandin among the floodlit emerald trees, I met M. Osusky, the Czech Minister. 'Quite satisfactory, quite satisfactory, the talks about Czechoslovakia. *Really* quite satisfactory,' he said. 'Any new developments?' 'No, no, nothing new, everything *quite* satisfactory.' One could see he was hiding something, and that he was not so sure that it was all *quite* so satisfactory.

At length, M. Flandin left Lord Halifax, and departed, with a big smirk on his face. Had Halifax told him about Runciman? What was he so pleased about? Flandin had, a month earlier, violently attacked Daladier for supporting the Spanish Government. Now he seemed to be *persona grata* at the Quai d'Orsay. Bonnet had by that time persuaded Daladier to follow Chamberlain's advice about the Catalan frontier; and, as for Czechoslovakia, Bonnet and Flandin were already seeing, more or less, eye to eye.

Exactly a week before the royal visit, Daladier had said: 'The solemn undertakings we have given to Czechoslovakia are sacred and cannot be evaded.'[1]

VIII. AUGUST: THE RUNCIMAN RESPITE

NOBODY had any serious illusions that Lord Runciman would bring about a lasting settlement of the Czech problem.

In France, opinion on the Runciman Mission was divided. Those who desired, above all, to preserve an extremely valuable ally in Central Europe, were greatly alarmed; those who wanted, above all, to avoid the danger of war looked hopefully to the Runciman Mission for at least a 'temporary' easing of the situation. In the Government itself these two opinions were held—the former by M. Reynaud and M. Mandel, the latter by M. Bonnet, M. de Monzie and others. M. Daladier was not quite sure what to think of it; for he knew that his military advisers were greatly perturbed at the thought of all that the Runciman Mission

[1] Speech in Paris, on July 12.

might eventually produce. Pertinax, representing the old Nationalist tradition, and voicing the opinion of French military experts, observed that in Anglo-French policy the lead had, up till then, been in the hands of France.

'The *primary fact* has, so far, been France's determination not to allow Czechoslovakia to be invaded. Now the lead has been taken out of France's hands, and the *primary fact* is now no longer the Franco-Czech alliance, but the results of the Runciman Mission; that is, the "Runciman Report".'

If Czechoslovakia and the Franco-Czech alliance were to be saved, it was necessary to secure an agreement between the Czechs and Sudetens which would still leave the military authority of the Czechoslovakian State unimpaired over its whole territory. The Sudetens, left to themselves, could certainly come to such terms with the Czech Government; but then the trouble was that they were not left to themselves, and that all the wires were being pulled by Germany, to whom a continued Czech military control of the Sudeten areas was the very thing that was not acceptable. But the only way of demanding from Germany that she accept a settlement compatible with the sovereignty of Czechoslovakia was to threaten her with war; and neither the French nor the British Government were prepared to do so, in earnest.

•   •   •   •   •   •   •

The preservation of the military mechanism of the Franco-Czech alliance—of 'the Bohemian bastion'—was, psychologically, a bad slogan for convincing not only British but even French public opinion. It was not enough to say that the Sudeten agitation for complete autonomy (for the question of the transfer of territory had not yet arisen at the time) had been artificially worked up by Nazi propaganda; the man-in-the-street was becoming gradually convinced that the Sudeten Germans were entitled to their claim; and the fact that the Czech crisis was, as it were, spread over a period of many months gave Germany the opportunity to impress gradually on the minds of the British and French people that the Sudetens *had* a good case for national autonomy; and once this had sunk into British and French minds, the next step was to impress upon them the fact that even with autonomy Czechoslovakia would still be a mess, and that it might be just as well to accept a clean cut—that is, the transfer of territory. Where persuasion—through the Press and in other ways—did not work, intimidation was resorted to.

The slow process by which French opinion was gradually demoralized was a masterpiece of tactics and propaganda. The Germans rightly guessed that, in spite of all the official assurances given to Czechoslovakia, there was, both in French political quarters, and among the French people themselves, a soil rich in war-weary pacifism. M. Bonnet, the French Foreign Minister, a man with a great influence both inside the Cabinet and with the Press, was himself strongly inclined towards the pacifist view, which he perhaps sincerely believed represented the innermost feelings of the greater part of the French people. He—as subsequent events were to show—did everything to discourage the revival of patriotic or militarist sentiments. But that did not become fully apparent until later.

· · · · · · ·

August was, in spite of everything, a holiday month in France. I went first to Brittany, which was packed with English tourists, and later down to the French Alps and the Riviera. Nobody seemed to be greatly worried. A widespread feeling was: 'Nothing much is likely to happen as long as Runciman is in Prague. *Qu'ils se débrouillent.*'

· · · · · · ·

And yet anyone lying on the beach at Juan-les-Pins would only have had to open any newspaper to see that the world was not faring well. Relations with Italy were as strained as ever. M. Bonnet thought the Italians ungrateful. Had France not done everything to please them?

Nevertheless, the Catalan frontier remained closed, both officially and unofficially, because M. Bonnet was still hoping to make friends with Italy. And it remained closed till the bitter end.

· · · · · · ·

Since the beginning of August the news from Germany was going daily from bad to worse. By the middle of the month there was no longer any doubt that at least 500,000 reservists had been called up; Germany had now 1,500,000 men under arms; civilian property was being commandeered on such a vast scale, on the eve of the great manœuvres on the Czechoslovak and French frontiers, that the public in Germany was becoming increasingly nervous every day, and talking more and more openly of war. A tremendous rush was being made to complete the fortifications in the west, and particularly along the Rhine. The Berlin correspondent of *The Times* reported that something like 300,000 men were working on these fortifications day and night. There was a heavy slump on the Berlin Bourse.

191

And even yet, French opinion was not unduly perturbed. On August 17, M. Blum wrote in the *Populaire*:

> French opinion remains calm, serious, and perfectly self-assured. The Government shows neither nervousness, emotion, nor precipitation.
>
> In my view, this is right in all respects. I believe that reflection and critical analysis of the facts lead to the dismissal of the hypothesis of an act of sudden aggression by Hitler against Czechoslovakia—even during the weeks when he will have ready in his hand an army whose exact strength is unknown. The most plausible conjecture is that Hitler is employing this menace to settle the Sudeten question peacefully, but nevertheless in his own way.
>
> The menace is suspended over France and England more than over Czechoslovakia. By making French and British opinion, which desire peace, aware of the war danger, Hitler reckons without doubt upon making London and Paris put a new turn of the screw upon Prague. The immediate danger is that this calculation should succeed. Nevertheless, I remain confident that neither London nor Paris will consent to be the instruments of Hitler's manœuvre.

In the *Figaro* M. d'Ormesson did not think it mattered. Hitler, he thought, needed a little excitement for his own prestige.

Henri de Kerillis took the threat more seriously, but thought that it could be checked, as it was on May 21, by a counter-threat, provided— he added significantly—'the nerve and the morale of our people are solidly forged.'

$$\cdot \quad \cdot \quad \cdot \quad \cdot \quad \cdot \quad \cdot \quad \cdot$$

It was at that time that the United States Government, unwilling to see matters drift any further, gave Germany a discreet first warning.

On August 16 Mr. Cordell Hull said on the wireless:

> 'To-day invasion of territory of sovereign States, destruction of lawfully constituted Governments, and forcible seizure of hitherto independent political entities and interference in the internal affairs of other nations, wholesale violation of established treaty obligations, attempts to adjust international differences by armed force—all these appalling manifestations of disintegration seriously threaten the very foundations of our civilization. . . .
>
> 'When the dignity of the human soul is denied in great parts of the world and when that denial is made a slogan under which propaganda is set in motion and armies take the field no one of us can be sure that his country, or even his home, is safe.'

And two days later, on August 18, Mr. Roosevelt said at Kingston, Ontario:

'We in the Americas are no longer a far-away continent to which eddies of controversy beyond the seas could bring no interest or harm.'

M. Blum no doubt smelling a rat at the Quai d'Orsay, thought that Mr. Cordell Hull's speech contained not only a warning to Germany but also one to England and France which, he said, 'must not acquiesce in a new defeat to the democratic cause without discouraging United States opinion and running the risk of alienating it.'

The Quai d'Orsay-ridden *Temps* was much more cautious:

It would be yielding to dangerous illusions to assume that at present the American people have rallied to a policy of active intervention in Europe. . . .

And so on. As if *that* was the point! But throughout the September crisis M. Bonnet consistently minimized the part America was playing; by declaring her material role in European affairs to be nil, he also implied that her moral role was of no importance. To the Foreign Affairs Committee and at other gatherings he would always say: 'You know, I spent a long time in Washington; and I know how isolationist they all are at heart. . . .'

.   .   .   .

In spite of more and more Czech concessions, the atmosphere in Central Europe was not improving, and a 'settlement' between the Czechs and the Sudetens was as little in sight as ever. On Saturday, August 27, Lord Runciman sent an urgent request to Henlein to call on him at Prince Clery's castle in Bohemia, where he was spending the week-end. The meeting between Henlein, Lord Runciman and Mr. Newton, the British Minister in Prague, lasted for two hours, but without any appreciable development for the better.

On that same day Sir John Simon made his Lanark speech—a speech for which the French had been waiting impatiently; for *at that stage* the view popularly taken in France was that if only Britain took a firm stand, Germany would be frightened to go too far. Sir John Simon's speech was, the French thought, fairly satisfactory, but not perhaps quite tough enough.

In his speech Sir John Simon reaffirmed Mr. Chamberlain's declaration of March 24 on the position of Great Britain in regard to Czechoslovakia. 'That declaration holds good to-day,' he said. 'There is nothing to add or to vary in its contents.' (That declaration, it will be recalled, was a warning that if war broke out 'it would be quite impossible to say where it would end and what Governments might become involved.') Sir John added:

'To find a solution for the controversy in Czechoslovakia contributions from all concerned are needed. We are convinced that, given goodwill on both sides, it should be possible to find a solution which is just to all legitimate interests.'

A serious shock to France came two days later—on August 29. That afternoon the startling news reached Paris that Hitler had just paid a surprise visit to the Rhineland. Accompanied by eight Generals of the General Staff, including General Von Brauchitsch and General Keitel, he had visited Kehl exactly opposite Strasbourg that morning. He had arrived at Kehl by road at 9 a.m.

'A quarter of an hour previously,' Reuter wrote from Strasbourg, 'the French people had been informed by the German authorities that the Chancellor was on his way, and both the French and German ends of the international bridge over the Rhine were closed.

'In Strasbourg the tour was taken very philosophically by the inhabitants, the majority of whom were unaware of the Chancellor's presence until after he had left. Only a few persons who were turned back at the bridge heard that Herr Hitler was on the opposite bank. Others only learned of the tour in the noon news broadcast.

'The inhabitants of Strasbourg recall that Field-Marshal Goering has also inspected the frontier fortifications.'

One is not so sure that the people of Strasbourg took it as 'philosophically' as all that; for it was soon after this 'surprise visit' to Kehl that the people of Strasbourg began to take their money out of the savings banks, and prepare to move farther inland.

IX. WAS MUNICH INEVITABLE?

IN ANY attempt to assess the proportion of blame due to France and Great Britain in the handling of the Czech crisis, one important fact should always be borne in mind: and that is that while France was an ally of Czechoslovakia, Great Britain was not. This fact was often forgotten— by the French themselves. The dispatch to Prague of the Runciman Mission, in the words of Pertinax, became 'fact number 1,' whereas until then 'fact number 1' had been the Franco-Czech alliance. But in reality, the lead had already passed into British hands some time earlier; the principle of British mediation had already been agreed to at the end of April; and I remember how in London, after the conclusion of the Anglo-French talks, I remarked to one of the shrewdest French journalists: 'Well, there is going to be one victim of these talks—and that is Spain,' to which François Quilici replied: 'You are wrong. There are going to be two victims; and the other one is Czechoslovakia.'

The firm Franco-British stand was successful on May 21; and that kept up the illusion for some time that a 'firm stand' might work again; but was not May 21 something of a fluke? In May, France and Britain had not been subjected to that intimidation which was to be practised on them so successfully in September.

But no sooner had the effects of May 21 worn off than Britain, supported by France, continued her pressure on Prague (which was, in effect, the form that her 'mediation' took at that time. But at that time France, at any rate, still assumed that a settlement would be reached and 'must' be reached in a manner compatible with the integrity of Czechoslovakia; and, after the appointment of the Runciman Mission, M. Bonnet instructed M. Corbin to tell the British Government that only a settlement within the present borders of Czechoslovakia and compatible with the continued sovereignty of the Czechoslovak State over all its territory, was acceptable to France. But it was really little good informing *the British Government* about it; such a statement was obviously only the expression of a pious hope, and no more, since Lord Runciman had already in effect been given *carte blanche*.

Then came August, and the great German mobilization. For a good long time France did *nothing* about that mobilization. She was just waiting. The Government, and particularly M. Bonnet, kept on suggesting that France could do nothing without being certain of British support. Sir John Simon spoke sufficiently clearly at Lanark on August 27. It was not until September 5 that the Maginot Line was properly manned. About one hundred thousand 'specialists' were called up. After that France sat back and waited for the Nuremberg Congress and Hitler's speech. It is not in the least surprising that, in the circumstances, the Nuremberg Congress should have produced what it did produce. It was all very well for Sir Nevile Henderson to 'warn' the Germans about Britain's attitude; the Germans did not believe that the French would 'march.'

And then, after Hitler's speech, came the French Cabinet meeting of September 13, which was a complete climb-down. In spite of everything, in spite of the firm 'authoritative statement' published in London two days earlier, it decided against mobilization; and Mr. Chamberlain was expected to settle matters somehow. Mr. Chamberlain went off to Berchtesgaden. After what had happened in Paris, one can well imagine Hitler's self-assurance.

By that time Mr. Chamberlain was, obviously, willing to accept almost any 'compromise.' For Mr. Chamberlain, as the French should have known, was in any case not a man particularly well suited for defending the interests of France's ally. But they did not care. They wanted him to shoulder the responsibility for the surrender of Czechoslovakia, and then be able to say that 'it was England's fault.'

It is curious that it was not until Berchtesgaden that Germany first demanded the cession of the Sudeten territory. Almost right up to the middle of September Germany had still spoken of Sudeten 'rights'; i.e., she still spoke in terms of a settlement *within* the limits of the Czechoslovak State—even though the rights demanded were no longer compatible with the integrity of that State. Even in his Nuremberg speech on September 12, Hitler still spoke as though he were ready to accept a settlement at least nominally *within* Czech limits, and his allusion to a plebiscite was left deliberately vague. It was not until the day when Mr. Chamberlain flew to Berchtesgaden that Hitler realized the extent to which Britain and France were frightened; and it was while Mr. Chamberlain was flying to Berchtesgaden that Henlein published his famous proclamation, saying *for the first time*, that the Sudetens wished to be incorporated within the German Reich. It was during Chamberlain's flight to Berchtesgaden that the autonomists became rebels.

Berchtesgaden really meant the end of Czechoslovakia; and France's responsibility for Berchtesgaden is immense.

After everything was over, a close associate of M. Daladier's told me:
'Notre erreur fatale, c'est de ne pas avoir pris position au bon moment.'

Prendre position: it was easily said. And the question arises whether Munich could have been avoided.

What could *prendre position* have meant? It could have meant this. Since France was Czechoslovakia's ally, it was for her to warn Germany *as early as possible* that, while willing to support such minority claims of the Sudeten Germans as were compatible with the sovereignty of the Czechoslovak State, she could not consent to a *territorial* change, or to a form of Sudeten autonomy which would in practice have amounted to the same thing.

If this warning alone failed to achieve the desired effect, France could have gone a step further. During the great German mobilization in August

196

she could *also* have mobilized. The whole atmosphere at the Nuremberg Congress would have been entirely different. Would Britain have opposed the French mobilization in such circumstances? It is, to say the least, extremely doubtful. But still the French would not budge. When, on the 12th, Hitler spoke, he was clearly convinced that since France had assumed an attitude of non-resistance, Germany could go on asking for more and more. But the French Government was unenterprising and did not want even to *risk* a war, and kept on saying that no support was to be expected from England, and that it was better to let England arrange things 'somehow.' Even on September 13, the day after Hitler's Nuremberg speech, France failed to mobilize, and hoped that Mr. Chamberlain would 'arrange things' at Berchtesgaden.

September was marked in France by an intense conflict between the 'pacifists' and the 'warmongers.' In reality the warmongers were the men who were trying to 'bluff' Hitler into moderation, into the acceptance of a solution acceptable to Czechoslovakia, and who in the last resort, were inevitably prepared to risk a war. They might have yielded in the end if Hitler had still demanded annexation, but at least they *tried* to dissuade him, in the only language he understood, from doing so. And the chances are that if they had taken a strong stand in time, and had rallied to France many of the other countries threatened by German hegemony, *it is not their bluff, but Hitler's, which would have been called. But their readiness to bluff and to take a risk came to nothing, because the pacifists kept on proclaiming that France would neither bluff nor take any risks;* and that if only Hitler was patient enough to wait a little, he would get everything or almost everything, without fighting. Since France was not going to risk a war, it was obvious that her concessions were going to increase in the same proportion as Hitler's demands.

One of the most astonishing things of all is that, *on the whole, the French Government was more 'pacifist' than the British Government. That is to say that, given the fact that France was Czechoslovakia's ally, she was, relatively, much weaker than was England as a non-ally of Czechoslovakia.* That is even truer if one compares not the two Governments, but the Press of the two countries, and in this case not only relatively but absolutely. If at any time in the first two weeks of September France had taken a strong lead in firmly opposing Germany's deliberate intention to destroy Czechoslovakia, the British Government and British opinion would have supported her. The British Foreign Office was clearly opposed to a surrender of Czechoslovakia; so also were certain members of the French Foreign Office—but only to be violently abused as warmongers in *Gringoire* and other papers of the

197

same sort—and that *with M. Bonnet's approval*. For immediately after Munich two of the three high officials attacked in *Gringoire* were got rid of by M. Bonnet. M. Pierre Comert, the head of the Press Department, was appointed to a much more obscure post, while M. Massigli was sent as Ambassador to Ankara. M. Léger[1] alone was left where he was: *le morceau était trop gros,* somebody remarked.

There was a moment early in September when an energetic French lead could in a large measure have revived collective security in Europe. Turkey, Jugoslavia, Rumania, and even Poland—though not perhaps M. Beck—were showing signs of anger and anxiety at the sight of Germany's immense war preparations; and Russia was, to all appearances, ready to support a policy of resistance. As for Italy, she was obviously wobbling. A bold French lead at that moment would probably have received support from England and the chief Eastern European States; and collective security might in a large measure have been restored. But this brief psychological moment—it lasted only a few days—was missed. No attempt of any sort was made in that direction, while Russia was deliberately discouraged from doing or saying anything. Mr. Duff Cooper's criticism of the British Government for its failure to mobilize the fleet or give Germany some other equally tangible warning long before the crisis had come to a head *could have been addressed even more effectively to the French Government.*

Instead, the French Government preferred to leave the fate of her ally in the hands of Mr. Chamberlain, who certainly did not think of Czechoslovakia in terms of France's treaty obligations. For, perhaps long before anybody else, Mr. Chamberlain had got the idea that the Czechs and the Sudetens could not live together much longer. He did not reason in general European terms. And the French *must* have known of Mr. Chamberlain's personal opinion on Czechoslovakia. His opinion had, in fact, been given considerable publicity in the American Press.

According to Joseph Driscol in the *New York Herald Tribune* of May 14, Mr. Chamberlain had, in the first week in May, discussed the Czech situation at a private luncheon given by Lady Astor to a group of American correspondents. The Prime Minister then already thought that frontier revision might be preferable to cantonal autonomy. The revision he envisaged was the cession of a 'fringe' of territory to Germany which, according to him, would transform Czechoslovakia into a smaller but sounder State.

As for the Prime Minister's belief that, after partition Czechoslovakia

---

[1] The permanent head of the French Foreign Office.

198

would be a 'smaller but sounder' State, it is conceivable that with the illusions he then still entertained on the possibilities of loyal co-operation with the Dictators, he *did* hold such a belief.

And so it was Mr. Chamberlain who, with the blessings of the French Government, was to handle the Czech crisis. One of the most remarkable features of French conduct was the discouragement given by M. Bonnet to any energetic move in Czechoslovakia's favour coming, not only from France, but also *from Britain*. Throughout September, M. Bonnet privately told everybody that *no* firm stand was to be expected from Britain; and when, at the height of the crisis Lord Halifax and the Foreign Office *did* take a strong stand, M. Bonnet did everything to suggest that it meant nothing. In effect, M. Bonnet spent his time suggesting to the British Ambassador that France would not 'march,' and suggesting to the French that the British could not be relied upon. As for the Russians, he claimed that they were no good at all—another point I shall discuss later. M. Bonnet *wanted* Munich; and he was not alone in wanting it. To the unfortunate Czechs alone he would not at first admit it, but on the contrary continued to assure them as late as the first week of September of French support. But the Germans knew what he really felt, and they acted accordingly.

In spite of all the arguments about the Czech Maginot Line and the Bohemian Bastion, France and Britain (and, in a large measure, French and British opinion) were led astray by the ethnical argument used with such tremendous effect by German propaganda. But it was an ethnical argument the futility of which was terribly difficult to demonstrate until the day when the Germans demonstrated it themselves by walking into Prague. The most that could be said against it in September was what Low said. He hit the nail on the head with his cartoon on the 'Procession of Nightmares'—the Nightmares being: Germans in Czechoslovakia, Germans in Rumania, Germans in Hungary, Germans in Alsace, German-speaking Swiss, Germans in America, and so on. *Nevertheless, the case for defending the integrity of Czechoslovakia was, if not exactly an unconvincing one, at least not a sufficiently clear one;* and the French Press—whether in some cases bribed by Germany, or, in others, simply reflecting a weary isolationist mood—had made every effort for months to confuse the issues in the French mind. It was somehow bad style to talk about the Czech Maginot Line; just as it was bad style to quote *Mein Kampf*; people replied: 'That's all very well, but——'; and *the fact that three million Germans 'wanted to be German,' was difficult to explain away by strategic arguments.* It was not until the last week of September that a large part of French opinion *fully* realized that in wishing to destroy Czechoslovakia Germany was striving to dominate Europe by the threat of its force. It was Hitler's bellowing on the wireless that convinced hundreds of thousands of Frenchmen of Hitler's evil intentions—Frenchmen whom no arguments about the 'Bohemian Bastion' or even the sacredness of France's signature could convince. Hitler made them angry. But there were millions of others who still did not see it, or who preferred to take a chance on it.

A point worth remembering is that pacifist, Flandinist and German-paid propaganda always made a special point of saying that *whoever favoured a policy of 'firmness' in relation to Germany was a belliciste— a warmonger—and wanted war with Germany.* That was Bonnet's argument and early in December (though not before that) it became Daladier's argument: *'La politique de fermeté c'était la politique de guerre.'*

X. THE PARIS PRESS IN SEPTEMBER

THE policy of 'no surrender' was advocated with great vigour by only five dailies and two of the important weeklies. These papers naturally criticized with great violence the Daladier Government, and in particular M. Bonnet.

The great *belliciste*[1] paper was the Communist *Humanité*, with its closely reasoned and unusually well documented foreign editorials by Gabriel Péri, the Communist deputy for Argenteuil, a man of great culture and with a fine polemical pen.[2] The evening paper, *Ce Soir,* was also *belliciste.*

Next the Nationalist *Epoque.* Henri de Kerillis,[3] the impetuous Nationalist deputy for Neuilly, described as the Cassandra of France by some, and as an 'hysterical woman' by others, represented what might be called the old traditional policy of French nationalism to which the

[1] Here and everywhere I use the words *belliciste* and *warmonger* for convenience, and ironically. Anybody who stood for a policy of firmness, and resistance, was branded a *belliciste.*

[2] Péri (whom I knew well) was shot as a hostage by the Germans at the end of 1941. His death was that of a French hero and patriot. (Author's note, 1942.)

[3] Now De Gaulle's representative in Canada. (Author's note, 1942.)

'Eastern Alliance' was an unanswerable dogma. Kerillis has no anti-Fascist prejudices; to him Germany, always striving for European hegemony, is simply France's hereditary enemy; *any* alliance—even with the hated Bolsheviks—is good if it can keep Germany in check. Apart from Germany, Kerillis is not hostile to Fascism; he wailed over sanctions which had made an enemy of Italy; but later he lost his long-cherished illusions about the fragility of the Berlin-Rome axis, and no longer even blamed sanctions for it, but admitted that Italy had, unfortunately, become Germany's satellite. In the early days of the Spanish war, Kerillis was passionately pro-Franco, but later complained bitterly because France had allowed Franco to be snatched away by Italy and Germany, and wished France had backed him from the start—overlooking the fact that Franco was already being backed by Berlin and Rome.

The *Ordre*, nominally a Right-Wing paper, is edited by M. Emile Buré. It consistently supported the Franco-Soviet Pact, and the maintenance of as many Eastern alliances as possible. 'After Sadowa, Sedan,' was, as it were, its slogan. Since the end of the *Echo de Paris*, which died in June 1938, Pertinax has been a regular contributor to *Ordre*. He differs from Kerillis (with whom he seemed to be in perpetual conflict on the *Echo de Paris* over the Abyssinian crisis) by his far wider knowledge of international affairs and by a clearer and less emotional presentation of his facts and arguments. The weekly, *Europe Nouvelle*, pursues the same policy as *Ordre*. The editor is Pertinax. It has specialized in devastating 'revelations' about M. Georges Bonnet.[4]

The *Aube*, edited by a brilliant writer, M. Georges Bidault, may also be classified among the 'warmonger' papers. It is the organ of liberal Catholicism, strongly opposed to Fascism on both religious and political grounds. Its views closely reflect those of Cardinal Verdier, the Archbishop of Paris. More ambiguous during the September crisis was the attitude of the other Catholic paper, *La Croix*.

An important weekly advocating the policy of firmness and 'no surrender' was the *Lumière*, edited by M. Georges Boris. Its contributors are mainly Socialists and Left-Wing Radicals like M. Albert Bayet. In the view of the *Lumière*, it is useless closing one's eyes to the fact that the battle in Europe is above all an ideological battle. M. Flandin's mentality has closer affinities with that of a German Nazi than with that of a true French democrat. A victory for Hitler means a victory for the French Fascists or *fascisants*. The *Lumière*, like some of the other 'war-

[4] Pertinax, Buré, Kerillis and Mme Tabouis are now in America. Mme Le Verrier, Editor of the *Europe Nouvelle*, and leading members of the *Lumière*, besides M. Louis Lévy of the *Populaire*, are in London. (Author's note, 1942.)

monger' papers, foresaw in the betrayal of Czechoslovakia a deadly blow to the democratic cause.

The Socialist *Populaire*, like the trade union paper, the *Peuple*, were both anti-Fascist and were intensely revolted by Germany's bullying of Czechoslovakia. But both papers showed some hesitation on the best way of dealing with the Czech crisis. M. Blum, though begging England to show 'firmness,' himself showed considerable hesitation in advocating a 'firm' policy. This has been attributed to a number of causes: first, to the knowledge that there was a large body of ultra-pacifist opinion in the Socialist Party, and that a breach within the Socialist Party could only be avoided by a cautious handling of the Czech situation; secondly, to Blum's own innate pacifism and the reluctance to take any war risks, and lastly, perhaps, to a certain self-consciousness created by the propaganda which consisted in saying that 'the Jews want war, because they hope to destroy Hitler.' Although he wanted to see Czechoslovakia saved, Blum praised Mr. Chamberlain for his 'noble audacity in his will for peace' when the British Premier took the aeroplane for Berchtesgaden; and when the dismemberment of Czechoslovakia was decided upon Blum said that he had received the news with 'mixed feelings of cowardly relief and shame.' But Blum's cautious and somewhat uneasy 'firmness' was offset in the *Populaire* by the altogether outspokenly pacifist articles of Paul Faure, whose argument was that 'war was, in any case, not a solution.'

Conflicting tendencies of the same kind were to be found in the *Peuple*, the organ of the C.G.T., except that its Communist members were more outspokenly 'firm' than the hesitating 'warmongers' of the *Populaire*. One hundred per cent 'pacifist' was *Syndicats*, the weekly organ of the syndicalist and anti-Communist section of the C.G.T. (Belin, Delmas, etc.).

It is curious to note that that great anti-Fascist satirical weekly, the *Canard Enchaîné* became, at least as far as M. Bénard's 'leaders' were concerned, almost rabidly pacifist in September, one of its principal arguments being: 'What do we care if 3,000,000 Germans want to be German?' A similar line was taken by M. Bergery in the *Flèche*.

The rest of the Paris Press, as we shall see, ranged from the half-hearted semi-official outlook (strongly inspired by M. Bonnet) to the plainly defeatist outlook which, in practice, was not very different. During the first week or ten days of September most of these papers were still moderately 'firm.' But by the middle of September all these officially inspired papers were ready to accept 'any settlement of the Czech crisis short of an invasion.' In the *Œuvre*, the 'warmongering' articles of

Mme Tabouis were cancelled out, as it were, by the 'pacifist' editorials of Jean Piot, the editor of the paper, and an ex-serviceman who loathed the very thought of another war; and even Mme Tabouis, who regarded the loss of Czechoslovakia and, 'consequently,' the loss of the whole of Eastern Europe as disastrous to France, actually said less than she would no doubt have liked to say; for the *Œuvre*, which had changed hands some months earlier, was now much less the great independent organ of militant Radicalism than it had been. The *Œuvre* tended more and more to reflect the views of M. Bonnet than those of M. Herriot. The two other Paris papers, which were at least nominally Radical, the *Ere Nouvelle* and the *République*, reflecting the views of men like M. Caillaux, were among the most 'defeatist' of all.

The conservative *Figaro* reflected a certain variety of views: while M. d'Ormesson was essentially *bonnetiste*, M. Romier took a rather longer view, while writers like M. Mauriac and M. Duhamel were, chiefly for moral and intellectual reasons, deeply perturbed by the deadly spread of the Nazi Anti-Civilization in Europe.

The two popular evening papers in Paris, *L'Intransigeant* and *Paris-Soir* were 'pro-Munich.' Very notable in this respect were the articles of M. Sauerwein in *Paris-Soir*.

The *Temps* was even more *officieux* than usual, and in the first half of September it did not hesitate to criticize openly the 'dilatory tactics' of Dr. Beneš. Later it shed crocodile's tears over the fate of Czechoslovakia. Much the same line was also taken by the *Petit Parisien*. However, it is only fair to say that both the *Temps* and the *Petit Parisien* refrained from the grosser forms of misrepresentation practised by certain papers of the Right, such as the *Jour*, the *Journal*, the *Matin* and the *Action Française*. Although M. Bailby in the *Jour* and M. Maurras in the *Action Française* betrayed brief moments of hesitation at the prospect of Germany's immense bloodless victory, all these papers, as well as the pro-Fascist weeklies like *Gringoire* and *Candide*—not to mention a plainly Nazi sheet like *Je Suis Partout*—were ideologically hostile to Czechoslovakia, even if not openly friendly to Germany and fully prepared to abandon Eastern Europe to its fate. They were also keenly looking forward to the political consequences in France itself of the surrender of Czechoslovakia. The *Matin*, in particular, was always playing on the 'anti-Comintern' string, and seemed to favour the destruction of 'Bolshevism' by Hitler. All these papers, more or less, believed in the virtues of the Four-Power Pact policy.

So also did the *Information*, the leading Paris financial paper. Controlled by the Banque Lazard, known to be in close contact with M.

Bonnet, the Foreign Minister, the *Information* counted among its principal contributors M. Fernand de Brinon, a leading light on the Comité France-Allemagne—a body working for the 'cultural' *rapprochement* between France and Nazi Germany. M. de Brinon had for many years advocated a *direct* understanding between France and Germany, had stood for Four-Power politics, and for the surrender of the whole of Central and Eastern Europe to German 'influence.' As long ago as 1933 he went to Germany to interview Hitler, and produced (with the approval of M. Daladier, the then War Minister) a sensational interview in the *Matin* with an almost extravagantly pacifist Hitler. M. de Brinon wrote, shortly after Munich, a sensational article demonstrating the virtues of 'self-determination' which since Munich, he said, had been accepted as an 'unchallengeable' principle. M. Ybarnégaray and others have publicly, in the Chamber of Deputies, referred to M. de Brinon with great contempt.[5] The paper of M. Doriot, the *Liberté* and the *Emancipation Nationale* were also entirely defeatist; the *Liberté* being the only paper that printed M. Flandin's poster on September 26, virtually inviting the people of France to resist mobilization.

As for Colonel de la Rocque, who from a budding and almost blossoming dictator in 1935 had now degenerated into a not very competent newspaper editor, he was, during some days in September, altogether incoherent. On the day after the Anglo-French acceptance of Hitler's Berchtesgaden plan, La Rocque proclaimed in his paper, the *Petit Journal*, that the authority and prestige of France had never yet stood so high!

The proportion of papers which advocated 'any old settlement' of the Czech conflict or a complete betrayal of Czechoslovakia was, it will have been noted, extraordinarily high. To say that this Press reflected accurately the feelings of the French people would be untrue; it reflected, above all, the influence of certain big financial and big business interests (not that big business in France was unanimous in its defeatism—thus the *Journée Industrielle* reflecting the views of a large part of the big employers, including some who had big interests in Czechoslovakia, was by no means wholeheartedly pro-Munich). Further, it reflected the views of M. Bonnet and many other leading politicians, many of whom were sincerely convinced that French opinion was not 'marching,' and that, in any case, it was not worth while risking a war for Czechoslovakia. It also reflected the wives of the *fascisant* elements,

---

[5] 'Crook' and 'scoundrel' were the terms applied to Vichy's present 'Ambassador' in Paris. (Author's note, 1942.)

who looked upon the Czech crisis as being, above all, an internal French issue: the betrayal of Czechoslovakia, they were conviced, *would completely discredit democracy in Europe,* and would enable them to gain greatly in influence, first, by stamping out Communism in France, and then Socialism, and then the democratic régime altogether. The *Gleichschaltung,* or even the vassalization of France did not unduly terrify these people. Kerillis has quoted a number of letters from people who said in effect that 'they would sooner be ruled by Hitler than by the Front Populaire.' The deterioration of the older *national* standards of France was very apparent from the Paris Press of September 1938.

At the same time, as has been rightly remarked, the French people were, in reality, far better than either their Press or their politicians. The readiness with which all the recruits joined their regiments, the absence of any 'incidents' during that day—and that in spite of weeks and months of 'defeatist' propaganda—was a surprise to those who were convinced that the French people would not 'march for Czechoslovakia.' A very high proportion of the French people felt instinctively, and in spite of everything, that it was not simply a case of marching 'for Czechoslavakia,' and that far greater issues were at stake.

Another point that will have been noticed from the above discussion on the Press is that there was no sharp division into Left and Right over the question of Czechoslovakia. As there were 'warmongers' among the Catholics (and their party, the *Démocrates Populaires*) and among the Nationalists (Pertinax, Buré, Kerillis, etc.—and Kerillis's influence was, in fact, far greater than is suggested by his isolated position in Parliament and the relatively small circulation of the *Epoque*), so there were also 'pacifists,' and advocates of 'peace at any price' on the Left, above all, among the Socialists and the Trade Unionists. Except for the Communists, who, on the face of it, at any rate, were completely unanimous in their policy of 'firmness' (though one would hesitate to vouch for the complete unanimity of their rank and file), all the parties, without exception, were divided, whether Left, Centre or Right. The Radical Party's feelings were, on the whole, well reflected in the hesitations and uncertainties and quarrels within the Daladier Government. Oddly enough, the two outstanding 'warmongers' were not Radicals, but two Centre Members of the Cabinet—M. Mandel and M. Paul Reynaud.

As for M. Daladier he was, as somebody remarked at the Chamber at the time of the crisis, the Mystery Man of France—'*bonnetist* one day and *belliciste* the next.' But, in reality, the *bonnetisme* was the stronger and the more lasting feeling of the two.

XI. SEPTEMBER: BEFORE BERCHTESGADEN

FRANCE was Czechoslovakia's ally; but nearly all that was happening during the first half of September was happening—outside France. In Prague, at Nuremberg, in the Sudeten country, and in London. In France, there were only 'reactions.' But little action. M. Bonnet alone was very active.

On August 24, Mr. Chamberlain, Lord Halifax and Sir John Simon held an important conference at the end of which it was decided to give a strong warning to Germany on the eve of the Nuremberg Congress—a warning to the effect that England would support France if the latter went to the aid of Czechoslovakia. Sir Nevile Henderson was instructed to convey this warning to the various Nazi leaders at Nuremberg. On August 25, the D.N.B., the German news agency, in a message from London denied 'on official authority' that any such British step was contemplated. Naturally, no such official denial had been given to the German agency. But, curiously enough, the Agence Havas published on the same day a message corroborating the German story.

In spite of this message, which was obviously 'officially inspired,' Sir John Simon made his speech at Lanark two days later.

It was on September 1 that Sir Nevile Henderson saw Ribbentrop. The story goes that, as on one or two subsequent occasions, Ribbentrop simply laughed in reply to the British Ambassador's warnings; but if so, did he not laugh because he was certain, not so much about Britain's determination to do nothing, as about France's extreme reluctance to 'march' for her ally? For if France was not going to 'march,' obviously Britain was not going to 'march' either.

On September 2, Paris was talking of a *détente*. Why? It sounds funny; on the previous day Lord Runciman had decided no longer to keep up the pretence of 'mediating' between the Czechs and the Sudetens, and had openly made Hitler a partner in the negotiations. Hitler had rejected the Czech Plan No. 3, but had accepted to continue negotiations. Whereupon Lord Runciman naturally pressed the Czech Government to produce Plan No. 4. That day, M. Bernus, in the *Journal des Débats*, had the sense to say that it was no use talking of *détente* because the German Press was a trifle less offensive than usual.

Nothing so gloomy in the *Figaro*, where M. d'Ormesson was happy to state that—

Whatever may be the interests and the passions, which are anxious to exaggerate their own importance, we must at any price demonstrate this one vital fact—the peaceful solidity of our country. Otherwise the risks will grow week after week.

In other words, it was no use demonstrating any kind of strength, or to warn Germany; it was enough to impress her with France's 'peaceful solidity'—whatever that meant. On the following day—September 3—the Press was a little more alarmed. In the same *Figaro*, the more clearsighted M. Romier wrote:

The Nuremberg Congress will show which course Hitler has chosen. *His choice will largely depend on the news he receives from abroad.*

Precisely. But no news was coming from France to impress him. The following day, Sunday, September 4, was, however, marked by an important event. That afternoon Mr. William Bullitt, the United States Ambassador, and M. Georges Bonnet 'celebrated' Franco-American friendship at the unveiling of the monument at the Pointe de Grave, commemorating the landing in France, in 1917, of the American troops.

Reference has already been made to the speeches made two weeks earlier by Mr. Roosevelt and Mr. Cordell Hull. Now it was Mr. Bullitt's turn to give a new American warning to Germany.

After exalting the ideals of freedom and democracy that were common to France and the United States, and recalling President Roosevelt's speech, Mr. Bullitt said:

'World peace is essential to us, for we know that a general war to-day would mean the destruction for a certain time of all the values of civilization accumulated with so much labour during the course of centuries.

'But if war breaks out in Europe once again *no man can say or predict whether or not the United States would be involved in such a war.*'

The Ambassador concluded:

'The colours under which Lafayette fought are the colours of liberty. These colours are those of France and the United States and several other countries; they are the old, old colours of common sense and human decency, of Christian charity and tolerance; they are the colours of freedom and peace.'

For a cold and calculating man like M. Bonnet and for one who claimed to know America so well and to be so certain of her fundamental 'isolationism' the speech he made on that occasion seemed extravagant and almost irresponsible:

'One is inclined to say that it is the fate of France's arms and

America's arms to be assembled under the same banners whenever they are called upon to defend those principles which our two nations consider to be the most precious heritage of mankind. The one friend is irresistibly compelled to rush to the help of the other friend who is in danger.'

Passionate opponents of M. Bonnet have gone so far as to suggest that this extravagant indiscretion was deliberate, and was calculated, in the most Machiavellian manner, to produce an isolationist outburst in America; an outburst which would discourage the British and French advocates of a 'firm' policy. Whether Mr. Roosevelt's Hyde Park statement on September 11, when he declared the interpretations of his European policy to be 'about one hundred per cent wrong,' was intended as a direct reply to M. Bonnet is not certain; but it may well have referred to certain articles published in America on the strength of M. Bonnet's extraordinary statement. In any case, it was a surprising statement—and a dangerous one—to make.

In the course of his speech, M. Bonnet referred to the Czech crisis. He placed Prague and Berlin on the same level, treating them as two equally naughty boys.

But his speech contained no warning to Germany, except for an assurance that 'France would faithfully carry out the pacts she had signed.'

A writer in the *Europe Nouvelle* later made the following remarkable allegation:

The British Government had by this time discovered that it had been pretty well left alone to carry the Czech baby; and it was becoming more and more puzzled by the extraordinary 'reticence' of the French Government. The British Foreign Office therefore specially asked M. Bonnet to include in his Pointe de Grave speech a declaration of loyalty to Czechoslovakia.

The semi-official *Intransigeant* wrote that evening:

One hopes that these elevated words may be heard and understood in Berlin. The two orators were careful not to utter any warning, and appealed, on the contrary, for conciliation. As for M. Bonnet, in a speech full of elevated thoughts, he displayed the most sincere desire for conciliation. He declared, however, that France would remain loyal to the agreements she had signed. Germany knows this well, even though some of Herr Hitler's advisers have tried to cast doubts on our loyalty and our resolution.

The *Humanité* was less pleased:

M. Bonnet yesterday declared that France would be loyal to the treaties she had signed. Very good. But not good enough. It was necessary in the present circumstances to dot the i's. M. Bonnet would have served peace better had he proclaimed that the integrity of Czechoslovakia and her independence were essential to France's security.

. . . .

In the meantime things were going from bad to worse in Czechoslovakia. After being informed of the Hitler-Henlein talks, Lord Runciman told London that he had 'not lost all hope.' At the same time Henlein was saying that there could be no compromise. 'The eight points of the Karlsbad programme are a minimum.' Clearly he was going to ask for more before long.

While he was saying this, all the bells of Nuremberg were announcing Hitler's entry into the town. The Congress started with a gala performance of the *Meistersinger*; in French, *les maîtres chanteurs,* the Blackmailers. An easy pun, but a singularly appropriate one.

It was during that same afternoon that the French Government at last published a *communiqué* saying that certain reservists had been called up to man the Maginot Line.

These measures should not disquieten the public, whose calm is one of the essential elements of peace.

Moreover, according to the latest news, the general situation seems to be developing towards a settlement.

What the last paragraph was based on was a complete mystery. Was the French public being deliberately doped into complacency and passivity?

M. Blum's comments in the *Populaire* on the military precautions are characteristic of the cautious and pacifist mood of the Socialist leader.

On the other side of the Rhine operations have for the last fortnight been in progress—operations which are called 'manœuvres.' Corresponding and 'adequate' measures in France would have been the calling up of all the immediately available reservists. *The Government has signed no such order, and in my opinion is right.* It has done nothing that would have looked like the beginning of a mobilization. It has confined itself to a few justified precautions. Was it right or wrong to have made these measures public? One may argue on this point. They are of so small a volume that they could have passed unnoticed both here and abroad. But, after all, why hide anything from the nation when there is nothing to hide?

Needless to say, Henri de Kerillis, boiling with Clemencist indignation, took a different view. He wrote in the *Epoque* on September 9:

The German game is successful beyond all Hitler's hopes. France and England failed to learn a lesson from their great victory of May 21.

Impressed by Germany's military display, they have been trying to keep her quiet with concessions. The Czechs are being constantly asked to capitulate; and our statesmen fail to realize that each new retreat by Prague is a new defeat for London and Paris, and a new cause for German exultation. Paris and London are frightened to answer Germany's military preparations by equal preparations. They should call up ten classes of reservists, build three lines of retreat behind the Maginot Line, begin the evacuation of Paris, concentrate the British and French navies in the North Sea. The moral side of the drama is being neglected, and mischievous campaigns have made disastrous progress on both sides of the Channel.

If this goes on Germany will believe that she can do everything. She will no longer be satisfied with a moral victory: she will want a material triumph. She will no longer be content with a Sudeten statute in Czechoslovakia; she will want to annex the Sudetenland. . . . Before it is too late, we must warn Hitler.

He concluded by saying that the defeatists were 'not France.'

Much has been written about the famous *Times* editorial of September 7, which, in suggesting the transfer of the Sudeten territory to Germany, acted as a tremendous encouragement to Hitler. It was wicked, and ill-advised, and all that, and Mr. Kennedy more than deserved the Government's *démenti* that afternoon.

But, actually, it was probably excessive to blame the British Government for Mr. Kennedy's thoughtlessness—which is, apparently, all that it was. Perhaps the pretty sentence with which he wound up his leader was only a sudden and unfortunate recollection of an argument he had at some time heard from somebody—who knows? But I have reason to believe that there was no sinister plot behind that *Times* editorial—though, I admit, it did look rather like it.

But although *The Times* is a famous paper, while the *République* is not, the article the latter published *not on the 7th, but on the 6th of September,* was in some ways more significant than *The Times* leader. M. Emile Roche, the president of the Radical Federation of the Nord, and the leader of the extreme right wing of the Radical Party, is a very close associate of M. Caillaux and—of M. Bonnet. And this is what M. Roche wrote in the *République* on September 6:

No! The talks between Prague and Karlsbad, and the talks between Paris, London and Berlin must continue. And a peaceful solution *must* be found.

Can Prague still persist in counting 3,200,000 *Germans among its loyal subjects? If so, all will be well.*

But if not, then the two races which cannot agree to live together within the framework of the centralized Czech State must be separated. Neither of them would die as a result, nor would Central Europe. We do not believe that they would like one another any better after millions of people had been killed in a war.

And that was the day on which the Czech Government, almost squeezed to death by Lord Runciman, produced its Plan No. 4. Did the French Government declare publicly, as it might well have done, that Czechoslovakia had now gone to the utmost limit of concessions, having almost accepted the entire Karlsbad programme, and that no more concession would be demanded from it by France? No. As we shall see, in the days that followed, France actually lent a hand in giving the Czechs another turn of the screw.

'Plan No. 4' of the Czech Government provided the Sudetens with a far wider autonomy than that enjoyed by any minority in Europe. Without German pressure the Sudetens should have been more than satisfied. Only two points of the Karlsbad programme were rejected by the Czechs—the two points that were essential to Hitler—namely point 3 which demanded the legal recognition of the German regions in one unit, whereas the Czech Plan proposed to divide them into three departments, and point 8, which demanded full liberty for German ideology, which would have meant the establishment of a totalitarian State within a democratic republic.

Paris was perhaps for the first time becoming aware of the full gravity of the situation. That night groups of ten or twenty people would be seen at various points discussing events in Czechoslovakia—an unmistakable sign of altogether unusual nervousness.

There was also great excitement in the Chamber lobbies; which in the last few days, had begun to fill up, even though Parliament was not sitting. People were wondering whether the Czechs had not gone *too* far, whether the Czechs would be able to keep full control over the districts controlled by German police and whether these districts were not likely to become hotbeds of Nazi rebellion. M. Frossard, M. Daladier's former Minister of Public Works, wrote in the *Homme Libre* on September 9:

> This is not a capitulation; it is a heroic sacrifice. . . . Lord Runciman had hitherto been able to exercise his pressure and influence only on the Czechs while the Germans and the Sudetens have not yielded one inch and have in practice not taken the slightest notice of Lord Runciman's 'mediation.'

And M. Blum, in the *Populaire*, wrote:

> British and French pressure in Prague cannot be driven any further.
> Paris must no longer act in Prague but in London, and London must
> no longer act in Prague but in Berlin.

But all eyes were turned to Nuremberg: would Hitler accept or
not? There was an uneasy feeling that he would not. On the previous
day Geneviève Tabouis had reported in the *Œuvre* that—

> Hitler had solemnly asked Ribbentrop to tell him whether Eng-
> land would march, if France marched; Ribbentrop replied that she
> would not; and that Germany could 'go ahead.'

No doubt M. Bailby was angry with Geneviève:

> How does she know what Hitler said in private to Ribbentrop?
> She wasn't there.

But there was a growing feeling that neither England nor France was
doing their job properly in impressing Hitler.

On the following day after the Morawska-Ostrawa incidents and the
rejection by the Sudetens of the 'final' Czech plan, M. Blum wrote, in
the *Populaire*, with a characteristic opening sentence:

> To act means, for the present, to speak. But we must speak clearly,
> dotting all the i's, and leaving no room for any error or misunder-
> standing or doubt in the minds of the German leaders regarding the
> real position of France and Great Britain. What is at stake is not the
> future of the Sudeten Germans, but the future of Europe, the future
> of Britain and France. If the great democracies express sufficiently
> strongly what they feel, they may yet save themselves, Europe and
> peace.

What was the French Government hoping for? It seems that two
things were still hoped for: one that England would 'warn' Hitler; another that the Czechs would allow themselves to be squeezed still more.

Here are the highly characteristic headlines of the officially-inspired
Paris-Midi of September 8:

> *Hitler, Goering, and Ribbentrop are examining Plan No. 4 which,
> in their view, can, at most, serve as a basis for negotiations. But since
> the Czechs have reached the limit of concessions, what will be plan
> No. 5? Will it be Runciman's plan or Hitler's plan?*

And on September 9, when the Slovaks, Hungarians and Poles began
to cause trouble, *Paris-Midi* came out with the superbly fatuous headline:

while in the *Journal* M. Alphonse de Chateaubriant[1] was going into raptures over the Nuremberg Congress:

> German youth! With what fervour they surround the master of Germany! How he feels what these young people want! An unforgettable sight, when, on his arrival, they saw him appear on the top of the station stair. There is a fixed look in his eyes. He looks at the cheering crowd, which surrounds him like a surging ocean. There is a grave look on his face. . . . War. . . . Peace. . . .
> The Germans say: 'Prague will decide.' Many Frenchmen think: 'He cannot avoid a war.' While others still say: 'He will go step by step.'
> 'No!' repeat unceasingly those who know him. 'He will place his genius at the service of the world, and he will give it Peace.'
> If only one could be sure. . . .

The important question between the 8th and 10th of September, when the crisis was rapidly coming to a head, was whether England would speak. For in French official quarters they were still shrugging their shoulders, saying that it was 'all very difficult' so long as England had not made her position sufficiently clear.

On the 8th the British Home Fleet assembled for naval manœuvres in the North Sea.

On the 9th the Sudetens proclaimed a state of emergency, and apparently waiting for Hitler's speech, suspended their talks with the Czechs, who, they said, were no longer capable of keeping law and order.

The French called up a number of naval reservists, and there was said to be great activity at Brest and Toulon, where the Atlantic and Mediterranean fleets were assembled.

On the 10th there were important ministerial consultations in London. The situation was becoming so serious that the Opposition leaders were summoned to No. 10. At the Foreign Office on the previous day Lord Halifax had already seen Mr. Eden; and Mr. Chamberlain had decided to send a note of warning to Hitler.

But nothing much was happening in Paris. The *Petit Parisien* warned Germany that if she invaded Czechoslovakia *'la riposte serait foudroyante.'* England, the United States, everybody would be against Germany. Whereupon, however, it hastened to add:

---

[1] In a book he wrote about the same time, M. de Chateaubriant went into raptures over *la bonté* of Hitler, his 'human kindness,' which, in all seriousness, he declared to be Hitler's most characteristic feature. (Author's note, 1942.)

If, on the contrary, the Reich does not depart from the road of peace, and collaborates sincerely at a friendly settlement which England and France are doing all they can to reach, then such a settlement will be reached before long.

Others, however, were clamouring for a British declaration.

The declaration came on September 11. It was the famous 'authorized statement' which, as was generally known, had been made to the Press by Mr. Chamberlain himself.

Great Britain could not remain aloof if there were a general conflict in which the integrity of France was threatened. . . . It is of the utmost importance that Germany should make no mistake about it: she cannot with impunity carry out a rapid and successful military campaign against Czechoslovakia without the fear of intervention by France and even Great Britain.

It was good enough. It was as good as the French could have expected. And it was a particularly useful warning after Goering's speech on the previous day.

On that Saturday night of September 10 Paris was in a state of jitters. The morning papers had said that, since Hitler was not going to speak until the Tuesday, it would be a *week-end d'attente*. It was a fine evening, and the Champs-Elysées were crowded with people.

'Paris-Soir! Paris-Soir!' the newsboys were shouting. *'Discours sensationnel de Goering!'* The papers were being snatched up. The result was —long, gloomy, anxious faces. In two-inch letters *Paris-Soir* announced:

VIOLENT DISCOURS
DU MARÉCHAL GOERING

and as sub-headings:

'We await the events that are inevitable. . . .'
'No army can enter German soil, and we are ready to make the last sacrifice.'
'The idea of frightening us is laughable.'
'It is intolerable that a nation of miserable pigmies—one scarcely knows where they have come from—should behave as it is behaving towards a great civilized nation. . . .'
'Instead of discoursing on peace, the British would do better to take care of their little Jewish State, of which they are in charge, and which is torn by civil war. . . .'
'We have never been so powerful. A blockade against us has become impossible.'

All in large letters on the front page. One can imagine the effect. Many a Parisian spent a bad night—the first of many to come.

On the Sunday, M. Bonnet went to Geneva, where he conferred with M. Litvinov and M. Comnene, the Rumanian Foreign Minister. He was going on the following day, to report his impressions to the Cabinet.

. . . . . .

Hitler was to speak at Nuremberg at seven o'clock on Monday.

That afternoon the French Cabinet met; I went down to the War Office to see the Ministers arrive. They all looked very grim and important. Two hours later they started coming out, one by one. As usual, the journalists wanted to know what had happened. But all were very reluctant to talk. Only M. Sarraut, looking mysterious, said that a great many things had been discussed—but mostly 'on a hypothetical basis—for we still do not know what Hitler is going to decide to-night.' I asked M. Sarraut what he thought of the British 'authorized statement' of the previous night. 'Are you satisfied, *M. le Président?*' '*Oui, je suis très, très satisfait,*' he declared, with a rattling *crescendo.* 'So you can't complain any more of insufficient British support?' 'Certainly not,' M. Sarraut replied.

A point worth noting. At the Foreign Office, in the Chamber lobbies and elsewhere, a lot of them had been saying: 'Oh, if only we could be sure of British support. . . .'

We waited for some of the other Ministers, but not all of them came out. After the Cabinet meeting, M. Daladier had retained M. Bonnet, M. Chautemps, M. Pomaret and M. de Monzie. A curious assortment: for these four were the principal advocates of an 'easy-going' policy. What were they talking about?

That Cabinet meeting was 'hypothetical.' All kinds of measures were discussed that would be taken if war broke out. Finishing touches were given to the mobilization plans; emergency measures of an economic and financial order were also discussed, including a possible moratorium on commercial payments, foreign exchange restrictions, and so on.

A strangely-worded *communiqué* was published after the meeting:

The cabinet meeting at the Ministry of War under the presidency of M. Daladier studied recent diplomatic documents and political events abroad, regarding which M. Bonnet made a statement.

The Cabinet paid tribute to the patriotism, calm, and *sangfroid* of the nation. It also received from North Africa and our colonial Empire the most moving testimony of fidelity to France.

215

This dignified and reasonable attitude of the country is of particular value for the defence of peace.

The tribute to the calm and self-assurance of the French people was well deserved. France had certainly kept remarkably calm—except for Goering's speech that Saturday afternoon.

Internal quarrels had become less noticeable; and the patriotic sense of responsibility was apparent from the remarkable fact that there had been little or no export of capital during the previous week; and—except in Alsace—no run on the banks and savings banks. Important also was the reference to the French overseas territories—a warning to Italy and Germany not to count on trouble in the French colonies.

What did M. Bonnet tell the Cabinet after his talks with M. Litvinov and M. Comnene? The Russian Foreign Minister had assured him at Geneva on the previous day that the U.S.S.R. would come to the aid of Czechoslovakia in the event of war, and after a decision by the League Council declaring Czechoslovakia to be the victim of aggression. This formality was provided in the Russo-Czech Pact, and was understandable, since Russia had no common frontier with Czechoslovakia; and it was necessary to give Rumania the legal right, under Article 16 of the Covenant, to allow Russian troops to pass through her territory. Although at that stage Rumania, naturally, did not wish to commit herself openly to allowing free passage to Russian troops and planes, there was no doubt that she would not deny Russia this right if it came to the point.

But M. Bonnet does not appear to have given quite that impression to the Cabinet, and, according to reports published both about this and subsequent Cabinet meetings, to have said in effect that the Russians and Rumanians had wrapped themselves up in League procedure, and, generally, to have shown little eagerness to help. Moreover, he is understood to have made the most of the 'decapitation' of the Red Army, and to have expressed great doubts as to its efficiency.

After the Cabinet meeting, and M. Daladier's talks with M. de Monzie, M. Bonnet, and the rest, the Premier held another conference with General Gamelin, the Head of the General Staff, General Georges and General Billotte, the Military Governor of Paris. He discussed with them the final mobilization arrangements, the evacuation of Paris and of the Paris suburbs, active and passive air defence, and so on. It all looked very earnest and sinister. What was Hitler going to say?

I had an hour before Hitler's speech, and dropped in at the Chamber. As I was leaving the War Ministry I saw M. Mistler arrive. The handsome young president of the Foreign Affairs Committee of the Chamber who spends his spare moments writing plays for the Odéon, was, during those days, one of the most active 'pacifists' in Paris. He and M. Flandin and M. Caillaux were pulling wires as hard as they could go. The first thing that must be prevented, they thought, was a mobilization.

In the Chamber lobbies that evening 'pacifist' propaganda was in full swing. One deputy was vociferating about *la jeunesse française*; France had no lives to spare for the sake of Czechoslovakia. *On sera tranquille derrière la ligne Maginot.* He spoke with conviction. He probably meant what he was saying. 'Only twenty years' respite since the last war—no, it isn't long enough. We must gain strength. If *la jeunesse française* is killed off it'll mean the end of France and French civilization. *Il n'y aura que des vieillards en France.*' Others were arguing about the French Air Force. 'How the devil can we go to war? Flandin has just been saying that we have only 600 aeroplanes which are any good at all.'

'Six hundred! He didn't say six hundred; he said sixty!'

I saw a reporter from the *Jour*. 'Well, are you dropping Czechoslovakia?'

'La Tchécoslovaquie—croyez-moi, on s'en fout éperdument. Beneš— il nous emmerde.'

I went home and turned on the wireless. There he was, already bellowing. Howls, howls, howls. Der Herr Beneš—more howls. I shall not tolerate—howls, howls, howls—that 3,000,000 unhappy Kreaturen shall be oppressed, and I ask the foreign Staathmänner—pfui! pfui! pfui!—to note that this is not an empty phrase. Howls, howls, howls. The Cathedral of Strasbourg (*con dolore*) means much to us Germans; but we have crossed it out, so that we may once and for all put an end to our eternal feud with France. Herr Chef-Ingenieur Todt and hundreds of thousands of German hands have been building fortifications on our western frontier. We are now invincible. More howls. Oh! the cannibal feast! And when the speech was over, the howls became deafening, and the Sieg heil! Sieg heil! went on interminably. And then the trumpets and drums played a sort of cannibal march—Siegfried motif—tum—tururum— tum tum—Siegfried motif—tum—tururum—tum tum. Wagner gone cannibal. Oh! turn off the bloody thing!

I went out into the street. Mme Bousquet, my concierge, looked out of her lodge. 'What's wrong with him?' she said. 'He must be off his chump. They *must* be a lot of savages. I had to turn it off, because Guy and Monique began to cry.'

I went back to the War Ministry. No, there was no Cabinet meeting; and there wasn't going to be one to-night. Three or four reporters were hanging about the entrance. 'Pretty bad, Hitler's speech, don't you think? Smells of war.' *'Pensez-vous,'* one of the reporters said. 'They're going to get a plebiscite, and that'll settle it.' 'Is that what the Government says? Didn't look like it this afternoon.' 'Of course, the Government will accept a plebiscite.' 'What about Reynaud?' 'Oh, he doesn't count.'

I went on to the Quai d'Orsay. Just my luck—here was Mistler again. He had seen Bonnet. 'What's he saying?' 'He hasn't had time to study the speech properly; but the first impression is that the door for further negotiations has not been closed. The speech hasn't improved the outlook, but hasn't made it any worse either.'

'What do you make of the story about the Rhineland fortifications?'

'Oh, there's a lot of bluff in that. We know what the fortifications cost us, and how long it took to build them. Besides, cement needs a good time to harden. I don't think the German generals would support Hitler's claim that the fortifications are impregnable. Still, we might have thought of all that on 7th of March 1936,' he added philosophically.

The telephone to London was a bother that night. The whole continent seemed to be talking to London via Paris. Especially Prague, which had only one or two direct lines to London—and these were constantly engaged by the British Legation and by Lord Runciman. It took an hour and a half to get through.

.   .   .   .

The day after Hitler's speech was, in a sense, the most decisive moment in the whole Czech crisis. The French Cabinet met; and it was clear that if a firm stand was to be taken, if a final attempt was to be made to stop Hitler from attacking or dismembering Czechoslovakia, it was now or never.

Yet the greater part of the Paris Press, partly under official influence, tried to take the rosiest possible view of the Nuremberg harangue.

'In the general interest of Europe,' M. Bourguès wrote in the *Petit Parisien*, 'the negotiations that are continuing in Prague under the guidance of Lord Runciman should go on uninterruptedly. The Beneš plan is really very liberal, and should lead to an agreement to both the Czechs and the Sudetens, on condition that confidence is restored on both sides, and that questions of detail are settled in a broadminded spirit.'

As if the Czech 'Plan No. 4' was not broadminded enough!

M. d'Ormesson in the *Figaro* thought that 'a door had been left open' for further negotiations.

M. Guérin, in the *Œuvre*, was less optimistic. 'One has to cling on to the last hope,' he wrote. And he saw the last hope in the fact that Hitler had mentioned the word 'settlement' and had not mentioned the word 'Anschluss.'

As for the *Matin*, it said quite candidly that France had no reason to make war if the Sudetens wanted a plebiscite.

The two great pessimists were, as usual, Kerillis and Péri.

The French Government had now come to the cross-roads. Resist or yield? Two men, M. Paul Reynaud, the Minister of Justice, and M. Mandel, the Minister of Colonies and old Clemenceau's disciple, were all for resistance; that is, for an immediate partial mobilization, which, they thought, could alone convince Hitler that France was meaning business, and would oblige him (since he obviously did not want war with France, England, Czechoslovakia and Russia) to accept a settlement which would leave the integrity of Czechoslovakia intact. Clearly, what interested him far more than the welfare of the Sudeten Germans (for what did he care for the Tyrolese?) was the destruction of Czechoslovakia as a military power, as an ally of France, as that platform near the heart of Germany from which (as Kerillis so often recalled) Berlin could be easily bombed—which it could not be from France or England.

M. Mandel and M. Reynaud knew that if France failed to react, Hitler's next step would be to ask for a plebiscite or an annexation of the Sudeten land. These two Ministers were, in some measure, supported by M. Champetier de Ribes, the Minister of Pensions, M. Campinchi, the Minister of Marine, and, to a lesser degree, by M. Zay, the Minister of Education, and M. Queuille the Minister of Agriculture.

But the 'pacifists' were in the majority. The principal 'pacifists,' who made no longer any secret of their belief that it was not worth while risking a war for Czechoslovakia, and who perhaps did not believe that Hitler could be intimidated, were M. Bonnet, the Foreign Minister, M. de Monzie, the Minister of Public Works, M. Pomaret, the Minister of Labour, and M. Chautemps, the Vice-Premier. Their views were not greatly dissimilar from those held by M. Flandin, M. Caillaux, M. Mistler, and others who had been pulling wires as hard as they could during the previous days.

Here is one of their arguments:

France is a war-weary country with a low birthrate, and provincial opinion is not prepared for a war over Czechoslovakia. It is not without significance that all the principal 'pacifists' represented rural constituencies in the Centre or West of France: M. de Monzie, and M. Pomaret represented the Lot; M. Caillaux the Sarthe; M. Bonnet the Dordogne;

M. Flandin the Yonne; M. Chautemps the Loir-et-Cher. In and outside the Cabinet they spoke, as it were, 'in the name of the French peasantry'; that peasantry which had always supplied the greater part of the army recruits.

The story goes that M. Bonnet—or was it M. Daladier?—produced General Gamelin's report on France's military possibilities in case of war; and read out to the Cabinet General Gamelin's enumeration of France's weak points—particularly her inferiority in the air; but omitted his conclusions which were to the effect that Czechoslovakia must not be abandoned, and that if unfortunately war could not be avoided, France could be sure of victory.

It has often been argued that France, as an ally of Czechoslovakia, could have been of little immediate use to the Czechs; for since the French Army, with its Maginot Line, was adapted to defence and not to aggression, and since the Siegfried Line had rendered an invasion of Germany practically impossible, France could only rely on a successful long war, at the end of which Germany would have been brought to her knees by a blockade. The principal military operations against Germany would have been done by the Czechs and Russians (whose support, M. Bonnet claimed, should not be relied upon). Actually, General Gamelin did not visualize the war as a motionless concentration of French and German troops on the two sides of the Rhine frontier; a French invasion of the Saar was contemplated; and it is remarkable that in his speech at Saarbrücken, on October 11—that is, *after* Munich—Hitler admitted that two zones of the German frontier still remained to be fortified—the zone of Aachen (Aix-la-Chapelle) and the Saar zone.

But, in speaking to the Cabinet, M. Bonnet is understood to have dwelt on France's weak points, and not on her strong points—or on Germany's weak points. And, again, he emphasized that the Russians were too far away, and their army was in any case, in a mess. At most, their air force could be of some nuisance value; but Czechoslovakia would be destroyed in a short time, and then the Russian Air Force would not be much good either. And it is reasonable to suppose that he also declared that Great Britain was neither ready nor willing to 'march'; and that a mere 'bluff' would not achieve the desired result.

M. Daladier wavered. He tried to weigh up all the pros and cons; France's military obligations, the possibility of a German climb-down, and, on the other hand, the millions of lives that might be lost if the bluff did not come off. He must have thought of his native Provence, of his two sons, of the quiet pleasant life under the olive trees. Was Czechoslovakia *absolutely* essential to the continued existence of France? Was it certain that if Czechoslovakia fell, Germany would automatically become the unchallengeable mistress of Europe? He wavered and hesitated, and in the end decided that there should be no mobilization—not yet. M. Chautemps was of the same mind; he also had two sons of military age. He had often said he would not let them die 'for Spain'; why should he let them die for Czechoslovakia? If Hitler had to be 'warned,' he should have been warned before Nuremberg; now it was too late; Hitler had committed himself too far. Why nothing had been done sooner, was another matter.

After the Cabinet meeting it was declared that more reservists 'may be called up'; a decree was signed by the President prohibiting the export of a long list of raw materials—notably iron, steel, scrap iron, raw wool, raw shrunk cloth, and skins and hides. M. Marchandeau, the Finance Minister, said that a number of financial and economic decrees had been prepared which would come into force in case of war.

But none of these measures was sufficient to impress Germany. Clearly, France was not 'marching.' Another rather more important decision was, however, taken by the Cabinet that day; and that was to prohibit all public meetings dealing with international questions. It seemed important to the Government not to allow the Communists, with their 'warmongering' to excite the populace, which in 1936 had given M. Blum so much trouble with its clamour for 'aeroplanes for Spain.'

During that day M. Daladier had two meetings with the British Ambassador, Sir Eric Phipps. It is said that after their first meeting that afternoon, Sir Eric reported to London on the great bewilderment he had found among the French Ministers.

That night Sir Eric Phipps was at the Opéra-Comique when he received a message from M. Daladier asking him to see him at once. The Ambassador jumped into a taxi and drove to the War Office. The situation in Czechoslovakia was growing worse every hour. At 5.30 p.m. the Sudetens had sent an ultimatum to the Czech Government demanding the revocation within six hours of the martial law measures that had been enforced in a number of Sudeten areas. What happened during M. Daladier's and Sir Eric Phipps's meeting that evening? Nobody quite knows; except that, in leaving the War Office, Sir Eric dropped the enigmatic phrase: '*Il faut que cette chamaillerie cesse.*' I rang up C——, and repeated to him the historic phrase.

'Ho-ho! Wonder if he's been told by London to pull his socks up?'

'So do I. Do you think they are going to stand up to Hitler?'

'Maybe—unless they propose to give hell to the Czechs instead.'

(It should be added that we did not know at that time what exactly had happened at the Cabinet meeting earlier in the day.) Later that night it was clear that it was again the Czechs and not Hitler who were going to be 'given hell.' A number of messages from Lord Runciman had been communicated to the French Government. The view expressed on the British side was that Runciman still remained 'the last hope.' And that night M. Daladier, taking the view that the *chamaillerie* was still an 'internal' Czech affair, sent another message to Prague urging the Czech Government in 'a firm and friendly manner,' to use the utmost moderation. The appeal was, clearly, being sent to the wrong address.

Il faut que cette chamaillerie cesse. Was it during that meeting on the night of September 13 that the 'direct contact' with Hitler was discussed? It is probable. M. Daladier had, in the past, often believed in the virtue of direct talks with Germany. And when, twenty-four hours later, the sensational announcement was made that Mr. Chamberlain was going to fly to Berchtesgaden in the morning, M. Daladier made the following statement:

> At the end of yesterday afternoon, in view of the rapid development of events in Czechoslovakia which rendered negotiations on the spot very difficult, I took the initiative to establish a personal and direct contact with Mr. Chamberlain with the object of examining with him *the possibility of adopting an exceptional procedure* which would allow for the examination with Germany of the most effective measures to assure a friendly solution of the differences which separate the Sudeten Germans and the Prague Government, and in consequence to maintain the peace of Europe. I am therefore particularly happy that the two Governments should see eye to eye.

It was said that M. Daladier had himself been surprised and rather taken aback by the announcement of Mr. Chamberlain's solo flight to Berchtesgaden; because he had imagined that he would take part in these discussions. But now Mr. Chamberlain was in exclusive charge of Czechoslovakia's fate.

One can well imagine Mr. Chamberlain's reasons for going alone. After what had happened on the previous day, it was clear to him that the French were not 'marching'; yet if he took Daladier with him, the French Premier would have felt obliged to ride the high horse, and speak of France's honour and treaty obligations—which might have made Hitler lose his temper and might have spoilt everything. Actually it is more probable that Daladier was only too glad that Mr. Chamberlain should have relieved him of all responsibility.

Be that as it may, the French had again, largely through their own fault, dropped out; and the lead was again exclusively in British hands.

XII. BERCHTESGADEN TO GODESBERG

UNTIL late in the evening, when wireless listeners learned with amazement that Mr. Chamberlain was going to Berchtesgaden (many at first refused to believe it—so fantastic did it seem) Wednesday, September 14, was a day of uneasy tension in Paris. The Press in Paris was either frankly pessimistic or frankly defeatist. M. Stéphane Lauzanne, in the *Matin*, was advocating a plebiscite.

> Ireland and Macedonia in the past, and Palestine to-day show that when two nations cannot live together any longer, they must be separated.

M. Blum, in the *Populaire*, had a brainwave—a Franco-British police force in the Sudeten areas. In a manner slightly reminiscent of the late Dr. Coué, he wrote:

> The Sudeten question can be settled: therefore it must be peacefully settled. If we have the will, peace will prevail.

M. de Kerillis was dramatic:

> I consider it my sacred duty to say that we have reached a point where we cannot yield another inch; and Germany must be told this. We are in the presence of a diplomatic Verdun.

A diplomatic Verdun! The French Government let Mr. Chamberlain fight the battle for them.

That Wednesday—the day on which the flight to Berchtesgaden was announced—will be well remembered in Paris; for it was on that day that the municipal carts began to deposit little piles of sand in front of the doors. Without warning, or almost without warning. Many concierges complained: 'They are just making a filthy mess of the pavement —what are we supposed to do with it?' Some were funny about it, saying it would be nice for the children; or nice for the cats. Some concierges took the sand down the cellar, saying they had no room for it upstairs, and that they weren't paid to trail buckets of sand up five flights of stairs. Statements were issued to the effect that if a two-inch layer of sand was put on the floor of the attic, or the top storey if there was no attic, incendiary bombs falling into the sand would go out automatically. If not, they would, within four minutes, melt metal over a radius of thirty yards. It all sounded too gruesome to be true. And anyway, what guarantee was there that the bomb would not miss the patch of sand on the top floor? Few people took it seriously and in the street people could be heard saying that it was all eyewash—the Government was trying to show it was doing something about A.R.P.—and others said it was just another municipal racket by the Topazes. A few days later, the papers said that the price of sand had gone up four times. 'Of course, it's just a racket.'

But somehow, at that stage, nobody was *convinced* that war was imminent; and the sand was treated as a bad joke. 'If they had provided masks instead, it might have done more good.'

And so, that night, a startled Paris learned that Mr. Chamberlain was going to see Hitler the next day. *'Un espoir se lève sur l'Europe,'* *Paris-Midi* announced the next morning.

M. Bourguès, in the equally inspired *Petit Parisien* used the words: 'a settlement on the basis of a free plebiscite, after the manner of the Saar plebiscite.' M. Bourguès went on to explain why M. Daladier was not going to Berchtesgaden.

That day the Chamberlain legend was born. The *Matin* and *Excelsior* thanked Mr. Chamberlain on behalf of France's mothers and France's children; M. Frossard, in the *Homme Libre*, wrote

This move, unprecedented in the history of the world, points to the tragic gravity of the situation, and earns for the grand old man the respectful admiration of the civilized world. I am now convinced that war has been rendered impossible.

M. Blum was also full of admiration, and even gave a share of his admiration to M. Daladier:

Mr. Chamberlain's resolution will stir the imagination of the world —and that means a great peace. In his will for peace he is showing a noble audacity.

The only discordant notes came from the *Ordre*, the *Epoque*, the *Humanité*, and from the *Peuple*, the trade union paper, which was not in one of its pacifist moods that day. M. Harmel promised 'to eat his hat if any good came out of the Chamberlain visit.'

Mr. Chamberlain is a cross between Machiavelli and Mr. Micawber; and when he goes on a mission of this kind, there is nothing to look forward to.

It is characteristic of the division in the French trade union movement that on the following day even before anything definite was known of the results of the Berchtesgaden talks, the *Peuple* published an article by M. Belin,[1] the 'moderate' trade union leader, which was in flat contradiction with M. Harmel's piece on the previous day:

[1] Now prominent as the chief labour leader in Vichy France.

I am grateful for the respite, even if it is only one of a few days. And I should welcome a settlement, even one with a great many drawbacks. A mediocre and even a bad settlement is better than even a victorious war.

Paris spent the 15th and 16th in a state of hopeful but uneasy expectation. The news from Czechoslovakia was bad. While Mr. Chamberlain was seeing Hitler, Prague, according to the papers, was 'very calm' and was 'calmly and firmly' rejecting any idea of a plebiscite.

News from Berchtesgaden was scanty at first. Blurred telephotos showed Mr. Chamberlain and Hitler and Ribbentrop and the British Ambassador sitting with blank faces round a tea-table decorated with flowers. Then, later in the evening, it was learned that Mr. Chamberlain was returning to London the next morning. Had the talks broken down? No, not exactly; but soon it was clear that Mr. Chamberlain was bringing back nothing better than an ultimatum. The officially inspired Press in Paris was almost cheerful. '*Détente. Ultimatum.*' *Paris-Midi* wrote:

> The *détente* in Europe has been created by Hitler's ultimatum. We have reached such a point of tension that the ultimatum has almost created a feeling of relief. For 'ultimatum' means 'delay.'

And the semi-official *Petit Parisien* was for the first time openly advocating the annexation of the Sudetenland by Germany.

This was no longer the *République*, a paper with no readers; this was the *Petit Parisien* speaking, the most widely read morning paper in France. One cannot help laughing when in his speech at the Chamber, on October 4, M. Daladier described the 'anguish' with which he and M. Bonnet learned from Mr. Chamberlain in London, on September 18, of Lord Runciman's conclusion that the Czechs and the Sudetens could no longer live together.

'*Avec quelle émotion!*' Until that time, he said, the French Government had always thought of a settlement 'within the framework of the Czech State.' Yet the inspired *République* (not to mention the *Matin*) had openly advocated the transfer of territory as early as September 6, while the even more semi-official *Petit Parisien* had proposed it on September 17. '*Avec quelle émotion!*'

And, in the meantime, M. Flandin was doing his little best, not only in Paris, but also in London. In the *Evening Standard* of September 16 he warned England that the French people would 'refuse to fight a war to save peace.'

There was a feeling in Paris during those two days after Berchtesgaden that Mr. Chamberlain was snubbing the French Ministers. On the day of Berchtesgaden the papers already announced that M. Daladier and M. Bonnet would probably travel to London at once to discuss the 'ultimatium.' It was not until two days later, after the British Cabinet meeting on Saturday, that an official invitation was received.

On Sunday morning, September 18, the two French Ministers flew to London. The great majority of the French Press had by this time already impressed on its readers that the transfer of the Sudeten territory was the only solution. There were still some, like the *Œuvre*, which spoke of an international conference, which would include Mr. Roosevelt and Stalin—a conference at which the Czech conflict and other matters might be settled; others, like the *Peuple*, called for the union of all the peaceful nations, who would 'enforce their will' on Hitler; but few had any illusion left. M. de Kerillis broke into lamentations:

> Oh, that journey! That journey! And to think that M. Daladier claimed the authorship of the idea! As if anybody could imagine that it would change the face of things! But alas! We are not living in the age of Corneille. . . . We are living in a hard, savage, barbarous age. Old England and Old France understand nothing about young Germany.

M. Péri, in the *Humanité*, was speaking of the coming betrayal, and of *the suicidal policy which consisted in buying a short respite at a colossal price.* But M. Lauzanne, in the *Matin*, was saying that if an invasion of Czechoslovakia was a crime, a refusal, at the risk of war to hand the Sudetens over to Germany would be an equally great crime.

.   .   .   .

The conversation at Downing Street, on Sunday, the 18th, lasted all day long. What took a long time was the French effort to persuade Britain to guarantee the new frontiers of Czechoslovakia. On their return to Paris the French Ministers claimed that it had been terribly difficult to get the British Ministers to agree to this. Maybe; *but were not the French asking for that guarantee simply in order to salve their conscience, or rather to whitewash themselves in the eyes of French opinion; and was not the reluctance of the British to give this guarantee due to their knowledge that the guarantee would inevitably prove a scrap of paper and so lower—for nobody would take such a guarantee seriously— the value of Britain's signature?*

There is little to suggest that the French put up any resistance against accepting the Berchtesgaden ultimatum, which now came to be known as the 'Anglo-French Plan.' Back in Paris, they claimed that they had been unable to resist, as Mr. Chamberlain was very firm in demanding their prompt acceptance; but it was later claimed by some critics of MM. Daladier and Bonnet that that was not exactly the case; that Sir Robert Vansittart and even Lord Halifax were by no means pleased with the plan, and that there were 'considerable possibilities of resistance.' M. Péri, in the *Humanité*, was particularly emphatic on this point.

. . . .

The majority of the Cabinet accepted the London Plan; but reservations were made, particularly by M. Mandel, M. Reynaud and M. Champetier de Ribes. M. Reynaud asked M. Bonnet to pledge himself not to bring any pressure to bear on the Czech Government; the Czech Government must be free to decide for itself. M. Bonnet agreed to this.

After the Cabinet meeting M. Bonnet had an hour's conversation with M. Osusky, the Czech Minister in Paris, and submitted to him the Anglo-French Plan. Why he needed a whole hour is not clear; for all the French Foreign Minister said in effect was one word: *acceptez.*

In leaving the French Foreign Office M. Osusky looked profoundly perturbed, and bitterly remarked to the journalists outside: 'Here you see the condemned man. He has been sentenced without even being heard.' M. Osusky's bitterness was understandable, it was he who in the previous two years had assembled the most impressive collection of French assurances of support, assistance, and loyalty to the Franco-Czech Pact.

How was the Anglo-French Plan received in Paris? By Péri, Pertinax, Kerillis and other *'bellicistes'* it was naturally treated as folly and as a betrayal both of Czechoslovakia and of France's vital interests. The Communist Party published a manifesto, a good deal of which to-day sounds prophetic:

> Repudiating the treaties bearing the signature of France and the undertaking they solemnly renewed only a few days ago, the Daladier Government have agreed to this new capitulation to international Fascism.
>
> After that Hitler will be able to demand French colonies and Alsace Lorraine, while Mussolini will ask for Tunisia, Corsica, Nice and Savoy.

The manifesto protested against the prohibition of public meetings and also against the Government's failure to consult Parliament on the grave decisions it was taking.

M. Blum, as he openly admitted, was much more divided.

> War has probably been averted. But it has been averted in such

conditions . . . that I cannot feel any joy, and am merely filled *with mixed feelings of cowardly relief and shame.*

But the semi-official Press no longer worried about the moral aspect of the affair; and demanded only one thing—Prague's immediate acceptance. The implication of most of the comments was that it was all the fault of the Czechs, anyway.

M. Sauerwein, in *Paris-Soir*, accused the Czechs of *aveuglement suprenant*, since they did not realize long ago that all this was inevitable.

M. Bailby, in the *Jour*, was even more explicit:

M. Hodza yesterday made a completely useless speech.[2] In the presence of facts, it is no use talking. No Frenchman will deny that the sacrifices demanded from Prague are atrocious, and there is no Frenchman who is not feeling profoundly sorry for the Czechs. But if Czech opinion was not informed sooner, and if the Prague Ministers did not make the necessary concessions in time, if, after the publication of the Karlsbad programme, they failed to accept the Sudeten terms, whose fault is it?

It was all pretty low. For, in fact, it was the fault of the French. Karlsbad programme? That dated back to April. Had not the French Government reaffirmed until the first week in September that they would support Czechoslovakia; had not M. Bonnet declared to the Foreign Affairs Committee of the Chamber two months after the Karlsbad programme, and to M. Corbin, nearly four months after the Karlsbad programme that the settlement of the Sudeten problem must be compatible with the integrity and sovereignty of Czechoslovakia—which the Karlsbad programme was certainly not? If the Czechs were blind, it was because they had been blinded by French assurances and promises.

M. Roche, in the *République*, reflecting the views of M. Bonnet, went even further:

If the Czechs reject the London Plan, it will be their own lookout. There is no treaty that we know of which would compel us to intervene.

As for the *Petit Parisien*, it dwelt on the British guarantee, which, it said, should make the London Plan much more palatable to the Czechs; and it urged the Czechs to accept: eighteen German divisions, it said ominously, were ready to attack Czechoslovakia.

The only comic relief that day was provided by our *confrère*, ex-would-be-Dictator, Colonel de la Rocque, who wrote in the *Petit Journal*:

[2] The Czech Premier had said that the Czechs would fight rather than accept a plebiscite.

The role our country has played in these last weeks will have been one of the wonders of our history. In spite of the pressure of the revolutionary warmongers, and of the pacifist climbers [?] our Ministers have known how to defend both our national honour and the peace of the world. . . . Eternal France alone was qualified for such an act of arbitration. Such is the noble tradition, the great destiny, the magnificent fortune of our country.

The Colonel was not joking; he was in dead earnest.

. . . .

On Tuesday, the Czech Government, after many hours of deliberation, virtually rejected the Anglo-French Plan, and proposed that the dispute be submitted to arbitration, in accordance with the German-Czech arbitration treaty. Mr. Chamberlain was in a hurry to fly to Godesberg, and the invocation of an old treaty, which Germany certainly regarded as a scrap of paper, struck him as fatuous and mischievous. Among the 'pacifists' in Paris there was the outcry that the Czechs were 'sabotaging peace.'

What followed was to be one of the most vital episodes in the Czech crisis. Paris that evening was in a state of great uncertainty. In London the Inner Cabinet met, and sat till 10.30 p.m. There were telephone conversations between London and Paris. Conversations with M. Bonnet alone, or also with M. Daladier? It is one of the obscure points in the story of the Czech crisis. All that is certain is that a couple of hours later, M. de Lacroix, the French Minister in Prague, who had already seen M. Krofta and other members of the Czech Government during the day, was instructed by M. Bonnet to call on President Beneš, together with Mr. Newton, the British Minister, and to inform him that if the Czech Government did not accept the Anglo-French Plan, it must do so at its own risk. France would not go to war if, following this refusal, Germany attacked Czechoslovakia. M. de Lacroix who, on the previous day, had already carried out the painful task of handing the Berchtesgaden ultimatum to M. Krofta, reluctantly obeyed his chief's orders. At 2.15 a.m., on September 21, the British and French Ministers drove up to the President's palace, and informed him of their Governments' decision.

To justify M. Bonnet's step, the *République* later made the extraordinary claim that M. Beneš had *asked* the French Government to threaten Czechoslovakia with non-support if she failed to accept the Anglo-French Plan. That alone, the *République* claimed, would have enabled Beneš to get the Czech people to accept the Plan. In reality this is a complete distortion of the facts. Dr. Beneš had simply asked for a *written* confirmation of France's decision not to abide any longer by the Czech alliance.

On the French Right it was later claimed that if, during the two previous days the Czechs were so 'difficult,' it was because they were hoping for a Cabinet crisis in Paris. One of the stories told was that M. Mandel had urged M. Beneš to resist; and that he promised to do his best to bring about a change of Government, with Herriot as Premier. It was even said that at Godesberg, Hitler had triumphantly announced to Mr. Chamberlain that he had gramophone records of the telephone conversations between Prague and London, and between Prague and Paris—conversations between Lord Runciman and the British Government, talks between Beneš and the French 'warmongers.'

Is it only gossip? In any case the French 'pacifists' tried to make political capital out of the stories that the French 'warmongers' had urged Beneš not to accept the London Plan, i.e., the Berchtesgaden ultimatum.

In Prague the acceptance of the ultimatum under French and British pressure aroused intense anger. There were violent anti-French demonstrations in the streets; and General Faucher, the head of the French Military Mission in Prague, resigned his post and placed himself at the service of the Czech Army. He returned all his French military decorations to the French Government. The story of this one and only French *beau geste* during the whole of the Czech crisis was virtually suppressed by the officially inspired papers. Some dismissed it as quixotic and theatrical.

On Wednesday, September 21, it was learned that M. Paul Reynaud, M. Mandel and M. Champetier de Ribes had 'offered' to resign from the Cabinet; or rather, that they had resigned, but that they had left it to M. Daladier to choose his time for making their resignations official. (M. Daladier had apparently asked them not to resign officially as it would create complications just on the eve of Mr. Chamberlain's journey to Godesberg.) If they wanted to resign it was because M. Bonnet, they said, had broken the pledge he had given to the Cabinet on the Monday; which was that he would not bring any pressure to bear on the Czech Government, and would not try to bully them into accepting the Anglo-French Plan. According to the *Canard Enchaîné* of September 28, M. Bonnet already *then* said, in reply to these accusations, that Beneš had 'asked' for this pressure; but the three 'warmongering' Ministers can hardly have believed it. It is curious that it was not until after Beneš's resignation from the Presidency that such an explanation was openly produced by the *République*.[3]

Needless to say, the pro-Fascist Press—the *Jour, Gringoire,* the *Action Française* and the rest of them did not fail to attack the three Ministers, whom they also accused of plotting against the Government.

. . . .

In the meantime Mr. Chamberlain was preparing to fly to Godesberg. On the morning of the departure *Paris-Midi* announced:

> Mr. Chamberlain is leaving for Germany with a plan in his pocket. Let Germany make no mistake about it: this plan provides for certain limits beyond which England will not allow Germany to go.

There was an uneasy feeling that Godesberg was not going to be a mere ceremony at which Mr. Chamberlain would announce to Hitler Czechoslovakia's acceptance of his ultimatum. For in the interval between Berchtesgaden and Godesberg, Hungary and Poland had put forward their own claims; and this was threatening to complicate matters. M. Litvinov's solemn announcement at Geneva on the day Mr. Chamberlain flew to Godesberg that Russia would fulfil her obligations to Czechoslovakia, if France did the same, was more or less ignored by the Great Powers, not least by England and France.

In Paris they were waiting for the results of Godesberg. I went to the Chamber that afternoon. Outside, I met N. 'Come on to the café instead,' he said. *'A la Chambre, ça pue le cadavre. Cette boîte me dégoûte.'* They were all, he said, so damned pleased about the way Bonnet had got the Czechs to surrender and had foiled the *bellicistes*. There was some talk of the disruption of the Cabinet in a day or two; some people were pushing hard for an Herriot Government; but Daladier did not wish to call Parliament; and it did not look as though there were going to be a change of Government. 'It's all pretty sickening,' N. said. 'If only we had a few faces like this in our Government,' he went on, pointing to the picture in the evening paper of General Sirovy, the leader of the Czech legionairies, with a black patch over one eye, who had just become Premier of Czechoslovakia in her 'supreme hour.' *'Une bonne gueule,* don't you think?' N. was a reserve officer and thought he might be called up at any moment. 'For Godesberg is not going to be such a simple business as all that.'

[3] The story of how Beneš had 'asked' for the French ultimatum was to be denounced as a fabrication in a letter published in the *Europe Nouvelle* of October 29. The letter was written by M. Hubert Beuve-Méry, the *Temps* correspondent in Prague, who had by that time resigned from the paper.

For the next twenty-four hours Paris waited for the results of Godesberg. One thing seemed clear—and that was that Hitler, satisfied with the way in which his methods had worked so far was now asking for more. And it is curious that, on the second day of Godesberg—the correspondent of *Paris-Midi* at Godesberg should have written that the talks between Mr. Chamberlain and Herr Hitler, and, on the other hand, the technical talks between Sir Horace Wilson, Sir William Strang and Ribbentrop, were in reality preparatory conversations calculated, if possible, *to prepare the ground for a conference to which at least France and Italy would be invited.*

Was it only a wild guess by a French journalist who did not know how to fill up his column? Or was 'Munich,' complete with Mussolini, already 'in the air' on the day of Godesberg? Or, lastly, was such a Four-Power conference the expression of the secret wishes of the French Ministers who up till then had been excluded (largely through their own fault) from all the talks with Hitler?

.   .   .   .

I shall not attempt to seek an explanation for that singular phrase in *Paris-Midi*. It is conceivable that, before everything had gone wrong at Godesberg during the afternoon of the second day, the possibility of 'Munich' *was* considered, and that after the breakdown of the talks, 'Munich' was no longer mentioned.

The other possible explanation is the 'fake theory'—namely, the theory that Munich was—regardless of the final 'breakdown'—firmly decided upon at Godesberg, and that the French mobilization, the mobilization of the British Navy, and Mr. Chamberlain's tragic broadcast of September 27, which was to send a cold shiver down millions of spines were part and parcel of a put-up show—the purpose of which was to get a panic-stricken world to accept the Munich settlement with gratitude and relief. No! Such a theory seems rather too Machiavellian for a man like Mr. Chamberlain—even though it *has* been put forward.

This theory received some support even from M. Fabre-Luce, an ardent admirer of Mr. Chamberlain and M. Bonnet. He described the *coup de théâtre* in the House of Commons, on September 28, as *une bonne farce!*[4] He may, however, have meant that Munich was in reality agreed upon a few hours before, and not five days before Mr. Chamberlain's House of Commons speech. Some sinister significance has also been attached to Mr. Chamberlain's words before leaving for Munich: 'It will be all right this time.' Supporters of the 'fake' theory have further

[4] *Histoire secrète de la négociation de Munich.*

said that since the fate of Czechoslovakia was sealed at Berchtesgaden it was surely 'unnatural' to mobilize and threaten war over some 'points of detail,' which, according to this theory, were all that the Godesberg conflict amounted to. This theory, though perhaps plausible on the face of it, minimizes three points:

(1) The great guiding principle in the Anglo-French attitude to the Czech crisis was that almost any settlement would do, so long as there was no armed attack on Czechoslovakia, which Hitler now wanted for military prestige. If there had been an actual act of aggression, France, in spite of everything, would have found it extremely difficult to remain aloof.

(2) It is possible that Mr. Chamberlain did believe—or at least tried to believe—that Czechoslovakia could continue a more or less independent existence under the Anglo-French Plan; while the Godesberg Plan clearly provided for the complete economic vassalization of Czechoslovakia with all her essential railways cut by German *enclaves*, etc.

(3) If the substance of the Godesberg Plan was accepted at Munich it was because after the *coup de théâtre* of September 28 war had become psychologically almost impossible, especially in England.

So, while there were some arguments in favour of the 'fake' theory, one still finds it difficult to accept—especially when the charge of 'faking' is made against Mr. Chamberlain. Such a 'fake' could have been only the work of a political chess-player of real genius—and unlimited cynicism.

XIII. FRENCH MOBILIZATION AND THE SCARE DAYS IN PARIS

IT WILL have been noticed that, up till the moment we have reached— that is, Friday, September 23—France's part in this vast conflict over the fate of her most reliable ally in Central Europe had been almost exclusively passive, except for minor mobilization measures, the distribution of sand to Paris householders, and M. Bonnet's 'ultimatum' to Dr. Beneš. Not a single speech was made between September 4 and Munich by either M. Daladier or M. Bonnet.

233

France's role as a dumb witness came to an end on Friday night, September 23. That evening, while Mr. Chamberlain was still at Godesberg, the French Government, in agreement with London (i.e., Lord Halifax and the Foreign Office) released the Czechoslovak Government from its undertaking not to mobilize. French 'pacifist' writers, like Pierre Dominique and Fabre-Luce, later claimed that both in London and Paris that day the 'warmongers' had gained the upper hand.

One good piece of news reached Paris that day; and that was Russia's threat to denounce her non-aggression pact with Poland, if Poland invaded Czechoslovakia. Though cold-shouldered by French and British alike, the Russians, it seemed, were doing their best. There were some people in Paris that day who thought that this Russian warning might prove a turning-point in the whole crisis, and a signal to all the democratic countries to pull themselves together, and to stop the rot. It was certainly the first gesture of 'firmness' coming from any potential enemy of Germany. And more gestures were to come.

That night a number of us were dining at the *Petit Riche* with a British Army man, who was explaining to us the technical difficulties of giving military assistance to Czechoslovakia. The atmosphere in Paris that night was one of depression and vague anxiety, but there was nothing unusual in the streets. We did not know yet about the coming Czech mobilization. People at the corner table were discussing the relative virtues of the old stock and the present stock of the *Petit Riche's* Santenay.

We later dropped in at Reuter's office. We met Gordon Waterfield on the stair. 'I am going home—anyone coming my way?' 'Going home already?' 'Yes, I am going home to get a pillow and a blanket. I have got to stay the night in the office. Anything may happen. They are expecting a French mobilization. Daladier is conferring with the Generals. The news has just come through that the Czechs have mobilized. And Godesberg is a washout. Chamberlain is coming back to-morrow morning.'

Here was a mouthful. In the Place de la Bourse all was quiet. Nothing startling anywhere. Café de la Paix crowded as usual. At the French War Office alone there was much coming and going. '*Alors, on mobilise?*' I asked a French reporter, who was taking notes on the arrivals and departures.

'*Il paraît*,' said he, adding facetiously: '*Mais la mobilisation n'est pas la guerre.*'

It was what they said in 1914.

．　　．　　．　　．　　．　　．　　．

Earlier that night Sir Eric Phipps had informed M. Daladier of the breakdown at Godesberg; and now M. Daladier was conferring with the Generals. General Gamelin had felt all along that France's diplomacy during the last months *had been completely out of proportion with her military strength:* and it was reported that he greatly resented the account given of his report both to the French Cabinet and to the British Government. General Gamelin now insisted on at least a partial mobilization of the French Army; and M. Daladier agreed.

Early next morning the *affiches blanches* were displayed on the *mairies* and other public buildings throughout France. The *affiche blanche* is associated in the popular mind with general mobilization; the use of the same poster for a partial mobilization was no doubt calculated to create a psychological effect in the country. This it certainly did—much more than had been done by the mobilization orders sent out to reservists individually earlier in the month.

Categories 2 and 3 were called up. The system of mobilization had been changed in France in 1936 (after the old system had shown itself to be too unwieldy at the time of the Rhineland *coup*); and these two 'categories,' which represented about 600,000 reservists, did not correspond to any 'classes.' The categories (*échelons*) into which the French Army reserve is now divided, comprise people of different ages, each *échelon* representing, as it were, a useful 'assortment' of all kinds of reservists. It is part of what is called 'vertical' mobilization, as distinct from the 'horizontal' mobilization, by classes.

The *affiche blanche* caused great commotion in Paris that morning. Although it was announced by the Government that this partial mobilization must not be considered as a first step towards general mobilization, everybody felt that it was singularly reminiscent of it. In food-shops, around underground stations, and in the streets generally, people assembled to discuss the partial mobilization order. Altogether it was accepted as something inevitable, and there were no protests and no attacks on the Government; on the contrary, the Government, many people felt, could not have done anything else. If there was any anger at all it was reserved for Hitler. In the Place Denfert, the old woman at a flower-stall looked wretched, but went on with her work as usual. Three of her four sons had been called up that morning. My landlord and his three brothers, all reserve officers, left for the eastern frontier that night. The only complaint—especially by the women—was that 'they don't give them much time to say good-bye to the family.'

The centre of life in Paris was the Gare de l'Est. Immense crowds had gathered there in the afternoon to see the reservists off. And with all the streets around the station blocked with people, traffic in that busy part of Paris was almost at a standstill. In front of the station a wooden barricade had been erected with a notice painted in green saying: 'Entrance for reservists,' and opposite it a notice-board on which was written in chalk: 'Last train for Strasbourg to-day, 4 p.m. Last train for Metz to-day, 4.30 p.m.'

Over the heads of the large crowds handkerchiefs were being waved to the reservists as they were disappearing inside the station. These were mostly young fellows—some well dressed, some poorly dressed, some still wearing the blue cotton trousers of the Paris mechanic. All were carrying little suitcases with their personal belongings. A number of reservists had already been put into field uniform in Paris.

Many were being seen off by women carrying babies and by young girls. Many of the women were weeping. The reservists looked earnest and a little grim, conscious of doing a painful but necessary duty. A few of the younger fellows smiled and even laughed as they waved good-bye, but these were rather forced, artificial smiles. One felt an undercurrent of anger against Germany. A lot of these people had heard Hitler bellowing on the wireless; they did not care much about Czechoslovakia, but they felt that Germany was throwing her weight about in an ugly, menacing manner. There was no singing and shouting, no 'Marseillaise' or 'Madelon'; no 'enthusiasm,' no illusions about the glorious panoply of war, but only a feeling of bitter necessity. Only here and there a few working-class lads were singing the 'Internationale.'

From time to time a little crowd of pacifists of the Marceau Pivert school would shout 'Down with war,' but they were coaxed rather than ordered by the policy to disperse. An old woman with an alcoholic face, perched on a bench, was screaming in a shrill voice, '*La guerre est une saloperie!* War is a filthy *business*. The profiteers are sending you to the front.' But nobody took much notice of her.

An elderly man, shaking his head, said he remembered 1914 when at the same Gare de l'Est people shouted '*à Berlin.*' Of course, he was imagining these things more than remembering them. In 1914 there were also plenty of weeping women at the Gare de l'Est. Nobody shouted '*à Berlin*' this time. It was rather sad and solemn, and nobody had any illusions about the romance of modern warfare.

The cafés all around the station were crowded with soldiers and reservists being seen off by their friends and families. Here was a middle-class family—a lad of twenty in a tweed suit, with heavily-rouged mamma who looked sulky and growled when a crowd of Communists marched past, singing the 'Internationale,' a pretty sister who said nothing, and a father with a white moustache and a heavy gold watch-chain who handed a bundle of notes to the boy and clicked glasses with him silently and with his cheeks twitching.

Obviously, nobody was *enjoying* it; but there was no terrible gloom and depression at the Gare de l'Est. Nor was there anything to indicate that the French people 'did not know (as was later maintained by some "pacifists") what it was all about.' At the Gare de l'Est that day nearly everybody spoke of *les Boches*.

The editor of the leading Paris evening paper sent his reporter to the Gare de l'Est that day, and told him to give as depressing an account as possible of the reservists' state of mind. The reporter returned to the office with his *papier*: 'I assure you they aren't in such a state of gloom and funk at all. Go and look for yourself.'

From the Gare de l'Est I walked down the Boulevard Sébastopol. There were crowds everywhere, strangely silent crowds. In cafés people sat sipping their drinks but saying very little to each other. All the shops were open—shoe- and hat- and fur-shops and stationery-shops advertising note-books for the opening of the schools next week; but wherever I looked in, there was not a single customer anywhere. The crowds outside were not thinking of shopping—though this was one of the great shopping streets of Paris.

As one walked through Paris that day and looked at the earnest and almost grim expression written on all faces, one was impressed by the deep unity of the French people in a moment of danger. The people were certainly showing an infinitely better spirit than either the newspapers or the politicians. On Saturday night the Paris building trade, who had been on strike—and they had good reasons for striking—sent a delegation to the Minister of Public Works and another to the Prefect of the Seine saying they would resume work at once and unconditionally for the sake of national defence and for the air defence of Paris.

And on the Sunday morning a similar announcement was made by the miners who had been on strike in the north of France.

.   .   .   .

On that Saturday evening I met a friend who had just come from the German Embassy. This, he said, was guarded by heavy police forces, and he found that the Embassy staff had been profoundly impressed by the change that had come over Paris in the last days—not least by the mobilization and the spirit of the people.

This hardening of the French attitude was regarded by many to be of decisive importance in averting a German attack on Czechoslovakia dur-

237

ing the next few days. The French mobilization had, at least, the effect of reducing the possibility of a 'localized' war—which Hitler would have welcomed.

And then came the four Scare Days.

It may, however, be said at once that during these four days—that is, until the Wednesday afternoon when Munich was announced—there were few people in Paris who regarded war as a certainty; to many it was a fifty-fifty chance. A great many others said knowingly that there would be no war. Only was it to be avoided by a German climb-down or another Anglo-French climb-down?

Two characteristic opinions are worth quoting; one from my friend, the one-eyed plumber in the rue de la Glacière, a good type of French artisan, chock-full of commonsense and very independent-minded. For three months in the year he abandons all work and goes home to fish. The plumber was convinced there would be no war, because, 'once you show the Boche that you are not frightened of him, he will inevitably give way.'

The very opposite view was held by my French bank manager, and in fact by all the clerks in the bank (i.e. those among them who had not yet been mobilized)—and that was that the French and British Governments were determined to yield, if Hitler did not give way.

These two opinions, roughly, correspond to those held in France during the danger week in September by (a) the optimists among the *peuple,* and (b) the optimists in business.

But to most people it was fifty-fifty. That, of course, was sufficiently bad to warrant anyone who had the slightest chance of doing it, of sending at least the children out of Paris.

The schools were to open on October 1, and many children had already returned from the holidays. In many cases, however, children who were still in the country were told to 'stay on.'

Paris has one peculiarity which London lacks. Nearly the whole *petite bourgeoisie* and the upper strata of the working class have still some connections with rural or provincial France. It automatically provides a piece of A.R.P.—and this was very evident during the four 'scare' days in September.

During those days Paris was cleared of a large part of its child population. *On ira chez grand'mère dans la Creuse,* or *chez ma belle-sœur du côté de Rouen,* or *chez ma cousine dans la Sarthe.*

The large-scale exodus, as we shall see, did not, however, begin until Monday, September 26.

•   •   •   •   •   •   •

M. Pierre Dominique later wrote that about that time M. Daladier had gone 'warmongerish'; and one certainly has the impression that during that day M. Daladier was beginning seriously to regret the weakness that France had, until then, displayed. Gossip-writers recorded that for some days afterwards he was hardly on speaking terms with M. Bonnet. During the previous week relations had already been slightly strained between the Premier and the Foreign Minister.

After the Cabinet meeting of September 13 (the Canard Enchainé related) M. Daladier wondered whether he shouldn't give a broadcast address to the nation; but, on second thoughts, he decided not to say anything: since he had no mobilization to announce, there was not much point in announcing a non-mobilization.

It was then that M. Bonnet coolly declared:

'If you are not going to talk, I'll talk.'

Edouard bit his nose off:

'If the Prime Minister has got nothing to say, the Foreign Minister has got to keep his mouth shut.'

Feeling much annoyed, M. Bonnet locked himself up in his study at the Quai d'Orsay.

Half an hour later, M. Stéphane Lauzanne joined him.

There were some who later insinuated that the famous article in the *Matin*, demanding the transfer of the Sudeten territory to Germany, was written by M. Georges Bonnet himself. . . . As if M. Stéphane Lauzanne could have allowed that![1]

And another bit of *Canard* gossip which I report of course, *sous toutes réserves*, told the following story about the Anglo-French meeting in London on Sepember 25 and 26:

On Sunday and Monday M. Bonnet wanted, on two or three occasions, to speak. But each time he was cut short by M. Edouard Daladier. For Edouard was feeling a bit sick. For had not Mr. Chamberlain in person said to him:

'Wasn't the Gamelin Report your Foreign Office sent us a bit incomplete?'

With a mischievous twinkle M. Daladier replied:

'Oh, that was nothing, Mr. Chamberlain. Our Foreign Office sent us, during one of our last Cabinet meetings, a British Admiralty report.'

And, after a pause:

[1] *Canard Enchainé,* September 21. Let it not be objected that I am using a frivolous source of information. The *Canard* is frivolous in form but not in substance and its political notes are written by some of France's best journalists, such as André Guérin.

'And it, also, was incomplete.'

M. Daladier, of course, is making no secret of the fact that he is fed to the back teeth with his Foreign Minister.

Which is also the feeling of M. Mandel, and M. Paul Reynaud, and M. Champetier de Ribes, and M. Gentin, and M. Queuille.

And sometimes M. Campinchi and M. Zay feel that way too. And, now and then, even M. Lebrun, especially after having had a talk with General Gamelin.[2]

It is significant that although M. Daladier was feeling energetic and rather defiant, and had regained much confidence from the good spirit shown by the reservists, and the successful manner in which the partial mobilization had been carried out, the Bonnet-inspired Press continued to preach moderation to—the Czechs, and to ask them for more sacrifices —namely to accept the Godesberg ultimatum as well.

M. Bourguès wrote in the *Petit Parisien* on Sunday, September 25: 'Faithful to her promises (!) France is ready to defend the integrity (?) of Czechoslovakia against an armed attack. England would certainly follow, and so would Russia. But, etc.'

It is curious that Russian help should have been mentioned for the first time in the officially inspired Press.

On the whole, however, the mobilization had not been without effect. Even M. Roche, in the *République*, wrote on September 25:

England and France are trying to avoid a conflict; they are doing it in a spirit of self-denial rare in the history of the world.

In this paper we have been indefatigable in defending peace. But peace with honour and dignity.

Before leaving for London, M. Daladier and M. Bonnet attended a Cabinet meeting at which greater unanimity was shown than at any of the previous meetings. The Anglo-French meeting in London was, in reality, a war council.

The last decision taken on the Sunday night was to summon General Gamelin to London early the next morning.

In the meantime the Czechs were preparing to resist *à outrance*; French 'pacifists' later accused the Czech Government of having wished to profit from the Godesberg ultimatum in order to go back on their acceptance, under British and French pressure, of the Anglo-French Plan of the previous week. The charge is silly; for if there was to be a

[2] *Canard Enchaîné*, September 28.

war, the Czechs were obviously not going to abandon their line of fortifications *before* the war had broken out.

. . . .

During that Sunday there were a number of other important developments. President Roosevelt telegraphed to Germany, Czechoslovakia, Great Britain, France, Poland, and Hungary urging that negotiations should continue, recalling the Kellogg Pact, and emphasizing the incalculable dangers of war to the social structure of every country.

It is curious how the Right in France, and even part of the officially inspired Press had constantly minimized Mr. Roosevelt's influence, and how even at the peak of the crisis, they preferred to see Mussolini come to Europe's rescue rather than Mr. Roosevelt.

These papers were, naturally, polite about Roosevelt; but no more. Thus, in its Press review, on September 25, *Paris-Midi* said ironically that that morning's *Peuple* (the trade union paper) was 'back at its hobby (*sa marotte*) again—another periodic appeal to Mr. Roosevelt!' But that was only the Press; and M. Daladier and Mr. Chamberlain replied at once, welcoming the President's move. In Germany the President's appeal was ignored. No mention of it was allowed on the wireless or in the newspapers, and it was not until twenty-four hours later that Hitler deigned to reply, putting in advance the blame on Beneš if war were to break out. Hitler cabled:

The possibilities for a just settlement are exhausted with the proposals of the German [Godesberg] memorandum.

Mussolini did not refer to the Roosevelt message in his speech. In Prague, on the other hand, it was immediately broadcast.

Poland, in the meantime, was becoming increasingly agitated and aggressive—and that in spite of Russia's threat to denounce the Russo-Polish non-aggression pact if Poland were to attack Czechoslovakia. Poland and Czechoslovakia were both France's allies; and now that one was preparing to attack the other, it was clear how low France's authority had fallen in Central Europe. The *Humanité* was fulminating against M. Bonnet for having failed to warn Poland that if she attacked the Czechs, the French would denounce the Franco-Polish alliance: Russia had set a good example; why was not France following it?

As for Mussolini, he made a speech at Verona in which he urged Britain and France to abandon the Czechs before war became inevitable.

. . . .

241

In London the British and French Ministers, while no doubt leaving themselves some loopholes, decided in effect that they would stick to the Anglo-French proposals.

It is fairly clear that M. Daladier and Mr. Chamberlain and Lord Halifax were feeling quite 'firm' on that Monday morning, after their talks with General Gamelin. As for M. Bonnet, he did not play an active part in the talks, and was being kept rather in the background by the Premier. He seems to have felt rather sore about it, for, if one is to trust a writer in the (usually reliable) *Europe Nouvelle*, he was so much impressed by the British firmness, that he thought it—almost excessive. Therefore, to cool the unexpected British ardour, he instructed M. Corbin to explain to the British Government that if war broke out, France would expect Britain (1) to introduce conscription immediately and (2) undertake to pay half the cost of the war.

General Gamelin stayed on in London after the French Ministers had left, and saw Lord Gort, Chief of the Imperial General Staff, and also consulted with French military experts at the French Embassy. The British Ministers were impressed by General Gamelin and by his account of the French Army; the weak point was the French Air Force; while the French, for their part, were sorry to find that, to begin with, England had no more than two divisions immediately available for France. The French wanted at least twelve; though General Gamelin, it appears, did not doubt that he could hold the Maginot Line almost indefinitely even without early British help on land, and even invade the Saar which had not yet been fortified.

.   .   .   .

That night Hitler spoke at the Sportpalast in Berlin—if it may be called speaking. The parts of the speech dealing with Beneš were like one long-drawn-out paroxysm of rage.

An outstanding feature of his speech was that at no moment did he give his audience the least suggestion that what he was threatening to produce was not a mere German march into Czechoslovakia, but a European war. Only on the following day did it begin to dawn on a large part of the German people how great the danger was.

But the speech was not made for internal consumption only. Hitler knew that millions of people all over the world were hearing him. Was not the 'animal roaring' at least to some extent, deliberate; was it not, like the insane outburst of rage with which he is said to have welcomed Sir Horace Wilson, Mr. Chamberlain's emissary, on the following day, calculated to create the impression, perhaps not least in the mind of

Mr. Chamberlain, that *Hitler was mad*; and that he would go to war even though he knew that Germany would be ultimately crushed by the Franco-Anglo-Russo-Czech coalition? Was not this simulation of madness the supreme bluff? Herr Abetz, one of the Germans who, on December 6, accompanied Herr von Ribbentrop to Paris, related, with a great display of joviality, how, on September 28, the day the British Fleet was mobilized, Hitler was 'literally in a blue funk', and was wondering 'how the devil he was going to get out of the mess without loss of face.' The French gentlemen of the Comité France-Allemagne, to whom Herr Abetz told the story, laughed themselves nearly sick.

The moral of the story is that if no desperate appeal had been addressed to Rome on the 28th, Mussolini would, if it had come to the worst, have undertaken to 'save peace' on his own initiative—in order to get Hitler out of the 'mess.' There is, in fact, reason to believe that Hitler had already told Mussolini of his worries on the 28th, and even before.

. . . .

THE 'FAUSSES NOUVELLES' AFFAIR

On the night of Hitler's speech, the British Foreign Office issued its famous authorized statement—a statement the like of which had never been made by Britain in time of peace before. The British Government was, clearly, anxious to avoid the charge made against Sir Edward Grey who, had he spoken sooner, would probably have averted the War in 1914.

> The German claim to the transfer of the Sudeten areas has already been conceded by the French, British, and Czechoslovak Governments. But if, in spite of all efforts made by the British Prime Minister, a German attack is made upon Czechoslovakia *the immediate result must be that France will be bound to come to her assistance and Great Britain and Russia will certainly stand by France.*
>
> It is still not too late to stop this great tragedy and for the peoples of all nations to insist on settlement by free negotiation.

Incredible as it may sound, the British *communiqué*, which would have aroused boundless gratitude and enthusiasm in France in 1914, was treated by a part of the Press as a forgery or a semi-forgery; while M. Bonnet allowed it to be understood that the British *communiqué* was of no vital importance.

The *communiqué*, as I happen to know on the best authority, was written by Lord Halifax in person, and was to have been broadcast that

243

night by the B.B.C. in German in such a manner that it would reach a very large number of German listeners; unfortunately, for some technical reasons, the broadcast did not quite 'come off.' But think of the impression it would have made in Germany on the very night Hitler was suggesting that France and England were 'against Beneš'!

But that is not all. M. Pierre Dominique, one of the great 'pacifists' of M. Roche's *République* published a book, several months after Munich, in which he denounced both the French and the British 'warmongers.' And in spite of all the official confirmation of the authenticity of the British *communiqué*, he glibly declared that these confirmations had to be made simply because Lord Halifax was a gentleman:

> There were many of us who on first seeing the British *communiqué* treated it as a forgery. No—it was *not* a forgery. But the *communiqué* was drawn up by Sir Robert Vansittart, the chief of the War Party at the Foreign Office, and was endorsed by an obscure underling. Out of sheer gentlemanliness (*délicatesse d'âme*), Lord Halifax did not wish to repudiate the document. In short, it was an act of bad faith.[3]

Chief among the other *fausses nouvelles* which was once again to arouse the fury of the 'pacifists,' was the Havas telegram from Berlin, on Tuesday, September 27, saying that there would be general mobilization in Germany at 2 p.m. on the following day. At *that time* the news was perfectly correct; if it was contradicted by the D.N.B. (the German official news agency) at 2.40 a.m. on the next day, *it was probably because in the interval Berlin had learned of the mobilization of the British Navy*. The 'general mobilization' story reported by Havas in rather milder terms than those used by the British Press, did not fail to arouse the fury of the 'pacifists,' i.e., the advocates of unconditional surrender to Germany; they thought it would produce a sharp 'militarist' and patriotic reaction among the French people. The *Action Française, organe du Nationalisme Intégral* produced the following piece from M. Léon Daudet:

> The scoundrel (*le misérable*), who is obviously affiliated with the war gang, and who launched this alarming piece of news, must be discovered, arrested and tried. Such a crime deserves merciless punishment. It shows up the war plot that is being hatched in the obscene darkness. The Sudeten affair (Hitler said so the other night in a speech that was extremely violent in relation to Beneš, and very restrained in relation to France and England) is a local affair which must be circumscribed and settled locally.

[3] Pierre Dominique: *Après Munich: Veux-tu vivre ou mourir?* (Paris, Stock.)

Léon Daudet was reacting to Hitler's speech in exactly the manner in which Hitler was hoping France to react. And this was the man who had written endless panegyrics in honour of Clemenceau! It was enough to make the Tiger pirouette in his grave. For here was the supreme synthesis of cold feet and frantic pro-Fascism—a pro-Fascism that had become completely blind to all that *nationalisme intégral* stood for. If such an attitude was understandable in the case of Bonnet and many other people, it was plainly indecent in the case of the *Nationalistes Intégraux*.

Daudet, however, tried to whitewash Clemenceau by implication. Clemenceau created the Czechoslovakia of 1919—complete with the Sudeten country—but the treaty of alliance was drafted by Philippe Berthelot and Dr. Beneš. And Philippe Berthelot was *un gredin vendu*.

> Some day we may know how much Beneš paid him. We already know that Rumania paid him 250,000 francs. Without a sou in the world this scoundrel (*scélérat*) had the most beautiful collection of obscene Japanese objects and drawings in the world.

. . . .

What did Paris look like during the great Scare of September 25 to 28?

I may as well begin by saying that air-raid precautions in Paris were negligible—or rather the 'passive defence of Paris,' as distinct from its 'active defence.'

Regarding 'active' defence, there were said to be seventy-two anti-aircraft batteries around Paris, representing several hundred guns; and a prominent member of the War Office assured me at the end of September that 'not one aeroplane in fifteen' would get as far as Paris. Which did not prevent 'pacifists' like M. Pierre Dominique from later claiming that there was not around Paris any 'active defence' worth mentioning, and that at the height of the crisis several anti-aircraft batteries had to be rushed to Paris from Toulon—which (he claimed) left the great French naval base in the Mediterranean as good as defenceless.[4] Probably the truth lay somewhere half-way between the two assertions. There were, naturally, also some anti-aircraft batteries on the Maginot Line and at various points between the frontier and Paris. The other form of 'active defence' was the French Air Force—but that is a matter which will be dealt with later.

Generally speaking, when the scare week began, there were plenty of cellars in Paris, but hardly any of them either bomb-proof or gas-proof;

[4] Pierre Dominique, *op. cit.*

245

there was some sand for extinguishing (with luck) incendiary bombs; extra trains were run to facilitate the 'voluntary evacuation' of Paris; there were no gas-masks, and few of the cellars had been propped up. Perhaps the 'active defence' would have chased away the enemy aeroplanes; but no one could tell.

The truth is that Paris felt pretty helpless.

It started on the Sunday. Thousands of cars were speeding west and south. The rich were, naturally, the first to go. On the great main roads to Dijon and Nevers and Rennes the hotels were beginning to profiteer on a big scale. A room that cost twenty francs fetched 100, which the motorists gladly paid. By Tuesday the price went up to 200. On and on they would drive away from the danger zone, and rent bungalows and cottages for a year on the Breton coast, and pay an exorbitant amount of rent in advance, and stuff up the cottage with food. Soldiers on the road would jeer at them as they drove past. *Embusqué, va!*

Children were a different matter. Many mothers would, on Sunday or Monday, take their children *chez grand'mère* in the Creuse, and come back to Paris on Wednesday morning. On the Tuesday the opening of schools was postponed from October 1 to October 10 ('October 10,' the pessimists reflected, 'wonder what Paris will look like on October 10!'). There was no longer any excuse for leaving the children in Paris. Train services were doubled and trebled; immense crowds were assembled at the railway stations, with people arriving two or three hours before the departure time of the trains. How reminiscent the stations were of the great holiday exodus at the beginning of August—and yet how different! The traffic in Paris largely consisting of taxis loaded with luggage, seemed faster than usual. Everybody seemed to be hurrying somewhere either to leave town or to make some last-minute arrangement. There were long, and at times, impatient queues outside the savings banks. The lights in the streets were being dimmed and at night the streets were almost completely dark. On Monday, all house painters were conscripted, and were busy camouflaging factories and railway stations. Trenches were being dug in the Parc Montsouris. In the Underground on Tuesday night I witnessed a strange scene in which a woman with a child was upbraided as 'inhuman' by the rest of the passengers for not having sent her child out of Paris. She explained apologetically that she was sending it the next morning.

·　·　·　·　·　·　·

How clearly I remember those last three days of the Great Scare. On *Monday* things still looked fairly normal. Mme Bousquet, my concierge, wondered whether she should take away the children to their aunt in the country, and in the end decided to wait for 'just another day.' She was more worried lest her husband should be mobilized. 'Like to look at the cellar?' she asked. 'It's a good cellar, and was used during the last war. Mme L., the *propriétaire*, has given strict instructions that only the *locataires* are to use it; she doesn't want any strangers dropping in from the street. Mme L. is going to the country to-morrow.'

Mme Fayolle, in the paper-shop, said I could buy my papers somewhere else for all she cared; *she* wasn't going to stay in Paris; she had already sent her little daughter away, and was going to follow. It was quite bad enough to have a son on the Maginot Line; the poor boy had sent a card saying he had had to spend two nights in a barn, and he had caught a bad cold. 'And you know how delicate he is."

My greatest fear was to be without tobacco, and I bought five packets that morning—to begin with. Ensor had come over from London that morning to 'have a look' at Paris. He thought war was a pretty safe bet, but 'not before Thursday.'

Went to the Gare de Lyon to look at the departing crowds, and also to recover an overcoat I had left in the train the week before. There was no coat, but plenty of crowds. But they were very conscientious at the *objets trouvés*, and went to no end of trouble to find my coat, and nobody suggested that there were more important matters to think about. Their job was to look for lost coats, and they stuck to their job. Later I joined some *confrères* at the Hotel Jacob, to see Hubert Ripka, who had just arrived from Prague. Ripka was the editor of the *Lidovy Novini*, and a close friend of Beneš. He looked worn out. 'Whatever happens, we are not going to abandon our fortifications,' he said with a desperate note in his voice. 'But you accepted the Anglo-French Plan.' '*Je m'en fous*. The Anglo-French Plan was cancelled by the Godesberg ultimatum.' He called the French Ministers a lot of names.

Edgar, who was also there, said triumphantly that he had discovered a firm that agreed to sell him three gas-masks. Perhaps they didn't do much good; but they acted like a mascot—gave you self-confidence. David thought gas-masks were a lot of British eyewash; you couldn't swamp the whole of Paris with gas. At the Deux Magots met Jacques G., an engineer who was going to be mobilized the next day. 'I hope to God we have the war *now* and get it over. It'll be far worse if we wait.' Frank dropped in at night, bringing with him a Czech refugee who had just come from Prague and was 'so glad to be in Paris. Everything in Paris,' he said, was 'so quiet and normal.' Naturally they wanted to hear Hitler's speech. I turned on the wireless. Hitler bellowed: '*Beneš und*

247

ich, Beneš und ich.' The Czech decided that there wasn't much to choose between Paris and Prague.

.   .   .   .

Tuesday. Called on old G. He and Mrs. were going to the station to book tickets for Thursday. They had some friends staying at Bagnoles de l'Orne, and had been offered a room. Mrs. G. was crying and packing up blankets and pillows and winter clothes. 'The house at Bagnoles is damp and cold—damn these Czechs,' old G. grumbled. 'It's no fun leaving home—heaven knows for how long. I don't mind so much myself, but my poor wife is desperate. Leaving the little nest to be blown to bits. You've got to understand women.'

Met Barsalou of the *Dépêche* and C., a member of Sarraut's *cabinet* for lunch in the Place des Victoires. Mme Barsalou had just returned from Arles, where she had dumped the children. Had a very good lunch, in spite of C.'s pessimism. He thought the wheels of war were already turning; people had accepted the idea of war; and that was fatal. We went on to the broadcasting station where C. was working; he produced some telegrams from Rome suggesting that Mussolini was up to something. In the Boulevard Haussmann saw whole family standing on the pavement with hampers and suitcases, waving desperately at 'engaged' taxis, as they dashed past. Taxis were making pots of money that day. Shops—except those selling trunks—were empty, and many assistants were mobilized. At the Parc Montsouris they were digging trenches of sorts, and at the Louvre pictures were being packed up. Went to the bank to take out enough money to last a couple of months—just in case. Monsieur S., the cashier, thought it was foolish of me. '*Vous allez voir,*' he said knowingly. He seemed genuinely unperturbed.

Some excitement in the Boulevards that afternoon. Two posters: one by Flandin, the other—a large yellow poster—by the Postmen's and Teachers' Trade Unions. Both pacifist *à outrance*.

M. Flandin's poster said:

ON VOUS TROMPE

and denounced the ideological war that was being prepared by the politicians of the Front Populaire. He also denounced the *fausses nouvelles* spread by the warmongers, and went on to say that all the quarrel with Hitler was now over a question of procedure.

There must therefore be no mobilization, which would only lead to the massacre of millions of Frenchmen. Parliament must be called and there must be an 'objective discussion' of the situation. *Pas de chantage au patriotisme!* All Frenchmen must unite in their determination to defend peace.

It was interpreted by some as a call to Frenchmen not to obey the general mobilization order, were it to come. The police tore down the posters, and the *Liberté* which had printed it that night on its front page, was confiscated. On the next day the *Action Française* spoke highly of the poster the ideas of which, it said, had been borrowed from the A.F. and protested against its laceration by *le gorille* Sarraut. The *Lumière* later claimed that the poster was printed *with the approval of at least two members of the Government*, and in February, M. Flandin claimed that *throughout September he had worked in the closest co-operation with the Government.*

And the postmen's and schoolteachers' posters said

> We do not want war.
>
> In these grave hours we are certain of expressing the wish of the immense majority of the French people by saying that we wish a peaceful settlement of the present international crisis.
>
> Only a few days ago a settlement was considered possible, and agreement had been reached on the principle of the dispute. How can we now tolerate that for reasons of procedure, *amour-propre* or prestige, the statesmen should break off the negotiations which have gone on for weeks, and plunge the whole of Europe into the most frightful of wars.
>
> We ask the French Government to persevere and not to be discouraged by new difficulties. We ask it in its negotiations to give expression to the ardent love of peace of the people of France who have lost so many victims on the battlefields of Europe.
>
> We ask that the rational message of President Roosevelt be listened to: 'It is better to make peace before the war than after the war. Armed force provides no solution for the future, nor for the good of humanity.'

At the Chamber people were in a blue funk; Flandin was asking that Parliament be called; he claimed that Parliament would never allow France to declare war on Germany because of Czechoslovakia.

That night I listened to German broadcast from the B.B.C. about mobilization of British Navy, A.R.P., trenches, gas-masks, evacuation of children, and what not. Then Chamberlain spoke. It was a tragic speech by an old man who seemed to have broken down.

> How horrible, fantastic, incredible it is that we should be digging trenches and trying on gas-masks here because of a quarrel in a far-

away country between people of whom we know nothing. It seems still more impossible that a quarrel which has already been settled in principle should be the subject of war.

'People of whom we know nothing!' What a sudden insight into Chamberlain's fundamental provincialism!

> He [Hitler] told me privately, and last night he repeated publicly, that *after this Sudeten German question is settled that is the end of Germany's territorial claims in Europe.*
> I was taken completely by surprise when I got back to Germany and found that he insisted that the territory should be handed over to him immediately, and immediately occupied by German troops without previous arrangements for safeguarding the people within the territory who are not Germans or who do not want to join the German Reich.
> *I am afraid I must say I find this attitude unreasonable.*

'Unreasonable,' what a superb understatement!
And then came the famous conclusion:

> *However much we may sympathize with a small nation confronted by a big, powerful neighbour we cannot in all circumstances undertake to involve the whole British Empire in war simply on her account. If we have to fight it must be on larger issues than that. I am myself a man of peace to the depths of my soul. Armed conflict between nations is a nightmare to me, but if I were convinced that any nation had made up its mind to dominate the world by fear of its force I should feel that it must be resisted. Under such a domination the life of people who believe in liberty would not be worth living.*
> *But war is a fearful thing and we must be very clear before we embark upon it that it is really the great issues that are at stake and that the call to risk everything in their defence when all the consequences are weighed is irresistible.*

The telephone rang. It was A., a French journalist. 'What do you make of it?' 'I couldn't swear to it, but it sounds to me like the beginning of a *dégonflage*. "People we know nothing about," and "not sure whether the Germans really want to dominate the world," and Hitler's assurance that "he won't ask for any more." ' But it was a moving speech for all that—it was tragic and human—and how different from Hitler's horrible bellowing the night before. As somebody remarked that night, it showed the whole world the difference between dictatorship and democracy.

And that night, how many people must have gone to bed wondering if it wasn't going to be their last restful night.

And then—Wednesday.

.   .   .   .

Wednesday. 'Black Wednesday.' Mme Bousquet, the concierge, went off with the children early in the morning. She came to say good-bye and said she would be back at the end of the week, if her husband wasn't mobilized in the interval. In the meantime an old woman, whose sister had a shop in the rue de la Glacière and who was staying in Paris 'for the present' would look after the house. Of course, if war broke out, she'd probably leave, too; 'but then you are not going to stay here either, will you?' I said I didn't know.

There was talk of the wholesale evacuation of Paris; but nobody quite knew when or where or how; people were preferring to go off on their own.

There was a suspicion in Paris that morning that not all was over— and that something was happening. The German ultimatum to Prague was going to expire at 2 p.m. Somebody was going to climb down— only, would it be Hitler or *us*? There were many who felt that Chamberlain's broadcast had, in effect, prepared the ground for a climb-down. Only—one couldn't be certain of anything.

The papers that morning were—if anything—less gloomy than on the Tuesday morning.

'*La Paix ne veut pas encore être vaincue. . . .' Paris Midi* wrote. And, below it:

The two last chances of peace: Roosevelt, Mussolini?

They put Roosevelt first. Only Roosevelt was proposing an immediate conference in a neutral country of the Powers concerned in the Czech Problem. Smelt too 'democratic'—too League of Nationish; what if the Russians decided to come? It all might not suit Hitler and Mussolini. On page three of the same paper there was a much more emphatic and explicit headline.

THE DUCE MAY YET SAVE EVERYTHING
BY PROPOSING HIS MEDIATION
(1) a 15 days' truce.
(2) a conference of the European 'chiefs'.

However, that morning several of the people to whom I talked did not take it seriously: 'the papers are just trying to prevent a panic.'

Took a bus to the Place de l'Opéra. The traffic seemed crazy. Everybody seemed in a desperate hurry. Terrific traffic-jams around the Gare St. Lazare. People were fighting for seats on the trains. Walked up the rue Lafayette; met a Russian *émigré* friend who worked in some kind of business. His *patron* had decided to close it down. 'I'll be all right—I'm too lame to go into the army; but they'll be only too glad to take me on in a munition factory at Asnières. Make quite a lot of money there.' He had already gone to inquire. Painters were busy camouflaging the works. Went into a shop to buy some toothpaste. Solitary assistant greeted me like a long-lost brother. 'It's twelve o'clock—I swear you are the first customer to-day. If only I were selling suitcases—or gas-masks!' Met Frank at the Rotonde for lunch. The place looked completely deserted —only two more customers besides us. The waiters looked *distraits*. 'Hell, I wish I was home in Omaha,' said Frank. I offered him the P——s' 'quiet little country house' at Sceaux; 'it's not far from the military aerodrome, but it's not too bad.' No, Frank didn't like the idea, and said he'd sooner be in Omaha.

     .   .   .   .   .   .

Went home to find that Peter had rung up—'What's wrong?' 'We are going to have a Press conference at my office at three. Z. from the Quai d'Orsay is coming to talk to us about Press arrangements during the war.' 'Is it as bad as all that?' 'Nothing like being on the safe side. Thomas and David are coming too.'

Rang up Richard Mowrer. 'What are you going to do?' 'I'm going to buy a bicycle.' 'A bicycle?' 'Sure. It ain't going to be much use living *in* Paris; so I'm going to find a place some ten kilometres out of town, and come in every day whenever necessary.' 'What about your car?' 'You never know about the gasolene. There mayn't be any, and they may also commandeer the car.'

I then went to Peter's 'Press Conference,' Monsieur Z. of the Quai was there.

We asked questions about the Censorship and about telephoning to London, and gathered that there would be a censorship, and that, in all probability, it would not be possible to telephone London.

And while we were talking, a Frenchman from next door came dashing in:

'Hitler and Chamberlain and Mussolini and Daladier are meeting at twelve at Mulhouse to-morrow.' *Coup de théâtre*; but—followed by a moment of doubt. 'Don't be absurd—why should they meet at Mulhouse? Are the French giving away Alsace-Lorraine?' 'Hell, I don't mean Mulhouse, I mean Munich.' That sounded more like it.

And Herr Dampfer, a German *émigré*, came in from next door and said: "Isn't it wonderful to think of the money Hitler could make on the Bourse if he wanted to!'

In the street outside the traffic seemed to have slowed down. Was it just imagination? In the Place de l'Opéra people were snatching up *Paris-Soirs* with giant headlines. But the feeling that afternoon was not one of exuberance. In the Café des Capucines I overheard two men talking:

'*Tout de même, quel soulagement!*'

'*Hm, oui, enfin. . . . C'est le soulagement qu'on éprouve le moment où on a fait dans sa culotte.*'

On my way home I saw a taxi laden with pillows and mattresses and wicker baskets driving up to a house. The people had *returned* from the station. They and the people on the first floor were waving frantically. '*Pas de guerre! Pas de guerre!*'

La mère Thiébauld was standing outside her house in the rue Broco. 'Have you heard?' I asked. 'Yes, of course,' she said, not sounding much impressed. 'All right if it's put off for a long time—but if it's only for a few months it's hardly worth it. *On l'aura dans des pires conditions.*'

La mère Thiébauld was an old peasant woman with a fund of common-sense; and although she read the *Journal* every morning, she had worked it all out for herself.

. . . .

That night Daladier spoke on the wireless. His voice sounded firm and authoritative:

I announced that I would make a statement this evening to the country on the international situation; but early this afternoon I received an invitation from the German Government to meet Chancellor Hitler, Signor Mussolini and Mr. Chamberlain in Munich to-morrow. I have accepted the invitation.

You will understand that on the eve of such an important negotiation, I must postpone the explanations I was going to give you. But before leaving, I wish to address my thanks to the people of France for its attitude, so full of courage and dignity.

I thank particularly the men who were called to the colours for their calm and their resolution.

My task is a hard one. Since the beginning of the difficulties through which we are passing, I never ceased for a day to work with all my strength for the safeguarding of peace and for the vital interests of France. I shall continue this effort to-morrow, with the thought that I am in complete agreement with the whole nation.

. . . .

What was it that had happened at the Quai d'Orsay on the night from Tuesday to Wednesday? It was later claimed that if Bonnet was not alone in 'saving peace,' he certainly played a 'decisive part' that night. It was even vaguely suggested that it was on his initiative that Munich was arranged.

On October 8 the *Intransigeant* claimed that it was M. Bonnet's two messages on the night of September 27-28, one to M. François-Poncet, the Ambassador in Berlin, the other to M. Corbin, the Ambassador in London, 'which were to spare the lives of millions of Europeans.' Mr. Chamberlain was not even mentioned—it looked as though Munich was the work of M. Bonnet alone. This is what M. Thouvenin, one of M. Bonnet's *hommes de confiance,* wrote:

On September 27 one did not yet want to believe in the imminence of the catastrophe.

That evening at 10 o'clock Mr. Chamberlain gave his famous broadcast. . . .

At 11 o'clock the British Government ordered the mobilization of the British Navy. The situation seemed to become more and more critical. M. Georges Bonnet declared to the British Ambassador, who again came to see him, that one must not lose heart, that one must persevere to the end and that peace could yet be saved.

The minister was now alone in his office. He was thinking hard.

Alone in his office, M. Bonnet reflected, weighing up possible decisions. After mature reflection, at 1 o'clock in the morning, he took a decision: he was going, at this hour of supreme effort to take a double step to save peace. He sent M. François-Poncet an urgent telegram in which he requested him to ask Chancellor Hitler immediately for an audience so that he could submit to him a compromise proposal. M. François-Poncet was instructed to recall to the Führer that the cession of the Sudeten territory to Germany had already been officially granted to the German Government, with the double guarantee of France and Britain, and that this guarantee was sufficient to dispel the doubts the Chancellor had expressed as to whether the Czechs would fulfil the agreement entered into in principle.

It now depended on the Reichsführer—and on him alone—whether peace was to be saved without Germany's losing the advantages that had already been agreed to.

A little later, at 2:50 a.m., M. Bonnet telegraphed to M. Corbin in London: the idea of a conference had been suggested; it was important that Signor Mussolini should be associated with it, and that Italy should urge Herr Hitler to support this proposal.

And so, two official telegrams left the Minister's office at the Quai

d'Orsay on that historic night; and they were to spare the lives of
millions of Europeans.

But here is a still better account of the "historic night" by another
'pacifist,' M. Paul Allard; for according to M. Allard, peace was saved
in the last resort not by M. Bonnet but by—M. Piétri, not even a member
of the Government!

> At 10 p.m. on the night of September 27-8 M. Bonnet expressed
> to Sir Eric Philipps (*sic*) the hope that on the following day Mr.
> Chamberlain would make another supreme effort; at 11 p.m. Mr. Bon-
> net sent M. François-Poncet a cyphered telegram instructing him to
> see Chancellor Hitler the next morning and to propose to him a prac-
> tical plan for the occupation of the Sudeten country—a plan which he
> had personally elaborated, during the day, with M. Daladier. (M.
> Allard's Daladier is rather more active than M. Thouvenin's.) At
> 2 a.m. M. Bonnet sent a telegram to M. Corbin inviting him to bring
> about a British *démarche* in Rome.
> It is established that at that moment the Duce alone was in a posi-
> tion to assume the role of a friendly mediator—and he proved to be
> a decisive factor in the calling of the Four-Power Conference.
> M. Piétri suggested to M. Bonnet that the idea be followed up of
> associating Signor Mussolini directly with an immediate conference.
> At the same moment M. Frossard (who had at the Chamber, on the
> same day, advocated a Four-Power Conference) telephoned to M.
> Bonnet, and a sort of three-men colloquy took place. Whereupon
> M. Bonnet wrote out his telegram (to whom? to Chamberlain, or to
> Corbin, to whom he had already telegraphed at 11 p.m.?). Mr. Cham-
> berlain appealed to Signor Mussolini. The Duce immediately tele-
> phoned Herr Hitler and threw, it is said (!), Italo-German friendship
> into the balance. . . . Peace was saved.[5]

These stories, the first of which at any rate was certainly written *ad
maiorem gloriam* of Georges Bonnet—call for two remarks. Mr. Chamberlain, in his House of Commons speech, on September 28, made no
reference whatsoever to any part played that night by M. Bonnet in the
calling of the Munich Conference.

Secondly, it would seem from these stories that the final surrender
was decided upon by the French rather than by the British; and that
at the very moment when, as a result of the mobilization of the British
Navy, Hitler was beginning to wonder how he was going to get out
of a hopeless mess without loss of prestige. The moral of these French
stories about the 'historic night' is that it was M. François-Poncet's

[5] Paul Allard. *Le Quai d'Orsay,* pp. 165–6.

communication to Hitler, rather than any British move which saved Hitler from a plight that was becoming desperate. It is true that the François-Poncet *démarche* ran parallel with Mr. Chamberlain's 'final' letter to Hitler, but this letter is not as obvious a surrender as the François-Poncet communication.

Mr. Chamberlain asked for 'a week' and asked that the Czechs be included in the talks. The French, however, accepted Hitler's date of October 1. If only they had waited a few hours longer, Hitler who, after denying the German mobilization order upon hearing of the mobilization of the British Fleet, was now obviously scared, might easily have accepted a Conference on Roosevelt lines, instead of a 'Munich.' The French *démarche*, much more than Chamberlain's 'last letter,' saved him from the unpleasant necessity of yielding. However, M. Bonnet's friends are very proud of it all, and claim for M. Bonnet the glory of Munich—a glory to which, they say, he is more entitled than are the British.

.   .   .   .

On September 29 the Press published a Havas message from Berlin describing, as follows, M. François-Poncet's historic visit to Hitler on the previous morning.

M. François-Poncet was received by Herr Hitler this morning. The conversations lasted about an hour.

It is said that the French Ambassador submitted to him some new suggestions from the French Government with a view to a peaceful settlement of the German-Czech conflict. According to well-informed sources, it is understood that the proposals provide for the occupation of the Sudeten country by German troops.

Immediately after M. François-Poncet had left Herr Hitler also received Sir Nevile Henderson, the British Ambassador.

It is further claimed that Signor Attolico, the Italian Ambassador was also received by the Führer, and it is said that he asked the Chancellor to prolong until October 1 the time given to the Czechs to evacuate the Sudeten country.

Although the exact meaning of the 'Sudeten country' is left vague, it is fairly clear from all this that it was already in Berlin on September 28, and not on the following day at Munich, that the substance of the Godesberg Plan was virtually accepted. And accepted by the French sooner than by the British. For the French 'new suggestions' certainly went beyond the Anglo-French Plan—a plan which, at least on the face of it, was still the basis of Chamberlain's 'last letter' to Hitler.

XIV. THE MUNICH TRIUMPH

O N THE face of it, Mr. Chamberlain and M. Daladier were in a very strong position when they left for Munich. The British Navy was mobilized; France had close on 1,500,000 men under arms, and it was known that German opinion was intensely perturbed at the discovery that the 'localized' war against the Czechs had in the two or three previous days threatened to develop into a war against a large European coalition.

Hitler himself seems to have wondered on the night of September 27–28, when he heard of the British naval mobilization, how he could get out of the hole. Mussolini came to his rescue; but, in addition to that M. François-Poncet already informed him, on the morning of September 28, that the French were prepared to accept almost anything—with the result that he had nothing to fear from Munich. On the face of it, and but for the French *démarche* of September 28, France and England could have insisted at Munich on Germany's acceptance of the Anglo-French Plan of September 18, and could have rejected Godesberg.

But, in reality, this was no longer practicable. The substance of Godesberg had already been accepted by M. François-Poncet, and, after the psychological 'no-war' shock on the afternoon of September 28, it was difficult for Mr. Chamberlain and M. Daladier even to bluff at Munich. British opinion, in particular, after being worked up to the realization that war was inevitable and after suddenly collapsing with relief, could not possibly be expected to face war 'over Czechoslovakia' once again. So, technically, Britain and France were in an extremely strong position at Munich; psychologically, they were in a very weak one. Especially England; for France, where the 'scare' had not been so great as in England, and where, consequently, the 'collapse' of Wednesday afternoon was not so devastating, could still put up some kind of resistance at Munich.

M. Daladier actually tried to do so at first; but received little support from Mr. Chamberlain. It is said that he went to Munich with the firm intention of 'standing up to the Dictators,' and that he 'stood up' to Hitler fairly well for the first couple of hours, though what he was 'fighting' for could, obviously, only have been details. Czechoslovakia had been sacrificed at Berchtesgaden, and England and France never even thought of going back on the 'Anglo-French Plan.' But after lunch Daladier's resistance weakened. Perhaps it was Mr. Chamberlain's fault. It may also be that Goering managed to fascinate him. Goering behaved with a kind of coarse, loud joviality, slapping Daladier on the back, and

257

saying that he liked and admired the French—'what fine chaps they were during the War!'—and that it was absurd for two great nations, which could be good friends, to quarrel over silly things like Czechoslovakia. Goering must have touched on one of Daladier's soft spots—which was his profound belief that France and Germany ought *somehow* to make friends and never go to war again. Later that day the Havas Correspondent asked Goering what he thought of Daladier: 'The very kind of chap I like,' Goering replied; and then added, *'und er ist so elastisch.'* The story goes that while Daladier 'passed' the message, though not without making a face, Bonnet, in Paris, stopped it from appearing.

An insight into Daladier's state of mind at the end of the Munich Conference is provided by the following account of how the Czechs were treated in Munich. This account, the summary of which I wired to the *New Statesman and Nation* and which was later published in full in the Paris *Ordre*, was based on first-hand information.

Dr. Hubert Masarik and Mr. Mastny were summoned to Munich to receive the Dictators' ultimatum about the future of their country. They arrived at Munich by aeroplane soon after three o'clock on September 29, were met at the aerodrome by a police car and, accompanied by members of the Gestapo, driven to the Hotel Regina, where the British delegation was staying. The conference was already in session and it was only at seven o'clock that they were able to obtain some conversation with Mr. Gwatkin. They tried to press certain economic and other problems on his attention. He was personally sympathetic but said they scarcely seemed to realize how painful it was to negotiate with Hitler, and made it clear that the plan under discussion was much worse than the terms of the Anglo-French Plan. At about ten o'clock the Czech delegates went into Sir Horace Wilson's room, where the plan was briefly explained to them, but no serious attention paid to their objections. They were warned that if the Czechs did not accept promptly they would be left to make their own terms with Germany and that the French might sound very sorry, and all that, but that they would certainly do nothing to help them. At 1.30 a.m. they were shown into the conference room. Hitler and Mussolini had gone, leaving Mr. Chamberlain, M. Daladier, Sir Horace Wilson, M. Léger and Mr. Gwatkin to inform them that the agreement had been signed. The French were obviously embarrassed; the agreement was read, but their protests and doubts about the definition of areas of 'preponderantly German character' and about the absence of safeguards for their vital economic and strategic interests, were brushed aside. Questions about proposals for supervision of the 'plebiscites' by international or British troops were referred to the International Commission. Mr. Chamberlain was tired out and yawned repeatedly, *while M. Daladier was too embarrassed to answer when they wanted to know whether the Czech Government was to have the opportunity of making any statement or giving any reply to the proposals. It was left to M. Léger to explain bluntly that no reply was expected from the Czechs* and that the agreement was regarded as already accepted. A Czech delegate was to be in Berlin not later than 5 p.m. on the same day to meet the International Commission, and an officer to go to Berlin to discuss the details of the evacuation of the first zone.

. . . .

It is certain that at Munich Daladier felt intensely unhappy about the result of the conference. Several correspondents who saw the statesmen emerge from the conference room have described their faces. Demaree Bess (*Saturday Evening Post,* December 3) said Daladier seemed 'sunk in the depths of despair,' Chamberlain had 'his usual poker face,' while Mussolini had a 'broad smile' and Hitler was 'walking on air.'[1] 'Depths of despair' seems to have been the impression Daladier gave everybody that night. When he returned to his hotel, a number of French journalists were waiting for him, and naturally went up to him to ask questions. There was a wild, vacant look in his eyes, he opened his mouth to say something, then changed his mind, and hastily walked to the lift.

Still, on the following morning, he tried to make the best of a bad job. Before leaving Munich he said to the correspondent of the D.N.B., the official German news agency:

I think the Munich meeting may prove to be an historical date in the life of Europe.

It was a great pleasure to me to find that there was no feeling of hatred or hostility towards France in Germany. I can assure you that there is no feeling of hostility towards Germany in my country; and that was true even during this last period of diplomatic tension and military preparations. The two nations must come to an agreement, and I am happy to devote all my strength to this necessary and faithful understanding.

According to Havas, 'all along the way from the hotel to the aerodrome M. Daladier was the object of warm ovations.' At the aerodrome, where he was received by General von Epp, the Statthalter of Bavaria, he reviewed a guard of honour, while the band was playing national

[1] Quoted by Hamilton Fish Armstrong, *Foreign Affairs,* January 1939.

anthems. Standing for a long time on the gangway of the aeroplane M. Daladier waved greetings to the cheering crowds.

When the aeroplane was in sight of Le Bourget an extraordinary thing happened. M. Daladier saw large crowds assembled near the aerodrome. He felt intensely uncomfortable. *How* were they going to receive him? But he soon realized that the people were cheering and waving. Well, since the people were pleased, it was no use looking unhappy. So in coming out of the aeroplane, M. Daladier, looking rather red in the face, waved as cheerfully as he could.

With the usual exceptions, the Paris Press that day had described Munich as an unspeakably happy event. And at one o'clock the French radio announced the exact route along which M. Daladier would travel from Le Bourget to the War Office. It was M. Bonnet's idea. Since Mussolini and Hitler and Chamberlain were going to make triumphal entries into their respective capitals, there was no reason why M. Daladier should not receive equal treatment. Otherwise Munich might look like a French defeat, like the Diplomatic Sedan the war-mongering Kerillis had announced in the *Epoque* that morning. A story told in Paris at the time is that Bonnet actually wanted all the churches to ring their bells during Daladier's entry into Paris; but that Cardinal Verdier, the Archbishop of Paris, would not hear of it. There were, no doubt, some who thought it would have been best for Daladier to sneak into Paris by *métro* with his hat well over his face; but it really would not have done.

I had forgotten all about the triumphal home-coming—it seemed so unimportant—when, about four o'clock in the Boulevard Haussmann, I saw a large crowd lining the pavements outside the Galeries Lafayette, and on the opposite side of the street, as well as all down the rue Lafayette. Several houses were decorated with flags, including some Union Jacks (probably a remnant of the royal visit). Shop-girls were standing on the balcony of the Galeries Lafayette holding tri-colour flags, and a facetious-looking street-sweeper waved a broom with a handkerchief tied to it—which caused much amusement in the crowd.

Some cried '*Vive la Paix!*' and others cried '*Vive la France!*' Nobody mentioned Czechoslovakia. A workman next to me remarked rather ironically, '*Vive la France malgré tout*,' and a messenger boy with a bicycle said that since the Boulevard Haussmann has been closed to traffic half an hour earlier there was now a terrible traffic-jam higher up the avenue where it runs into the Grands Boulevards, and the drivers were all 'cursing like blazes.' A grimmer touch of irony was added a few minutes before M. Daladier's car drove down the rue Lafayette by the appearance of a brewer's lorry labelled *'La Sedan, Bières Extra-Fines.'*

And then, at last, came a small open car, with Daladier standing up in it and looking rather red and bewildered. Next to him, with a self-satisfied smirk on his face, sat M. Bonnet. *'Vive Daladier!' 'Vive la Paix!' 'Vive la France!'* And the girls on the balcony of the Galeries Lafayette waved their little flags.

In spite of the cheering, in spite of the profound relief that war had been averted, there was an undercurrent of uneasiness in Paris and the cheering itself had a rather conventional quality. And one doubted whether the leading article in the *Paris-Soir* that night really reflected the feelings of the man-in-the-street.

> As a result of this terrible crisis (it said) France could have died or might have come out much reduced in authority. She has come out of it with her head erect, with her friendships strengthened, with the Anglo-French friendship definitely sealed, and with new friendships in prospect.

And, illustrating this article, was a photograph showing Hitler and Goering looking on patronizingly as Daladier was signing the Munich agreement. One wondered how many people in Paris looked at this photograph that afternoon with any sense of historical perspective.

There was, altogether, much nonsense in that issue of *Paris-Soir* they were selling on the afternoon of M. Daladier's return from Munich. That day it opened a public subscription for a villa in France to be presented to Mr. Chamberlain, *'le Seigneur de la Paix.'* The villa was to be near some river where the Premier could fish. It also announced that a Paris town councillor had already proposed that an avenue in Paris be named after 'September 30.' There were other suggestions for an avenue Chamberlain and an avenue Daladier, and even an avenue Mussolini; however, nobody went so far as to propose an avenue Hitler—not even M. Flandin. Two days later *Paris-Soir* announced:

> *Dans un élan magnifique*
> *nos lecteurs*
> *continuent de nous adresser des dons pour*
> *'La Maison de la Paix,'*
> *qui sera offerte à M. Chamberlain.*

In twenty-four hours, it said, the subscription had exceeded 100,000 francs (£550). The subscription was open for a month; £1,500 was all that they managed to collect. In the end, the money was handed over by Mr. Chamberlain himself to some ex-servicemen's organization, when he came to Paris at the end of November.

Although at the Bon Marché and the Printemps and in other shops they continued for some weeks to sell 'lucky umbrellas' in the form of clips and brooches it was soon found that the supply was greatly in excess of the demand. And in my working-class district I dropped, several weeks later, into a paper-shop, and the old woman asked me appealingly to buy a photograph of Mr. Chamberlain. 'I have had it for two months, and nobody will buy it—I'll give it you for one franc instead of 2.50.'

.   .   .   .

It may be said at once that the Anglo-German declaration which came immediately on top of Munich created an extremely unpleasant impression in Paris, and damped what Chamberlain enthusiasm may have existed in the country. Even the Right, who, for ideological reasons, had been looking forward to a 'Four-Power Pact' Europe, were annoyed; it looked as though both Chamberlain and Hitler were beginning to treat post-Munich France as a negligible quantity. Although in reality, there was nothing so very sinister in the Chamberlain-Hitler declaration (for Chamberlain was particularly anxious to get some such declaration in view of the two veiled threats Hitler had uttered in September to denounce the Anglo-German Naval Treaty) the French felt cheated. England had got something concrete out of the Munich meeting, while France had nothing to show. They thought the Germans were already busy driving a wedge between France and England, with a view to isolating France, in accordance with the recipes of *Mein Kampf*.

And Henri de Kerillis, on October 2, quoted the words said to him, some time earlier, by a prominent Englishman (his description suggested that it was Mr. Churchill):

> The Czechoslovak affair may have much graver consequences than is imagined. For three centuries British policy has been based on the balance of power in Europe. We have always fought against the hegemony of any one Power. But this policy was possible only because we always had a strong point of support which we used as our basis. In reading your papers, in looking at your reactions, we are for the first time beginning to wonder whether such a point of support exists any longer. It is therefore possible that the time will come when we may be obliged to break away from our traditional policy, and instead of resisting against the dominating Power in Europe we shall endeavour to come to terms with it.

M. de Kerillis added to this:

> It is only fair to say that he did not add 'at your expense.' But nevertheless his words have worried me greatly; and I also remem-

bered *Mein Kampf* with the isolation and destruction of France as Hitler's ultimate aim.

A stranger demonstration even than Daladier's entry into Paris on the day of the Munich agreement took place in the Champs-Elysées on the following night, when, at the suggestion of the Paris Association of Ex-Soldiers, M. Daladier rekindled the flame on the grave of the Unknown Soldier. Enormous crowds gathered around the Etoile that night, and the traffic was held up for over an hour. As on Armistice Day, the Arc de Triomphe was decorated with a large tricolour banner, illuminated by a searchlight rising high into the sky. And with strange fervour thousands of people that night sang the 'Marseillaise': *'Le jour de gloire est arrivé.'*

To those who, like Pertinax, felt that 'France had retroactively lost the world war at Munich' the ceremony seemed sacrilegious; to many it was a rather personal thanksgiving ceremony; to some it was a political demonstration. The Champs-Elysées crowd—as readers of my last book will remember—is predominantly a '6th of February' crowd; and on that night, when Munich was celebrated round the Arch that had been built to commemorate the battle of Austerlitz (in what was still remaining of Czechoslovakia!), hundreds of young men stretched out their right arms in the Fascist salute. Daladier, their villain of the 6th of February, had now become their hero of the 30th of September.

And, there is something ironical in the thought that in both cases it just happened—without Daladier having desired it. He did not desire the 6th of February riots; nor did he, at heart, desire Munich. In spite of himself he became first, *le fusilleur,* and now the Man of the Munich Peace.

.   .   .   .

Parliament was called for a brief 'exceptional' session on October 4. The whole debate on Munich lasted barely six hours; and technically it was only a discussion on the motion of adjournment approved by the Government.

Although it was one of the *grandes journées* of Parliament, and the Chamber was crowded, everybody felt that the calling of Parliament was, to the Government, little more than an unpleasant formality. The whole crisis had occurred without Parliament having been consulted at any moment—in spite of numerous requests that Parliament be called. These requests, incidentally, came chiefly from the 'pacifists' who were convinced that the majority of the Chamber and Senate was 'pacifist' like themselves. M. Flandin was particularly firm on this point; and one of the principal arguments used against a 'firm' policy was that the Chamber would in no circumstances consent to declare war on Germany even if Czechoslovakia were invaded. The argument certainly reflected to some extent the state of mind in French Parliamentary quarters at the end of September, that is, *before* the guns had gone off; what Parliament would have done once the war had actually started can be only a matter of speculation. Even an ardent 'pacifist' like M. Pierre Dominique was not certain that Parliament would not have been swept off its feet by the reaction of public opinion to an actual outbreak of war. But one thing is certain: and that is the desperate fear of the majority of the French deputies of being suspected of *bellicisme*; a charge of 'warmongering' might prove fatal in the next Election. And it is significant that, although opinion was greatly divided in every party on the merits of Munich, the motion of adjournment (which, in effect, implied the approval of Munich) was voted unanimously with the exception of the Communists, and of M. de Kerillis. There were one or two abstentions. Unlike the Labour Party, the French Socialists, though profoundly divided, all voted 'for Munich.'

The electoral aspect of the vote is well illustrated by the interruption made by a Right-Wing deputy during M. de Kerillis's speech: 'Remember Neuilly!'—Neuilly being M. de Kerillis's constituency, which as a *belliciste* he was now considered to be certain to lose.

M. Daladier spoke that day with great self-assurance, though not perhaps without a slight touch of uneasiness. He began by saying that when his Government was formed the Czech-Sudeten conflict was already in progress. The Anschluss had made the conflict an acute one.

> We did what we could from the outset to avoid anything irreparable. Several times I defined the position of my Government: 'We are animated by two equally strong feelings: the desire not to be compelled to take military action and the will never to betray our word if, unfortunately, our hopes were to be deceived.'

After briefly recalling the London meeting in April and the crisis of May 21, 'which was overcome thanks to the effective collaboration of the peaceful wills of all the Powers concerned,' M. Daladier referred to the pressure brought to bear on the Czechs.

In September the situation became truly dangerous, and on the night from the 13th to the 14th M. Daladier told Mr. Chamberlain that he thought direct contacts between the responsible statesmen to be more useful than any diplomatic notes. 'Mr. Chamberlain, who had the same feeling, went to Berchtesgaden.'

There followed a tribute to Mr. Chamberlain which was cheered by the greater part of the House, most of the deputies rising to their feet.

In this account M. Daladier had already skated over a great deal of thin ice; and in the rest of his speech there were to be many gaps. No mention was made of the critical French Cabinet meeting of September 13; and in what was to follow, the whole story of Godesberg and of the two London meetings in September was left very obscure. Nevertheless, M. Daladier made the remarkable claim:

> Perhaps for the first time in the history of the world was everything done and said in public. And I think I may say that if peace was saved, it was because we never had recourse to the methods of secret diplomacy. We acted in broad daylight, under the control of the Nations; and I wish to assert that the nations, all the nations, desire peace.

After briefly mentioning Berchtesgaden M. Daladier described 'the great emotion' with which he and M. Bonnet heard of Lord Runciman's conclusion that the Czechs and Sudetens could no longer live together.

> But it was necessary to look the facts in the face. We were in the following dilemma: we could have said No, and so encouraged Czech intransigence and German aggression, or we could have looked for a compromise. . . . If we had taken the former course, who could assert that the integrity of Czechoslovakia could be maintained even after a terrible but victorious war?

The French ultimatum of September 21 was naturally discreetly omitted. Instead a tribute was paid to the 'heroic devotion of the Czechs to the cause of peace' with which they accepted the London Plan.

But at Godesberg Herr Hitler put forward new claims, in the form of 'modalities of application.'

Then came an interesting definition of the attitude of the French Government:

> During those days of anguish there were two currents of opinion in France. Both could be found inside every political party, one might even say in the heart and conscience of every Frenchman: one was the hope in further negotiation, the other the faith in intransigent firmness. As the head of the Government I recognized from the outset that both these movements of opinion represented the infallible instinct of the French people; and I felt that the truth lay in the synthesis of these two currents of opinion and not in their juxtaposition. What the French people desired was that the irreparable should be avoided. The

irreparable was German aggression. If this had happened we, for our part, would have asked you to fulfil France's obligations.

The phrase suggested that he was not sure whether Parliament would have agreed to a declaration of war on Germany if Czechoslovakia had been attacked.

But the theory of the 'synthesis'—whether, on close analysis, it makes any sense or not—is in curious contrast with M. Daladier's later claim in December that 'the policy of firmness meant the policy of war.' For, in spite of his self-confident manner on October 4, M. Daladier had not yet been fully converted to the view that Munich was both good and completely inevitable.

After referring to the mobilization of September 24, M. Daladier claimed that the General Staff had

'placed France's armed forces in a position to carry out their supreme duty towards the country. . . .'

And then came the confirmation, which caused visible embarrassment on the Right, and loud cheers from the Left, that the *fausse nouvelle* about the official British statement of September 26 was perfectly authentic.

A reference was then made to President Roosevelt; and the ovation that the mention of his name produced on nearly all the benches, but particularly on the Left, was greater than that produced by the mention of Chamberlain. And, significantly enough, a later reference to Beneš was received with almost complete silence by the Right.

Then came M. Daladier's account of the 'historical night' of September 27–28. On that night

'we decided to make a last effort. We asked our Ambassador in Berlin to request a personal interview with Chancellor Hitler; and we instructed our Ambassador in London to ask Lord Halifax to give instructions to the British Ambassador in Rome to ask Signor Mussolini to support the idea of a conference.'

And giving Mr. Roosevelt's intention a rather loose interpretation, M. Daladier added:

We responded in this manner to the spirit of the second message of President Roosevelt who made such a generous contribution towards a peaceful solution of the conflict.

M. Daladier continued:

At 11.15 a.m., on September 28, M. François-Poncet was received by the German Chancellor and submitted to him in the name of the French Government certain proposals of a precise nature and capable of immediate and practical application. Herr Hitler did not reject these suggestions, and said he would reply in writing.

Two points might be emphasized.

These proposals 'capable of an immediate and practical application,' which meant in reality the virtual acceptance of an immediate German occupation of at least certain Sudeten territories and of other demands contained in the Godesberg memorandum, and which were submitted to Hitler 'in the name of the French Government' had not been discussed by the French Cabinet. They were agreed upon by M. Bonnet and M. Daladier. From M. Daladier's account it would appear that the brainwave to call Mussolini to the rescue was also a French brainwave; and that it was M. Bonnet (and M. Daladier?) who suggested this solution to the British Government. As already said, there is no reference to any French move on the night of September 27–28 in Mr. Chamberlain's speech on the afternoon of September 28.

'I accepted the invitation to Munich,' M. Daladier went on. 'It was not a question of discussing procedure or of submitting counter-proposals. [What an admission!] It was a question of saving peace which many considered to be definitely lost. I said "yes," and I regret nothing.' (Loud and prolonged cheers on many benches.)

'No doubt, I would have preferred that all the nations directly concerned be represented. But there was no time to lose. The least delay might have been fatal. Was not a frank conversation with Herr Hitler and Signor Mussolini better than any such proposals [what proposals —Roosevelt's?] or any written discussions? You know the results of the Munich meeting, which was a useful conversation rather than a formal conference. We avoided the use of force. We produced, without out a shadow of doubt, a Peace Plebiscite in the four countries. . . . It was an effective victory of peace, and a moral victory of peace. Also a human victory, for thanks to the reciprocal concessions and to the goodwill of all (!) Munich is an unquestionable improvement on Godesberg.'

The 'improvement' was, however, described only briefly:

'It contains stipulations for organizing the right of option for individuals, and it *eliminates all the provisions which might have figured in an armistice imposed by the victor on his defeated foe* (!). *England and France have given complete guarantees, and Italy and Germany have promised to give their guarantees as soon as the question of the Hungarian and Polish minorities is settled.* I am convinced that thanks to direct conversations, a just and honourable settlement will soon be found.'

To think that in the weeks that were to follow England and France remained completely aloof from the 'honourable settlement' of the Hungarian claims! The Czechs did not even condescend to invoke the Franco-British guarantee when Germany went on taking away territories for the transfer of which no provision had been made at Munich. They were the first to consider the Anglo-French guarantee as a scrap of paper.

'No doubt,' M. Daladier said, 'Munich has reduced the territory of Czechoslovakia. *But the Czechoslovak Republic can continue her life as a free country, and we shall do our best to help her.'*

There followed compliments to the spirit of peace and heroism and self-sacrifice of the Czechs.

These compliments were, in turn, followed by a discourse on the mutual esteem France and Germany felt for one another. 'One can no more think of intimidating Germany than one can think of intimidating France.' Daladier's ambition had always been a *rapprochement* with Germany; and he dwelt on this *rapprochement* at length even in the speech that followed immediately upon France's 'diplomatic Sedan.'

M. Daladier added, of course, that in seeking friendship with Germany France had no intention of 'substituting new friendships for old.'

Peace, he said, had unfortunately not been

definitely saved; and we must go on defending it every day. . . . It is possible, as some have written, that at Munich the face of the world had been changed in a few hours. However that may be, one thing is certain: France must meet a new situation by developing a new sense of duty. (Loud cheers on the Right.) Peace will not be maintained unless our production enables us to speak as equals to the people around us. We can maintain peace only with healthy finances. . . . We must reach a general settlement in Europe, and build it on new principles; and having avoided war in Central Europe, we must make it retreat in all parts of the world where it is still in progress. . . . This country is in need of a moral transformation. This unity was achieved during a few days among the mobilized forces. My dear friends, let us not allow this unity to be scattered through idle quarrels and unimportant polemics.'

M. Daladier then announced that he was going to ask Parliament for plenary powers; 'the interest and the very life of the country are at stake.'

He was, naturally, going to secure these plenary powers on the following day. They were to be valid until the 5th of November; the Communists voted against them; the Socialists, after being promised by the Government (so at least they claimed) that Parliament was to be called by the middle of November, abstained.

The discussion that followed M. Daladier's speech—technically it was on the motion of adjournment—was a rather tame affair.

M. Edmond Miellet, Vice-President of the Army Committee, complimented the Government on the Munich agreement, which, he said, was the best possible solution to the Czech problem.

M. Michel Walter, an Alsatian with mildly autonomist tendencies, dwelt on the grave consequences of the crisis which had completely upset the economic life of Alsace; and while Alsace was loyal to France, it was necessary for France to pay the greatest attention to Alsace's economic plight; the prosperity of Alsace would not be restored unless the threat of war ceased to hang over her, as it had now done for years. Such a threat must be eliminated for ever.

Alsace-Lorraine appeals to France and to her Government not to refuse *a priori* to take the new road of the new diplomacy.

Meaning, of course, Four-Power Pact diplomacy.

A flood of home truths on Munich and of charges of unpardonable weakness came from M. Péri, the Communist speaker, and from M. de Kerillis, the upholder of the Nationalist tradition, who was frequently cheered—by the Communists only. At one point M. Flandin interrupted him, and reminded M. Herriot, the Speaker, that M. de Kerillis was exceeding his time limit. These were the only words uttered by M. Flandin during that post-Munich discussion. Probably he did not wish to embarrass the Government; and perhaps he also felt uneasy because the truth was beginning to leak out about the telegram of congratulation he had sent to Hitler (as well as to Mussolini and Mr. Chamberlain) on the day of the Munich settlement. And—worse still—Hitler had answered his telegram and had told him encouragingly that *he had watched M. Flandin's activity for the past year with great interest and sympathy.*

Through the indiscretion of a post-office official the copy of the telegram was to be read out before the Foreign Affairs Committee of the Chamber some time later.

It created a fearful uproar—here was Hitler treating Flandin as though he were a kind of potential Seyss-Inquart. Several members resigned from the Alliance Démocratique; and even M. Maurras, in the *Action Française,* which had approved of the famous Flandin poster of

September 27, now declared that Flandin 'had not understood the first thing about the real meaning of Munich'; and added that he had, in fact, always thought him to be rather an ass.

In the discussion on Munich, M. Marin, the old Lorrainer who had supported Poincaré through thick and thin at the time of the Ruhr, spoke with sorrow but with a feeling of helplessness and futility. His main argument was that the Government had left France completely in the dark about the negotiations. M. Daladier's statement had not explained anything. Without the British White Paper and the Commons Debate and the Czech documents, France would be in absolute ignorance of what had actually happened.

M. Blum's statement, which he made in the name of the whole Socialist group, with all its conflicting tendencies, was inevitably vague and colourless—except for its final passage, which was of considerable significance.

He blamed the men who in the past had refused to treat with Weimar Germany, he spoke of the noble example of Jaurès, who never despaired of saving peace; he expressed joy because Peace had been saved and sorrow because Czechoslovakia had been sacrificed, and said that if France's will for peace was so deep and general it was largely thanks to the Socialists. And in deploring the sad fate of Czechoslovakia, M. Blum said that if only his proposal for a National Government in March had been accepted, all might have been different.

'Perhaps one understands better than one did then why certain statesmen persistently refused to follow us.' France, M. Blum said, 'must now be honest with herself and examine all the treaties to which she is a party and frankly denounce those which she does not intend to fulfil.' Europe must be built up on the basis of 'equity, concord and solidarity and may France take the lead in bringing this about.'

'But once again we ask whether such an initiative can be effectively taken without the support of the French masses; and for the third time we say: no. You can neither organize peace nor prepare war without the support of the people.

'*We are ready in advance to struggle against any attempt to exploit the European Crisis for the benefits of political Reaction; and we proclaim that the lesson to be learned from the last crisis is that the unity of all the forces of liberty, progress and justice—which are the real national forces—is more essential than ever.* It is with these feelings and with this hope that the Socialist group is prepared to vote for the motion of adjournment.'

Blum's proposal meant that it was more important than ever to form a real National Government, complete with the Socialists. And his fears that if this was not done France would, after Munich, go along the road of political reaction was, as we shall see, not unjustified.

The Right were determined that Munich should be followed by a long spell of political reaction. Not only in home affairs, but also in the handling of foreign affairs. For the next two months at least home policy was dominated by anti-Communism, and foreign policy by *rapprochement* with the dictator countries.

THE NEGLECT OF RUSSIA

Before starting on the story of the post-Munich period, it may be advisable to inquire more closely into two important points which have hitherto been mentioned only incidentally.

One is the cold-shouldering of Russia by France and England throughout the Czech crisis; the other is the state of the French Air Force in September—whose weakness was widely declared to be one of the principal reasons why the Munich surrender was inevitable.

Although Russia was tied to Czechoslovakia by a treaty of mutual assistance concluded in 1935, in terms of which the signatories were bound to help each other in the event of an unprovoked aggression by a third party, provided that the Franco-Czech treaty had entered into force, Russia was ignored throughout the Czech crisis by both England and France. So much so that even Dr. Beneš refrained from establishing too close a contact with the U.S.S.R. lest he confirmed the impression that Czechoslovakia was an 'outpost of Bolshevism in Europe.'

The two reasons for the cold-shouldering of Russia by France and England were (1) the deep antipathy felt for Russia in the greater part of the British Conservative Party and, for that matter, among wide sections of French opinion, (2) the deplorable effect created in Western Europe by the 'purges' in the Red Army, and the belief that a 'decapitated' army could be of little use. But actually, this judgment on the Red Army was largely encouraged by natural antipathy for the U.S.S.R.; and no serious attempt was made by either England or France to find out what the Russian Army or Air Force was really worth. Staff talks were consistently refused; and, instead, questionable sources of information, like Colonel Lindbergh, were used in high quarters in London.

In British and French Government quarters it was frequently suggested that Russia had neither the intention nor the means of helping Czechoslovakia. There is no ground for this suggestion. Her air force would, in any case, have been an important factor—in fact, the only

271

direct help that Czechoslovakia could have obtained immediately from abroad in case of war. To move a Russian army into Czechoslovakia, would, of course, have presented greater difficulties; but it is not true that (*a*) Rumania would have refused transit. On September 11, though without wishing to commit herself at that stage, M. Comnene, the Rumanian Foreign Minister, nevertheless clearly indicated to M. Bonnet that there would be no difficulty once the war had started and (*b*) that the Russians had made no military moves at all during the September crisis.

The Riga Correspondent of *The Times* wrote on September 6 that the view held in Moscow was:

> that the Red Army, especially the air fleet, will intervene if Czechoslovakia asks for help. The reorganization of the Kiev and White-Russian military districts is interpreted as preparation for this, especially as these commands have been strengthened to nearly a war basis, and all frontier garrisons have been reinforced.

Later in the month, on September 25—i.e., at the time of Russia's warning to Poland to denounce the Russo-Polish nonaggression pact if the Poles invaded Czechoslovakia—foreign observers estimated (the Riga Correspondent of the *New York Times* wrote) that

> in the Kiev and White-Russian military districts, there were 330,000 to 350,000 Soviet troops, with artillery, tanks, chemical sections, and 2,000 aeroplanes, mostly heavy bombers and fast fighters of the newest type. At other places there were five cavalry corps and two tank corps (2,000 tanks) ready to break through at the start of hostilities.

This, in itself, does not prove that Russia would have been of great military help to Czechoslovakia; but it rather suggests that there was no ground for the assertion that the Russians were 'doing nothing.' Considering that the French scarcely did anything before September 24, and that the Russians did not receive the slightest encouragement from the Western Powers, their military preparations appear to have been more substantial than could have been reasonably expected from them by France and England—who had simply ignored Russia throughout the crisis.

THE FRENCH AIR FORCE

The weakness of the French Air Force was one of the chief arguments used in favour of surrendering Czechoslovakia. That France's Air Force was inadequate in September is true enough; but her helplessness in the air was deliberately exaggerated for political ends. General Gamelin himself admitted that France was extremely weak in the air; but his conclusion, nevertheless, was that France was fit to fight a successful war, if, unhappily, this could not be avoided.

To understand the reasons why the French Air Force was so weak, one has to look some years back. Between 1929 and 1938 France had spent an equivalent of £200,000,000 on her air force, and of this about £150,000,000 since 1932 alone. Why, then, had she so little to show for it? It was alleged in some quarters that the French General Staff had for a long time urged the Government to spend as much as possible on the army and as little as possible on the air force, and that the air force suffered from a lack of funds. That is true, but it is not the complete explanation.

What, then, had been the trouble, even allowing for wastage, incompetent handling—and even graft, which in France is a popular explanation for so many things? One of the main sources of trouble was the simple fact that the aeroplane is the least standardized of all weapons and is in constant progress; and the difficulty of catching up with this progress has been felt in other countries, and not only in France. But in France, for a variety of reasons, this difficulty was particularly great. There was also some bad luck, as the following case will show.

The most ambitious French air programme since the foundation of the Air Ministry in 1928 was decided upon by General Denain, who was Minister of Air from February 1934 to January 1936. At the beginning of 1934 France had 1,665 aeroplanes, nearly all of out-of-date makes. Denain's programme provided for 1,050 new planes, mostly fighters. But here was the tragedy: when in 1934 the plan was set in motion General Denain rather went on the assumption that 250 km. per hour was a speed not likely to be exceeded for many years. And it was precisely during 1935 and 1936 that enormous technical progress was made in aeroplane construction. This knocked the Denain programme on the head long before it was completed.

But it is obvious that once a plan is in motion it cannot be suddenly stopped—with nothing ready to replace the plant set up at great cost. (In England, as distinct from France, the expansion of plane construction luckily began after the great 'step forward.') Adjustments were attempted in France, and various excellent prototypes like the Morane-Saulnier 405 fighter were built, but the mass production of an entirely different category of planes from those provided in the Denain programme was found to be impossible. As it is, the Denain plan, which should have been completed in July 1936, was not completed until a year later. It is true that in the meantime the Pierre Cot programme was, as it were, superimposed on the Denain plan; it provided for 1,500 planes—that is, an addition of about 500 planes to the Denain programme. But progress was slow. The aeroplane industry suffered directly or indirectly from the great strike movement of 1936, and while the nationalization of most of the aircraft factories that year had no adverse effect on production, the (admittedly useful) decentralization of many of the works concentrated until then in the Paris area rather upset production for a time. Shorter working hours also had a bad effect. In the whole of 1936 only 500 military planes were produced.

In 1937 little progress was made as regard quality, and the total output for the year was only 470 machines or an average of under forty a month. But most of these, at least, were thoroughly modern machines.

M. Guy la Chambre, who succeeded M. Cot in January 1938, produced a new plan for 2,617 first-line planes; this again was superimposed on, rather than added to, the Cot plan. After the Anschluss, no less than 3,000,000,000 francs of special credits were granted to the Air Ministry, which out of this sum ordered new plant for 1,300,000,000 francs. Shortly, after taking office, M. Guy la Chambre claimed that French production would be increased to 250 planes a month within a short time.

What was the strength of the French Air Force in September? There are no official figures, but according to reliable sources the entire French Air Force consisted of about 3,500 planes, of which 1,400 were first-line. Naturally only a small proportion of these 1,400 planes were completely modern; a large part still consisted of planes built under the Denain plan. These old bombers, flying under 250 km. an hour, could not, of course, be dismissed as 'useless'; they were quite fit to do night-raid service, only the danger of being destroyed on the return flight was much greater than with faster bombers. The modern French planes, like the immensely fast Morane 405 single-seater fighter, the Potez 63 are among the best in the world, and the Lioret bombers and Dewoitine fighters are also considered to be excellent. But there were not enough of them. As in other branches of industry, France had achieved remarkable quality but what she lacked was mass production. However, the suggestion that the French are 'incapable' of mass production is absurd: until 1931 France was the biggest maker of mass-produced cars in Europe.

At the time of the September crisis France was producing little more than 50 military planes a month. What happened between September and the spring of 1939 was briefly this:

Experts at the time of the crisis had declared that with her present plant France would not be able to exceed 250 planes a month; and that if she wanted to build up a large air force rapidly foreign purchases were the only solution. This solution was partly adopted; and M. Reynaud, the Finance Minister, said in February that with the capital that had returned to France during the previous months France would be able to buy 6,000 aeroplanes abroad.

It was, of course, a theoretical figure in the sense that even the United States could not deliver 6,000 aeroplanes as though they were a pound of butter. But the phrase could, nevertheless, be regarded as the statement of a policy; for France, left to her own resources, could never rival Germany in aeroplane production, and the fact was admitted. She lacked both the plant and the skilled labour; and it was clear that it would take at least two years before Germany's output of 500 a month could be equalled—and what would Germany's output be then?

But that period was, according to M. de Torres, a well-qualified writer, still a *période de démarrage*—a 'starting period'—in which the mass production had not yet come into its own. He claimed that the plant purchased in 1938 would be in full working order by the middle of '39, and that France would then be able to turn out 250 to 300 military planes a month. But if this figure was to be maintained or exceeded, important new investments would be necessary.

Also, there was a dangerous shortage of French engines, particularly of the high-power engines required in the case of the ultra-rapid modern planes; the French production of engines in January 1939 was only 237 a month; and unless the whole system was reorganized France was going to continue to import a large proportion of her aeroplane engines from abroad. Already, in January, France was buying several hundred engines abroad, mostly Rolls-Royces.

XV. THE CONFUSION AFTER MUNICH

LIKE every country in Europe, France heaved a physical sigh of relief at the thought that war had been averted. But what were the *rational* reactions to Munich? On the whole, it may be said that while everybody in France *must* have felt a little humiliated, the humiliation was keenly felt by only an important section of the working class, by some traditional nationalists in the army and elsewhere, and by a number of intellectuals. In October, Paris was described by some onlookers as being in a state of mental confusion, by others as being in a state of *abrutissement*, inertia and resignation. No member of the Government had the honesty to say that Munich was a fearful defeat for France. Why could they not have admitted it freely, and said to their people: 'It *was* a defeat, but now, let us pull ourselves together and work for a better France, so that it doesn't happen again.' Such an admission would have been a basis for some kind of National Unity. But they went on praising and praising Munich—*because some lacked moral courage; while for others it was necessary to do so for internal political reasons. It was part of the reactionary offensive.* Jouhaux said in October: 'They lied and lied before Munich, and they have gone on lying.'

And yet, except among an important part of the working class and in certain nationalist quarters, Munich was accepted with astonishing ease. M. Duhamel was one of the few men who was profoundly conscious of the moral wound Munich had inflicted on France, and had realized how dim her authority had grown in the world. France—source of all generous ideas! He was one of the few who openly said that what France had lost was not only her Maginot Line in Central Europe, but also what he called her Descartes Line. French schools were closing down in Czechoslovakia; Munich was not only a diplomatic Sedan but a cultural setback of immense importance. Her century-long spiritual leadership of Europe seemed at an end. And it is strange to think how little the loss of the 'Descartes Line' affected the Government, and even many intellectuals, especially of the Right. It looked as though these intellectuals were ready and eager to conduct France along the spiritual groove of Fascist ideology. Maurras might well speak of Germany as being 'the mad dog of Europe'—but the soul of the *Action Française* was like the soul of Goebbels.

It is curious that while England suffered from a guilty feeling which expressed itself in the enormous contributions—totalling some £400,000 —to the Lord Mayor's Fund for Czech refugees, there was no such reaction at all in France. The *Temps* collected a few thousand pounds— and that was about all. While, after Munich, hundreds of thousands of 'Penguins' on Czechoslovakia continued to be sold by bookstalls throughout Great Britain, France lost all interest in her former ally. With a curious lack of sensitiveness the Government-inspired Press continued to praise M. Daladier and M. Bonnet to the skies. A remarkable demonstration of complacency and insensibility was provided by M. Bonnet at a reception organized in his honour by his constituents at Périgueux. The officially inspired Press made much of this reception: the accounts of it were calculated to show that *la province* was a hundred per cent 'pro-Munich.' Here are a few specimens from the four-column account in the *Petit Parisien* of that 'unforgettable day':

> Already outside the station thousands were shouting, '*Vive Bonnet! Vive Bonnet!*' Périgueux will not soon forget this cry. Bunches of flowers were piled round him in his open car. Women—mothers and young girls—went on crying: '*Merci, Bonnet! Merci, Bonnet!*' Looking a little pale, the Foreign Minister answered these greetings with his hands and with his eyes,[1] while, behind him, enormous bouquets continued to be presented to Madame Bonnet whose charming modesty was also being loudly cheered.[2] And the triumph of the people began. . . . In the Place du Théâtre three little girls recited a compliment, which no one could hear, so loud were the shouts of enthusiasm. And the din was dominated by that cry of gratitude: '*Merci, Bonnet! Merci, Bonnet!*'

And, later, speaking with the voice of injured innocence to a number of ex-servicemen and local worthies, about the unjust attacks that had been made on him, M. Bonnet said:

> 'There is one criticism which I refuse to accept: and that is that France was not loyal to her signature. France's signature is sacred. Czechoslovakia wasn't invaded, was she?'

To which the local worthies replied: 'Of course she was not! *Vive Bonnet! Merci, Bonnet!*'

Guy de Maupassant would have made a pretty story of this Périgueux apotheosis.

That was on the 8th of October. On the 9th Hitler made his Saarbrücken speech which rather tended to damp the post-Munich and Four-Power Pact enthusiasm. If before Munich he threw bouquets at France, and gave her Strasbourg Cathedral as a present and tried to flatter her into inactivity, he now made no mention of France whatsoever—though he was speaking at only four miles from the French frontier. All he said was that the two gaps in the Siegfried Line—the gap at Aix-la-Chapelle and the Saar gap (the latter had figured prominently in the plans of the French General Staff)—would now be filled up. The French Munich enthusiasts felt cheated—though not entirely discouraged. From their point of view there were some good points in the Saarbrücken speech.

[1] Such is the journalistic style of officially-inspired enthusiasm.
[2] Ditto.

For instance, this curious post-Munich novelty: Hitler declared, in effect, that he could not allow England to be ruled by Mr. Churchill or Mr. Eden or Mr. Duff Cooper; if these came into office there would be trouble. This suited the more cynical among the Munich enthusiasts perfectly. As we shall see, the 'Hitler veto' was actually going to become an important factor in French home affairs, and was to be used by the supporters of certain Ministers as an argument for maintaining them in office. On the eve of the Radical Congress at the end of October, M. Lamoureux, one of M. Bonnet's close political associates, published in a local sheet of the Allier, a statement alleged to have been made by Hitler to François-Poncet, the retiring French Ambassador, when he went to take leave of the Führer at Berchtesgaden:

> So long as men like M. Daladier and M. Bonnet remain in office I am confident in friendly relations between our two countries.

Just like that. The Radical Congress could put it in its pipe and smoke it.

The wave of political reaction that was to reach its height in December, began during the days that immediately followed Munich. It was a phenomenon to be expected. Munich was the work of the Bonnets and Flandins and the greater part of the Right—and the support given to the 'Munich' policy by these people was not so much dictated (as in the case of many Socialists and trade unionists) by an innate pacifism, or even by provincialism, as, to a large extent, by rather precise political motives. The battle between pacifists and *bellicistes* was not only a battle over foreign policy; it was a much more complex affair. It is characteristic that almost the very first reaction of the Press of the Right after Munich was to start an anti-Communist campaign:

'There are accounts to settle,' the *Matin* wrote on the very day after Munich. Doriot's *Emancipation Nationale* also wrote: 'There are accounts to settle.' The *Action Française*, on the very day of Munich, wrote a little nursery rhyme, inciting its readers to murder the *bellicistes*:

> S'ils s'obstinent, ces cannibales,
> A faire de nous des héros,
> Il faut que nos premières balles
> Soient pour Mandel, Blum et Reynaud,

and, like the other, it went on shouting: *'Comptes à régler!'* even though M. Maurras suddenly became rather less pro-Munich, and declared that it was not such a great 'victory' after all. And Doriot's *Liberté* declared on October 4 that it was high time the *belliciste* Ministers in the Cabinet were turned out.

Some days later it was reported that two hundred-odd papers in France had published a sort of manifesto demanding the dissolution of the Communist Party. All this was pretty well orchestrated.

. . . .

The Chamber votes on Munich and on the plenary powers were of the greatest importance in encouraging the reactionary campaign. The Communists were the only party to have voted against Munich: it was 'positive proof' that the Communists had *wanted* war. Although the Socialists voted for Munich and merely abstained in the vote of the plenary powers, the papers of the Right thought it good enough. The Front Populaire, they said, was now completely and irretrievably lost; even in a purely nominal parliamentary sense. They urged Daladier to draw the only possible conclusion from the two Chamber votes—and that was that he must sever his connection with the Left completely and form and alliance with the Right and Centre. As usual, Daladier hesitated. He hesitated for nearly a month.

These hesitations were not confined to M. Daladier alone. The public was rather muddled. Daladier's first idea was to fight an election on the Munich and *'anti-belliciste'* issue; but this would have meant the dissolution of the Chamber; and this met with much opposition from the deputies themselves who did not much care to risk their seats and, in any case, to go to a lot of expense. The Senate was lukewarm in its support of dissolution; and M. Maurice Sarraut, the influential editor of the *Dépêche* of Toulouse, and a sort of Father Confessor of the Radical Party, was altogether hostile. The dissolution proposal was advocated most strongly by part of the Right Press, notably by the *Temps* which hoped to see the Socialists and Communists both beaten and driven into Opposition. For at that time it was still uncertain whether Daladier had finally severed his connection with the Left.

It is true that on October 13 the Bureau of the Radical Party passed a violently anti-Communist resolution, in which it said that the Communists had, through their two Chamber votes, wilfully abandoned 'the formation to which they still claim to belong'—which meant that the Radical Bureau considered the Front Populaire at an end. But information from the constituencies suggested that the Bureau did not fully reflect the feelings of the Radical rank-and-file. The resolution also attacked M. Flandin, and suggested the formation of a 'concentration' Government comprising everybody except M. Flandin's followers and the Communists. This made little sense, and was scarcely practicable. The Right would, clearly, not abandon Flandin's followers, and at the same time agree to co-operate with the Socialists; and, though in a rather indiscreet form, Flandin represented, after all, much the same foreign policy as M. Bonnet, one of the great men of the Radical Party.

It was enough to confuse anybody—not least M. Daladier. In the days that followed, M. Daladier, however, consulted both M. Marin and M. Blum with a view to forming a wide national coalition; but while M. Blum was favourable, and M. Marin reserved at first, he informed the Premier, after the Senate election of October 23, that he would not enter a Government containing Socialists. For the Senate election had shown a notable swing to the Right.

During October M. Daladier was, in fact, being carefully pushed into an alliance with the Right and Centre. It is true that there were other ideas in the air. Many people felt that France needed something different from the existing parliamentary form of Government—though, heaven knows, Parliament, which had played no part whatsoever throughout the Czech crisis, had fallen pretty low, and M. Flandin could, not without an element of truth, declare in his open letter to Kerillis, that France was now a 'parliamentary democracy only in name.' On the Right (and also among some people on the Left) the real question was whether a 'new form of Government should be established on the basis of the existing institutions, or whether the pretence of "parliamentary democracy" should be discarded.'

The irrepressible Kerillis demanded a Government of National Safety, presided over by a General, and working in close contact with the working class. But Parliament, he said, should be sent on holiday for two years, and his plan provided for a censorship and for a number of other drastic measures of the same sort. Regarding Parliament, he remarked, not without justice, that 'it was not playing any part anyway.'

And M. Henri Pichon, the leader of the Union Fédérale des Anciens Combattants, the principal 'Leftish' ex-servicemen's organization with 2,000,000 members, and claiming to speak in the name of 6,000,000 ex-servicemen, also advocated, in a statement made on October 11, a Government of *salut public*, which would be 'Republican, but without party labels.'

The statement caused something of a row. Other ex-servicemen's organizations, particularly those of the Right, claimed that M. Pichon had no right to speak in their name.

The statement was, however, typical of that post-Munich atmosphere in which many felt that 'this could not go on any longer,' and that France must turn over a new leaf.

Among important sections of the Left, a 'public safety' Government—

though not with Daladier at its head—was, if anything, welcomed. It seemed better than the sort of reactionary 'parliamentary' Government into which the Radicals were being gradually driven. It is curious that about the middle of October rumours were current to the effect that several leading Socialists were considering favourably the formation of a 'public safety' Government with General Noguès, the Resident-General of Morocco, at its head. They thought that a respected army man heading a 'public safety' Government and working in co-operation with the trade union leader—that is, working not 'against' but 'with' the working class, would, despite parliamentary appearances, be less 're-actionary' than the sort of 'Radical-Centre-Right' Government the Right were having in mind.

. . . .

A typical post-Munich phenomenon was the campaign for a large air force. This campaign came from different directions. M. Frossard, M. Daladier's former Minister of Public Works, who had resented Daladier's suppression of the 40-hour week, and had resigned from his Government in August, and who was, in October, considered to be a coming man—one who could, with advantage, replace M. Daladier at the head of a 'Leftish' National Government—launched in his paper, the *Homme Libre*,[3] the slogan for '5,000 aeroplanes.'

But the Government would not allow him a monopoly in his clamour for '5,000 aeroplanes.' The Government-inspired Press ran a similar campaign; and by the 20th of October the campaign was in full swing. Giant headlines: *'Des avions! Des avions!'* shrieking from every newspaper kiosk in Paris, were a typical post-Munich sight.

In the case of M. Frossard he was inspired partly perhaps by personal ambition, but chiefly by the sincere and gloomy belief that without a large air force France would be helpless against more German black-mail. In the case of the Government Press the campaign was partly calculated to justify the surrender of Czechoslovakia, but, above all, to impress upon the public that what France was needing, above all, was a very strong Government, and one which, among other things, would abolish the forty-hour week. The articles naturally suggested that M. Da-ladier, the Premier and War Minister, and M. Guy la Chambre, the Minister of Air, were the right men in the right places. In those post-Munich days a 'strong Government' was a slogan that was bound to be universally accepted: only *what kind of strong Government?*

[3] He was, some weeks later, to be squeezed out of the *Homme Libre* which became the personal organ of M. Bonnet.

By the end of the month it became clear that M. Daladier had finally decided to break with the Left—and not only with the Communists, but also with the Socialists. At the Radical Congress at Marseilles, on October 27, M. Daladier attacked the Communists with extraordinary violence. He accused them not only of having hampered the international talks that preceded Munich 'by grossly insulting Mr. Chamberlain' but also of paralysing French production by their propaganda among the workers. In short, the Communists were to M. Daladier the agents of a foreign Power, and Public Enemy No. 1. As for the Socialists, they were not mentioned at all. The speech delighted the French Right and all the anti-Comintern enthusiasts in France and abroad.

In Germany the Press almost suggested that France had as good as joined the anti-Comintern Pact!

.   .   .   .

November and especially December were the two months during which France seemed to be sinking more and more deeply into the quagmire of political reaction. The *Temps* openly declared on the very day after Munich that the Franco-Soviet Pact and the Franco-Polish alliance had now 'lost much of their practical value'; and in November and December the 'free hand in the East' policy reached its height with the campaign in the *Matin* and other papers in favour of *La Grande Ukraine*. The *rapprochement* with Italy being slow in coming, France was playing the German card.

The anti-French demonstration in the Italian Chamber on November 30, when the deputies rose like one man and shouted: 'Tunisia! Corsica! Nice!' opened in reality a new chapter in French foreign policy—and had, as will be seen, a wholesome effect. For it created a certain *sursaut* of French public opinion, which at the time of the Ribbentrop declaration had sunk into a state of gloomy inertia. It will be objected that the Ribbentrop declaration came a week after the Italian 'Tunis-Corsica' demonstration: but such was the *gleichschaltung* of the French Press in those days that the news of the Italian demonstration was, if not suppressed, at any rate enormously minimized, and it was not until about a fortnight later that the general public became fully aware of the real significance of the Italian demonstration.

During the weeks that followed two distinct policies in relation to Italy seemed to exist: the Daladier policy of firmness, and the Bonnet policy of 'appeasement.' While Bonnet did his best to suppress in the Press all the unpleasant news from Italy, Daladier went on his voyage to Corsica and North Africa, and said in effect that the Italians could go to hell. The Italian campaign against France was in reality a tremendous setback for the Flandin policy, which consisted in saying that France could become an 'Empire Power' instead of pursuing a Continental policy. It was largely on this assumption that the Right in France welcomed Munich: and now it looked as though the Axis Powers were preparing a new Munich not at the expense of Poland or Rumania or Russia, but—at the expense of the French Empire with Spain as the big trump in their game.

. . . .

During a few weeks which followed Munich the French Government and the inspired Press heavily backed the Italian horse. Compliments were showered on Mussolini for having 'saved peace'; and the withdrawal from Spain of 10,000 Italians—mostly war-weary invalids—in the first week of October, was treated by the official Press as the beginning of a happy settlement of the Spanish problem and as the beginning of a Franco-Italian *rapprochement*, and of a happy co-operation between England, France and Italy. All objections were met with the most optimistic hopes and assurances.

And it was curious how in all the flattering articles on Mussolini's 'pacifism' the awkward question of Germany's co-operation with Italy in Spain was completely ignored.

It is significant that all this outburst of flattery of Italy coincided with Hitler's Saarbrücken speech, which, as we have seen, was a disappointment to the Munich enthusiasts. During those two months French diplomacy tried, without much success, in playing off Rome against Berlin or Berlin against Rome—though without at the same time abandoning the Four-Power idea. Only this idea did not and could not work well: for the tactics of Rome and Berlin consisted at the same time in playing off London and Paris against one another. In October, just after the Hitler-Chamberlain declaration, Italy encouraged France to court her; but in November, while the *rapprochement* between France and Germany was in progress, relations improved between England and Italy, and became extremely strained between England and Germany! The Four-Power harmony was being constantly disturbed by Italy and Germany in this curious manner.

In October, as already said, Italy was the object of France's particular attentions. The sacrifice of Spain on the altar of Franco-Italian friendship was going on. In accordance with the promise given by M. Daladier to Mussolini during their meeting at Munich, the French Cabinet appointed M. François-Poncet, who had been Ambassador in Berlin since

1931, to Rome. M. Coulondre, who had for a year been Ambassador to Moscow, and, before then, Director of Economic Relations at the Quai d'Orsay, was appointed to Berlin. Together with these two appointments went the 'purge' at the Quai d'Orsay. M. Massigli, one of the most prominent 'pro-League' men at the Quai was sent to Ankara, and M. Comert, the head of the Press Department was *limogé*—and appointed to the relatively obscure post of assistant director of the American Department. M. Bonnet, clearly, wished to be surrounded in Paris by people more in sympathy with his new policy. M. Comert was succeeded at the Quai d'Orsay by M. Bressy, a councillor at the French Embassy at Warsaw; he was very much 'Bonnet's man,' an 'appeasement' enthusiast, with little experience, and a profound distrust, of the Press, especially the British press.

Unfortunately, the Italian Government missed no opportunity of displaying their bad humour towards France; and took an abnormally long time to grant their *agrément* to the appointment of the new French Ambassador. But at last the *agrément* came, and on November 7, M. François-Poncet arrived in Rome. According to Reuter, a crowd of Italians applauded him as he drove from the station. That same night it was announced in Rome that the Franco-Italian visa restrictions would be removed—which indicated an end of the tourist war, which had gone on since August. 'The decision is the first outcome of the arrival of the new Ambassador,' Reuter said. On the following day Reuter said that since M. François-Poncet was accredited to the 'King of Italy and Emperor of Ethiopia,' it was probable that Franco-Italian negotiations would be shortly resumed; and that the Italians were very anxious to clear up a number of points relating to the Suez Canal, the port of Jibuti and the Jibuti-Addis-Ababa railway. The Reuter message said that the French Ambassador was expected to visit Count Ciano shortly, but added cautiously that 'for the present there is no authoritative indication that negotiations will be resumed.'

The real sequel was to come on November 30.

.   .   .   .

If, during November, the French Government was playing about with 'appeasement' and Four-Power Pact ideas, the same was even truer of the British Government.

On November 1 Mr. Chamberlain, still flushed with the Munich triumph and feeling very strong in the country—Mr. A. D. Lindsay had just been beaten in the Oxford by-election—spoke in a dictatorial manner which Opposition speakers found insufferable. It was the speech in

which the Prime Minister attacked the Opposition for 'fouling the nest.'
Regarding Eastern and South-Eastern Europe, Mr. Chamberlain said
that it was quite natural for Germany to have a 'dominating position'
there. And the Four-Power *motif* was played with great gusto.

> . . . We shall never get far in this way unless we can accustom
> ourselves to the idea that democracies and totalitarian States are not
> to be ranged against one another in two opposing blocks but that they
> can, if they choose, work together not merely for the settlement of
> differences after they have arisen but also for the operation of a con-
> structive programme which will facilitate the international exchange
> of goods and provide for the regulation of international relations in
> various ways for the good of all.
> That is the policy which is sometimes called a policy of appease-
> ment; that is the policy to which this Government intends whole-
> heartedly to devote itself.

Mr. Chamberlain said nothing about colonies; and that disturbed the
Opposition; for it was well known that Germany was about to make a
new bid for colonies. As Sir Archibald Sinclair said:

> Whatever the solution, it must not be the offer of a colony in order
> to buy a few months' peace from Germany. It must be part of a general
> settlement, and the acid test of the sincerity of that settlement must be
> the measure of general disarmament.

Although Mr. Chamberlain's speech was very much in M. Bonnet's
'line,' it caused considerable uneasiness in France, not only on the Left,
but among important sections of the French Right.

The absence of any reference to France in Mr. Chamberlain's speech
was resented by many other people. One French commentator remarked
that day: 'With all our faults Mr. Chamberlain should still remember
that we provide Great Britain with an army—it is no good putting us
on the same level as Italy and Germany.'

On November 8, at Munich, Hitler raised the question of colonies;
and so pushed the question to the foreground of European politics.

> Beyond the colonial question Germany has no demands to make on
> France and Great Britain.

. . . .

What was the attitude of the French Government to colonies during
that post-Munich honeymoon? M. Bonnet was desperately anxious to
secure a Franco-German 'no war' declaration; and negotiations on the
subject were in progress. It was important to do nothing that would

hamper the Franco-German talks. At the Radical Congress at Marseilles, M. Daladier had spoken of colonies; he had referred to 'a vast zone of security outside Europe which France will defend as she will defend her home territory.' What exactly did this 'vast zone of security' mean? A person working in close touch with M. Daladier put forward the view that this did not mean every French possession in the world, but rather all her possessions in Africa which formed a vast single *bloc*—with the exception of a few British enclaves (Nigeria and the Gold Coast being the most important) and three unimportant Spanish enclaves, besides Liberia. According to this view, this African *bloc* was considered by M. Daladier to be 'unalterable.' It was true that it included the former German colonies of Togoland and the Cameroons, but if these were returned to Germany, France's strategic position in Africa would before long be rendered hopeless, and such a transfer of territory might lead to no end of new trouble.

But since Germany had more or less (or so at least M. Daladier's friend thought) admitted the principle of substituting territories of equivalent value for those that once belonged to her, it was possible that, if he found sufficient general reasons for doing so, M. Daladier would be willing to consider the transfer of certain other French territories to Germany—territories lying outside the 'security zone,' and which would be equivalent in value to Togoland and the Cameroons.

But these ideas did not go far. The German demand for colonies produced a surprisingly sharp reaction in France—perhaps an unconscious and belated reaction against 'Munich,' and against German bullying. Scarcely a month had passed since Munich, and here he was again asking for something else! It annoyed people.

On November 9, the day after Hitler's speech, the Marin group (or Fédération Républicaine) passed unanimously a strongly-worded resolution which asked the Daladier government to state its position with regard to the colonial question. It was alarmed by the coming visit to Paris of Mr. Chamberlain, and declared that it would vote against the Government if it failed to make such a statement.

There was an enormous amount of excitement at the Chamber that day. A Socialist deputy, and M. Monnerville, a Negro deputy, wrote to the chairman of the Colonial Committee demanding that no decision be taken without the approval of Parliament. M. Moutet, the former Minister of Colonies in the Blum Government, demanded on behalf of the Socialists that this committee be called immediately. A Radical deputy, M. Gerent, announced his intention to question the Government on its colonial policy at the first opportunity.

President Lebrun himself indirectly joined in the campaign by making a speech in which he referred to 'the magnificent unity of our Empire' and to the loyalty and devotion to France of the natives. He implied that it would be monstrous to hand them over to the mercies of Nazi Germany.

It was during that week that the pogroms in Germany were at their height. On November 7, a seventeen-year-old Polish Jew, Herschel Grynspan, wounded fatally a secretary of the German Embassy in Paris. To all appearances the boy had been driven desperate by the sufferings inflicted on his parents in Germany; though some of the circumstances of the murder were mysterious, and there were many who believed that Grynspan was another Van der Lubbe. Vom Rath, his victim, died three days later; and the result was a fearful Government-organized pogrom throughout Germany. All the Jewish shops in Berlin were smashed in the middle of the night by bands of hooligans; all the synagogues were burned, and thousands of Jews—men and women of every age—were dragged out of their houses, and beaten up and sent to concentration camps, and their houses demolished.

Although the greater part of the French Press was instructed by the French Foreign Office not to 'play up' the pogroms, and not to offend Germany in the midst of the Franco-German negotiations, the pogroms were of considerable importance in providing the opponents of any surrender of colonies to Germany with an unanswerable argument. M. Monnerville, the Negro deputy, was extremely active in protesting against any attempt to hand Negro people over to German rule. But it was not until November 16 that the Government made its position perfectly clear; it was after a meeting between M. Daladier and M. Taittinger, the vice-president of the Colonial Committee and a leading member of the Right, that the following *communiqué* was published:

> The Government has not waited for the present campaign over colonies to make its position clear on this question. No surrender of territory was ever, or could ever be, considered. No negotiations have therefore been entered into.
>
> The Government hereby renews the denial of the false news suggesting that the question of colonies will be discussed during the coming Anglo-French talks.

This *communiqué* was emphatic enough; but it was strange, all the same, that it should have taken the Government fully a week to produce it. It was suggested, after its publication, that M. Bonnet was not by any means pleased; in pursuing his policy of *rapprochement* with Germany, he almost certainly wished to keep colonies in reserve as a possible bargaining counter. But M. Daladier knew that the campaign against the surrender of colonies could no longer be ignored; and he took his decision for various reasons. He knew for instance that in the Senegal and other Negro colonies French officials had been distributing pamphlets with translations into the Negro languages of certain passages of *Mein Kampf* concerning the 'apishness' of the Negroes. The effect was devastating.

And so the colonial question was shelved—at least for a time—as far as France was concerned. The only danger, many Frenchmen thought, might come from the visit to Paris, during the following week of Mr. Chamberlain and Lord Halifax. But, actually, nothing happened. Anti-German feeling in England was running so high at the time that there could be no question of conceding colonies to Germany.

XVI. DALADIER BREAKS THE GENERAL STRIKE

THE Daladier Government obtained plenary powers from the Chamber on October 4. These were to expire on November 15. M. Daladier had stressed the extreme gravity of the financial situation; the mobilization had cost several milliards: business had come to a standstill during the crisis; production was low, and France was faced with a deficit of forty or fifty milliard francs in 1939. Like other ministers before him, he declared that the time had come for drastic remedies.

But nearly a month passed, and nothing happened; and nobody knew what use the Daladier Government would make of its plenary powers. M. Daladier himself did not seem to know. At last, on the eve of the Marseilles Congress M. Gentin, the Minister of Commerce, dropped an interesting hint which caused much excitement: the time had come, he said, to adopt a policy of *économie orientée*. This was understood to mean that the Government had decided in favour of an economy which would be half-way between liberal economy and planned economy (*économie dirigée*). Without saying what he had decided, M. Daladier made a resounding speech at Marseilles, in which he declared that he had 'chosen his road.' *'J'ai choisi mon chemin; la France, en avant!'*

But three days later a violent campaign was suddenly let loose in the *Petit Parisien*, in the *Action Française*, in a number of other papers against—M. Marchandeau, the Finance Minister, of all people. Marchandeau, who had had the reputation of a gentle, cautious, over-orthodox financier was now accused of taking part in a revolutionary plot against France. The *Action Française* spoke about a Blum-Marchandeau conspiracy; and even the more sober *Petit Parisien* charged him with being almost revolutionary, and with borrowing his policy from the defunct Blum Plan of the previous April. It said that he was planning to establish a camouflaged form of exchange control (despite the assurances given to the contrary to Parliament before the plenary powers were granted), two kinds of currencies—one 'loyal' to the Tripartite agreement, and the other a purely internal currency, of wishing to resort to large-scale credit inflation, to increase income tax to 'absurd' proportions, and to subject companies to some kind of capital levy. In short, M. Marchandeau was accused of being as unorthodox and as anti-capitalist in his quasi-totalitarian schemes as was M. Blum's plan which the Senate had angrily rejected six months earlier. Was that the road M. Daladier had chosen?

In any case the Cabinet met on November 1, and after a stormy meeting that lasted several hours it was announced that M. Marchandeau had resigned from the Finance Ministry, or rather, had swopped jobs with M. Reynaud, the Minister of Justice. 'Liberal' finance had triumphed, and was going to be given another chance.

M. Reynaud was hated by the Right on account of his foreign 'anti-Munich' policy; but as a financier he was welcome both to the Right parties and to High Finance generally.

Personally, he had always enjoyed a considerable measure of goodwill from the Left, who well remembered his courteously devastating criticisms of Laval and who appreciated his hostility towards M. Flandin; but if he did not become Finance Minister in April, when the Daladier Cabinet was formed, it was, at least partly, because his financial remedies were too unpalatable to the Left parties, whom, nominally at any rate, Daladier still desired to keep inside his Government majority. Now that the Communists had dropped out the majority, and the Socialists, in abstaining, had half-deserted it, there was no longer any parliamentary reason for not appointing M. Reynaud to the Finance Ministry. M. Reynaud locked himself up in the Ministry of Finance for a week, and on November 12 produced his decrees.

In addition to a long and detailed report to the President of the

Republic, on the state of France's finances and economy, M. Reynaud gave a dramatic broadcast on the night of November 12.

'You wish to know the truth about your finances,' he said. 'I shall tell you. Your situation is very grave. The good news is that we are certain to get over the situation.

'The main evil is not in the finances of the State; it is in the country's economy. We are in the last rank of industrial production. France is using up her reserves; she is living on her capital.

'Besides this, we are affected by a serious malady. I refer to armaments. I am asked for 25,000,000,000 francs (about £140,000,000). How can I refuse it?'

Turning to the question of large public works, M. Reynaud said that in 1939 about £140,000,000 would be spent on armaments. 'We cannot simultaneously offer ourselves the luxury of big public works.'

Referring to the new taxes and the economy cuts, and the reduction in the number of government employees (including 40,000 railwaymen), Reynaud said that the deficit on the ordinary Budget had been wiped out and the deficit on the railways had been largely reduced. 'We have wiped out to-day a deficit of some £114,000,000. Apart from a few milliards of francs, our only borrowings now will be for national defence.

'However hard all this may appear, it is but the beginning. After this first week's battle we shall have many others to fight. Our final salvation is not for next week or next month, or even for the coming year.'

As regards production, M. Reynaud declared that it must increase by between thirty and forty per cent. Therefore more hours must be worked.

'Do you think that with Europe as it is to-day France can at one and the same time maintain her standard of living and spend 25,-000,000,000 francs on armaments *and take two days' holiday a week? People abroad are listening to me and I tell you that the "week with two Sundays" has ceased to exist in France.* The decrees which have just been signed are only the first step on our way. Our plan is a three-year plan.'

The decrees were well received by the Bourse, where *Rentes* and industrials boomed. But they, naturally, met with angry criticism from the Left, and particularly from the C.G.T., whose Congress met at Nantes that week. The Left Press considered that disproportionately heavy sacrifices had been asked from the poor man; nothing serious had been done to fight tax evasion in the case of the rich; the flat two per cent super-tax on all earned incomes, no matter how small, was a thoroughly undemocratic measure; the compulsory overtime gave arbitrary power to the employers; and the general abolition of the five-day week was absurd, as in many factories there was scarcely enough work for four full days.

M. Blum thought that the whole plan was far too much based on the 'return of confidence' principle, and so was unsound. For one thing, he said, it was enough for one of the Dictators to frown to shake this 'confidence.'

.   .   .   .

M. Jouhaux spoke at the C.G.T. congress at Nantes on November 16; and, rather carried away by the hostility shown towards the decrees by a large part of the rank-and-file, threatened the Government with a General Strike, 'if this were to prove indispensable.'

> 'Trade union labour,' he said, 'is ready to take a large share in a programme of sacrifices but it does not accept sacrifices that are contrary to the general interest. A sound economy cannot be built on the basis of "Get rich, you capitalists, and may the working class sink lower than ever. . . ."'
>
> 'The decrees in their present form are unacceptable. The system of overtime introduced by M. Reynaud aims much more at the restoration of the employer's authority than at any economic restoration.'

M. Jouhaux concluded that the C.G.T., the trade-union federation, should work out in minute detail the use of 'its supreme weapon,' the general strike, in case its use became indispensable.

The mention of a general strike was made rather cautiously; but the idea was to take shape in the days that followed—largely under the influence of events, and of extremist—mostly Communist—agitation.

The truth is that, although the decrees were extremely unpopular, they did not warrant the use of the 'supreme weapon'; and the general strike was determined by a large number of considerations: to the Communists, in particular, the general strike was above all, a mass protest against the Government's growing reactionary tendencies at home and the increasingly pro-German policy abroad. It should be remembered that what was ultimately called was only a twenty-four-hour strike i.e. a demonstration or a warning, and it was not intended to be a fullfledged general strike; and essential services like electricity, water and gas were never to be suspended; a point conveniently overlooked by the Government, which tended to represent the strike as a revolutionary rising.

The general strike was a complete failure; and that for a number of reasons. For one thing, M. Jouhaux had threatened the Government a fortnight before it actually happened; and in the interval the Government had been able to take all the necessary precautions. Secondly, the issues were extremely confused. Officially it was a protest strike against the decrees; but everybody felt that these were not an adequate reason for resorting to the 'supreme weapon'; and if the Communists and a considerable part of the rank and file—who were, after all, the descendants of the Communards who in 1871 had rebelled against the capitulation of Frankfort—were smarting under the humiliation of Munich, this feeling was not shared by everybody. The increasingly domineering attitude of some of the big employers—who felt that the day of reckoning had come after all the humiliations they had suffered in 1936, and who now made a point of eliminating trade union labour from their works as far as possible—also increased the discontent among certain sections of the working class. But, all this was not sufficient to make the strike a success. In the last analysis it is probably also true to say that, disillusioned in the Front Populaire, the working class were not feeling sufficiently heroic about anything to risk losing their jobs—especially after the Government had requisitioned all the public services and was threatening prospective strikers with severe reprisals.

The real trouble started on November 23, first in the north of France, and on the afternoon of the 24th, in the Paris Region. That day, while Mr. Chamberlain and Lord Halifax—who had already been welcomed at the Gare du Nord on the previous night with loud cries of '*A bas Munich!*' and '*Vive Eden!*'—were being fêted at the Paris Town Hall, a vast stay-in strike broke out at the Renault works with its 33,000 workers. Simultaneously, a number of other works were occupied. The stay-in strike at Renault's was a challenge to the Government; for no Government had ever even attempted to evacuate by armed force a factory even half that size. A year earlier M. Chautemps had sent the *garde mobile* to Colombes to evacuate the much smaller Goodrich Tyre works; but the strikers had threatened to resist; there was danger of serious bloodshed, and the Government withdrew the troops. The strike was ultimately settled after lengthy negotiations. But now there were no longer any Socialists in the Government; and M. Daladier, without even attempting to negotiate an evacuation, sent 10,000 *gardes mobiles* to the Renault works and ordered them to 'chuck the strikers out.' He told them, if necessary, to use tear gas. By midnight the works were cleared, with comparatively little bloodshed—about a dozen people were badly hurt on each side.

The word 'requisitioning' has a curious effect on the French mind.

A requisitioning order is too much like a mobilization order to be ignored. And M. Daladier was completely successful in requisitioning the railways and the public services; on the day of the general strike nearly everybody was at work on these services. For two days before the strike of November 30—which was called on the 25th, the day after the Renault evacuation—the Socialists fulminated against the Government, saying that everything would have been settled by the arbitration of Parliament—but Daladier, they said, had deliberately failed to call it, for fear of being overthrown. They declared that he had broken his pledges to them—which was to call Parliament on November 15. They also accused him of deliberately provoking the working class.

But Daladier was determined to break the strike—if it occurred. On the 27th he made the following broadcast:

> When Mr. Chamberlain and Lord Halifax were examining with us the common problems of our national defence and the consolidation of peace in Europe, strikes and illegal occupations of factories were launched in Paris and the North of France.
>
> When on Friday we announced the forthcoming Franco-German declaration which is to guarantee the integrity of our frontiers, we were confronted with the threat of a general strike. Why these movements when all occupations of factories have been declared illegal? Why these threats when the humblest will be certain to suffer most? Why paralyse all public services? The pretext is that we are about to destroy existing social legislation.
>
> The general strike has no material or moral justification. We have not threatened the liberty of the people. We intend no dictatorship, no Fascism. The sacrifices demanded are necessary to the life of the country. Yet one party opposes these sacrifices and prepares to offer violence and is attempting to blackmail the Government.

The speech was sharply anti-Communist. It was clear that M. Daladier was banking on a split within the C.G.T. itself.

M. Reynaud also spoke, in rather milder and more appealing terms. M. Daladier was right: the trade unions were sharply divided.

On November 27, M. Henaff, one of the Communist trade union leaders still spoke in the most categorical terms:

> Not a single train will run in France and the postal service will be stopped. If the Government wishes to requisition the workers it will create conditions suitable for stay-in strikes.

But a day later—after the requisition orders had been issued—it was fairly clear to everybody that the strike would not succeed.

But Daladier was determined to win in what he called 'this trial of strength.' A delegation of ex-servicemen and M. Frossard, fearing the evil effects of antagonizing the working class, attempted, on November 28 and 29, to mediate a settlement between the Government and the C.G.T. But in vain; Daladier even refused to see them. In the meantime Jouhaux and the other more clear-sighted trade union leaders were becoming desperate; and by the night of the 29th were praying for some face-saving device that would enable them to call off the strike which was obviously going to be a fiasco. But a face-saving device was the one thing Daladier would not provide them with. He wanted his victory. And the Communist leaders in the C.G.T. would not agree to Jouhaux's proposal to call off the strike 'in any case.'

    ·   ·   ·   ·   ·   ·   ·

The strike was a failure. On the railways and in the public transport services the number of strikers was less than two per cent. Teachers, postmen, and the other *fonctionnaires* were nearly all at work. In Paris, shops, restaurants and banks were nearly all open, and although the strike was almost complete in the building trade and in the docks, in private industry it did not exceed an average of fifty per cent. It is curious that, as distinct from the Communist railwaymen, few of whom struck, the Socialist miners were nearly all on strike. They were less in sympathy with the strike order than the Communists, but followed it largely in virtue of an older trade union discipline. It is true that the railways were 'requisitioned,' while the mines were not.

At noon I went to the headquarters of the C.G.T. and saw M. Jouhaux. He looked rather gloomy and, trying to make the best of a bad job, he said:

> For two hours this morning there was a complete stoppage in the bus and Underground services, but owing to the requisition order and the military measures taken by the Government work was resumed at eight o'clock. We do not deny it.
>
> In many factories, as in some of the Government offices, the crossed-arms strike is in progress. It may be invisible from outside, but is effective for all that. Eighty per cent of the miners are striking. Among the dockers and in the chemical and metal industries the stoppage is almost complete. The movement will continue unless something exceptional happens.

His last sentence suggested that the possibility of calling off the strike at noon had been discussed. Actually, in the case of the Post Office, the strike was called off at noon. Not that many postal employees had struck in the morning, but it was possible that there were some belonging to the afternoon shift who might, and who would thus unnecessarily expose themselves to reprisals.

The failure of the strike was certainly a severe blow to the Communist Party—though the Government did not go so far as to dissolve it—and also to the C.G.T. The tension between the 'syndicalists' and the 'Communists' became very severe, the syndicalists, like M. Belin, openly admitting the strike to have been a failure and an error—an error which, they said, was made under Communist pressure, and against the better judgment of the 'true' syndicalist leaders. The C.G.T., whose membership had soared from 1,200,000 to 5,000,000 in 1936, and had gradually declined to some 3,500,000 during 1937 and 1938, was estimated to have lost at least another million in the weeks that followed the General Strike. Widespread dismissals and other reprisals followed the strike—particularly in private industry. The 'ringleaders' were the principal victims. The Government refused a complete amnesty, and it was not until February that a bill giving the Government certain discretionary powers in this matter was passed by the Chamber.

M. Daladier was intensely pleased with himself. One had the impression during those days that he had at last achieved his long-cherished ambition—which was to prove in practice that he was a 'strong man.'

．　　．　　．　　．　　．　　．　　．

When, on December 9, at the end of the debate on the Government's general policy, M. Daladier rose to speak, he looked almost a new man. He now betrayed no hesitation, no uncertainty on any subject. He spoke as the strong man of France, as the man of law and order. The firm but quiet, almost Baldwin-like, manner that was his in the days when he was War Minister in the first three Front Populaire Governments had given way to a pugnacious and truculent manner which only now and then was relieved by moments of emotion.

Throughout he was loudly cheered by the Right and Centre and by part of the Radicals.

In the very first sentence M. Daladier declared that his 'brutal frankness' might hurt some feelings. He was sorry, but it was better than hypocrisy.

> The Chamber must decide to-day whether the Government is to continue in office. I am responsible for my own actions and am not the prisoner of any man or any party.

The general strike of November 30, M. Daladier said, turning to the

Communists, was political in character, and the objection to the decrees was only a pretext.

The Premier then produced a large pink folder and proceeded to read some of the more explosive utterances of trade union leaders before the strike. With his face turned to the Communists he read out the quotations with a triumphant air. One of the quotations said that 'Munich and the decrees are inseparable.' He said scathingly:

> You wanted to paralyse the country, you wanted to stop all trains and buses, you thought that this stoppage would lead to the fall of the Government whose foreign policy you dislike. You call that a professional strike.

M. Daladier now spoke with much grimness. He said:

> When factories are occupied they must be cleared. Democracy has one sovereign, and that is the law. The police of every country in the world use tear gas, and I ordered tear gas to be used. You need not blame the Prefect of Police or the commander of the Mobile Guards; it was not they, it was *I* who ordered the use of tear gas.

And with a grim jocularity that slightly reminded one of Dr. Goebbels's witticisms, he added: 'I wish I could have given them laughing gas instead.'

His next point was rather more difficult. It was when he defended the legal action taken against the Renault workers who had been arrested that night. He admitted that 'a certain confusion was inevitable' in the scuffle that accompanied the evacuation of the Renault works, but he made no serious attempt to justify the weighty charges made against the summary trials of the 300 strikers, nearly all of whom had automatically been sentenced to terms of imprisonment.

Several leading lawyers in France had protested against the manner in which these trials were conducted. One of them, M. le Trocquer, the Socialist deputy, rose to his feet and interrupted M. Daladier. He said that the judge had sentenced the men on a general charge without any evidence on the individual cases and without even a police report on the circumstances in which each man had been arrested. Some had been arrested outside the factory and claimed not to have had anything to do with either the stay-in strike or the disorders.

There were many at the Chamber who felt that M. Daladier had here a good opportunity of proposing an amnesty for all the imprisoned strikers—some of whom at least were certainly innocent (and M. Daladier almost admitted as much)—but he did not seize this opportunity.

There was some heckling from the Communists, one of them saying something about the 6th of February riots against Parliament, which had driven the Daladier Government of 1934 out of office. M. Daladier made a quick retort: 'Yes—when the Communists were rioting against Parliament side by side with the *Action Française*.' (Loud cheers on the Right.) One wonders, however, what would have been M. Daladier's reply if the 12th of February instead of the 6th of February had been mentioned. The 12th of February, 1934, was the date of the general strike, which laid the foundations for the Front Populaire—that Front Populaire which played so decisive a part in M. Daladier's political fortunes.

Be that as it may, M. Daladier's 'strong man' speech on the strikes was impressive in its own way and was certainly an able piece of Parliamentary oratory—full of platform effects, which had not previously been in M. Daladier's manner.

The second part of his speech was much less substantial. He defended Munich with greater determination than on October 4, when there was still a note of apology in his voice. The policy of 'firmness,' he now declared without hesitation, was in reality a 'policy of war.' Were millions of French peasants to be sacrificed again?

It was a strange remark. Large numbers of rural deputies rose to their feet and cheered, and in the midst of the cheering a war cripple rose from the Communist benches and angrily shouted something at M. Daladier. 'I am sorry if I used this phrase,' M. Daladier said. 'I spoke as an old infantry-man. For after 1915, ninety per cent of my company were peasants.'

The slip was almost certainly deliberate. The Daladier régime—for one can actually speak of such a 'régime'—was becoming, more and more, based on the support of the peasantry. The Munich policy had more support from the peasantry than from the working class; the decrees demanded heavy sacrifices from the working class and from the middle class—but, apart from the rises in indirect taxation, next to nothing from the peasantry. One could not help remembering Napoleon III and his plebiscites.

After referring to Anglo-French friendship and deploring the sarcasm that the Communists were exercising at the expense of that 'great old man' Mr. Chamberlain, and referring to 'peace with Germany which I and every ex-serviceman wants,' Daladier ended on a note of emotion:

> The man who speaks to you has been the same for twenty years (ironical cheers on the Left). I am a son of France, of the people of France; a little rough, perhaps, but a free man who has never betrayed his party. I am the son of a workman, and I am a patriot.

I want to ask you two questions: Does one cease to be a Republican by desiring law and order to be respected? Does one cease to be a patriot by refusing to lead one's country down the war path?

He then recalled the storms France had weathered in the last year; and sometimes, he said, he longed to be back under the olive trees, in his native Provence, with his boys, far away from Paris.

The speech was made shortly after two important international events: the anti-French demonstration in the Italian Chamber of November 30, and the signing of the Bonnet-Ribbentrop declaration on December 6. The former was not mentioned by Daladier at all, the latter only briefly.

XVII. RIBBENTROP IN PARIS

M. BONNET had worked very hard, almost since Munich, for a Franco-German 'no war' declaration. But the Germans were slow in reacting to his advances. Why did he want such a declaration? Surely, nobody could seriously believe in the value of a German non-aggression pledge. And yet, he wanted it. For one thing, he thought that even if of little practical value in the long run, such a declaration would be of a certain psychological value, and might even be of practical value, at least for a time. If Germany was up to more mischief, it was better that her mischief be directed towards the East, than towards the West. Besides, Mr. Chamberlain had at Munich signed his 'no-war' declaration with Hitler; and if Bonnet managed a parallel Franco-German declaration, it would look good, and increase his personal prestige, and—improve his chances for the Premiership.

The *gleichschaltung* of the French Press which was never so apparent as during November and December—that is, for some time before and for some time after the Bonnet-Ribbentrop declaration—was largely due to this ambition. First it was necessary not to do anything that would disturb the Franco-German negotiations; and later, it was important not to spoil the 'moral effect' of the agreement. In December, Bonnet's desire to prevent Franco-Italian relations from becoming unduly strained became another reason for 'keeping the Press in order.'

How can the Press be 'kept in order'?[1] I am here on delicate ground. But the Press in France was, in a large measure, muzzled by a technique which must be familiar to all French Foreign Ministers, but which was never practised, at least since 1919, more extensively and more effectively than by M. Bonnet. The Government has all kinds of means at its disposal for 'influencing' the Press. First of all, the secret funds, which are, in many cases, heavily supplemented by funds placed at this or that Minister's disposal by various financial and business interests. Parallel with funds received from or *via* the Government, certain papers are alleged to have been receiving important 'subsidies' from foreign Governments; and Germany is alleged to have been quite unusually lavish with her money in Paris not only at the time of the Czech crisis, but also during the few months that followed. M. de Kerillis, invoking a high American authority, claimed that £2,000,000 had been spent by German propaganda in France during the greater part of 1938. But there are other ways of influencing papers. The Government can resort to intimidation, or flattery, or certain other methods. The Havas Agency has a quasi-monopoly of agency news in France; and it is officially subsidized by the Government. The Foreign Office, therefore, has a considerable hold on Havas. It is able—especially in cases when the news is not likely to leak out elsewhere in France (for if it leaks out abroad it does not necessarily matter)—to get Havas to suppress some unpleasant piece of news—the suppression of such news in France was done on a very extensive scale, especially at the early stages of the anti-French campaign in Italy; an attempt was even made not to 'release' the story of the anti-French demonstration at the Italian Chamber on November 30. But the story was too big to be suppressed altogether; and it was merely toned down. Apart from papers directly subsidized, and to which the Government can give 'friendly advice,' certain Ministers have also a personal way of influencing the Press. Personal relations exist between Ministers and newspaper editors; and these are asked by *Monsieur le Ministre* not to play up this or that piece of news. The editor—or his 'diplomatic correspondent,' for that matter—cannot easily refuse, if he values the Minister's friendship, even if he is financially independent of him. It was in these various ways that during the great Franco-German *rapprochement* the bulk of the Press was *gleichgeschaltet*; extraordinarily little was said, for instance, about the pogroms in Germany. On another occasion, a paper with a very large circulation

[1] This was written in Paris in 1939—hence the present tense and also the cautious wording of all references to corruption in the French press. But my meaning is sufficiently clear. (Author's note, 1942.)

299

was specially 'requested' not to publish a big *reportage* it had prepared on German refugees in France. King Carol's visit to Paris on November 19–20, while the Franco-German negotiations for a 'declaration' were in progress, was virtually ignored by the semi-official Press; in the past, the *Temps*, which now gave the visit only a few lines, would certainly have written ponderous editorials on '*L'Amitié Franco-Roumaine.*' When the bulk of the Press can be *gleichgeschaltet* by these methods, the Opposition Press becomes, in itself, less dangerous: for its aggregate circulation becomes negligible compared with that of the 'semi-official' Press. The one sells in millions, the other only in hundreds of thousands.

But there are ways of dealing with the Opposition Press, too. Thus, a small paper belonging to a former Cabinet Minister which more or less depended on Government subsidies, became rather rebellious after Munich. The subsidies were stopped, and the paper passed into other hands, which wrote exactly what *Monsieur le Ministre* wanted to be written.[2] Then there is the case of a political weekly of high standing, but run at a substantial deficit. The deficit is 'covered' by one or two wealthy patrons who are not out of sympathy with the paper's 'anti-Munich' policy. But it so happens that the patrons are invited to lunch; and there they meet *Monsieur le Ministre*; and *Monsieur le Ministre* is perfectly charming; and during coffee he remarks casually that such-and-such a journal is doing the country a great deal of harm, and that its patrons are really very ill-advised to spend their good money on such a mischievous publication.[3] Sometimes it does not work; but sometimes it does. Similar methods—though not by *Monsieur le Ministre* personally—are applied to big advertisers. M. de Kerillis, in the *Epoque*, has referred to the advertising revenue his paper has lost through such pressure on the bigger advertisers.

I hasten to add that such Government pressure on the Press was not by any means limited to France before and after Munich; 'friendly admonition' and 'friendly requests' and lunch invitations to Editors and similar tricks have been applied on an extensive scale in England, too. Advertisers, whether directly inspired from above or not, have also tended to boycott papers which were 'too gloomy,' and not sufficiently in agreement with Mr. Chamberlain. But the *gleichschaltung* has never been quite so blatant in England as it was in France, especially during

[2] The reference is to Frossard's *Homme Libre*, which was taken over by Bonnet in this fashion. (Author's note, 1942.)

[3] I refer here to the *Europe Nouvelle*, which was nearly sunk by Bonnet. (Author's note, 1942.)

November and December 1938. For one thing, English papers are financially independent of the Government.

To reinforce this *gleichschaltung* of the Press, M. Bonnet conceived two decrees which he desired the Government to approve; but M. Marchandeau, the Minister of Justice, refused to sign them. These two decrees were calculated to protect the Dictators against attacks. Under the existing Press Law heads of foreign States and (this was added by a Laval decree to oblige Mussolini) heads of foreign Governments may ask the French Government to take action against a paper which has published anything which they consider offensive. In terms of the decree drafted by M. Bonnet this action could be taken without any complaint from abroad, but on the initiative of the French Foreign Minister. This proposed decree had vast implications. The other decree proposed that any trials likely to have 'international repercussions' be heard *in camera*: the purpose of this was to keep a trial like that of Grynspan, the Jewish murderer of the Secretary of the Germany Embassy, out of the Press. The counsel for the defence was obviously going to say some unpleasant things about the Nazi régime; and, for the sake of Franco-German friendship, it was better that all that sort of thing should not be given any publicity.

.   .   .   .

It was on November 22, on the eve of Mr. Chamberlain's and Lord Halifax's arrival in Paris that M. Bonnet received the Press (who were ushered in by his friend, Percy Philip), and announced that the terms of the Franco-German declaration had been agreed upon. 'There are some,' he said, not without a touch of bad humour, 'who do not want friendship with Germany; but I am not one of them.'

Mr. Chamberlain, on the following day, naturally declared himself to be in full agreement with the French Government, and said that he greatly welcomed the Franco-German declaration.

It may be said that if, after creating some difficulties in October, the Germans were now much easier to deal with, it was for a number of reasons, one of which was a very curious one; the pogroms had created a tremendous wave of anti-Nazi feeling in England and the United States; and by getting Ribbentrop feted by Democratic France, Germany was made to look more or less 'respectable' again in the eyes of the world. If the French Government was friendly, and treated the pogroms as an 'internal German affair,' why should England and the United States be so squeamish? From the German point of view, the declaration also had other advantages: it helped her propagandists to convince her Eastern

301

neighbours that France had lost all interest in Eastern Europe; or, as Kerillis was to put it, it was calculated to disgust Eastern Europe with France, and to neutralize it if, by any chance, Germany desired to tackle the West. Ribbentrop's visit was to have taken place on November 28; but was postponed owing to the general strike; and he arrived in Paris on December 6.

Already on the day before his arrival a part of the Press 'interpreted' the real meaning of the Franco-German declaration in a manner that was eminently suitable to the Germans. Thus, M. Sauerwein wrote in *Paris-Soir* that no one should imagine that France would ever attack Russia—oh no! if Germany attacked Russia, France would not betray her Russian friend, she would remain neutral. Such, at any rate, seemed to be the meaning of his words, which read as follows:

> It should not be difficult to show that by seeking appeasement with Germany we are not going to enter into any coalition against Russia.

With such comments in the French Press, Ribbentrop could well gain the impression that Germany could help herself to the Ukraine, at least in so far as the Russians would let her.

And two days later, after the declaration was signed, the *Matin* explained that the third clause of the declaration—with its reference to 'special relations with third Powers'—did not really mean what it seemed to mean.

> In the course of their conversations, M. Bonnet and Herr von Ribbentrop tried to find out whether within the framework of their commitments towards third parties it would not be possible for them to allow one another a certain liberty of action in order to extend and develop the premises of the Franco-German agreement.

. . . .

There was a strange unreality about that German visit to Paris—and yet what a big occasion it would have been in different circumstances!

There is nothing since the War that the average Frenchman had in his heart desired more than a real understanding between France and Germany. Briand was popular because for three or four years—at least until Stresemann's death—he held out the hope of such an understanding. Melancholy thoughts of missed and wasted opportunities in the past must have run through many a Frenchman's mind when he read in the evening papers the official, polite, but rather embarrassed descriptions of Herr von Ribbentrop's arrival in Paris that morning, and when he observed the total indifference with which the people of Paris treated what in other circumstances would have been a great day in the history of France, Germany and Europe.

This indifference was understandable, for Ribbentrop was not paying a visit to the people of Paris, and the French Government, indeed, made it clear that it did not wish the people of Paris to have anything to do with the visit. Lest they should give Ribbentrop the wrong kind of welcome, it was better that they should not give him any welcome at all.

There were no public reactions of any kind—simply because there was no public. The couple of hundred people who, from a respectful distance, were allowed to see Herr von Ribbentrop arrive at the Hôtel Crillon, just looked on curiously, expressing neither approval nor disapproval.

At the reception, given by M. Daladier in the afternoon, and by M. Bonnet at night the two 'non-Aryan' members of the French Government—M. Mandel (the Minister of Colonies) and M. Zay (the Minister of Education)—were not invited. This left many people with a bad taste in the mouth. The *Populaire* indignantly asked whether Hitler's racial laws had been accepted by the French Government and whether Ribbentrop was to be left with the impression that France already discriminated between 'Aryan' and 'non-Aryan' Cabinet Ministers.

A number of persons invited refused the invitations, including the wife of a Cabinet Minister, who declared that she was dining instead at the Czechoslovak Legation.

Bonnet and Ribbentrop had a long conversation in which they 'reviewed all international problems, particularly those directly concerning their two countries.'

The Franco-German declaration was signed, with great solemnity, in the famous Clock Room of the Quai d'Orsay—the room where the Kellogg Pact was signed in 1928.

The declaration read:

1. The German and French Governments have come to the unanimous conviction that friendly and good-neighbourly relations between Germany and France are one of the most essential elements of a consolidation of the good relations in Europe and of the maintenance of a general peace. Both Governments therefore will do all in their power to safeguard such a formation of relations between their countries.

2. Both Governments state that there are no more questions of a territorial kind between their countries, and they solemnly recognize as definite the frontier between their two countries as it now runs.

3. The countries are resolved, without prejudice to their special relations to third Powers, to remain in touch with one another as regards all problems concerning their two countries, and to enter into negotiations if the future development of these problems should lead to international difficulties.

In testimony of this the representatives of the two countries have signed this declaration, which comes into force immediately.

GEORGES BONNET,
JOACHIM VON RIBBENTROP.

Signed in German and French in Paris on December 6, 1938.

The statements Bonnet and Ribbentrop later made were taken down on gramophone records and broadcast. The two statements differed considerably in tone. Whereas M. Bonnet expressed the pious hope that the Franco-German declaration would do good to the cause of peace in general, Ribbentrop said nothing whatsoever of European peace but dwelt merely on Franco-German relations.

Ribbentrop said:

With to-day's declaration France and Germany, taking into account the solid basis constituted by the friendship which binds them to other States, have agreed to put an end to their secular frontier conflicts, and, by recognizing reciprocally their territory, to facilitate the road to mutual recognition and the consideration of their vital national interests.

As partners equal in rights, two great nations declare themselves ready, after serious differences in the past, to establish relations of good neighbourliness for the future. With this declaration of their goodwill they express the conviction that there exists in fact between them no opposition of a vital nature to justify a serious conflict.

I hope to-day's declaration will open a new era in the relations between our two peoples.

M. Bonnet said:

The efforts of the French Government, like those of its predecessors, are always sincerely inspired with the aim of maintaining and organizing peace. The arrangement of relations of good neighbourliness between France and Germany and the expression of their common desire to develop peaceful relations constitute essential elements in this undertaking.

That is why I am very glad about the signing of this Franco-German declaration, which, by solemnly recognizing existing frontiers, ends a long and historic debate and opens the way to collaboration, which must be facilitated by the conviction that there exists between

304

the two countries no difference of a nature to call in question the peaceful basis of their relations.

Furthermore, I do not doubt that this common declaration will bring to general appeasement a contribution of which the future will confirm the full value. It marks a particularly important stage in that work of co-operation and reconciliation to which France ardently hopes to see all peoples associate themselves.

The lack of spontaneity in the Franco-German protestations of friendship, the numerous mental reservations that certainly existed at least on the German side, the police wall that separated the representative of Germany from the people of France, certainly made any enthusiasm over the Franco-German declaration very difficult.

Herr von Ribbentrop was conscious of this strained and rather artificial atmosphere when in his statement he expressed the hope that 'not only' the Government but also the people of France would approve the declaration of friendship.

And what was the net result of the Franco-German meeting? The French papers, including those most favourable to a Munich policy, betrayed an unmistakable feeling of uneasiness. The uneasiness was chiefly due to the anti-French agitation in Italy.

Not without much humming and hawing the semi-official Press tried to suggest that Ribbentrop had expressed disapproval of this Italian agitation, and had even suggested that it had no support from Germany. But coupled with the violent outburst of the German Press on that same day against the anti-Italian demonstrations in Corsica and Tunisia, Ribbentrop's 'disapproval' of Italy failed to convince. Even the ultra-reactionary *Action Française* declared that it 'didn't believe a word of it.'

As regards Spain, there was the same humming and hawing in the semi-official Press. Herr von Ribbentrop was supposed to have said that he fully sympathized with the French view that the Spanish problem ought to be 'cleared up,' but in reply to the remark that it would be desirable to establish some kind of 'neutral' régime in Spain he was reported to have said that 'while he appreciated this point of view and while Germany no longer took very much interest in Spain, she would still like to see General Franco win.' Obviously, no great step towards a 'settlement.'

Nor did Ribbentrop commit himself in any way to hastening the withdrawal of the 'volunteers' on Franco's side. Instead, he made the usual remarks about the menace of Bolshevism.

Colonies were not discussed, except that, according to one report, the Germans expressed the desire to be given a share in the management of

Tangier. Apart from that, however, the Germans were anxious to give France the impression that France and Germany were 'facing different ways as regards territorial interests,' France being primarily a Colonial Power and Germany primarily a Continental Power.

On the face of it the declaration contained nothing which would allow Germany a free hand in the East and cancel the Franco-Polish alliance or the Franco-Soviet Pact. Nevertheless, both the German Press and a part of the French Press clearly suggested that France was no longer interested in Central or Eastern Europe.

Bonnet tried to make the most of the Franco-German declaration. According to one report of the meeting of the Foreign Affairs Committee of the Chamber on December 14, he claimed that Ribbentrop had said to him:

> If in signing the Franco-German declaration we Germans have abandoned Alsace-Lorraine, do you imagine that we are going to attack France not for the sake of Alsace-Lorraine but simply in order to help out Italy?

During some weeks Bonnet seemed to treat the Franco-German declaration as the corner-stone of his whole policy; and, far from regarding it as useless in the light of the Italian claims, he considered it all the more valuable. His point of view at that time may be reasonably summed up as follows:

He held that peace on the Rhine must be secured whatever else happened. This was all the more important since British aid on land could only be negligible at first and slow for several months afterwards. He felt that France could not pursue a Continental policy unless there was conscription in Great Britain and a large expeditionary force, and that without these it was not even certain that France could conduct a successful defensive war for more than a few months—especially if Italy also intervened on Germany's side.

In fact, he felt that while France could hardly help Eastern Europe, Eastern Europe could hardly be expected to give important help to France.

According to M. de Kerillis, who is himself a member of the Foreign Affairs Committee, M. Bonnet gave, on December 14, the following remarkable answer to his question whether France would intervene in the event of a conflict in Eastern Europe: 'If Poland, Russia, and Rumania defend themselves, why, then we shall go to their aid.'

This remarkable statement implied that—

1. M. Bonnet was not convinced that Poland, Rumania and Russia were fit to defend themselves against Germany.
2. That he anticipated a number of 'peaceful' German conquests in Eastern Europe.
3. If Poland and Russia and Rumania were to put up a good fight against German aggression and so prove their value as military Powers, why, then the questions of France's military 'commitments' in Eastern Europe could be reconsidered.

Altogether, in the heyday of the Franco-German *rapprochement* M. Bonnet appeared to believe that while Germany was busy in Eastern Europe France need fear nothing on the Rhine and could even afford to take a high hand with Italy.

And it was about that time that the *Matin* printed a most impressive series of articles on *La Grande Ukraine*, in which Biscupski, Skoropadsky and other adventurers and Nazi puppet hetmans were treated in all seriousness as Ukrainian nationalists and patriots. In the early part of December, France's sense of responsibility had fallen to its lowest point. The 'let's-be-last-on-the-menu' policy was never advocated with such blatant cynicism; and this virtual acceptance by a certain part of the Press of the 'vassalage' principle ran parallel, in a curious way, with the creation of a December 1851 atmosphere in France itself. Some months later I lunched with three prominent French journalists—and they all agreed that December was 'something of a nightmare'; the atmosphere in France had never got nearer a 'Fascist' atmosphere than during those days. The *Canard Enchaîné* referred to M. Daladier, the baker's boy, as *'Daladier, fils du Général Boulanger.'*

Not content with the *gleichschaltung* of the greater part of the French Press, the French Foreign Office began to treat distinguished foreign correspondents, who had always been good friends of France, as though they were her enemies, simply because they commented candidly on the policies of the French Government. M. Bonnet came to hate the bulk of the American Correspondents (with the exception of P. J. Philip), but the worst thorn in his flesh was the British Press. Not only was a whispering campaign started which consisted in saying that such-and-such British journalists (I was one of them), were on the 'blacklist,' and would 'soon' be expelled from France; but, certainly not without official inspiration, *Gringoire* started a violent personal campaign against Thomas Cadett, the Paris Correspondent of *The Times*, who, because he had lunched a few times with M. Blum when the latter was Premier, was accused of being 'Blum's spokesman' and a frequenter of 'Bolshevik drawing-rooms.' *Gringoire* demanded his expulsion—a thought that was perhaps son to M. Bonnet's wish, if one may say so. But since such an expulsion would have created a fearful scandal in London, where questions would certainly have been asked in the House of Commons, a few rather perfidious attempts were made instead to pull wires from the London end to get Cadett 'recalled.' It was a typical instance of the December atmosphere. Some reasonable advice ultimately put an end to the campaign; though it was to flare up again for a short moment in February, when, one day, in a message to *The Times*, Cadett commented, not without a touch of impish irony, on the striking difference between M. Daladier's public utterances on Italy's claims on France and M. Bonnet's semi-private utterances on the same subject. But that was perhaps only a flash in the pan. For after the second half of December this oppressive atmosphere in France began to improve somewhat—largely, it is only fair to say, thanks to M. Daladier and, indirectly, thanks to Count Ciano.

XVIII. 'TUNIS! CORSICA! NICE!'—THE END OF THE SPANISH WAR—THE END OF MUNICH

THE Italian campaign against France was at last beginning to annoy the French; and French opinion was at last beginning to shake off that drowsy torpor into which it had sunk as a result of Munich and the Franco-German declaration. 'Little France' feelings may have been strong in France; and it was even possible to persuade French opinion—or part of it—that 'a free hand for Germany in the East' was a sound policy. Had not M. Flandin said that France would be 'an Empire Power rather than a European Power'? And if, two months after Munich, the very existence of this Empire was, for the first time, being openly challenged—then, surely, somebody must have been wrong; and the whole problem of peace was not as simple as all that. That France should be selected as the *next* victim—immediately after Czechoslovakia—that was really too much! One day I remarked to a Left-Wing and rather anti-Munich Radical: 'If you didn't risk a war for the "Czech bastion," are you going to risk a war for Jibuti?' His reply was instantaneous: *'Djibouti, c'est à nous.* It isn't the same thing at all. In the case of Czechoslovakia most people didn't know what it was all about. It may seem absurd to you, *mais c'est comme ça. Djibouti, c'est á nous!'* he repeated. It reminded one a little of the joke about Chamberlain who after giving away Czecho-slovakia, refused to leave Hitler his umbrella as a souvenir.

'Oh, no, you can't have that : it's British.'

'Djibouti, c'est á nous!'

.   .   .   /   .   .   .   .

Mr. Chamberlain and Lord Halifax came to Paris as the official guests of the French Government on November 23, and stayed till the morning of the 25th. At the Gare du Nord their arrival was marked by an anti-Munich demonstration apparently organized by the Communists. On the following day the two Ministers attended various functions, and the political talks lasted only a few hours. But the visit was of great impor-tance to the Daladier Government. On the 22nd, to save the Govern-ment from a moral defeat, M. Daladier took an extraordinary course ; if, he said, the Finance Committee did not approve the decrees, he would telephone London and call off Mr. Chamberlain's visit ! Thanks to this threat, he secured a majority of one on the Committee ! What was ulti-mately going to save the Daladier Government was its victory over the General Strike ; but until then its position remained very shaky.[1]

The talks during the Chamberlain-Halifax visit were of no great importance. Perhaps the most important talks related to Anglo-French defence problems. The French urged upon the British the necessity of constituting an expeditionary force ; while the British pointed out to the French that the French Air Force was still in a mess. The conclusion on both sides seems to have been 'we'll see what we can do.' The other talks were rather general. Regarding Eastern Europe, they agreed on a policy of 'wait and see' ; 'wait and see—and hope for a Franco victory' seems to have been the 'decision' taken on Spain ; and the Left were kept quiet by the assurance that the two Governments were going to stick, as before, to the London Plan, and that 'there could be no question, before the withdrawal of volunteers, of granting belligerent rights to Franco.' The Ministers already felt that the matter was no longer of any decisive importance in one way or the other, and that they could well afford to sound firm and fair on this point.

One had, however, the impression during that meeting that there

[1] At the end of the debate that followed the strike M. Daladier secured a majority of seventy-four—the entire Right, including even M. Chiappe and the eight members of the P.S.F. (the ex-Croix de Feu) voting for him. There were three hostile Radical votes, and thirty-three Radical abstentions (including M. Delbos, M. Cot, and M. de Tessan). This meant the New Majority had come officially into existence.

was a certain reserve—particularly on the British side; and that Mr. Chamberlain was not exactly 'falling over' his French hosts. And it is curious that there was one very important piece of news which, to all appearances, he withheld from them—and that was his decision to go to Rome in January. He probably knew that the French had good reason to advise him against such a move. But, as he was to say at the famous London Press dinner on December 13:

> Next month Lord Halifax and I have planned a visit to Rome for the purpose of discussing with the head of the Italian Government and his Ministers all matters of common interest and concern. *It may be that some will once again be speculating upon who is the winner and who the loser in these talks. That is not the spirit in which we propose to undertake our journey.*

And he added the somewhat undemocratic remark, which sounded almost like a—wholly undeserved—apology for the Nazi outrages:

> I find it difficult to rouse much excitement over different systems of government, apart from particular actions which may not necessarily be inherent in the system.

'Who will be the winner and who will be the loser' in the Rome talks seemed unessential to Mr. Chamberlain. The French did not look at it quite in that way—for Mussolini obviously wished them to be the losers. Mr. Chamberlain's famous speech was not made until a fortnight later; but the French Ministers must have had a pretty good idea of Mr. Chamberlain's theory about 'winners and losers'; for the announcement on November 28 of the Rome visit came to the French—or at least to many of them—as a rather unpleasant surprise. Even M. Bonnet apparently received the news with slightly mixed feelings.

The effect in Italy of the announcement of Mr. Chamberlain's visit was immediate. Two days later, Count Ciano made a speech before the Italian Chamber. First he praised the British Government, and then he said:

> The prime objects of our policy is *to safeguard with unshakable firmness the interests and natural aspirations of the Italian people.*

At this point, rising to their feet almost like one man, the black-shirted deputies burst into loud cries of 'Tunisia! Corsica! Nice!'

M. François-Poncet, the French Ambassador, was in the diplomatic box. Instead of standing up and leaving, he stayed. The announcement of the Rome visit, without any consultation on the subject with France, gave the Italians the idea that the French could now be squeezed in the name of 'appeasement,' and that Mr. Chamberlain would consent to 'mediate.' Italians in Tunis were already saying—though half-jokingly: 'We want Runciman! We want Runciman!'

The anti-French demonstration aroused comparatively little attention in France at first. A member of the Havas Agency told me that the Quai d'Orsay's first move was to try to suppress the news of the anti-French demonstration in the Italian Chamber altogether; but it was found that one or two papers had already received the news from their own correspondents in Rome, and that complete suppression was impossible. But the Quai tried, nevertheless, to reduce the damage to a minimum, first by getting the news toned down in the Press as far as possible; and then by declaring, on December 5—after assurances had been received by M. François-Poncet that the Chamber demonstration was spontaneous and did not represent the official policy of the Italian Government—that 'the incident was closed.'

Instinctively, the French people refused to be so easily convinced. Not that they took the Italian campaign very seriously at first. Except in Corsica and Tunisia, where some angry anti-Italian demonstrations took place in the first week of December, the demonstrations elsewhere were little more than student rags. In the Latin Quarter the students carried posters and shouted: 'We want Vesuvius!' 'We want Venice!' and in the Place de la Sorbonne a youthful orator defended the 'natural aspirations of the Youth of France'—their most natural aspiration being to take their girl-friends for a holiday to Venice or Naples without having to bother about visas and passports. '*A nous Venise!*' '*A nous le Vésuve!*' It was all a joke—but a rather significant one to come from the very students of Paris who, three years earlier, had forced Professor Jèze to abandon his lectures at the Faculty of Law because he was legal adviser to the Emperor of Abyssinia. If the anger was not greater, it was very largely because there is a time-honoured tradition in France not to take the Italians seriously—least of all as soldiers.

But in Corsica and in Tunisia it was all taken considerably more seriously. On December 5 M. Daladier published a statement saying that he had 'since last Thursday' (i.e., since the very day after the Rome demonstration) received a great number of telegrams from Corsican municipalities and associations, from groups in the island itself, and from all parts of the French Empire.

But although the Italian Government had declared itself to be 'entirely foreign' to the anti-French demonstrations, the Press campaign in Italy grew daily in intensity.

Gayda, in the *Giornale d'Italia*, on December 12—sounding rather more moderate than usual—demanded a free zone in the port of Jibuti and the cession to Italy of the shares in the Jibuti-Addis-Ababa Railway. But, at the same time, the Italian papers declared M. Daladier's coming voyage to 'Italian Corsica' to be an 'intolerable provocation.' And Gayda declared, already early in December, that the Franco-Italian agreement of 1935 had become 'worthless.'

The clamour for Corsica and Nice was, of course, not taken seriously. But with 95,000 Italians in Tunisia, Italy was obviously trying to turn Tunisia into a 'problem.' That there were over 100,000 Frenchmen in Tunisia and over 2,000,000 natives who (whatever their grievances against France), were unanimously anti-Italian, made no difference. The Jibuti port and railway were a different matter; nobody denied that, since the conquest of Abyssinia, Italy had a reasonable claim in respect of these. But why discuss Jibuti in *such* a tone? Regarding Tunisia, a number of writers were prepared to accept Italy's challenge.

Thus, M. Viénot, who was Under-Secretary for Foreign Affairs in the first Blum Government, wrote in the *Œuvre* on December 13:

'Italy intends to obtain for her 95,000 nationals living in Tunisia the right to organize a "national community"—after the manner of Henlein's original demands. In this way Italy hopes to lay the foundations for her eventual conquest of Tunisia.

Let us reduce the Italians in Tunisia to the status of aliens by putting an end to their present privileges. The Franco-Italian Convention of 1896 is in force only by virtue of its tacit and automatic renewal, and we may denounce it at three months' notice. Let us, before waiting for new claims, denounce it. Let us at the same time take the necessary measures of self-protection; let us expel Italian agitators, dissolve the Fascist organizations and prohibit their paper, the *Unione*.'

The 1935 agreement was actually denounced by Italy a few days later —on December 17; but, naturally, the French Government did not take advantage of this to apply to Tunisia the drastic remedies advocated by M. Viénot.

This repudiation was, in fact, a brutal reply to the conciliatory speech M. Bonnet made before the Foreign Affairs Committee of the Chamber on December 14, when he said that, in spite of the attacks on the 1935 agreement in the Italian Press, France still considered it valid; and that there was no question of 'retorting' by depriving the Italian settlers of their existing privileges. M. Bonnet repeated several times that the anti-French outcry in the Italian Chamber 'did not represent the official policy of the Italian Government.' He added, however, that France would not surrender an inch of territory to Italy.

That is to say that not a single one of Italy's *territorial* claims would be considered; but there were also *non-territorial* claims; and these M. Bonnet did not mention.

We are going to hear a lot more about this distinction.

On December 19 M. Bonnet spoke to the Chamber itself. He was even firmer than before about Italy's territorial claims. Not a single inch of French territory, he said, would be given up.

> Any attempt to achieve such ambitions can only lead to an armed conflict. And when I speak of French territory I include in it Tunisia, the French possessions on the Somali coast in their entirety, Corsica, Nice, and Savoy.

By speaking of 'the French possessions on the Somali coast in their entirety,' M. Bonnet must have had in mind certain suggestions tentatively put forward in London—such as a 'free zone' for Italy in the port of Jibuti.

Apart from that, however, his speech rather suggested that there were signs of a *détente* between France and Italy.

This speech was made on the 19th; and it was actually on the 17th that Italy had repudiated the 1935 agreement. At the meeting of the Chamber on December 29 M. Bonnet was going to be publicly accused of having deliberately concealed from the Chamber, in his speech on the 19th, this new development of extreme gravity. The news finally leaked out in the *Ordre* on December 22; and it was only then that the fact was officially admitted by the French Foreign Office.

M. Bonnet was accused of excessive timidity, which, his critics thought, would only encourage Italy in her demands. The French Government, they said, should frankly state that if the agreement of 1935 was null and void, then the status of the Italians in Tunisia was now again subject to revision by France at three months' notice.

It was also said that the French Government should demand the return by Italy of the 2,500 shares in the Jibuti-Addis-Ababa Railway which were handed over to her in 1935.

Further, it was proposed that all the territories which had, actually or nominally, passed under Italian sovereignty under the 1935 agreement, should be promptly returned to France.

But the French Government preferred to 'go easy,' and not to 'dramatize' matters. Although in view of the dangerous-looking troop movements in Abyssinia and French Somaliland, a gunboat and two battalions of Senegalese troops were sent on December 28 to Jibuti, at the request of M. Mandel, the Minister of Colonies, the French Foreign Office claimed that these dispatches were 'a matter of routine' and had nothing to do with reports of alleged Italian troops movements. In reply to allegations that Italian outposts had already been occupying, for some time past, various points thirty or forty miles inside the frontiers of French Somaliland, the Foreign Office declared that it had decided to send there a commission of geographers who would find out exactly where the frontier was. Pertinax replied to this that the geographers had returned from there several months before and knew 'exactly where the frontier was.' It was an open secret that M. Mandel had played this little trick on M. Bonnet by giving the information to Pertinax.

On December 29 M. Bonnet was asked at the Chamber why he had concealed from it, in his speech ten days earlier, the repudiation of the 1935 agreement. M. Bonnet looked rather embarrassed.

Significantly enough, this onslaught on the Government by the Left received the strongest support from the Right. M. Marin declared that it was not enough to say that France would not yield an inch of territory. One had to teach people to respect other people's property acquired at the cost of blood and tears and milliards of money.

M. Vallat, another leading member of the Right, supported M. Marin, while M. Gouin, a member of the 'Socialist Union' asked that the sitting should be suspended so as to indicate to M. Bonnet that a reply was desired.

Although M. Campinchi, the Minister of Marine, asked that the discussion of the Budget should be resumed, the suspension was voted by 309 votes to 279.

This was a blow to the Government—even though it had not made the vote a question of confidence. M. Bonnet then spoke. He began by saying emphatically that he had learned of the Italian repudiation of the 1935 pact after his speech in the Chamber. Then, however, he added that 'even if he had heard of it before he could not have mentioned it, as it had not been discussed by the Cabinet.'

His critics were having the time of their lives. '*Il mentait comme un arracheur de dents,*' a French journalist later irreverently remarked in the Lobbies.

For some days, and especially during M. Daladier's triumphal visit to Corsica and North Africa, M. Bonnet's stock had fallen very low. The Premier, now genuinely infuriated by the Italians, was also dissatisfied with his Foreign Minister's 'over-cautious' handling of the conflict with Italy. M. Bonnet, as we shall see, was going to come into his own again, once the enthusiasm of Ajaccio and Bastia and Tunis and Algiers had subsided. Largely, by converting M. Daladier to his own outlook—at least for a time—particularly on the question of Spain.

.   .   .   .

On board the *Foch*, which was escorted by the cruiser *Colbert* and three destroyers, M. Daladier sailed for Ajaccio on New Year's Day. If there was anyone in Italy who doubted Corsica's loyalty to France he must have been completely disillusioned, after the truly Mediterranean enthusiasm with which M. Daladier and his suite were greeted at Ajaccio and Bastia.

Corsica is politically one of the most clannish of French provinces. Every Corsican is a politician, and there are long-standing party feuds in every town and almost in every café, but all Corsicans, whether they belonged to the 'Piétri clan' or the 'Landry clan,' or to the 'Campinchi clan,' welcomed M. Daladier with the same joyful unanimity. For on that occasion he represented one thing only, and that was France.

At Ajaccio, in replying to the words of welcome by the Mayor of the town, M. Daladier said:

> France has no need to be aggressive or threatening, she has no need to shout. You have asked us to reflect with solicitude on the destinies of your island. You can count on us. You can be assured that the Government of France thinks of you with particular tenderness, for French history, rich as it is, is further enriched by your history.
>
> You gave Bonaparte to France and France gave you back Napoleon, but you also gave France 40,000 lives in the Great War, and this blood proves your unbreakable attachment to your Motherland.

And he added, in characteristic Daladier style, that he himself had blood bonds with Corsica: half the blood in the veins of his two sons was Corsican.

In Tunisia the reception given to the Premier was equally impressive —M. Daladier drove through the streets of Bizerta, densely packed with people shouting *Vive la France! Vive Daladier!* Women in top-storey windows threw flower petals into his car. Later the sentiments of the people were to be translated into words by the Bey, who told M. Daladier:

> You can be certain that all Tunisians will, if necessary, rally to France. I give you this assurance here. France has the right to the infinite thanks of the people of Tunis for the work it has done here, and Tunis will show her gratitude.

The one jarring note was a demonstration outside the Bey's palace as M. Daladier was leaving. A party of natives, carrying a banner inscribed *'Vive le Destour'* (Destour is the Tunisian Nationalist Party), was roughly handled by the Bey's guards and several arrests were made. The crowd expressed strong disapproval of the demonstration.

The Italian language paper, *Unione,* published in Tunis, did not mention the visit, but published an article discussing the community of feeling between Arabs and Italians. All other papers welcomed M. Daladier, the Arab Press in particular declaring that Rome received a shock from the reaction of Tunis and Corsica to the 'mad Italian claims.'

On the following day M. Daladier inspected part of the 'desert Maginot Line' which guards the frontier between Tunis and the Italian colony of Libya. This system of defences, known as the Mareth Line, was designed by General Morin, one of the chief engineers of the Maginot Line, and M. Daladier, as War Minister, was specially anxious to see it.

From Gabet, in Southern Tunisia, M. Daladier gave a broadcast:

'Since dawn,' he said, 'I have been going from village to village, or rather from blockhouse to blockhouse, on the fortified line built to defend our Tunisian frontiers. I remember above all the review, remarkable for the enthusiasm of the soldiers and people, and perhaps more so for the presence there of the chiefs of the Southern tribes, who came voluntarily with their men. They told me, "If one day France has need of us again we will come with all our force, all our soul, and all our love for her!"'

M. Daladier also gave Tunisia assurances that France could keep an eye on her economic problem. This was important, for Tunisia has certainly been handicapped by the tariff system under which Tunisia is, as it were, an open market to French exports, but France is not an open market to Tunisian agricultural exports.

But whatever their economic grievances against France, the Arabs infinitely preferred her to Italy. They knew, for one thing, that they were incomparably luckier than their fellow Arabs in Libya; and French official quarters made at that time a point of 'rubbing it in' that while in fifty years of French rule in Tunisia the native population had doubled, in Libya it had declined by sixty per cent in twenty-five years of Italian rule. Moreover, the Italians in Tunisia provided much of the cheap labour in the docks and mines, and they were in sharp competition with the native workers.

A French friend of mine who was travelling in Tunisia shortly before the Munich crisis, told me the following significant story. He was staying in Southern Tunisia as the guest of a local chief. The outlook in Europe was very serious. The Frenchman asked his host whether he thought Tunisia would supply any troops to France in case of war. After much humming and hawing the Arab chief said that it would be 'very difficult to get his men to go and fight in France.' 'But supposing,' the Frenchman said, 'they have to fight not Germany but Italy?' The Arab's embarrassment vanished instantly. 'Oh, that's quite different,' he said. 'You have only got to supply the rifles. *Tu n'as qu'à nous donner des fusils.*'

One of the effects of the Italian agitation against France was to reduce to a large extent the importance of the Neo-Destour, the organization of the Tunisian Nationalist extremists. Another effect, in the few weeks that followed the Montecitorio demonstration, was to produce in Tunisia 25,000 Italian applications for French citizenship.

The native population of Algiers greeted M. Daladier with the same enthusiasm as the native population of Tunis. The visits had been arranged at short notice, and, without the totalitarian police mechanism at their disposal, the French authorities could obviously not have 'cooked' such native demonstrations in which hundreds of thousands of people took part.

M. Daladier himself was carried away by it all, and at Algiers he made a speech of which only expurgated versions were published in the Quai d'Orsay-controlled Press. They regarded it as contrary to 'appease-ment' and its final phrase as a fairly obvious criticism of M. Bonnet's more cautious policy:

> 'France wants peace with all countries. . . . But if anyone inter-prets her attitude as a sign of weakness or abdication then I cry "Halt."
> 'When I said, "I maintain the integrity of the French Empire," I not only said I would not yield an acre of its territory, but I meant I would not be led into juridical procedures which some people would like to set on foot.'

The phrase was also a warning to Mr. Chamberlain not to try and drag France into any Four-Power Pact scheme or into a Mediterranean Munich after his talks with Mussolini.

. . . .

Paris was delighted with the journey. It was like a fresh wind blowing through the stale 'pre-Fascist' hothouse atmosphere that had developed in the last three months of 1938. In spite of the humiliation of Munich, France, it was felt, could still speak in a clear loud voice. Even the Press of the Left spoke with great approval of the North African tour. The

317

journey cured France to some extent of her growing inferiority-complex. During the days that followed the Tunisian voyage, Daladier's popularity and personal prestige were greater than they had ever been. He had become something of a national figure—even though the Left Press liked to point out that what the people of Corsica and Tunisia and Algeria had cheered with such impressive unanimity was not M. Edouard Daladier, but the Representative of France.

It was believed for a time that, taking advantage of his enhanced position and his genuine popularity in the country, Daladier would attempt to form a 'real' National Government; but soon after his return to Paris the Right-Wing influences again began to make themselves felt. Besides, internal problems soon became confused as a result of the *débâcle* of Catalonia. It came as an unpleasant reminder that the 'defence of the Empire and the Empire routes' was not perhaps as simple a matter as some of the North African speeches had suggested.

The Italian authorities were certainly angry with the French as a result of M. Daladier's successful tour, and stopped even distinguishing between the pro-Fascist and anti-Fascist among the French. So much so that M. Tharaud, the pro-Fascist writer, was arrested at Genoa on January 5 and sent back to France just as he was going to board an aeroplane on his way to Jibuti.

Nevertheless, the success of the voyage was not without some effect in Italy. Although the *Tevere* 'spat' on France, the *Telegrafo Fascista* of Leghorn, belonging to the Ciano family, though fulminating as much as ever against France, said on January 4 that—

> although circumstances may arise in which the claims to Corsica, Tunis and Jibuti may have to be 'soft-pedalled' for a time, this will not, however, mean that these claims have disappeared from the tenacious memory of the Italians.

Although this sounded like an Italian climb-down, the abuse in the Italian Press went on as strong as ever.

But it was significant that even so semi-official a paper as the *Petit Parisien* should have given the greatest prominence on its front page to the famous *Tevere* article 'We spit on France.' France was no longer frightened. And M. Bailby boldly addressed his condolences to Mussolini on having such a stupid son-in-law, without whose clumsy indiscretion M. Daladier would not have gone on his triumphal tour—a tour which had made France 'Empire-conscious.'

That sounded very good: and the Munichois did not fail to interpret it as the crowning achievement of their policy: had not M. Flandin proclaimed long before that France should be 'an Empire Power rather than a European Power'? Only—in the last resort, the security of the Empire still depended on three things: (1) no German hegemony in Europe, and (2) no German support of Italy's claims, and (3) no extension of the Berlin-Rome Axis to Spain.

· · · · · · ·

Barely a couple of days after M. Daladier's return to Paris this last point was going to become a question of the most immediate importance. M. Daladier returned on January 6, and on January 8 Mr. Chamberlain and Lord Halifax left for Rome, and, on their way they stopped in Paris for a cup of tea. The tea party took place in M. Bonnet's study at the Quai d'Orsay. It will be remembered that the Montecitorio demonstration took place exactly two days after Mr. Chamberlain's visit to Rome had been announced; which showed that the Italians were preparing the ground for a 'Chamberlain mediation' to their own advantage and at France's expense. But at the end of December the French Government officially requested Mr. Chamberlain not to attempt any 'mediating' between France and Italy during his visit to Rome. Apparently rather reluctantly, Mr. Chamberlain agreed; and he confirmed this promise to the French Ministers during his tea party at the Quai d'Orsay on January 10.

The Rome visit was a remarkable failure; since Mr. Chamberlain could not commit himself to 'mediating' a settlement with the French, the visit was of little interest to the Italians. Mussolini assured him that he would withdraw his troops from Spain 'after the final Franco victory' —but that was about all.

Lord Halifax had gone to Geneva, and there he saw M. Bonnet. According to reliable accounts, Lord Halifax was greatly dissatisfied with the Rome visit, and gave M. Bonnet a gloomy view of the future prospects of 'co-operation' with Italy. But being as devoted as ever to 'appeasement,' M. Bonnet, in receiving the French Press at Geneva that night, gave them a rather rosy version of what Lord Halifax had told him.

· · · · · · ·

The Spanish tragedy was, in the meantime, moving to its close. On January 11, Franco's troops were within fifteen miles of Tarragona. A few days later Tarragona fell. By January 22 Barcelona was in sight. Within thirty-six hours the hungry city was bombed nineteen times. How was the French Government reacting to Franco's advance?

It started with a rather nasty bit of hypocrisy. On January 10—it was the day of the Chamberlain tea party—it was solemnly announced at the Quai d'Orsay that on the initiative of M. Bonnet (the point was strongly emphasized) the French Government had, at its meeting that morning decided to send 45,000 tons of French flour to the Spanish Government —'a purely commercial transaction,' it was explained, 'fully compatible with the non-intervention agreement and answering the elementary demands of humanity.'

That was on January 10; and one may say at once that on January 24 —two days before the fall of Barcelona—700 tons out of the 45,000 had left for Spain. Señor Pascua, the Spanish Ambassador in Paris, remarked bitterly that these bags of flour were 'tied up with red tape.'

Certainly M. Bonnet had no desire to see the Spanish Government win, or even prolong their resistance.

The position of M. Daladier was rather less clear. On Saturday, January 14, he received two visits; one from M. Blum, the other from the British Ambassador. M. Blum pleaded for the Spanish Government, and said that France would be in grave danger if Franco was allowed to win with Italian and German help: could not an eleventh-hour attempt be made to save the Spanish Government? M. Daladier who had, a week earlier, returned from Algeria, and who was full of ideas on the Empire and on Empire Routes, was much perturbed; and Blum left with the impression that Daladier had made up his mind to do something to help the Spanish Government. And, for a day or two afterwards, it was whispered in the Chamber lobbies—perhaps simply in order to keep the Left quiet—that 'two munition trains had left Toulouse for Catalonia last night.'

But on that same Saturday M. Daladier also received a visit from Sir Eric Phipps, who had seen Mr. Chamberlain that morning on his home journey from Rome. That night Havas published the following highly significant statement:

After seeing Mr. Chamberlain the British Ambassador gave M. Daladier an account of the Prime Minister's impressions of his Rome visit. He emphasized particularly the repeated assurances that Signor Mussolini gave Mr. Chamberlain of his intention to withdraw the Italian forces now in Spain, in the Balearics, and in other Spanish territories after the final victory of General Franco.

The emphasis placed on these assurances left little doubt that Mr. Chamberlain was desiring a rapid Franco victory and was hoping that nothing would be done by the French to delay it.

But M. Daladier was wobbling. On the following day, January 15, the *petit congrès* of the Radical Party met; and the majority of the delegates were greatly alarmed and excited about Spain. The mention of M. Bonnet—who was at Geneva at the time—was booed; and the thousand delegates cheered unanimously when Senator Berthod said:

> Last April Italy undertook not to keep any hold on Spain or on any Spanish possessions. Judging from the manner in which she has observed her other obligations we can only feel very anxious about the whole thing. For if Italy remains in possession of the Balearics on the main French sea route to North Africa, it will clearly mean the end of the French Colonial Empire.

M. Daladier himself did not touch on the Spanish problem in his speech before the Congress, but it was widely assumed that he had, in advance, given his approval to Senator Berthod's speech.

It is curious that even the *Petit Parisien*, which had been consistently pro-Franco, should on January 16 have published a message from Rome admitting that

> in certain Fascist quarters the view is taken that after a Franco victory Italy's diplomatic position will be very much stronger for trying to achieve what is called in Rome 'the natural aspirations of the Italian people.'

London was apparently becoming alarmed by these signs of an 'evolution' of French opinion on the Spanish question. The *Agence Economique et Financière* reported from London on the same day that the Radical Congress had caused great excitement in 'responsible British quarters.'

And M. Bonnet and M. Flandin and the Right generally thought that it was high time to 'stop this nonsense'—all the more so as even on the Right there were men like M. Raymond Laurent, the Catholic deputy, who had recently come back from Barcelona, together with M. de Tessan and a number of other deputies, and had been giving highly favourable accounts of the tolerance and humanity of the Spanish Government. It may be added that among the French Catholics there were large sections who during 1937 and 1938 had developed an intense dislike of General Franco, and resented his pretensions to being the 'Soldier of Christ,' while allowing the German and Italian auxiliaries to bomb open towns and to machine-gun women and children. The two outstanding attacks on Franco from the Catholic side were made by M. Mauriac, in a memorable article in the *Figaro* in June 1938, and by M. Georges Bernanos in his magnificent piece of polemical writing—*Les Grands Cimetières sous la Lune.*

M. Bonnet hurried back from Geneva on Monday, January 16, and the 'reaction' against the mood shown by the Radical Congress started in full earnest. In fact, it was so complete that one has the suspicion that the demonstrations of righteousness at the Radical Congress were little more than a flash in the pan.

In the semi-official Press the 'solemn promise' given by Mussolini to Mr. Chamberlain that the Italians would clear out of Spain and the Balearics once the war was over was given the greatest prominence. The report, according to which Count Ciano said something that was very nearly the opposite, was dismissed as a fabrication. The fear of 'entanglements' in Spain and the fear of 'provoking' Italy and Germany and of offending Mr. Chamberlain were being cultivated to the utmost. At the same time happy visions were conjured up of the future co-operation between France and the new Spain. There was a sudden clamour for the sending of a diplomatic representative to Burgos.

At the same time appeals were made to instincts of decency and humanity—'it would be inhuman to prolong the war'—and the same old story was told over and over again that Spain would be Spanish and that the Spaniards would never be run by foreigners. In the Chamber lobbies it was whispered all over the place, 'Chamberlain is a wise bird. He has got his agreement with Franco in his pocket—so no wonder he does not want us to interfere.'

And in M. Bonnet's *entourage*, night after night they were producing stories of how the Spaniards loathed the Italians; how at Tarragona there were fearful rows between the two, and how Spanish women would empty their chamberpots on the Italian troops as they marched past. The effect of all this propaganda soon became very noticeable at the Chamber. Already on January 17—the second day of the foreign debate —the Chamber was in a completely unheroic mood; and seemed to be only too glad to take the line of least resistance. Thus, M. Flandin's speech on Spain received much wider support than could have been expected a few days earlier. He was cheered by half the House—that half which formed part of M. Daladier's majority. It almost looked as though these people were lapping up gratefully the arguments with which he was supplying them for leaving the Spanish Government to its fate.

M. Blum, who attacked M. Flandin with unusual vigour and charged him with hypocrisy, was loudly cheered by the Socialists and Communists and by about half the Radicals. But the other half of the Radicals seemed unimpressed. It was an altogether different reaction from that of the Radical rank-and-file at the Radical Conference two days earlier.

M. Flandin's great argument was that 'non-intervention' as he understood it, was something quite different from what some people imagined it to be. 'If we have agreed to non-intervention,' he said in effect, 'it means that we will not intervene even if the others break their promise.'

M. Blum, intervening in the debate, said that he could not accept M. Flandin's way of reasoning. The purpose of the Non-Intervention Agreement was to prevent all Powers from taking part in the Spanish war, and this agreement demanded reciprocity. Germany and Italy, in joining the agreement, had given a definite pledge to England and France. How could France look on complacently now that the pledges made to her and to England were being grossly violated?

M. Flandin, speaking almost like an Italian newspaper, said that M. Blum had not himself observed non-intervention as pedantically as all that, and he remarked that in March 1938, in particular (during the great Aragon offensive) M. Blum had 'relaxed' the frontier control and 30,000 tons of war material had reached Government Spain.

M. Flandin then returned to his 'moral' argument.

'If we send any munitions to Spain now,' he said, 'the Spaniards will be able to say, "Our fathers and brothers and sons have been killed by French shells." '

This 'moral' argument was reinforced by the 'intimation' argument:

'If you thought that Italian intervention in Spain could damage France's vital interests, why did you tolerate it for two years? Why are you choosing this moment for putting an end to non-intervention, —the very moment when we have been solemnly warned that French intervention would lead to a general war?'

Once France started sending armaments to Spain, he continued, there would be no end to it. Sooner or later she would have to send troops as well (an argument suggesting that Italy's resources were inexhaustible).

These arguments, providing *an easy 'moral' case for doing nothing*, carried the day—all the more so as, in London, Mr. Chamberlain was taking exactly the same line.

On that same day, January 18, the French Cabinet met and decided to stick to 'non-intervention.' As *Paris-Soir* put it, the policy of the Government would consist of 'neutrality in the affairs of Spain but vigilant defence of the Empire and of the Empire communications.'

There were some people who felt that this might be a little easier if only instead of taking Mussolini at his word, Mr. Chamberlain had asked for certain guarantees—for instance, an international occupation of the Balearic Islands, for without such a precaution anything might happen to France's 'Empire communications.'

It was a curious debate. It began on January 13, and went on for six whole sittings until January 26. In fact, apart from Spain, the whole dispute between the *Munichois* and the *anti-Munichois* was exhausted on the very first day. The *Munichois* speaker was M. Montigny, M. Caillaux's henchman; and his ideas—as M. de Kerillis later said— were, in effect, the ideas of M. Bonnet.

M. Montigny's main argument was that while as a result of Munich, and especially as a result of Italy's hostility, France was no longer able to conduct a big European policy, she was together with England, invincible in a defensive war.

It is an argument which may be questioned. As M. Paul Reynaud said in the famous foreign debate in February 1938: 'No line of fortifications can hold out indefinitely against an indefinite accumulation of guns and tanks'—not to mention the various ways of turning the Maginot Line.

But the invincibility of France in defensive war was the corner-stone of M. Montigny's argument. Nevertheless, he betrayed some uneasiness, for instance, when he said that 'the pro-Munich people would never accept a form of German hegemony which would mean the vassalization of France.'

He also denounced German propaganda in Alsace, which he said must be stamped out—another remark pointing to some doubts about the real value of the Franco-German 'no war' declaration.

M. Montigny said that the Italian people did not want war with France, and he expressed the hope that for this reason Italy's claims would in due course, once normal relations had been re-established between France and Italy, be examined firmly and calmly.

As regards France's Eastern alliances, M. Montigny thought that these no longer counted for much, since the League Covenant, with which they were linked, had become a dead letter.

In reply, M. de Kerillis, the great *anti-Munichois*, recalled all the disturbing things that had already happened since Munich—Hitler's speech at Saarbrücken in which he vetoed Mr. Churchill and Mr. Eden, so intervening in British home affairs; the Italian campaign against France; the pogroms in Germany; the manœuvres in favour of an independent Ukraine, and so on. If this sort of thing continued,

324

he said, France would be left alone in Europe 'with no ally except a soldierless England.' That, he said, was the policy of the present Government.

An alternative policy was to agree right away to become a vassal of Germany—such a solution had at least the advantage of avoiding war.

Finally there was the policy of bringing all the nations threatened with German aggression together, for only such a coalition could prevent Germany from destroying the nations of Europe one by one. He went on:

Without Eastern alliances there can be no balance of power in Europe. The Russian alliance remains a necessity. It was hoped after Munich that M. Bonnet would go, like M. Barthou in 1934, on a European tour. He did not. King Carol and the Regent Paul came to Paris instead and went back in a state of discouragement.

M. Bonnet, interrupting, said that, on the contrary, they went back in full agreement with the French Government.

M. de Kerillis then said that Colonel Beck, the Polish Foreign Minister, had been cold-shouldered. He was recently in the South of France but he was not invited to Paris; he was instead invited to Berchtesgaden.

Hitler's ambitions were unlimited. The only question was whether he would first go east or west. It was no longer certain that he would go east, for he was doing his best to neutralize the east through Colonel Beck.

'Germany will never fight a European coalition again,' M. de Kerillis said. 'Hitler has said so. Therefore the only way of preventing war is to create such a coalition.'

M. Bonnet was going to speak—but it was always 'at the next sitting.' His speech was announced four times; it was not until January 26 that he spoke. It was the day on which Barcelona had fallen. It was the *fait accompli* for which he had been waiting for a fortnight: it was no longer any use discussing the pros and cons of sending help to the Spanish Government.

On the previous night I saw Del Vayo off at the Gare d'Orsay. He was going back to Barcelona. 'Come and see me soon in Barcelona,' he said with a false note of bravado in his voice. He got no farther than Figueras. The game was up. Most of the other passengers on the train were going to the winter sports with their skis.

     •   •   •   •   •   •   •

On the day Barcelona fell, most of the people at the Chamber looked rather miserable and bewildered. Even the Right looked puzzled: for while Franco's Spanish and Italian troops were marching into Barcelona, Mussolini was addressing a crowd of 40,000 outside the Palazzo Venezia, on 'the splendid victory of Barcelona'; and the crowds shouted: 'Tunis!' 'Corsica!' and 'To Paris!' That afternoon Bonnet made a completely empty speech.

He said that France had done everything to make friends with Italy. He praised Mr. Chamberlain and Lord Halifax and repeated Mussolini's pledge to the British Premier. France, he said, would maintain intact her sovereignty and her territory everywhere. He even added that the undertakings connecting France with Poland and Russia remained fully in force. France was doing all she could for the refugees; no country had done more for refugees. France would not allow any of her interests to be harmed in the Far East, and she ardently desired to see peace restored in Spain.

M. Bonnet criticized those French journalists who had attacked him and said that the Communists wanted France to 'intervene everywhere —in China, in Spain, in Central Europe.' This remark created an uproar which lasted nearly half an hour, the Communists shouting all kinds of insulting remarks at M. Bonnet and demanding that he should 'produce a text.'

In the end M. Bonnet was able to complete his speech. The radiance of France's prestige, he said, was now as great as ever, and if anybody counted on France's decadence he was preparing for a rude disappointment.

Daladier's speech was of a different order. He spoke with great emotion, suggesting that in the coming year France would have some very dangerous corners to turn. While accepting the idea, put forward by M. Blum, for an international conference—that is, something different from Munich—he declared that nothing would be given away under the threat of force: 'Not an acre of our territory, and not a single one of our rights.'

A notable passage in his speech was that in which he paid a warm tribute to the Italian people, and protested against flippant remarks in various papers to the effect that the Italians were not soldiers. His speech ended on a tragic note—so tragic that many listeners wondered whether M. Daladier was not taking the blackest possible view of the developments in the days to come.

It was noticed that while M. Bonnet said that not an inch of territory would be given away, M. Daladier added 'and not a single one of our rights.' One rejected merely Italy's territorial claims, the other both her territorial and her 'non-territorial' claims.

· · · · · · ·

326

Why was Daladier's speech so strikingly tragic in tone? Why did he speak of 'the hard and heavy task that lies ahead'? Why did he say: 'A free nation cannot argue over the sacrifice to be made if this sacrifice is indispensable to the maintenance of its dignity and independence'?

Was he overdramatizing the situation? On the following day, the *Homme Libre*, the mouthpiece of M. Bonnet, began its leading article with a veiled criticism of Daladier:

> M. Bonnet defined French foreign policy yesterday. There are moments in the life of a great nation when it is best to avoid fireworks and empty phrases and grandiloquent perorations and when it is best to be like a meticulous accountant carefully adding up all the facts of a given situation.

But did not M. Daladier know of something which he did not wish to disclose openly, but which had deeply disturbed him?

The Diplomatic Correspondent of the *Manchester Guardian* wrote on January 27, reporting German troop movements and the danger of a German attack on either Holland or Switzerland. And during the days that followed the atmosphere in Paris was an 'alarmist' one; and it was not until January 30, when Hitler 'merely' demanded colonies, that Paris heaved a sigh of relief. As a Frenchman remarked to me that day: 'We are all so scared of Hitler that if he does not conclude his speech with the words: "And now, fellow-Germans, my bombers are on their way to London and Paris," we consider it a "moderate" speech.' But the causes for immediate anxiety were still there. During those first days of February the general public was not aware of any serious danger; but President Roosevelt knew that the Germans were preparing a *coup*—possibly against Holland; and his famous statement before the Military Committee of the Senate was calculated to be a warning to Germany. 'Our first line of defence is France.' It was believed that the 'leakage' of the Roosevelt statement was deliberate. Mr. Chamberlain, a few days later—on February 6—added his own warning; it was calculated to discourage Italy's belief that England would not support France were Italy to attack her in the Mediterranean and North Africa. This warning was repeated by Lord Halifax on the 23rd of February.

· · · · · · ·

In the meantime General Franco had practically won the war, and France hastened to apply 'appeasement' to Spain.

Franco's victory was hailed with loud cries of joy from all the Right papers. How they revelled in the '*débâcle des rouges.*' How they poured buckets of mud over the vanquished Republican army—vanquished by hunger and 'non-intervention.'

And when the French Government decided that it could not, after all, drive back the retreating army with machine-gun fire, and allowed the 170,000 women and children and the 270,000 soldiers and civilians to enter France, with what howls of rage they were greeted by *Gringoire* and the rest. *Gringoire* published a loathsome drawing of a burglar and murderer, with a large bag of stolen art and church treasures on his back, entering France, and saying: 'I'll find plenty of work here.' *Le Jour* wrote—'Will France open her door wide to the murderers?'

And the foulest phrase of all was produced by the *Matin* which said that France must not allow herself to be 'blackmailed with pity' (*le chantage à la pitié*). But I shall say no more. Nor shall I attempt to describe the sufferings of these hundreds of thousands of refugees. The first few weeks at Argelès and St. Cyprien were hell. But the French have perhaps been blamed unduly for this. It was a stupendous problem to receive nearly half a million people within a few days. Many died for want of care. Thousands lived for weeks in conditions of incredible filth. At first there were no shelters—they dug holes in the wet, filthy sand, and slept there. But there were many French doctors and nurses and many other people; yes—mainly *le peuple*—who did for the refugees a thousand little acts of kindness. Also some of the *gardes mobiles*—not all, but many. The refugees were not all good soldiers; among 300,000 people one gets every kind of people—'heroes and jailbirds, and poor bewildered peasants, and hungry women and children and many wounded with fearful wounds and gangrenous limbs,' as M. Sarraut was to say at the Chamber on March 14. People of every kind—good, bad and indifferent. An ocean of suffering.

.   .   .   .

The French Government felt that they ought to be got rid of as quickly as possible. Repatriation was the word. One had to make sure that Franco took them back without delay. Except those who might be shot. Only what was the criterion? France and England hoped that Franco would grant a generous amnesty. It would have solved an immense problem for the French. But nothing could be extracted from Franco. 'How many can *not* go back?' M. Sarraut asked on March 14. And he added: 'I haven't the slightest idea at present.'

The Right, fully supported by M. Bonnet, clamoured for the immediate recognition of Franco. Well, obviously, since France and England had done so much to secure his victory, it was little use not recognizing him now. Only it was foolish to imagine that they could now lay down conditions. They still had the idea that Franco would 'need money,' and so would eat out of their hands. But when M. Bérard went to Burgos he at once found that there was no great *empressement*. M. Bérard was an aged senator, a former wit and boulevardier, a great admirer of General Franco, and an intimate friend of M. Laval's. He had a very long nose, and one paper published a cartoon showing Bérard and Bonnet touching noses—an *arc de triomphe* through which Franco walked. Bérard went twice to Burgos; but Franco was not available. Each time he was received by General Jordana, Franco's Foreign Minister. It was a great disappointment to the Right Press, who thought that a Franco-Bérard meeting could be produced as proof that their policy was right. According to Havas from Burgos, Bérard's last meeting with General Jordana 'was not merely cordial, it was affectionate. General Franco's Foreign Minister shook him by both hands, and said how glad he was to have negotiated with him a settlement of such vital importance.'

It may be said that this settlement provided neither for an amnesty nor for any 'moral' undertaking of neutrality; nor even for the withdrawal of the Italians. The French, as far as one could see, got nothing. But the Spaniards, according to the Burgos version of the agreement, were promised not only the return to Spain of all the war material brought to France by the Republicans; but also the £7,500,000 of gold which had been denied the Republican Government some months before, besides all the other Spanish property in France. When M. Bérard returned from his first visit to Burgos, it was suggested in responsible French quarters that the armaments (including fifty up-to-date aeroplanes) and the gold would be used for paying for the refugees. But the Burgos version of the agreement said nothing about this; and at the French Cabinet meeting, on February 27, M. Daladier refused to give any information on the contents of the Bérard-Jordana agreements.

The truth is that the French Government decided to recognize Franco unconditionally. No arrangement was reached even about the return of the refugees. M. Sarraut and his paper, the *Dépêche de Toulouse*, had protested against such unconditional recognition; for at Toulouse they were worried at the thought of living next to the 'third hostile frontier.' But Bonnet's advice prevailed.

Daladier got over the difficulty very nicely. On February 24, at the Chamber, Daladier announced that he was determined to recognize Franco precisely *because* he did not wish his 'third frontier' to be hostile. And when the Cabinet met three days later to approve the recognition of Franco, M. Sarraut said no more. In any case, what more could he say? Amid a storm of applause from the Right and Centre and part of the Radicals, the Chamber had ratified the recognition in advance by 323 votes to 261. In the *Populaire* Blum burst into lamentations: 'To think that the Front Populaire Chamber of 1936 could have done *this*!' But it was a groan rather than an argument. One need hardly add that the Government partly justified its decision by saying that the British Government had no intention of delaying the recognition; while Mr. Chamberlain said, in effect, a few days later: 'We didn't start it; it was the French.' The truth is that Daladier read into the British communication of February 22—to which Daladier referred in his speech—precisely what he wanted to read into it—and what Mr. Chamberlain had wanted him to read into it.

·　·　·　·　·　·　·

A few days after the recognition of Franco, Bonnet was reported to have told to the Foreign Affairs Committee of the Chamber a cheerful story to the effect that at the Barcelona parade Franco said to the Italian commander as the Italian troops were marching past: 'I'd like you to regard this magnificent parade as a farewell revue in your honour.' The story naturally got into the Press, and made first-rate pro-Franco stuff —and most cheering news. But at 1 a.m. the Quai d'Orsay issued a statement saying that 'only the official *communiqué* of the Foreign Affairs Committee must be regarded as accurate.' Which had the advantage of allowing the Barcelona story to get about, yet without engaging anybody's responsibility.

The French Government had in the meantime taken a bold step. 'A stroke of genius,' some said when they heard that Daladier had appointed Marshal Pétain Ambassador to Burgos, the Hero of Verdun, a national figure if ever there was one. It was a little as if Chamberlain had sent to Burgos a member of the Royal Family. Many felt it was much too great an honour to render to Franco. But in official quarters they said: 'It's got nothing to do with Franco. It's in order to foil the Germans.' It wasn't quite clear *why* this was going to foil the Germans; but it sounded very Machiavellian.

But the Spanish response to this unprecedented honour was not brilliant. The person sent to Paris was a Senor Lequerica—nothing more than the Mayor of Bilbao; and worse still, alleged to have been associated for a long time with the *ABC*, a Madrid paper noted for its violently pro-German and anti-French sentiments. It is true, that Lequerica had treated Bérard to lunch during his first journey to Burgos; an important fact which the *Jour* produced as though it were positive proof that Lequerica was *un ami de la France.*

A few days after the 15th of March, the extraordinary piece of news reached Paris, namely, that Marshal Pétain had been for a week at San Sebastian but had been unable to travel to Burgos 'owing to a snowstorm' (in Spain and in March!). According to a less official version, General Franco was refusing to see the Hero of Verdun so long as the Republican fleet, which, after the Casado *coup* on March 5 had sailed from Cartagena and was interned at Bizerta, was not returned immediately to General Franco. It was a national affront if ever there was one. Franco refusing to see Pétain! Was the French Government going to recall Pétain? No. It decided to hand over the fleet.

. . . .

During that first fortnight in March optimism was running high in both Paris and London. Franco was not perhaps as appreciative as he might have been, after England had conquered Minorca for him and France had sent him Pétain; but it was thought that he 'would be all right in time—he had to keep up appearances with regard to his allies, and not sound ungrateful so soon—but he would soon want some money.'

And Poland and Rumania seemed quite energetic. The Poles were showing a renewed interest in the French alliance and the Polish Army was said to be splendid. And King Carol was full of energy; Codreanu was dead; and Calinescu was the worst enemy of the Nazis. The Italian claims on France could be ignored. Chamberlain was behind France; and Daladier had told Italy to go to hell. The Italians would, it was thought, be only too pleased if they got the shares of the Jibuti Railway—something to show for their efforts—but if they wanted them, they must ask for them politely, the French said. And Cardinal Pacelli had been elected Pope—what a biff in the eye for Hitler and Mussolini! the optimists said. And beyond the sea, Mr. Roosevelt had uttered his grave warning.

Optimism was running high. There was no spot in Europe, it seemed, at which Hitler or Mussolini could strike with impunity. Even the Hungarians had gone anti-Nazi. Even the anti-Munich *Aube* thought that France and England were 'turning out to be luckier than they deserved to be.'

It seemed to have occurred to nobody that Hitler might strike at— Czechoslovakia. Poor Czechoslovakia! She had been forgotten. It was, somehow, assumed that she was now a vassal of Germany, and of no importance any longer. The Czechs were being *so* tactful, trying not to do anything to offend Germany. Moreover, had not Hitler said at the Sportspalast, on September 28: 'I don't want any Czechs'?

Had everybody forgotten the Bohemian Bastion? Had everybody forgotten that it was not an end but a means—that bastion which, in September, it was such 'bad style' to mention. M. Bonnet knew, on March 11, what was coming. And yet, on March 14, in the *Homme Libre*, the organ of the French Foreign Minister, the unspeakable M. Thouvenin in an article entitled *Fausse Alerte!* thundered against the 'lies' in the British Press about the strange things that were happening in Slovakia.

> Some day it will become necessary to discover who the people are who are deliberately spreading these mischievous stories—and why they are doing it. . . .

And he added that the 'reassuring news' from Slovakia was 'the best justification of the Munich policy'! And then came March 15. The Great Lie of Munich was in ruins. The policy of Appeasement, of Peace in Our Time, was shown up. That policy which was a blend of well-meaning British gullibility and French *facilité*—and some worse things.

. . . .

March 15 was a rude awakening for France. In the days that followed it was clear that Mitteleuropa—and more than Mitteleuropa—was coming into being. Wherever the victorious German armies went without firing a shot, they brought with them the gospel of the Concentration Camp.

And yet the reaction in England was sharper than in France. When Lord Halifax proposed the peace front, French official quarters were polite about it at first; but the old pro-Munich Press soon began to pooh-pooh it—'That's all very well, *but not with the Soviets!*'

The first reaction to the Prague *coup* of M. Bressy, Bonnet's right-hand man, was to say rather cynically, '*Ça vous étonne?* It is, after all, only a consequence of the blunders made in 1919.'

As for M. Daladier's first reaction, it was to ask Parliament for plenary powers 'for the defence of the country.' *Pleins pouvoirs*—and completely unlimited. The Left, including a number of Radicals, tried to argue: 'Will these powers apply to the freedom of the Press? Will they enable the Government to put Parliament in cold storage, not merely for eight months but for years?' M. Daladier refused all explanations. He dismissed all objections as 'byzantinism.' 'You will go on with your hair-splitting discussions even with the enemy at the gates.' And M. Daladier added contemptuously: 'This is not a time for words; it is

a time for action. Democracy must cease to be a régime of contradictions'
—a strange phrase singularly reminiscent of certain totalitarian formulæ.
And he said that he could not attach as much importance to parliamentary speeches as to the words that reached him 'from the very bowels
of the country'—which was, in effect, a reference to his fan-mail—a fanmail which, for some time, Daladier had come to consider as the best
barometer of what the country felt and thought.

Parliament gave way; it was no use risking a Cabinet crisis at a time
like that. The Chamber passed the unlimited plenary powers, valid until
November 30, by a small majority; while the Senate passed it by a large
majority. M. Daladier had refused to commit himself to any interpretation of his plenary powers; and all the Senate could do was to explain
unilaterally, through M. Caillaux and M. Gardey, the spirit in which it
was granting M. Daladier these powers. In the course of these discussions hardly any reference was made to Czechoslovakia. Only on the
second day did M. Daladier express his sympathy for the Czech people.
As for M. Bonnet, he remained silent; he sat on the Government bench,
with his thin lips tightly shut, and with a cold, lizard-like look on his
face. Like a lizard expecting to be attacked.

Prague—German trade agreement with Rumania—Memel—all within
a few days; and what more was in store? London was active. Mr. Chamberlain proclaimed the British guarantee to Poland: late, terribly late,
the man who had given the League its *coup de grâce* in dismissing
Eden was becoming converted to collective security. Hitler had said he
would not allow Germany to fight on two fronts again. Poland was to
become the Second Front. But Russia? How much was Poland worth
without Russia? Mr. Lloyd George stressed the point and questioned
the value of the Anglo-Polish Pact, with Russia's position remaining uncertain for a number of reasons. For, obviously, Russia alone could give
Poland direct and immediate help.

Mr. Chamberlain guaranteed Poland not only in the name of England, but also in the name of France. In the Chamber lobbies that day
people looked a little scared—what if it was going to provoke Germany
and precipitate a world war? 'What if they are going to bomb Warsaw
to-night?' they asked. Kerillis alone was delighted. '*Votre pays est
épatant!* The guarantee to Poland is going to save peace. And even if it
does not, the Germans will be beaten!' But strangely enough, the French
Government said nothing. It had allowed Chamberlain to commit the
whole French nation; but neither M. Daladier nor M. Bonnet made a
single public utterance on the subject. More than that—in the days that
followed, M. Bonnet's paper, the *Homme Libre*, at first refrained from

333

making any comment whatsoever; but then it came out with a long article demanding British conscription: not only, it said, was it impossible for France and England to pursue a big European policy with nothing on land except the French Army; but it was not even certain that France could hold out indefinitely against the onslaught of the German and Italian armies, three times more numerous than the French. The Germans, it said, could not, economically, afford to fight a long war; their only chance was a rapid victory. As at Verdun, they would try to break through at any price. And what if they launched against some new Verdun three or four or ten times as many men as they had hurled against the old Verdun? Could France hold out without important land reinforcements from England?

There was some truth in it. And it expressed a feeling which was shared by the large majority of Frenchmen—who thought that it was not fair that the French should have to do all this dirty work. Only, this British Conscription propaganda also had a slightly nasty aspect—it was like the last kick of the retrenchment policy. But what was much worse, the *Homme Libre* also proceeded to print ultra-pacifist articles by M. Compère Morel, saying that 'we must not oppose force by force,' and proposing mere economic pressure on Germany in the event of an attack on Poland! Daladier, however, was not in agreement with all this.

On March 29 Daladier answered Mussolini's speech of March 26. He was firm, but left the door open to negotiations on Jibuti, the Suez Canal, etc. But it was too late. For after Italy had been allowed to gain control of Spain, she could, clearly, no longer be bought off with little concessions like that. She was now completely tied to the Axis. No retreat seemed possible now. As Michelet had said of Napoleon—'*C'était la fuite en avant.*' Whether she liked it or not, Italy was now Germany's prisoner. And she seemed to like it; for she felt that she was backing the winner.

The map of Europe early in April could hardly bear looking at. Italy established in Albania—threatening to cause endless trouble in the Balkans; Jugoslavia caught between Germany and Italy; the Balkan entente in danger of collapse; Germany spread beyond the Carpathians, and with Hungary as her vassal; Rumania in a legitimate state of jitters; Poland strategically weakened through Germany's conquest of Czechoslovakia and through her stranglehold on Lithuania after the capture of Memel; Holland and Denmark and even Switzerland in danger of a lightning invasion; Spain hostile to England and to France.

·   ·   ·   ·   ·   ·   ·

But Britain was beginning to wake up. With an energy that created a profound impression on French opinion, Mr. Chamberlain and Lord Halifax proceeded to build up a vast Peace *bloc* in Europe. Daladier, never at heart a Munichois, and in whose hands the most vital decisions of foreign policy now rested, followed wholeheartedly. Defeatism seemed to be played out. French opinion, so divided at the time of Munich, now realized that there was no other way.

If the Peace *bloc* complete with Russia, and with the support of the Democracies implied in Mr. Roosevelt's great message of April 15, could be built up in good time, peace, it seemed, might yet be saved—and, what is more, an honourable peace. The smaller nations of Europe, so bitterly disappointed in England and France, were now ready to resist; all they wanted to know was whether England and France were this time really in earnest. They seemed to be. Especially after France had gradually mobilized nearly a million men by the middle of April, and Britain had sent her fleet into the Mediterranean, and had introduced conscription.

And on April 21 M. Paul Reynaud was able to declare on the wireless, and this time on behalf of the French Government, that 'the phantom of the *repliement impérial* had vanished' and that France 'had not abdicated in Europe.'

Only it was late—terribly late. Russia had been cold-shouldered for the last four years, and had lost faith in a fruitful alliance with France and Britain—and in their genuine desire for it. Litvinov was succeeded by Molotov. The *Action Française* joyfully gloated over the idea that Litvinov was now going to be 'bumped off.'

The *Angriff* wrote in the same vein.

EPILOGUE

I. THE SEEDS OF VICHY

S UCH is the story of France till the summer of 1939. Once the Germans had started their propaganda campaign against Poland, war had become almost a certainty. It was doubtful that the British guarantee to Poland would stop it. What, one felt, might still stop it would be an alliance with Russia; but after the manner in which Britain and France had ignored all her advances, the chances for such an alliance seemed none too good. The dismissal of Litvinov in May 1939 spelled alarm among those who still believed that war might be averted.

The summer of 1939 was one of tension. Many people in Paris took their holidays early that year—in June, or July. On September 1 the expected happened. Germany attacked Poland.

Then, after eight months of the 'phoney war,' France herself was overrun; and for nearly two years now she has been partly under German occupation, partly under the rule of Vichy.

What happened? Perhaps it is useful to recall some of the major developments of the last six or seven years of the Third Republic, as related in this book.

＊　　＊　　＊　　＊　　＊　　＊　　＊

To say that the collapse was the work of a small Fascist clique who betrayed France and her people would be an exaggeration. To say that the Fifth Column and the Fascist clique prepared France psychologically for the collapse, and then took advantage of it would be nearer the truth, but it would not be a full explanation either. The causes of the collapse are numerous, and not all apparent. The French people themselves are partly responsible for what happened; and not only the leaders.

Vichy is the ultimate crystallization—a crystallization brought on by disaster—of many things in the past with which close observers of France have been familiar for a long time. The Third Republic which was born at Sedan in 1870 was also mortally wounded at Sedan in 1940, and died a month later.

Perhaps the primary cause of it all was the war-weariness of the French people; that war-weariness which resulted from the fearful blood-bath of 1914-18, when France lost nearly 1,500,000 of her men. The

337

thought of another war continued to fill French hearts with profound dread. The pacifism of France, of the French people, was such that it often smothered their old instinct of national self-preservation. As the power of Nazi Germany grew, the pacifism of France became, if anything, increasingly acute.

In 1936 Goebbels boasted with impunity: 'If we had been in the position of the French, and they had put a Hitler in power, we should have made war on them.' But no suggestion of a preventive war could have received the slightest support from the French people. The opposition to preventive war against Nazi Germany was quite independent of any political or juridical scruples.

From 1933 to almost 1939 Hitler had no great difficulty in persuading the French people that he wished them no harm. Of course they did not really believe him when he promised them eternal peace; but they did believe that he had no intention of attacking France in the near future. The most blatant example of France's loss of her instinct of self-preservation was her failure to react to the German re-occupation of the Rhineland. This does not excuse the utter blindness of the British Government and of British opinion to the significance of the Rhineland *coup* of March 1936; but the fact remains that the French people themselves were unwilling to consider its full implications.

Munich was another example. The French had a solemn treaty of alliance with the Czechs; yet they felt fewer scruples about letting the Czechs down than we did, who had given them no solemn undertakings. In the light of the collapse of France, the story of the Czech crisis makes very illuminating reading to-day. All the seeds of the present collapse were already there: the pacifism of provincial France; the pandering to Hitler among certain French politicians; the 'anything rather than war' propaganda in the Press; the widespread conviction that France was not equal to fighting Nazi Germany; the thought that *la jeunesse française* must be saved from war, if France was to survive at all; the agitation to the effect that England, though full of righteous indignation, was unprepared to fight—except 'to the last French soldier.'

· · · · · · ·

The building of a vast system of frontier defences, later to be known as the Maginot Line, began in 1928. The decision was, in itself, a confession of weakness; and a manifestation of the French dread of another invasion. France's whole war machine was in fact, defensive, and not offensive. But it was a point which could still be argued so long as the Rhineland was demilitarized; the French Army, it seemed, was still

338

capable of striking at Germany's vulnerable Western flank if Germany attacked any of France's eastern allies. But the Rhineland *coup* was, in reality, the knock-out blow to France's system of alliances. In *The Destiny of France*, a book I wrote in 1936, I suggested that the day France acquiesced in Hitler's occupation of the Rhineland she condemned herself to the position of a second-class power in Europe. This was perhaps putting it a little crudely; but the idea was clear. M. Crû, the London correspondent of the *Temps*, in reviewing my book, got very angry, and said that the British public would not be 'taken in by such nonsense,' which, he said, reminded him of the nonsense in the German Press before 1914 which used to treat the French as a degenerate people.

Yet, as Delbos was to discover in December 1937, the authority of France had, since the Rhineland *coup*, declined in a terrifying manner. There was a growing conviction in Eastern Europe that France, encouraged in this by certain currents of opinion in Great Britain, would fight only if she were directly attacked: a view which was strongly to be confirmed at the time of the Czech crisis.

. . . .

One of the chief reasons given by many leading French politicians at the time of Munich for not fighting for Czechoslovakia was that France *could not* fight, because her armed strength was inadequate. It was a good excuse, rather than a reason. It is true that while Germany had been building up and organizing her army and air force day and night since 1933, France's armaments production, especially after 1935, failed to increase in anything like the German proportion and actually severely declined in 1936, 1937 and 1938, especially in the all-important branch of aircraft.

. . . .

So here are three indirect and distant reasons why France was not well prepared for the war: (1) the long-standing dread of war among the French people; (2) the defensive nature of the French war machine, with the Maginot Line as its basis—and the consequent loss of all the Eastern allies, and (3) the inadequacy of equipment, particularly in the air—the result, partly, of routine methods among the French High Command, and partly, of the Front Populaire period which had the effect of severely lowering and disorganizing the output of armaments, especially in comparison with Germany.

The reluctance of the French people to go to war was thoroughly exploited by a group of politicians who, not many years after Hitler's advent to power, began to think of France in terms of a 'new European order.' M. Déat, M. Montagnon, M. Marquet and other Neo-Socialists were among the first to think in such terms as long ago as 1933, when they broke away from the Socialist Party, and proclaimed the new slogan: 'Order, Authority, Nation.' M. Montagnon used to go about the Chamber lobbies, proclaiming: *'Nous vivons en pleine période révolutionnaire.'* M. Montagnon lost his seat in the 1936 election, and was lost sight of for some time; but, oddly enough, he made his reappearance in April 1940 as the right-hand man of M. Frossard, the Minister of Information in the Reynaud Cabinet. M. Déat had, since 1933, distinguished himself as an ultra-pacifist on many occasions. His article, 'Die for Danzig,' published in the *Œuvre* in May 1939, created a great stir in France and produced an angry denunciation of M. Déat by M. Daladier, the Premier. M. Marquet, after a short spell of office under Doumergue in 1934, reappeared in the limelight again as Minister of the Interior in the Pétain Government which signed the Armistice. The Neo-Socialists had no great following either in 1933 or later; but they were a significant symptom of new ways of thinking—and on the Left at that.

· · · · · · ·

In 1933, the first year of Hitler, France still seemed an unshaken and unshakable democracy. Yet, even in 1933, apart from the split in the Socialist Party, there was at least one interesting 'New Order' development—a striking departure from the traditional foreign policy that France had pursued for many years past: and that was the acceptance 'in principle' by M. Daladier and M. Paul-Boncour, his Foreign Minister, of the Four-Power Pact, proposed by Mussolini, no doubt in agreement with Hitler. The idea was warmly supported by Mr. Ramsay MacDonald—who was over-impressed by Mussolini and his troops, and who really saw no harm in it. But it was more surprising that the French, who *should* have realized all the New-Order implications of the proposal, could have agreed to it. This acceptance badly shook France's allies in Eastern Europe, and even M. Barthou's earnest efforts a year later to convince the Poles that France could be trusted to pursue her traditional policy did not succeed. The Four-Power Pact was quashed by parliamentary opposition; but Daladier's and Paul-Boncour's first reaction to it suggested that something new was in process of development since Hitler's arrival at the Chancellery in Berlin. Later, Daladier still went on hoping for a direct Franco-German understanding.

· · · · · · ·

Now, the 6th of February, 1934, is a day which the *Action Française*, the various Fascist and semi-Fascist organizations in France who developed chiefly after that date, and the Neo-Socialists have often described as 'the beginning of a new French era.'

Some have dismissed it simply as *'un événement bien parisien,'* which provided the dynamic youth of the capital with a lot of rough fun; others have called it a 'Fascist conspiracy.' There was in it a little of both. A very high proportion of the 50,000 people who threw stones and iron bars at the police in the Place de la Concorde, though dissatisfied with the Government, had no clear idea of overthrowing the Republic, still less of setting up a Fascist dictatorship. But the people working and directing the 'military operations' behind the scenes had some rather clearer intentions.

Were there any schemes for setting up a new kind of government other than a plain National Government after the Poincaré model? The evidence shows that there were. A number of Right-wing politicians, both before and immediately after the 6th of February, indiscreetly spoke of setting up a government at the Hotel de Ville—'if the Daladier Government failed to resign.' Many people had a share in organizing the 6th of February. First, the *Action Française* leaders; then Chiappe, who was, among other things, doing his Corsican vendetta on Daladier; and a great many more. Chiappe was the chief of the *Gringoire* gang; his brother-in-law, Horace de Carbuccia, was the owner of that disastrous paper. When the Germans entered Paris, in June, they promptly accepted Chiappe as the virtual chief of the Paris town council, and are said to have shown him great courtesy and consideration.

While the riots were in progress outside, the Chamber went on with its stormy sitting, which continued to drag on, largely owing to the obstructionist tactics of the Right. The continued presence of the Deputies at the Chamber naturally added fuel to the furious flames of the riot outside. It is perhaps significant that the chief obstructionist at the Chamber was M. Henry-Haye, who in 1938 became an active member of that very peculiar organization, the *Comité France-Allemagne*, and who in 1940 was to be appointed Ambassador to Washington by the Pétain Government.

.   .   .   .

The Croix de Feu, whose development was one of the principal consequences of the 6th of February riots in 1935, claimed a membership of about two millions.

What exactly La Rocque's programme was would be hard to explain. The conception of the 'family' as an electoral and civic unit, was opposed to that of the 'citizen.' The 'corporatist' *motif* was inspired by the example of Italy, though otherwise the Croix de Feu denied being Fascists. Their 'corporatism' and their 'family' vote idea, however, implied a drastic revision of France's republican constitution; and both ideas have been adopted by the constitutional and trade union reformers of Vichy. The courtship of the peasantry, 'the backbone of France,' and of the small *bourgeoisie* as opposed to the 'Communist' working class, was also apparent in the Croix de Feu propaganda; though, like the Nazis before them, the Croix de Feu placed great store on the support they were supposed to be getting from a part of the working class.

La Rocque, however, was a cautious man, and the more extremist movements, such as the Cagoulards, and, to some extent, Doriot's *Parti Populaire Français*, were the outcome of the impatience existing among the more violent Croix de Feu men.

. . . .

Laval was in genuine sympathy with the Croix de Feu, whom he privately declared to be the 'finest element of France.' It was also in 1935 that Laval expressed his private belief that 'parliament could function only in normal times.' Laval, the ex-Socialist, was, indeed, a representative figure of the French *bourgeoisie*, perhaps the most fully representative figure, despite his plebeian origin, his Socialist past, and his lack of personal polish. Laval already then pursued a policy of appeasement towards Italy and Germany, and had no faith whatsoever in the League of Nations or in collective security. His hostility to England, though never openly expressed, was certainly real.

. . . .

But it is no use blaming Laval entirely for the Abyssinian fiasco. The Socialists and the Radicals—particularly Herriot, though a member of the Laval Cabinet—were violently hostile to Laval, both owing to his anti-British policy, and to the patronage he was giving to the Croix de Feu. But at heart neither the Radicals—who, after the fall of Sir Samuel Hoare, followed suit and broke up the Laval Cabinet—nor the Socialists were ready 'to go the whole hog for the Negus.' At heart, they felt it was most regrettable that the League should be put to the test over so unfortunate a case as Abyssinia; and they really felt that the primary purpose of the League was to keep order in Europe—and to protect France against Germany.

. . . .

I need not recall here the story of the great Front Populaire movement in France. Charles Péguy once drew a famous distinction between *politique* and *mystique*; the latter being a policy with a spiritual and emotional inspiration. The anti-Fascism of the Front Populaire was not merely a policy; it was a genuine *mystique*. Later, however, like the Dreyfusard *mystique* of the past (Péguy's favourite example), it degenerated into *politique*—and a *politique* conducted entirely by the Communists. Whatever the motives of Moscow in turning the Communist Party in France into a nationalist, patriotic, jacobin organization, the support this nationalism and jacobinism received from wide sections of French opinion was perfectly genuine.

The Radicals, egged on by Republican opinion in provincial France (particularly by the *instituteurs*), were at first, for the most part, favourably disposed towards the Front Populaire. The first waves of strikes had, indeed, all the qualities of a *mystique*. But as the strikes continued, Radical and even Socialist opinion became alarmed; while the upper *bourgeoisie* got into a genuine panic.

At this time the *bien-pensants* might well have chosen as their slogan: 'Fascists of the world unite.' It went even farther. The Cagoulard movement, which made its first spectacular appearance in Paris on the 9th of September, 1937, when two houses were wrecked by bomb explosions in the Étoile district, was a strange flower of that funk and Fascism which found its clearest expression in the phrase 'Hitler rather than the Front Populaire.' Henri de Kerillis, who saw the full implications of the phrase, never ceased to dwell on it in his denunciations of the French *hitlériens*. The Cagoulard organization was largely composed of some wild men who had been driven underground by the dissolution, in June 1936, of the Fascist leagues. Panic-stricken *grands bourgeois* supported it financially: for they saw in it a promise of protection against Communism. The Cagoulards worked in close contact with German and especially Italian and Spanish agents; and Baron Aloisi was widely spoken of as their secret chief. The gruesome murder of Carlo Roselli, the great anti-Fascist Italian journalist, and of his brother, was one of the first acts of the Cagoulards. General Duseigneur, and numerous French business men, were more or less mixed up in the case; among them was M. Watteau, a close friend of General Duseigneur, and later a judge on the Supreme Court at Riom. It was whispered that General Weygand, noted for his sympathy for the 6th of February people, had contacts with Cagoulards; but there is no direct evidence of this. The Cagoulard affair, which, apart from few arrests, was thoroughly hushed up by the Press and the legal authorities, was not perhaps very important in itself, but it was symptomatic; and so also was the sympathy the accused men received from a number of papers, notably the *Action Française*, the *Jour*, and *Gringoire*.

.   .   .   .

After Munich the anti-Red crusade became the real aim of men like Bonnet, both at home and abroad. Flandin was preaching 'retrenchment' behind the Maginot Line; Bonnet was fraternizing with Ribbentrop. Bonnet promised Ribbentrop what was virtually a free hand in the East; the *Comité France-Allemagne*, with Fernand de Brinon, Bonnet's *homme de confiance*, the Abetz, the chief Nazi agent in Paris, as its leading personages, was a centre of political activity; Mr. Percy Philip was *persona grata* with Bonnet, while Mr. Thomas Cadett, the Paris correspondent of *The Times*, and the present writer had the threat of expulsion from France suspended over them.

.   .   .   .

This pre-Vichy atmosphere in the days of the Ribbentrop visit, when France already seemed to have accepted the status of Germany's vassal, with a *gleichgeschaltet* Press, anti-Red and anti-semitic campaigns and what-not, was dispelled by M. Daladier. Daladier was not devoid of healthy national reflexes. The illusions of Munich were rapidly dwindling; and on the 15th of March the greater part of France realized that the policy of appeasement had broken down. Nevertheless, Bonnet continued to send secret emissaries to Berlin and Rome. M. de Brinon went to Berlin and met Ribbentrop, with whom he talked without the knowledge of the regular ambassador, M. Coulondre. When the latter heard of it he nearly resigned. M. Baudouin, who often went to Rome, was believed to go there with secret messages from Bonnet. Bonnet, in effect, begged the Italians not to take Daladier too seriously.

.   .   .   .

Then came April 1939—the point at which my main narrative was broken off. Since the guarantee had been given to Poland, it was necessary to supplement it, if possible, with a Russian alliance. It was late—very late. The Russians distrusted Mr. Chamberlain and M. Bonnet. Daladier was all in favour of the alliance, and accused Mr. Chamberlain of unnecessary haggling: '*il marchande comme un épicier,*' he once angrily remarked. Actually the responsibility for the breakdown of the talks is divided. But that is another story.

.   .   .   .

France was actively preparing for war. Daladier, who had felt very pessimistic since January, took upon himself the task of preparing France for it, both materially and psychologically. The stock of the Communists had fallen very low; what remained of the C.G.T. was in open revolt against the Communists who had got it landed in the strike fiasco; and Daladier, assuming dictatorial airs, was behaving toughly to everybody.

Il faut en finir is a fair summing up of what the average Frenchman felt between January, or at any rate, March 1939 and September. The French were fed-up—fed-up with the constant partial mobilizations, Hitler's arrogance, and the economic uncertainty. Only, is fed-upness the best possible incentive to war?

. . . .

France, especially peasant France, wanted to see a strong hand at the helm; and it had faith in Daladier with his hard, harsh, peasant manner. Daladier flattered the peasantry; more than once he treated them as class-one citizens who provided the Army with the greater part of its recruits. He elaborated a 'Family Code.' The Daladier regime had its poet-laureate in Jean Giraudoux, who, in his book with the significant title *Pleins Pouvoirs*, published in July 1939, gave coherent expression to Daladier's revivalism. Like Daladier, he felt bitterly that '*le Français se fait rare*,' and he advocated the creation of a more orderly, more coherent French culture, with spectacular monuments, a lot of children, and rather fewer *métèques.* There was a streak of Vichy-ism in the book, as there was in Daladier. But Family Code or no Family Code, Daladier really knew that he was building on sand. He saw the war coming, and knew that the Family Code, with its cash premiums on every new French baby, would not be properly applied until after victory.

This revivalist mood coincided with an unusual vogue, among the younger people of the educated class, of the writings of Charles Péguy. Why Péguy? Why this religious approach to France, why this French messianism? Why this sudden discovery of France's Christian and civilizing mission? Was it not a healthy reaction against the degenerate 'nationalism' of Charles Maurras, whose '*nationalisme intégral*' had joined the Fascist international and had supported Munich? The *Nouvelle Revue Française, Esprit, Politique*, and other monthlies were packed with references to Péguy, and quotations from Péguy. If France had any spiritual and ideological guidance of a positive kind in 1939, and not merely the negative '*il faut en finir*,' it came from Péguy. Only —the appeal was heard, after all, by only a part of the educated class. It never reached the ears of the ordinary soldier, or of the general public.

345

The writings and the strange destiny of the fiery French crusader against the German beast, of the man who was killed by a German bullet on the Marne in September 1914, were unknown to the ordinary Frenchman.

. . . .

Otherwise, the war had no great positive basis. The recruits went off to the Maginot Line in the last days of August and the first days of September, with a feeling of anger against Hitler, but with a heavy heart. I was in Scotland at that time. I got a letter from a French peasant woman, who had watched the troops drive past in their lorries towards Orléans. *'Le cœur serré, je les ai vus patir.'* It was everywhere like that. To France the war was a tragedy, a universal, general tragedy— but above all, a tragedy for every man, woman and child. Five million men were said to have been called up—practically every man from 20 to 49. There was a grim acceptance of the war; but there was no enthusiasm. *Il faut en finir,* so as to have peace later on. But an ideological basis, or even a sentimental basis? No. It was just *'quel malheur, quel malheur,'* as my peasant woman wrote. The political parties, as *Politique* remarked in December 1939, revealed their complete ideological bankruptcy on that occasion. Even the argument that the existence of France was at stake was not presented with sufficient conviction. And then there was all that trouble with the Communists. The Russo-German pact had a devastating effect on the French working-class, the only class which, until then, had been powerfully, violently anti-Hitler. The Daladier Government dealt with the whole matter with a great lack of tact and discrimination. Not only were the Communist leaders thrown into prison— apart from those who escaped abroad—but the Government started a large-scale persecution of local party and trade union officials. The war was unpopular with the *bien-pensants*; but the persecution of the Communists was an extremely popular pastime. Daladier, who himself was rabidly anti-Communist, kept the Right appeased in this manner. The effect was bad. Had the Communist leaders been given enough freedom to defend Stalin, they might have made themselves very unpopular with the workers, who would have swung round in favour of the war. But all this persecution aroused in them feelings of party loyalty; and their attitude to the war became increasingly morose and sceptical. Thus the anti-Nazi working class, which might conceivably have remained anti-Nazi in spite of the Stalin-Hitler pact, became pacifist.

. . . .

The soldiers, in the meantime, were getting bored. They sat in their casemates on the Maginot Line; they were billeted in out-of-the-way Lorraine villages. True, during the first few weeks, there was some activity on the Maginot Line; the Germans were compelled to evacuate Saarbrücken; but after the evacuation by the French of the Warndt Forest, the 'phoney' war became really 'phoney.' Some 30,000 men on the Maginot Line were engaged in patrol activity; and that was about all. The spirit among the troops varied considerably. Some continued to be full of fight; others thought it all a deadly waste of time. On the whole, however, the spirit was not bad. There was a true *jacobin* atmosphere in many parts of the army; there was much open discussion among the soldiers—much more open than in the rear; and a genuine spirit of camaraderie among all the ranks. Men who came back from the Front thought that one of the effects of the 'phoney' war was to create something of a gulf between the Army and the rear; between the men who would go on living indefinitely an abnormal life, and those living a normal life; and they prophesied that after the war France would be recreated by the soldiers. How long could they endure the 'phoney' war? Some said a year; others eighteen months; after that the Germans would have to be provoked into attacking. There was, of course, much dissatisfaction of a private kind. The soldiers were paid only 75 centimes a day; and the German propagandists would bellow about the British privates who were getting 17 francs. In Paris, soldiers would use up their ten days' leave driving taxicabs or acting as office messengers in order to make a little money for themselves and their wives. Soldiers' families were poorly paid. A woman and two children, though living rent free, received only 16 francs a day in the provinces and 21 francs in Paris. There was some haggling on whether, in taking work, a soldier's wife forfeited her military family allowance.

What were the politicians' reactions to the war? There were some who still tried to stop it. On the 2nd of September the Chamber voted the declaration of war on Germany only by implication; it was when it agreed unanimously to the opening of military credits amounting to 500 milliards. A few, notably M. Bergery, seemed very restive; but they were not given a chance to speak. Only, behind the scenes, some anti-war agitation still continued. The most notable example of this was the attempt made by Bonnet, the Foreign Minister, to stop the British Government from declaring war the next day. He had been in constant communication with Ciano, and the Italian Government were proposing another 'Munich' on the 5th of September. Poland had already been invaded; and, unlike the British Government, Bonnet was willing to go to the conference without a German withdrawal from Polish territory. The tension between London and Paris became so acute that day that, after war was declared, Daladier was obliged to remove Bonnet from the Quai d'Orsay. He, however, kept him in his Cabinet as Minister of Justice. Bonnet's behaviour on that Saturday greatly embarrassed Mr. Chamberlain, who was made to face a storm in the House of Commons.

.   .   .   .

Daladier had a variety of people in his Cabinet—some of them more or less sharing Bonnet's ideas—notably de Monzie and Pomaret. Outside the Cabinet the opposition to the war was more outspoken. After the conquest of Poland, Flandin said to the Foreign Affairs Committee of the Chamber: 'Is it really worth going on with?'

The two men in the Cabinet who took the war most seriously were Reynaud, the Finance Minister, and Mandel, the Minister of Colonies, who was working night and day to increase the war contribution of the colonies, both in manpower and in food and raw materials. Reynaud's two speeches in November and December at the Chamber and Senate, as well as his later broadcasts, were remarkable. He warned France that if the war was to be won, it *must* be a long one; and that she must face enormous sacrifices. He warned her against easy optimism. He advocated severe rationing in France, too. But other men in the Cabinet preferred to take an easier line. M. Queuille, the Minister of Agriculture, reflecting the views of rural France, was opposed to large-scale rationing; and no really important rationing measures were ever introduced. And, in contrast with Reynaud, de Monzie said: 'This war *must be short.*'

Daladier was War Minister; he had been War Minister for nearly four years, and had also held the post before that. He talked with great confidence of military problems, and seemed to have the greatest faith in the Maginot Line. He assumed that the war would be a long one; and that Germany would, in the end, be worn out by the blockade, or would smash her head against the Maginot Line. In December he declared with great satisfaction, *'La France n'a pas été envahie'*; and he recalled that, while in the corresponding period in the last war France had lost 415,000 men, she had now lost 1,600. He added that the northern extension of the Maginot Line was reliable; and was being worked on all the time. *'Nous sommes avares du sang français,'* he said, amid a storm of applause from the deputies, each of whom was thinking of his own constituents, to whom he could repeat the magic phrase. It was pathetic and understandable from a human point of view; but the trouble was that the conception of the 'bloodless war' became deeply engrained in the minds of many Frenchmen; and when the *blitzkrieg* came, they were psychologically unprepared for it. Even with poorer equipment, the French Army would have put up a better show in September 1939 than it did in May and June 1940.

While all was quiet on the Western Front, war broke out in Finland. The French 'pacifists' who had been lying low during the early stages of the war in the West, and who even paid lip-service to the anti-Hitler cause, now saw their chance. The invasion of Poland by Russia was bad enough; but the attack on Finland was intolerable. The *Temps*, the *Matin*, the *Action Française* and several other papers proclaimed that the *équivoque* ought to be put an end to; it was senseless to fight Germany and yet to maintain diplomatic relations with Russia. War on Russia, the *Temps* argued, would provide the Allies with a great many strategic opportunities they were now lacking. An attack on Baku was almost openly discussed. There was, behind all this, an attempt to patch up a peace with Germany, and to turn the guns—possibly German and Allied mixed—against the Soviets. There were many who, without being keen on fighting Germany, were eager to fight Russia. Catholic peasant recruits from Brittany and Normandy were said to be anxious to be sent to Finland to fight the Bolsheviks. The failure of the Government to help Finland aroused the fury of the Right-wing Deputies; and the Daladier Government was virtually defeated, and resigned.

It is true that the anger did not last long; and the Radicals, in particular, deeply regretted the fall of Daladier when they saw who had succeeded him. The Right felt equally bad about it. Instead of Daladier, Reynaud—'England's man'—was now at the head of the Government. A number of 'doubtful' people, such as Bonnet, had been cleared out of the Cabinet; instead, Reynaud gave three Cabinet posts and three undersecretaryships to the Socialist Party. The reception given by the Chamber to this war-to-the-bitter-end Cabinet was anything but encouraging. The Right, howling their heads off in a true 6th of February spirit, charged Reynaud with having plotted with Blum against Daladier. The votes cast for this Government were only two above the aggregate number of hostile votes and abstentions; and it was even whispered that Herriot, the Speaker, had made a mistake, and that in reality Reynaud had been defeated.

Daladier was still War Minister; but his attitude to the new Premier remained ambiguous. The first day the new Cabinet appeared before the Chamber, Daladier was not present at all; his absence was like a cue to many Radicals to vote against the new Government—which, indeed, they did, with Bonnet as the leader of the anti-Reynaud drive among the Radicals.

Daladier continued to be in a bad humour. When Reynaud went to London for his first Supreme War Council, Daladier refused to accompany him. It was on that occasion that Reynaud signed the French pledge not to make a separate peace with Germany. Oddly enough, Daladier had always refrained from giving such a pledge to England. Émile Buré recently expressed the view that Daladier had, at heart, continued to hope right through the 'phoney war' for a patched-up peace with Germany. That is not certain. The impression one had of Daladier during the early months of 1940 was that he did not know what to do. He was, especially after his riding accident in January, in a morose kind of state, and very irritable, bad-tempered and almost inaccessible—an additional reason, by the way, why he was so unpopular with the deputies, who love to hobnob with Cabinet Ministers.

During the first weeks of its existence, the position of the Reynaud Government was extremely shaky. It—or rather its Socialist members— were violently attacked in papers like *Gringoire*; and, about a fortnight after its formation, I met Marcel Déat at the Chamber of Deputies, who announced that he was going to interpellate the Government, and that the chances of overthrowing it were considerable. Déat thought that at least thirty of the Socialists—those in sympathy with Paul Faure's pacifism—would vote against the Government. It is well known that the visit of Mr. Sumner Welles to Europe raised high hopes among the French pacifists—Paul Faure, Déat, Flandin, Laval, Bonnet and others. M. Paul Faure in his paper, *Pays Socialiste,* wrote an article, entitled *'J'ai fait un rêve insensé,'* in which he advocated, in effect, an economic roundtable conference at which Daladier, Chamberlain, Stalin, Hitler, Mussolini and the rest would discuss the economic reconstruction of Europe. For Paul Faure thought of the war in purely economic terms. His argument was that all the differences which had resulted in the war could be amicably settled by economic discussion. The part he gave England in his economic scheme was not clearly defined; like Brunet, one of his followers, he thought of the economic reconstruction of Europe chiefly in *continental* terms. Paul Faure was to become one of the principal supporters on the Left of the Pétain armistice. It was even announced at first that he had entered the Pétain Government as Minister of Labour. Paul Faure has always been something of a defeatist. This great Socialist—whose love affairs had, at one time, filled the gossip columns of *Gringoire* and *Candide*—lacked confidence in an extraordinary degree. I remember lunching with him in 1935, at the time of La Rocque's greatest vogue. Paul Faure was very nervous, and thought a successful Fascist *coup* by the Croix de Feu highly probable. His faith in the Republic then was no greater than his faith in France five years later.

.   .   .   .

What saved the *belliciste* Reynaud Government was the war in Norway. With a certain lack of responsibility and perspective, Reynaud made tremendous political capital for himself out of the first naval battle of Narvik, when seven German destroyers were sunk in one day; and drew, both before the Chamber and the Senate, an overwhelmingly optimistic picture of the progress of the Allies in Norway. Narvik, Narvik, Narvik—for a fortnight nobody talked of anything but that. And then, towards the end of April, the reaction set in. The evacuation of Andalsnes did not look so pretty; and when, in the second week in May, the disaster of Norway had become only too apparent, and when the resignation of Mr. Chamberlain became a matter of hours, the position of the Reynaud Government was also severely shaken. For a moment it seemed that Reynaud would be even more badly shaken than Chamberlain; which prompted a Labour M.P. to remark that Norway might lead 'to the survival of a bad British Government and the fall of a good French Government.'

But, actually, this prophecy proved incorrect. Mr. Churchill succeeded Mr. Chamberlain; but M. Reynaud remained in office. Not without a great deal of trouble, though. The fall of Mr. Chamberlain would automatically have been followed by the fall of M. Reynaud, but for the invasion of Holland and Belgium. On the day this happened, Daladier's plans for revenge had ripened; and he would have succeeded Reynaud had not the latter succeeded in persuading M. Marin and M. Ybarnégaray to enter his Cabinet. The entry of these two leaders of the Right into the Government strengthened Reynaud's position; for the Government now assumed the appearance of a real National Government stretching from the extreme Right to the extreme Left. Marin, the old Lorrainer, certainly entered the Reynaud Government in a purely disinterested patriotic spirit. What were the motives of M. Ybarnégaray in entering it is more doubtful. His past record suggested that he was a sincere patriot—an impression which was scarcely altered by the prominent role he played in the Croix de Feu movement, and even by his close association, during the Spanish civil war and after, with General Franco. And yet, Ybarnégaray's conduct during the weeks that followed, and especially before and after the signing of the Armistice, makes one wonder whether he entered the Reynaud Government on the 10th of May in a purely patriotic spirit, and without any ulterior motives. For there were others in the Reynaud Government whose defeatism became blatant in May. Baudouin, Pomaret, de Monzie, and others, and, of course, Pétain.

II. VICHY

THERE is the purely military story; but I am not a military expert; and to the layman in Paris[1] only the following points were clear:

(1) In the Low Countries, the Allies were overwhelmed by the force of the German onslaught and the novelty of the German technique; above all, by the number of their tanks and their almost complete command of the air. France's 3,500 tanks were scattered all over the front, and were never effectively used for any counter-offensive.

(2) The lessons of the campaign in Poland, which was a first application of these principles, had been ignored and neglected on the easy assumption that the Poles are Poles and the French are French. Actually, everything tends to show that as an individual soldier the Pole was superior to the Frenchman.

(3) While there were some remarkable cases of French resistance—notably at Rethel and at a few other more or less isolated points during the great German drive from the Meuse to the Channel Ports and also at Dunkirk, and a week later on the Somme—the general level of French morale was considerably lower than in 1914 when Germany at first also enjoyed an indisputable superiority in equipment.

(4) Both the morale and efficiency of the French officers were, again, unequal to 1914–18; and human life, generally, was prized too highly both by the French command (*'avares du sang français'*) and by many of the individuals directly concerned. I am merely stating a moral factor in France's collapse; I am not, as a civilian, presuming to criticize men each of whom faced far greater dangers and hardships than any of us

[1] For a first-hand account of Paris during the invasion of France and for the rapid disintegration of the Reynaud Cabinet see the Author's *The Last Days of Paris*.

civilians ever did; but the fact remains that, in many cases, the old spirit of Verdun was lacking. And the same is true of the women. They wept too much from the very day the Germans invaded Holland and Belgium.

(5) Was there 'Fifth Column' activity in the Army? There is no doubt that the Germans had numerous agents; and that bogus telephone calls, for instance, played a certain part in the disorganization of the French. But whether there were many officers and men who were consciously handing their country over to Germany is something about which I have no evidence; and I doubt whether plain treason played any great part in the German advance. But discouragement and—in the later stages of the war—the belief that the struggle was hopeless, and that if France was to survive she must 'accommodate' herself to her defeat, were important factors, which largely account for the subsequent attitude at Bordeaux of men like Pétain and Weygand.

(6) Lastly, it is clear that the real trouble, psychological and material, arose from the sudden collapse of the 'Maginot' system on which the whole organization of the French Army had been based, and which every French—and British—citizen had been taught to trust implicitly. The French had had the miracle of the Maginot Line drummed into them for years; perhaps it was lucky, from the point of view of morale, that the British soldier had heard of Maginot only a few months earlier, and also knew from direct experience when he arrived in the north of France earlier in the war that there was really nothing in the way of fortifications worth writing home about. The fortifications built by the British between the Channel, and, roughly, Hazebrouck, were in fact, never attacked, but turned. The Germans broke through the French sector of the 'extension'; and this had been the subject of the most deplorable and irresponsible optimism.

.   .   .   .

The decision not to defend Paris has often been criticized. I have no opinion on the question whether a successful defence of Paris was militarily possible; what evidence there is suggests that it was not. But there was the same psychological element in the decision not to defend Paris as in the formula *'avares du sang français.'* Even a conquered France was better than a physically annihilated France, France might, in time, emancipate herself if her people were allowed to live on and rear children; and Paris might still be Paris provided it was not razed to the ground. To put it a little crudely: the old slogan of the Jacobins, *'Liberté ou la mort'*, had been abandoned for *'Esclavage—plus ou moins provisoire—plutôt que la mort,'* on the ground that what was most important to save, if anything could yet be saved, were the seeds of national, or rather, racial survival. In all this, there was a vague conception of 'regeneration through suffering,' and there was the strangely Chinese-like belief that 'France could not be destroyed.' There was also a tendency to take a very long, and very philosophical view of the whole thing: the French, as men of a higher civilization, would eventually absorb and convert the German conquerors; and pleasant parallels from history —how the Franks were civilized by the Gallo-Romans and how in the twelfth century the Kingdom of France was reduced to a tiny bit of country round Paris—appealed to many minds in these moments of distress. Already for a few years—particularly after Munich—writers like M. Detoeuf had liked to play about with such ideas of the inevitable regeneration of France through conquest and humiliation. Others, like Marcel Déat, went much further, and were, in effect, prepared to make the best of a bad situation by accepting wholeheartedly the New Order of Hitler and Mussolini, and by begging the supermen for a little place— oh, quite a little place—in the new scheme of things.

. . . .

The motives that prompted the Bordeaux Government to surrender to Germany are, in fact, numerous and very mixed. The motif of expiation and renovation through suffering was present in some minds—and this perhaps was the most respectable of the motives. Others were prompted, either by cowardice or by what they believed to be their self-interest, to bow to the German demands, in the hope that the Germans would allow these people to become, as it were, the ruling caste in France—a caste which could now wreak vengeance on its political opponents. On the soil of defeat and disaster the seeds of Vichy had rapidly developed into a great monstrous flower. Here was something of all the things that one had already seen sprouting, especially since 1934. The 6th of February spirit; the anti-liberal and anti-parliamentary spirit, which was not merely critical of the abuses of the French parliamentary system, but absolutely hostile to the parliamentary, democratic idea; the cultivation of the peasantry—that good French peasantry which had already supported Napoleon III through thick and thin, as against the turbulent industrial proletariat; the shouts of *La France aux Français* which had in the heyday of the Croix de Feu and Jeunesses Patriotes and Solidarité Française resounded up and down the Champs-Elysées; the Nazi-inspired anti-semitism of *Gringoire* and *Je Suis Partout*; and the more authentically French anti-semitism of the *Action Française*; the anti-Freemasonry of the old Stavinsky days; and, above all, the anti-British explosions of *Gringoire* and the anti-British sentiments of many of the ordinary people, and also of the Lavals, the Bonnets, the Déats, the Paul Faures.

It was all there; the feeling that the British were selfish imperialists, who were ready to fight to the last French soldier; that the British had not sent enough troops and had let the French down. And even as late as the 16th and 17th of June, the men of Bordeaux were still full of pernicious illusions about Italy and Spain; even though Italy had declared war on France, and General Franco had converted his neutrality into nonbelligerency. The Latin *bloc*—the *bloc* of the Latin Nations, which would, in the long run, offset and cancel out Germany's hegemony on the Continent—this Latin *bloc* was still a favourite idea with Laval and Baudouin, and the aged Marshal Pétain. Daladier had sent him to Spain as French Ambassador in March 1939; he had allowed himself to be flattered and blackmailed by the Spaniards, and was ultimately persuaded by them that Hitler would offer him, the 'Hero of Verdun,' an honourable soldier's peace.

.   .   .   .

Was it possible for France to continue the war after the fall of Paris? The answer is yes; provided France was in a truly heroic mood. It would have meant grim sacrifices and fearful risks. In Weygand's view there was no line in European France which could be held successfully for any length of time. All the great industrial centres had fallen, or were about to fall, into the hands of the Germans. The only chance was to continue the war in North Africa. What did that mean? It meant first, that European France would be left entirely in the hands of Germany; and what fearful blackmail could the Germans not exercise on the Government of North Africa and the soldiers and sailors there? Anything from the massacre of the two million war prisoners to the massacre of the entire French population. Was such German blackmail—though perfectly compatible with the Nazi character—ever attempted? I do not know; but it is characteristic that stories of such blackmail should have been current *at Bordeaux* during the few days that preceded the armistice. The continuation of the war in North Africa would have been perfectly feasible; but it meant two things, both of which were distasteful to the men around Pétain; *it would have meant the perpetuation of the alliance with 'democratic' England, and it would have meant that the war would be primarily fought against Italy.* And even the idea of a *revanche* on Germany *through the (relatively easy) defeat of Mussolini's Italy* was intolerable to the Lavals, the Pétains, the Ybarnégarays, the Baudouins, the De Monzies, and the rest who had, for years, been longing for Italy's friendship, and had been day-dreaming of the Latin *bloc*. Their political ideal was precisely Mussolini's Italy. These pernicious illusions were encouraged by the astonishingly mild armistice terms presented by the 'victorious' Italians to France, and, later, by the lack of haste they showed in enforcing them.

.   .   .   .   .   .

There was a variety of motives behind the French decision to surrender. But whatever the different motives, all the men round Pétain shared, more or less, in the illusion that by surrendering to Hitler and by being polite and humble to Italy, they could build up a France of their own; that authoritarian *bien-pensant* capitalist and small-freeholder France in which they would rule under the more or less benevolent glance of Hitler and Mussolini. This France, they thought, would be anti-Liberal, anti-British, but (unlike Germany) not necessarily anti-capitalist, or non-capitalist. It would be the France of *la France aux Français*. The grim and ugly paradox of the whole thing was that the slogan *La France aux Français* became the more or less official slogan of the French Government on the day when two-thirds of France's territory were under German occupation; and that this slogan, *La France aux Français,* was essentially one symbolizing the attempted fraternization of France with the Nazi conquerors! Equally grim is the thought that the 'National Revolution' should have triumphed on the very day when France had departed from her true national tradition further than she had departed from it in a thousand years.

.   .   .   .   .   .

What has happened in Pétain France so far is sordid, grotesque, and yet, in many ways, sad and pathetic. The Constitution of 1875 was abolished, and with it, the older slogan of *Liberté, Egalité, Fraternité.* Some of the noblest things France had contributed to European civilization were being gleefully and almost savagely discarded. Instead, the *Führer* principle was being adopted, and embodied in the 85-year-old Marshal Pétain. To appeal to French sentiment, the Marshal was going to take up his residence at Versailles—if the Germans would allow him to do so. Shades of Louis Quatorze! But the Nazis, who had their own ideas about Versailles and Paris, preferred him to stay at Vichy, the home of decrepit invalids. The Chamber was abolished and the Senate was abolished, to be replaced by rubber stamp bodies to be constituted in accordance with Führer Pétain's wishes. The *départements* were going to be replaced by the *ancien-régime* provinces; a sentimental idea with which La Rocque had played, nobody quite knows why. Already, in 1935, I saw a map of France divided into provinces hanging in La Rocque's office in Paris. Irresponsible nonsense was written in the Vichy Press about decentralization, and, at the same time, about the great example of Richelieu—as though Richelieu, the maker of the French State, had been a décentralizationist! The split-up of France into provinces only played into the hands of the Germans, who promptly took up the fantastic idea of an 'independent Brittany,' an independent state of Flanders—not to mention Alsace-Lorraine which was already virtually annexed, even before any peace treaty.

Everything in France ultimately depends on the outcome of the life-and-death struggle between Germany and Great Britain. The state of affairs in France in the months that followed the Armistice was certainly abnormal and, in every respect, provisional. The Vichy Government attempted, very unconvincingly, to persuade the stunned and bewildered French people that a 'National Revolution' was in progress in France. What 'National Revolution' was possible, with two-thirds of the country, including the entire Atlantic coast, occupied by Germany? Those who signed the Armistice foolishly imagined that France would rapidly 'return to normal.' Before long the Germans made it very clear that this was a naive illusion. In the rich, occupied parts of France—in Normandy, Brittany, the Beauce, the Vexin, the Yonne, and all the other grain and meat and sugar and dairy regions—the Germans bought up with doubtful notes all they could lay their hands on. This food, a large part of which normally went to Southern France, in exchange for the wine of the Midi, now went to Germany. Already in the middle of July the *Temps* complained of the 'great wall of China' the Germans had set up to separate occupied France from unoccupied France. There was scarcely any traffic between the two, and scarcely any trade. Refugees had great trouble in returning to their homes. Lucien Romier in the *Figaro* and even the pro-Fascist Fernand Laurent in the *Jour* admitted that Pétain France was completely at Germany's mercy. 'Everything depends on what the Armistice Commission at Wiesbaden decides,' M. Fernand Laurent wrote. 'So long as Article 17 of the Armistice continues to be rigorously enforced, that is, so long as no food and other commodities can be brought from the occupied zone to the unoccupied zone, there can be no return to normal.'

Laval asked the Germans to allow the French Government to settle in Paris; all in vain. To add insult to injury, the Germans appointed Abetz virtual Ambassador to France and *Gauleiter* of Paris—the chief spy who had been ignominiously thrown out of France two months before

357

the war. He had been a great friend of Bonnet and Mme Bonnet; but that did not make him any friendlier to the Vichy Government now. On the contrary, his behaviour to Vichy was thoroughly insulting; and the Germans suspended over the Pétain Government the constant threat of a 'rival' government in Paris. Already the local German-controlled Press was, with the help of men like Doriot, carrying on Nazi propaganda, particularly among the bewildered French working class; National-Socialist propaganda, with the emphasis on the second word. The Vichy Government were accused of being rusty reactionaries, representing nobody, and as a set of crooked politicians in league with capitalism, and 'with mysterious threads stretching out to England.' No doubt, the ineffable Alphonse de Chateaubriant who, already in the days of Munich, slobbered over the great human *bonté* of Adolf Hitler, wrote in the Paris Press that the Axis doctrine was France's only salvation; while Marcel Déat was preaching the wholehearted adherence of France to the New Order. And another person—a M. Coutrot—in the *Œuvre* even went so far as to write that 'June 1940 was a great victory for both Germany and France; the two peoples, abandoning their national enmities, can now live and work together for a happy future.' And M. Ybarnégaray, the Minister of Youth and Family, set up labour camps where the youth of France would live and work *'dans la joie et dans la santé.'* Only none of this impressed the Germans, or the ordinary people of France. The *National Zeitung* of Goering said that while a few Frenchmen sincerely wanted an understanding with the Führer, the French people had not realized yet that the Armistice was not peace and that 'penance must yet be done.'

It also opposed to the cringing of the writers in the *Œuvre* the arrogant theory of the *Herrenvolk*; and added that this theory was diametrically opposed to the French 1789 theory of equality among men, nations and races. As for the Vichy clamour for a 'return to normal,' the clearest answer was given by the *Berliner Börsenzeitung*, which suggested that Southern France was an underpopulated country; that most of the refugees would do better to stay where they were, and leave the rich North and West of France to German colonization.

The worst piece of self-abasement was the Riom trial, in which the Vichy Government decided to judge the 'war criminals'—the politicians 'responsible for the war.' Bonnet was to appear as chief witness for the prosecution. Georges Bonnet was going to produce evidence, not only against Mandel but also against Daladier who had kept him in office for years, against his better judgment. Hitler, who had protested for years against the 'war guilt lie' in the Treaty of Versailles, could only rub his hands at the sight of the French accusing their own politicians of having started the war. In 1919 the Germans had carefully refrained from trying their own 'war criminals'; and to them the Riom trials were, indeed, a pleasing demonstration of France's lack of national solidarity—a solidarity which they themselves possessed in an extraordinary degree, even at the worst moments.

Riom was too much for the French people to swallow, and Vichy kept on postponing the Trial.[2]

What are the feelings of the French people? There is everything to suggest that they are wretchedly unhappy, both in their bodies and in their souls. They are being robbed and despoiled of everything by the Germans; and M. Déat's theories about the New Order must be cold comfort to them. Already in August 1940 Déat complained of the Anglomania which, he said, was still widespread in France—Anglomania being the hope—in M. Déat's view, the idle hope—for a British victory over Germany. Whatever their past grievances against England, however deep the anger widely caused in France by the Oran battle, very many people in France knew already then that if France's soul could still be saved, it could be only through the defeat of Germany.

* * * * * * *

Vichy had, from the outset, been violently anti-British in its propaganda; it said that Britain had deserted France; and after the Oran incident in July, anti-British feeling was, indeed, more widespread in France than it had been for many years. But gradually, the change came. It is true that, after September, the Germans relaxed the frontier regulations, and a high proportion of the seven million refugees from Belgium and Occupied France were allowed to return home. It was a concession to the French—because the French were becoming desperate, and the Germans feared that if they persisted in their refusal to allow the refugees to return, even Vichy might rebel. Pétain was still at that time able to hold suspended over the Germans the threat of a revolt in North Africa. And the Germans also knew that, from September onward, pro-British feeling in France was beginning to take on alarming proportions.

At the time of the Armistice, many Frenchmen believed that Britain would soon surrender. But then came the Battle of Britain and the bombing of London, and the French realized that not all was lost; that England was continuing the war in dead earnest, was inflicting severe

[2] When it finally was held, it went off the rails—from the German point of view. Instead of saying why France had *entered* the war, it merely attempted to explain why she had *lost* it. (Author's note, 1942.)

losses on the German air force, and that the Germans had failed to bring Britain to her knees. Such being the case, there remained the living hope of a better future.

Laval, who had backed the German horse from the start, became nervous. If France went pro-British, if North Africa rebelled, it would be the end of him. He induced the Marshal—by a ruse, it is said—to meet Hitler at Montoire; and the Marshal reluctantly agreed to the 'principle of co-operation' with Germany.

But the Battle of Britain had been lost by Hitler; and the presidential election in America was near. The prevalent feeling even at Vichy at that time was that France should not commit herself too deeply, and try to play for time. In Paris, the scum of French journalism were doing their quisling propaganda with Laval's blessing; but this propaganda was not popular in France. The man-in-the-street whistled the B.B.C. ditty:

> Radio-Paris ment, Radio-Paris ment,
> Radio-Paris est allemand.

After the Germans had lost the Battle of Britain, Pétain showed some initiative when, in December 1940, he refused to sell out completely to Germany, at Laval's instigation, and even dismissed Laval. But the threat that a rival Nazi government, under Laval, Doriot, and Déat, would be set up in Paris forced Pétain two months later (February 1941) to give way again. True, Laval was not reinstated, but Darlan took his place. Darlan, the ambitious, mediocre man who could already see himself head of the Navy of the New European Order, favoured an all-out policy of co-operation with Germany. If there were limits which he was still obliged to respect, it was because General Huntziger, the War Minister and General Weygand had not yet been won over to all-out co-operation, and because French public opinion, especially in Occupied France, had, by that time, become almost unanimously pro-British. The French people knew that all the Germans wanted to do in France was to rob and loot; and the national conscience of France preferred them to do so openly, without any polite new-order camouflage. Many months later, it was this national conscience which pulled the trigger of the revolver that wounded and nearly killed Laval.

It was the signal and the symbol of a French awakening.

Germany tried to retard this process by shooting hostages and also by ordering Vichy to dismiss Weygand; while Huntziger was killed in a mysterious air crash about the same time.

But the French people are sound, so sound that Darlan has been obliged to set up a Gestapo of his own to supplement the German terror in the Occupied zone. Only it will not work. Vichy Gestapo chiefs will continue to be found dead on railway lines, and in the dark streets of Paris German soldiers will be, more and more, in fear of their lives. Laval must feel an unhappy man, with a very uncertain future.

And whatever doubts may still have existed in French minds must have been removed by America's entry into the war. Even the tone of Pétain's speeches suddenly changed.

.   .   .   .

It is inevitable that Britain should have felt bitter about France during the past two years. How much easier would Britain's strategic problems have been with a French North Africa solidly on her side, and with Indo-China free of the Japanese. But for the Japanese springboard of Indo-China, Malaya might not have been lost. Vichy may yet change its tune, and sound less eager to co-operate with Germany.

But it co-operated with Germany in England's darkest hours.

And it was also in one of those dark hours—perhaps the darkest of all—that General de Gaulle and his men came to England. They, at least, had the courage and the faith to say 'No' to the infamous snarling victor of Rethondes.

These men will form the nucleus of a new, free and better France. And in France, there are millions of men already working at home for the day when the Germans are driven out.

What vengeance the Germans may yet wreak on France, on Paris and the two million Frenchmen in prison camps, we do not know. France will emerge from this war shaken and weakened. She will have a great task before her—that of a real national revival. Perhaps the tragic lessons of recent years will not have been in vain.

The future of Europe needs—as the posters in the 1936 election used to say—a Free, Strong and Happy France; a France whose creative genius will once again shine across the world after years of twilight and darkness.

INDEX

365

DATE DUE